Normativity and Naturalism in the Philosophy of the Social Sciences

T0270864

"This book picks up a core current debate over whether normativity and naturalism can be reconciled in social science, and extends and deepens it. No philosopher of social science should ignore it."
—*Don Ross, University of Cape Town, South Africa*

Normativity and Naturalism in the Philosophy of the Social Sciences engages with a central debate within the philosophy of social science: whether social scientific explanation necessitates an appeal to norms, and if so, whether appeals to normativity can be rendered "scientific." This collection brings together contributions from a diverse group of philosophers who explore a broad but thematically unified set of questions, many of which stem from an ongoing debate between Stephen Turner and Joseph Rouse (both contributors to this volume) on the role of naturalism in the philosophy of the social sciences. Informed by recent developments in both philosophy and the social sciences, this volume will set the benchmark for contemporary discussions about normativity and naturalism. This collection will be relevant to philosophers of social science, philosophers interested in the rule following and metaphysics of normativity, and theoretically oriented social scientists.

Mark Risjord is Professor of Philosophy at Emory University, U.S. and the University of Hradec Kralove, Czech Republic.

Routledge Studies in Contemporary Philosophy

For a full list of titles in this series, please visit www.routledge.com

Normativity and Naturalism in the Philosophy of the Social Sciences

Edited by Mark Risjord

LONDON AND NEW YORK

First published 2016 by Routledge

2 Park Square, Milton Park, Abingdon, Oxfordshire OX14 4RN
52 Vanderbilt Avenue, New York, NY 10017

*Routledge is an imprint of the Taylor & Francis Group,
an informa business*

First issued in paperback 2019

Library of Congress Cataloging-in-Publication Data
Names: Risjord, Mark W., 1960– editor.
Title: Normativity and naturalism in the philosophy of the social sciences /
    edited by Mark Risjord.
Description: 1 [edition]. | New York : Routledge, 2016. | Series: Routledge
    studies in contemporary philosophy ; 77 | Includes bibliographical
    references and index.
Identifiers: LCCN 2015037247 | ISBN 9781138936621 (alk. paper)
Subjects: LCSH: Social sciences—Philosophy. | Naturalism. |
    Normativity (Ethics)
Classification: LCC H61 .N57 2016 | DDC 300.1—dc23
LC record available at http://lccn.loc.gov/2015037247

ISBN: 978-1-138-93662-1 (hbk)
ISBN: 978-0-367-23513-0 (pbk)

Typeset in Sabon
by Apex CoVantage, LLC

Contents

1 Introduction

Mark Risjord

THE QUESTION OF NORMATIVITY IN THE SOCIAL SCIENCES

"Sociology begins by disenchanting the world," wrote Alvin Gouldner, "and it proceeds by disenchanting itself" (1968, 103). As this Introduction was being written, the United States Supreme Court decided that the right to marry is enshrined in the Constitution. The global trend toward state endorsement, or at least tolerance, of same-sex marriage is strongly resisted by those who see marriage as embodying moral and religious values. Opposite-sex marriage, on these views, is the morally correct social form. The social sciences, by contrast, have been disenchanting marriage and other social relationships for almost two centuries. People do not get married because they ought to, but because socially sanctioned sexual relationships satisfy a variety of biological, psychological, and social needs. The social sciences thus disenchant the world by replacing the commonsense tangle of explanation and justification with empirically robust theory. In so doing, the social sciences have not fully disenchanted themselves. Social scientific accounts routinely appeal to social, moral, and aesthetic values, as well as rules, conventions, practices, standards, commitments, regulations, and laws. What are we to make of the normativity that figures in the social sciences? Is appeal to normativity a vestige of pre-scientific thought that will disappear as our theories become more sophisticated? Or is normativity an irreducible dimension of the social world that the social sciences should not ignore?

Questions about the place of normativity in the social sciences instantiate some of the oldest metaphysical and epistemological questions in philosophy. While philosophy has primarily been concerned with the relationship of moral 'oughts' to nonmoral facts, philosophical thinking has always—implicitly or explicitly—encompassed theories of the social world. When the social sciences budded off from philosophy in the nineteenth century, the philosophical divide between those who took norms to be irreducible and those who sought to naturalize them persisted. The philosophical question of whether 'ought' can be reduced to 'is' was thus played out in the context of increasingly empirical and causal social theories. In the last several decades, inquiry into social phenomena has been richly informed by evolutionary, neuroscientific, and cognitive theory. Extensive theoretical and methodological mixing has produced fields like evolutionary psychology, cognitive anthropology, and behavioral economics. These developments provide a host of new challenges to and resources for the traditional questions about normativity. At the same time, late twentieth-century philosophy has seen a resurgence of interest in normativity, and new arguments and analyses have become available. The essays in this volume bridge recent work in the social sciences with that in philosophy in order to approach anew the ancient questions about the place of norms and values in a mechanistic world.

'NORMATIVITY' AND 'NATURALISM' IN THE PHILOSOPHY OF SOCIAL SCIENCE

Like all philosophical questions with a long history, the very terms in which the issue is cast have become part of the debate. It is no surprise, then, that in the papers below much of the discussion turns on how to properly understand 'naturalism' and 'normativity'. In order to engage the questions debated in this volume, it is necessary to recognize the range of senses these words have taken on.

'Naturalism' is used to mark a position in at least three debates. The first is a meta-philosophical debate, one that concerns the methodology of philosophy. In this sense, naturalists are those philosophers who see philosophy as continuous with the sciences. Naturalists hold that, at the very least, philosophers need to take scientific results and methods seriously and consider their consequences for philosophical issues. More ambitiously, some naturalists adopt methods, theories, or conceptual frameworks from the sciences. A philosophical naturalist need not take the sciences at face value, of course. Critical reflection on scientific practice is an important part of the philosophical naturalists' program. To oppose naturalism, in this metaphilosophical sense, would be to hold that philosophy is prior to, or otherwise independent of, scientific inquiry. It is probably safe to say that all of the essays of this volume are naturalist in the metaphilosophical sense.

In the second sense, 'naturalism' is used to mark a central question within the philosophy of the social sciences: What is the relationship between the social and natural sciences? Should (or must, or can) the social sciences adopt the methods, conceptual frameworks, or explanatory forms of the natural sciences? In this debate, naturalists hold that there is continuity between the social and the natural sciences. Anti-naturalists argue that humans have some feature—e.g., free will or rationality—that requires methods, concepts, or forms of explanation that make the study of humans distinct from the study of non-human objects. Recognition of values and adherence to norms are distinctive of human beings, and therefore, this *epistemic* sense of naturalism is integral to the discussion among the contributors below.

The third sense of naturalism relevant to this volume might be called *metaphysical* naturalism, as it concerns the place of norms and values[1] in a world of causes and material objects. Some metaphysical naturalists take an eliminativist stance, arguing that talk of norms and values should ultimately be replaced by a psychological or sociological descriptive vocabulary. Other metaphysical naturalists look for ways to reconceptualize norms to make them consistent with the picture of human capacities that is emerging from biology, neuroscience, and cognitive psychology. On the latter sort of metaphysical naturalism, norms are real features of the natural (causal-material) world that emerge from or supervene on human capacities and interactions. There are many who regard both of these projects as impossible. Normativity has features that resist any sort of reduction to causal-material processes. While metaphysical anti-naturalists take values to be independent of facts, they do not all hold that norms are a distinct kind of substance. Many of the authors in this volume who are identified as 'normativist' want to find a place for norms in the natural world. Whether their views count as metaphysically naturalistic is one of the hotly debated topics below.

'Normativity' is intended to cover a wide range of phenomena paradigmatically expressed as rules or obligations, though of course norms need not be explicitly formulated by anyone. There is broad agreement among the contributors to this volume that anything normative must satisfy the Wittgensteinian desideratum: if x is a norm, then there must be a difference between something being right (correct, justified) according to x and something seeming right according to x. Several features of norms follow from this requirement. First, norms cannot be flatly identified with regularities. If there is an account of normativity that is naturalistic (in any of the senses identified above), the difference between being right and seeming right will have to be constructible in terms of human capacities and interactions. Second, anything subject to norms is subject to correction, sanction, praise, or blame. And, of course, any sanctions may themselves be judged correct or incorrect. This introduces a further feature of norms: there is a way in which they 'point beyond themselves'. Normativity is a teleological notion, not in the sense of a spooky causal pull from the future, but in the sense that a norm's demands are never fully determined by past judgments. Whether something is now correct depends on judgments to be made in the future.

Since the title of this volume invokes a contrast between naturalism and normativity, it is natural to treat the debate as having two camps: the naturalists and the normativists. The foregoing discussion should show that such an opposition is not a simple dichotomy. The broadest question of this volume is whether the central features of normativity are consistent with the demands of either an epistemological or metaphysical form of naturalism. Some of the essays below argue for a negative answer, and conclude that there is a forced choice between naturalism and normativism. It is important to recognize, however, that the antithesis of naturalism and normativity is a position within the debate, not a shared presupposition of the debate. The normativists in this volume argue for the importance, or even indispensability, of norms in understanding the social world. But to answer the main question in the affirmative is to argue that there is no forced choice. Many of the authors in this volume who are described as normativist thus accept some form of epistemological or metaphysical naturalism. The problem is whether they can coherently do so.

THE CONTEMPORARY PROBLEMATIC AND ITS ORIGINS

In the nineteenth and twentieth centuries, the battle line in the naturalism-normativity war was drawn around the difference between the natural sciences and the social sciences. The phenomenon of normativity was used to argue that the social sciences have a distinctive object and method. The natural sciences, it was argued, explained phenomena by fitting them within law-like regularities. The human capacity to bind ourselves to laws and to act on the basis of rules disappears when it is treated as an instance of law-like or causal regularities. Hence, the human sciences required a form of understanding—Dilthey's *verstehen* or Collingwood's reenactment—that was distinct from natural scientific explanations. These nineteenth-century and early twentieth-century arguments for epistemic anti-naturalism relied on a neo-Kantian metaphysics of normativity wherein value is closely associated with rationality and does not reduce to fact or causal law.

In the mid-twentieth century, rationality became the focus of debate. Hempel's seminal paper on explanation, "The Function of General Laws in History" (1942), put instrumental rationality into a natural scientific explanatory framework. Dray (1957) objected on the grounds that treating instrumental rationality as a psychological law failed to capture the agent's reasons. The reasonableness of an action, from the agent's point of view, is not simply the fact of desiring the outcome, but that the outcome is desirable. Also opposing a conception of scientific theory and explanation that relied on subsumption under law-like regularities, Winch (1958) used a neo-Wittgensteinian analysis of rules to argue against the scientific explanation of human behavior. Winch's arguments expanded the debate to theoretical rationality, and it encompassed economics, anthropology, and sociology as well as history.

The traditional debate in the philosophy of the social sciences has been made more complex in the last several decades by three developments. First, philosophical views of the *natural* sciences have become more sophisticated. It is no longer plausible to think of the natural sciences as all following the pattern set by Newtonian mechanics. Biology, chemistry, and physics exhibit considerable variation in their methods, theory structures, and ontological commitments. In addition, few philosophers of science argue that natural science must be strictly value free. This further effaces a source of difference between the social and natural sciences. Second, within the social sciences, appeal to biological, neurological, and psychological mechanisms has become increasingly powerful and widespread. These explanations seem to advance the cause of naturalism insofar as they close the methodological and ontological distance between the natural and social sciences. Moreover, they provide new resources for the social scientific understanding of normative phenomena. These two developments have made any simple dichotomy between natural and social sciences impossible.

The third development lies in recent accounts of normativity. There has been a revival of interest in neo-Kantian accounts of the metaphysics of normativity. This work tends to be anti-naturalistic in all three senses articulated above. While philosophically important, it has not been taken up by the social sciences. Two alternative accounts of normativity, rational choice theory and the expressivist-pragmatic view, are of particular interest to the current debate over naturalism. Both views have traction within the social sciences and both have metaphysically naturalistic credentials (though these credentials are subject to debate below). Rational choice theory (decision theory and game theory) has been an inspiration for accounts of normativity since Lewis's *Convention* (1969). In recent decades, a number of philosophers and social scientists have drawn on the growing body of experimental work to develop more psychologically plausible rational choice models of normative phenomena. With respect to the expressivist-pragmatic analyses of normativity, there is a strong conceptual affinity between these philosophical theories and the social theories of Pierre Bourdieu, Anthony Giddens, and other 'practice theorists'. The essays below respond critically to all three accounts of normativity, and the latter two provide important resources for those who want to construct a naturalistic view of normativity.

THE CONTEMPORARY DEBATE

Understood against the background of the recent developments, the questions "Is an appeal to norms and normativity required for an adequate understanding of ourselves?" and if so, "Can appeals to normativity be rendered 'scientific'?" take on a new significance. These questions frame the entire volume and the essays by Turner and Rouse present two poles of the dispute. Turner's essay argues that social scientific explanations have rendered appeal to any transcendental norms, and in particular moral norms, superfluous in the explanation of human action. Writers for this volume are generally unsympathetic to the idea that normativity requires an ontological status outside of the world of human interaction. However, they do not agree that such disenchantment expunges normativity. Many of the authors argue that paying due attention to the normative dimension of human societies is indispensable for an adequate account of us humans as social beings.

The difficult questions concern how this normative dimension of human societies is to be conceptualized, and why it is indispensable. The essay by Joseph Rouse sketches a powerful answer that treats normativity as resulting from an ecological niche of mutually accountable practices. The bulk of the essays respond directly to the dispute framed by Turner's and Rouse's contributions.

Within the broad problematic set by the Turner and Rouse essays, four subsidiary issues come to the fore in this volume: explanation, instrumental rationality, agency, and methodology. In his critique of Rouse, Roth contends that "nothing normative can or does do real explanatory work." The first issue, then, is whether an appeal to norms can have any value as an explanation. This issue runs throughout the volume, with Turner, Roth, Henderson, Paleček, and Ylikoski and Kuorikoski developing arguments against explanatory normativity, while Rouse, Peregrin, Stueber, Okrent, Eriksson, and Risjord argue in favor. The ground on which this issue is debated has shifted as the social sciences have begun to appeal to models from evolutionary biology and cognitive psychology. To what extent can the explanatory role for norms be discharged by biological or cognitive mechanisms that enable social interaction? And to what extent do such explanations satisfy the purported need for normativity in the social sciences? The essays by Risjord, Stueber, Dinishak, and Paleček explore the relevance of cognitive and neurological mechanisms to understand explanatory appeals to normativity, while Rouse, Peregrin, and Okrent develop models that draw on evolutionary biology.

The second issue concerns instrumental rationality. Deliberate action is instrumentally rational. *Prima facie,* then, normativity is required to account for intentional action. Moreover, decision theory and game theory seem to embed the normativity of instrumental rationality into their models. Can the normativity of motive, reason, or utility be accounted for in naturalistic terms? Here again, the traditional question has been put in a new light by recent scientific developments. Behavioral economics and similar programs call into question the adequacy of rational choice modeling, and indicate that at the least, these models need to be supplemented with other resources. And research into the psychology of decision and intention has called into question our folk-psychological understanding of motives and choices. The essays by Eriksson, Koreň, Ylikoski and Kuorikoski, and Stueber explore the question of whether instrumental rationality, understood either folk psychologically or through the lens of rational choice theory, requires a commitment to normativity that cannot be naturalistically captured.

The issue of whether the social sciences must be distinct from the natural sciences has both conceptual and methodological dimensions. The issues of agency and interpretation respond to these two dimensions of the (epistemological) naturalism problematic. Different ways of thinking about agency in the social sciences has been at the root of the arguments over whether the social and the natural sciences share a unified ontology. What must people be like, if they are to be moved by reasons? What sort of understanding of agency is needed to account for the normative aspects of human action or social interaction? Fitting persons within a fully causal system of the world has long troubled normativists and naturalists. And here again, both psychology and biology have helped change the conversation about the ontological distinctiveness of the social sciences. In their essays, Stueber, Risjord, Paleček, and Koreň examine the ways in which specific cognitive mechanisms provide the basis for new ways of thinking about agency, and how these new conceptions might be embedded within social scientific theorizing. Dinishak uses recent work on autism to call into question the idea of like-mindedness, thereby challenging presuppositions about agency and our ability to explain the behavior of others. Okrent, Peregrin, and Rouse look to the resources of biology to conceptualize natural beings that are responsive to norms, and thereby dissolve the dualism of normative agents and non-normative animals.

The epistemic dimension of the naturalism issue in the philosophy of the social sciences often focuses on questions of methodology. Arguments for a distinctive method typically begin by identifying some feature of humans that cannot be captured by causal regularities. Normativity is a leading candidate, so the possibility of a metaphysically naturalistic account of norms has direct consequences for the plausibility of epistemological naturalism. Koreň reflects on the methodological consequences of fitting traditional rational choice models to the new experimental evidence about choice behavior. Paleček's contribution tries to methodologically split the difference between naturalism and normativism, giving rules a descriptive role complemented by (non-normative) cognitive explanations. Participant observation has often been presented as necessary for understanding the normativity of human interaction. Zahle engages the question of whether the epistemology of participant observation requires or motivates an anti-naturalist position.

The themes of explanation, instrumental rationality, agency, and methodology crisscross in the essays below to such an extent that it is impossible to arrange them in thematic clusters. The authors are responding to a closely related set of questions, and are often arguing directly with one another. The essays have therefore been arranged dialectically; for the most part, each essay is followed by another that argues for the opposite answer to one of its central questions. Reading through the chapters in order is not necessary, but doing so will trace an intellectually satisfying path through some of the central terrain of the philosophy of the social sciences.

NOTE

1 Contributors to this volume do not distinguish systematically between norms and values. Henceforth, the qualifier ". . . and values" will be dropped.

REFERENCES

Dray, William. 1957. *Laws and Explanation in History*. Oxford: Oxford University Press.

Gouldner, Alvin W. 1968. The Sociologist as Partisan: Sociology and the Welfare State. *The American Sociologist* 3(2):103–116.

Hempel, Carl. 1942. The Function of General Laws in History. *Journal of Philosophy* 39:35–48.

Lewis, D. 1969. *Convention*. Cambridge, MA: Harvard University Press.

Winch, Peter. 1958. *The Idea of a Social Science*. London: Routledge and Kegan Paul.

2   The Naturalistic Moment in Normativism

Stephen Turner

INTRODUCTION

Arguments for normativism are notoriously diverse, just as the normativities that are asserted by them are. So is the role attributed to normativity. In this paper I will focus on a question about one role: the explanatory role of normativism or normativity in relation to ordinary "scientific," meaning social scientific, explanations of actions and beliefs, especially the empirical, observable, or empirically relevant aspects of human conduct. My concern will be with a narrow question. When social scientific explanations are complete, is there something left over—a gap in the explanation—that can be filled by appeals to normativity, or needs to be? My specific initial concern, however, will be even narrower than this; it will be with a particular case, namely, normativists' claims to have something special and additional to say about motivation above and beyond what social science says. This is a relatively clear case of overlap or conflict between normativism and social science. Motivation is an element of the usual kinds of explanations of human action. Normativists—or at least some of them—claim to have a non-natural motivator that actually accounts for action and serves as a motive, like the natural motives of social science and psychology, as part of the causal world.

I will call this a "naturalistic moment," a place where normativism makes factual assertions about real processes in the natural world. In this case, it is the claim that moral reasons, by virtue of their normativity, or because of the goodness of the reasons, have some sort of explanatory force beyond the mere "natural" fact of people's beliefs and desires. The kind of normativisms I will consider here are those primarily found in ethics, which is where I will begin. But they appear as well in related forms in the extended kind of ethics that figures in semantic approaches to normativity, which I will return to at the end of the paper. Rather than reconstructing these arguments at great length, which is pointless given the fact that these authors agree on little about the specifics of their claims, I will to try to identify the specific point of apparent connection, and conflict, with the concerns of normal social science explanation. The basic issue with these accounts is what I will call their dualistic structure: for every normative account, there is a social science or naturalistic alternative, which explains the same thing, or the empirically equivalent thing. The normativist must claim that there is some super-added normative element that cannot be accounted for naturalistically or by social science. What I will show is that these claims fail: they merely serve to push the conflict back so that it reappears at the next level because the super-added element *also* has a social science explanation that parallels the normative one. Although the examples of normativism I will work with here are highly specific, the basic structure of the problem is generic.

LIMITING THE TERMS

The term "normative" is especially problematic. Commentators have made the point that the term "normative" tends to be used more or less indiscriminately in much of this discourse to apply to everything with ideational content. But to set some sort of limit to this discussion, I will make two stipulative restrictions, which I will explain and justify briefly, in the full recognition that in this literature there will be (a few) reputable philosophers who reject even these restrictions, and others who, we will see, overstep them in the course of their arguments.

The restrictions attempt to exclude, or problematize, two groups of claims. Rudolf Carnap observed that science proceeded in accordance with certain habitual ways of thinking. His project of rational reconstruction into artificial languages was designed to make the thinking of science explicit, consistent, and so on, but also *better* because it was explicit, consistent, and so on ([1950] 1992, 73–4). Carnap never thought he was representing what was implicit in scientific thought or explaining natural language with formal methods. Like rational choice theorists talking about the naïve reasoning of ordinary people, he considered scientific thought to be a good start, but something that could be improved on by representing it formally. A rational reconstruction was a self-conscious idealization, not an explanatory psychological or social science project. Idealizations are thus excluded in what follows. This is the first restriction.

My second stipulation is to restrict the notion of "normative" in relation to thought or inference to those forms of thought or inference that are not shared with infants and animals. Squirrels figuring out how to get the food out of a bird feeder and making conditional inferences to do so, monkeys imitating other monkeys using tools, monkeys paying joint attention and recognizing that the other monkey is attending, or monkeys finding a tool to use in the first place, are not normative, even if their thought processes can be reconstructed in accordance with the laws of logic or rational choice theory. An infant in the crib solving the false belief problem is not thinking in a norm-governed way even if it conforms with what can be reconstructed as norms. Similarly, making oneself understood is a practical, non-normative achievement, accomplished by infants; in contrast, speaking "correctly," meaning in non-accidental accordance with an ideal or standard, is a normative one. Anticipating consequences of one's actions, likewise, is not normative, but predictive and empirical; applying sanctions in conscious conformity with a rule is normative. The issues are with the many things that fall between these broad limits.

What is "tacit," such as the habitual reasoning Carnap was reconstructing, is not normative, because, more generally, if the thing that has been acquired was acquired by normal causal means of habituation, trial and error, pragmatic testing, or other means available to infants and animals, or is part of our inherited capacities or tendencies, it is not "normative." A way of doing things can become "normative" by virtue of a belief about it—that it is the *right* way to reason, dress, speak, or behave, for example. "Moral" propensities, like the propensity to feel shame when others shame us, or altruism, or sympathy, might seem to be an exception to this: they are both natural and might be thought to be intrinsically "moral" apart from any beliefs we have about these feelings. But "normativisms" as I have defined them here, although it might acknowledge these propensities, doesn't depend on them: real normativity requires for them an added ingredient beyond human nature.

Hegel, notoriously, thought that habit was already ideational. Today he would say "normative." My third stipulation is to exclude this usage and the reading of normative notions into "natural" forms of inference and action. Mosquitos are able to catch birds in flight and extract blood from them. If we were to design systems that simulated this remarkable capacity we would rely on a lot of calculus, and even more in the way of mathematics. But it is not appropriate to say that mosquitos possess the concept of integrals and operate correctly in relation to its normative character. If characterizing the thing you are calling normative depends on an analogy to a formal or ideal version of the same thing, there should be independent evidence that the possession in question should be attributed to the mind in question. It is possible to do experiments on squirrels and humans, for example, that exhibit features of their reasoning. Transcendental arguments to the effect that they have to have such and such mental content are likely to fail the mosquito test. This means, for example, that attributing concepts from modal logic to non-formal contexts, such as habits of mind, is not legitimate. Similarly, one can give evidence that squirrels think several steps ahead of their actions, and make choices based on this, so it is legitimate to say that they think conditionally—but not that they "possess modus ponens."

THE PROBLEM OF MOTIVATION

When normativists speak of motivation, this is an apparent reference to something that social scientists, or psychologists, take to be their business to explain or to use in their explanations. Similarly, when normativists discuss such notions as possessing a concept, this presumably also refers to some sort of actual psychological or social process in the world of cause. I take it that a central point of normativism is that the relations, facts, properties, and so forth that concern it are not reducible to, explicable in terms of, eliminated by, or otherwise absorbable into the world of social or psychological explanation. So why would normativists be concerned with motivation?

The reason predates social science and "scientific" psychology. It is deeply rooted in the response to Kant, and not surprisingly there is a Kantian element in much of the normativism that I will discuss. The nineteenth-century response to this problematic was this attack, from the dominant figure in the Philosophy of Law in Germany, Rudolph von Ihering:

> You might as well hope to move a loaded wagon from its place by means of a lecture on the theory of motion as the human will by means of the categorical imperative. If the will were a logical force, it would be obliged to yield to the power of a concept, but it is a very actual existence which you cannot budge by purely logical deductions, and one must have actual pressure to set it in motion. This real force which moves the human will is interest.
>
> (Ihering [1877], 1913, 39)

"Interest," in this passage, is something that explains and is more permanent than pro-attitudes or desires, the proximal "push" explanations of action (Turner 1991).

But Ihering's conception of interest is not quite a social science conception, and this is an important distinction that reappears as an issue in relation to present writers, such as Joseph Raz, who will be discussed shortly. For Ihering, who was a Benthamite, "interest" was a concept with "normative" significance as well. Interests were "real interests" in the Marxian sense: not merely what people took to be their interests, but parts, as Ihering understood it, of human nature. One could understand the evolution of law as the successive replacement of coercive schemes that led to the greater fulfillment of these interests. And this also meant that one had a standard for judging one legal order to be better than another. This was "desirable" because the interests were the source of desires themselves: when one worked one's way up the causal regress explaining desires, one arrived at these facts of human interests.

We get a social science account of interests with Max Weber, who uses the language of interest to make a quite different point:

> Not ideas, but material and ideal interests, directly govern men's conduct. Yet very frequently the "world images" that have been created by "ideas" have, like switchmen, determined the tracks along which action has been pushed by the dynamic of interest. "From what" and "for

what" one wished to be redeemed and, let us not forget, "could be" redeemed, depended upon one's image of the world.

(Weber [1915], 1946, 279)

The phrase "material and ideal" is critical: the term "ideal interests" refers to such interests as salvation. The term points to the huge variety of "moral" or normative motivations found in the actual history of morality, including those in the "honor" or "recognition" family, and how these actually work. There is no assumption that there are genuine interests and pseudointerests, or that if this were so it would be relevant to the explanation. On the other hand, to explain someone's actions in terms of their belief in salvation through the means of rituals or magic, or in terms of a complicated theology of predestination, as Weber did in *The Protestant Ethic* ([1904–5] 1958), is a complex historical and "sociological" task, involving an account of the related beliefs of the agent, the historical situation in which these beliefs came to be compelling, the psychology involved in applying the beliefs in action, and to the particular historical situations in which action occurred. We can take this explanation as a paradigmatic bit of social science.

A simple example of an account of norms in social science in terms of motivation is found in Jon Elster, in part of a much more elaborate discussion of social norms. I present it in this truncated form to indicate what the rival account to normativism looks like. He first explains the function of norms:

> that they have the effect of focusing and coordinating expectations. . . . If the norm to do X is shared within a community, each will expect others to do X. An alternative means of focusing expectations is by psychological salience or prominence.
>
> (Elster 1989, 105)

He then adds a motivational claim:

> A norm, in this perspective, is *the propensity to feel shame and to antici-pate sanctions by others at the thought of behaving in a certain, forbid-den way* . . . this propensity becomes a *social* norm when and to the extent that it is shared with other people . . . the social character of the norm is also manifest in the existence of higher-order norms that enjoin us to punish violators of the first-order norm.
>
> (Elster 1989, 105; emphasis in the original)

So norms are propensities to feel such things as shame or to expect sanctions, which can be shared, and can also be backed by higher-order norms that justify, but also motivate, the punishment of violators.[1]

This definition deals with motivation: indeed, it defines norms in terms of motivations. But it tells us nothing about such things as how people recognize "violations," leaving that to psychology, nor about the validity of the higher norms that apparently justify—the word is not used—but motivate the act of sanctioning. Avoiding this kind of "normative" problem allows this definition to apply very generally. Such primitive normative notions as tabu and fetishes assimilate the "normative" to the dangerous by regarding the punishment befalling the violators of a tabu as a mechanical consequence of the act, independent of human action or the thinking of a deity: the determination of what is a violation is wholly empirical: either the mechanical consequences occur or they do not. Yet both work nicely to produce the functional consequences that are the first part of the definition.

The fact that so much of morality is close kin to the ideas of purity and danger that are part of the notion of tabu, from the caste system to high school notions of sexual morality, should alert us to the smallness of the distance between "empirical consequences" of violation and "incorrectness," and to the ongoing motivational sources of the actual moral psychology of garden-variety norms. With respect to correctness, the reason the social science account gives us no answers is that the determination of what is a correct application of a norm, or what is normatively correct, is not a matter of theory, but is entirely empirical: what is correct avoids sanctions, and what is incorrect incurs them. The advantage of this way of thinking about correctness is that it avoids a puzzle about how correctness is learned: in this account, it is learned empirically, through the reactions of others to one's own actions. It is obscure how it could be otherwise, even if there were such a thing as a generic normative motivation or set of motivations of some sort. One would still need to account for the fine-grained application of norms in actual societies.

THE ZONE OF CONFLICT

The kinds of normativism I will be discussing here are explanatory normativisms: theories which assert that there is some sort of distinctive fact, property, source of validity, or force (for example, the force that is behind inferences or the binding character of law or the psychological force impelling people to fulfill obligations) that is normative as distinct from causal (perhaps irreducible to the causal or otherwise not part of the ordinary stream of explanation), but which nevertheless has some sort of causal force. These kinds of normativism unequivocally reject the kinds of accounts of norms, ideal interests, and so forth given in social science: for this kind of normativist, these at best are about conventions, beliefs, and the like, and not about real normativity, which is a property, quality, or fact of some sort that accounts for validity, meaning genuine validity and not merely believed-in validity, assumed validity, and so forth. This property is claimed to be irreducible, intrinsic, and indispensable for the proper description, understanding, and explanation of normative phenomena.

The problem with this property is one that we have already glimpsed: it always appears in conjunction with, or hidden within, some sort of "natural" or non-normative thing, such as norms as described by Elster, as the mere beliefs corresponding to the "normatively valid" ones that motivate action, and so forth. The narrowness of the gap between the thing described by the normativist and the thing described by social science means that the issue is very often little more than a problem of description: the issue with an Elster-type description of a norm, or a Weberian description of an ideal interest, is that it fails to capture the element of validity. The question this raises is whether the element of validity does any explanatory work. Normativists of the kinds we are considering here insist that it does. Some normativists, whom we might call non-explanatory normativists, do not: the mere claim that normative properties are ordinary factual properties ascertainable by reason, which could be considered a form of normativism, implies nothing about the explanatory role of these properties in relation to action, or in addition to the different fact of the agent's belief that there are such properties.

As a starting point, we can use some arguments provided by Robert Audi, who makes the same basic distinctions I will make, in his discussion of the mental and the moral. The core question for Audi is simple. Does the goodness of a good reason matter to its explanatory or causal role? Audi's answer is that

> whenever we explanatorily invoke a moral property, it will be in part on the basis of, or at least in the light of, some belief or presupposition to the effect that one or more natural properties is playing an explanatory role in relation to the phenomenon being explained. We are thus in a position to rely—often unselfconsciously, to be sure—on those other properties to do the explanatory work, and it is arguable that they, and not any moral property, are in fact what does it.
>
> (Audi 1993, 62)

He gives this example: that in the end it was because Richard Nixon was morally corrupt that he was run out of office (1993, 61). He notes that "this explanation is plausible, but if it is successful then such moral properties as corruption seem to have causal power" (1993, 61–2).

The problem is this: What explains Nixon's being run out of office is not his moral properties, but people's beliefs about his moral properties. Whether they were right about this is immaterial. Nixon would have been run out of office whether or not he was "truly corrupt," or whether or not there are such things as moral properties. All that the explanation needs is the beliefs of the agents. As Audi puts it:

> One cannot know (and normally would not even believe) that there is such corruption except through some awareness of, say, lies, hypocrisy, and cover-ups. But these are just the sorts of non-moral

(social-psychological) factors that, in their own right, we suppose (on the basis of our general knowledge of social forces) can perfectly well explain an official's being forced to resign. They also seem to have causal power in a quite intuitive sense. We understand quite well, for example, how lies, when discovered, lead their victims to retaliate. Perhaps it is on the basis of pragmatic reasons—for instance, out of a desire to combine explanation with moral assessment—that we cite the moral factor as cause.

(Audi 1993, 61–2)

There is, as Audi concedes, an indirect sense in which

there could not be beliefs with this content unless someone had moral concepts; for this reason explanations by appeal to such beliefs might be said to be indirectly moral. Such cases show another way in which the moral plays a role in explaining events, but not that a moral property is a causal variable in any explanatory generalization or that some moral phenomenon, as such, has explanatory power.

(Audi 1993, 63n13)

The conclusion here is familiar to social science, because it is Weber's: for pragmatic reasons, it makes sense to use such concepts in explanation, if one keeps in mind that the specifically "normative" content does not do any explanatory work.

This is precisely the way of constructing the problem that normativists routinely deny. An especially clear formulation is found in Joseph Raz. The premise is apparently innocuous: "Acting with an intention or a purpose is acting (as things appear to one) for a reason" (Raz 2009, 184). The next step differs only slightly from Audi:

The reasons referred to above are normative reasons. A normative reason is a fact which, when one acts for it, gives a point or a purpose to one's action, and the action is undertaken for the sake of or in pursuit of that point or purpose. Reasons, and this is the common view among writers on the subject, have a dual role here. They are both normative and explanatory. They are normative in as much as they should guide decision and action, and form a basis for their evaluation. They are explanatory in that when there is a normative reason for which an agent acted then that reason explains (that is, it features in an explanation of) that action.

(Raz 2009, 184)

The conflict is over the "dual role" and its relation to explanation. The question that divides Raz from Audi is this: does the fact that some reasons are, in addition, normative—still explanatory, but normative as well—add to, or qualify, their explanatory significance? For Raz, the answer is "yes."

The dual role of "normative reasons enables them to play a certain explanatory role, and thus . . . the way they function as explanatory reasons presupposes that they are also reasons in a different sense" (Raz 2009, 187).

"Presupposes that they are reasons in a different sense" is the key move. The fact that they are "normative reasons" is what "enables" them to explain. But they could not function in their explanatory role unless they were also *good* reasons—and normative here means "good reasons," as distinct from merely explanatory reasons, which would include bad reasons. The problem is to ground the distinction between good and bad reasons. And to do this we need to move up one step in the regress of justification, where the distinction is presumably clear.

> One may say that reasons for a belief are those facts which explain the believing, meaning the acquisition of the belief when it was rationally induced. But this view allows that 'reasons' is ambiguous between explanatory reasons, which, presumably, can explain all beliefs, and normative reasons for belief, which also explain those beliefs which were rationally arrived at, that is beliefs arrived at because of reasons for the beliefs (and the same can be said of the explanation of why one rationally sustains certain beliefs when the explanation invokes reasons for those beliefs). Regarding the latter kind of reasons their ability to explain the believing depends on the fact that they are normative reasons, reasons which can justify a belief, whether or not they also explain it, and which explain beliefs as rational or justified because they are normative reasons.
>
> (Raz 2009, 189)

Rationally arrived at beliefs can explain *because they are already explained by the reasons for them*. In short, the trick of substituting "believed x" for "x" that was central to Audi's way of making the distinction does not work on the level of explaining belief itself. There we find real reasons, not just "believed to be" reasons.

Good reasons thus deliver us to an explanatory dead end: they are justified and explained by further "normative reasons" which need no further explanation. Normative reasons have the inherent feature of being warranted.

> Reason explanations explain action and belief by reference to their inherent features. After all, it is inherent to beliefs that those having them take them to be warranted, and would abandon them had they thought that they were unwarranted. Similarly, by their nature intentions to act involve belief in reasons for the intended action. Hence reason-explanations deepen our understanding of intentions, actions and beliefs, by contributing to an understanding of whether they have the features which they purport to have.
>
> (Raz 2009, 198)

What does "deepen our understanding" mean here? Raz has his own way of answering this question, and it depends on the liberal use of terms like "inherent." He claims that evaluative issues deepen our understanding of action by telling us whether the agents are right about what they think they are doing, and further claims that this deepening is "relevant" to ordinary explanations. Why does "an understanding of whether they have the features which they purport to have" (Raz 2009, 198) matter to explanation? On the surface, it is merely a matter of adding a normative endorsement to the reason that does the explaining. If it was something else, such as our independent investigation into the truth and our discovery that the reasons are valid, it would be irrelevant to explaining how the agent in question acted—these would be our reasons for believing the agents' reasons were valid, not his. So it seems that all we are doing that is at all relevant to the explanation when we decide the agent is right is to agree with him. This doesn't deepen our understanding of the action at all—we had to already understand the reasons the agent had, which are the reasons that do the explaining. Raz denies this, and gives the following "argument":

> It may clarify things if we return to explanations of actions done in the belief that there is reason (or that there is undefeated reason) for them when that belief is false. Observing common explanations offered in such cases we distinguish several types:
>
> (a) The agent did it because he believed that R
> (b) The agent did it because he mistakenly believed that R (where 'R' has the required content for a reason explanation).
>
> It would be a mistake to think that (b) is the same explanation as (a) as the reference to the fact that there was no R is explanatorily idle. Rather (b) is a more comprehensive explanation than (a). (a) is adequate to a certain range of interests in why the agent so acted. (b) is adequate for a wider, perhaps one may say here, deeper range of interests. Similarly, when the belief which led to the action was true we still have two possible types of explanation:
>
> (a) The agent did it because he believed that R
> (c) The agent did it for R
>
> (c) entails that he believed that R. (a) is still a good explanation, but for the reasons explained (c) is a better, more comprehensive explanation, one which answers a wider range of interests in the action.
>
> (Raz 2009, 198)

The argument, then, is that normal non-normative explanations are better, because they are adequate for a deeper range of interests. The question remains: are these explanatory interests, or merely normative ones—an interest in endorsing a reason as valid?

This pseudoargument boils down to a series of equivocations. Better and more comprehensive in what sense? Explanatory or normative? And this is just the beginning of the equivocations, which are equivocations between normative and non-normative senses of the same terms. Is the deeper range of interests a matter of "real interests," or what the person takes to be her interests? One may ask whether these interests are interests in the sense of Weber, the social science sense, meaning our historically situated, culturally generated interests in explanation, or something less relativistic. But Raz does not ask this, because he thinks that "interests" provides the dead end that justifies the previous assertion that normative reasons are an explanatory dead end. Instead, the justification is circular: our non–social science "interests" that are supposed to ground these claims turn out to be nothing more than the normativists' partisan interest in validating particular reasons.

The same problem arises with "reason" itself. Is reason "inherent" in something, or are the reasons people use to justify their reasons things that they take to be reasons? Behind these questions is a simple equivocation over "reason" and Reason with a capital R, or genuine reason, which Raz does not directly address. The relation between intention and action requires only that the agent take something to be a reason. It requires a belief—not a true belief. The belief that something is a reason is just another belief. So is the belief that something is a genuine reason. Because Raz cannot imagine that reason is a contested concept, that different people or different groups take different things to be reasons, he cannot see the equivocation.

Nor does he think it matters how people came to their beliefs: This is why he dismisses the idea that "reasons for a belief are those facts which explain the believing, meaning the acquisition of the belief when it was rationally induced." He sees that this just pushes the question back to whether the inducing was rational. But rather than going back in the explanatory direction to ask *why* they thought it was rational he goes directly to the normative concept, and argues that the explanatory work is done by appealing to the normative reasons themselves. He acknowledges that "none of the above constitutes an explanation of the productive process which leads to awareness of the reason and from there to the motivation and the action" (Raz 2009, 200). But he goes on to say:

> That is, of course, true, but I doubt that it is a drawback. Welcome as such explanations are, they are not needed for an understanding of the normative-explanatory nexus. Indeed, so far as that goes they may do too much. As stated the nexus is sufficient, for those who understand it, to distinguish cases in which an action is done for a normative reason (and can be explained relying on the nexus) from other cases.
>
> (Raz 2009, 200)

In short, once we have worked our way back to a case of genuine reason, which he imagines the reason-action nexus to be, the work is done.

Explaining the provenance of the beliefs in question is "too much." But none of this helps Raz. One needs some further argument that genuine reasons explain without additions and other reasons, non-genuine reasons, explain only if something is added. The problem is still there: bad reasons explain just as much as good ones do. So the "normativity" of the normative-explanatory nexus adds nothing.

Raz nevertheless provides a useful, and crucial, guide to the point of normative arguments about motivation, and allows us to see exactly what they are supposed to do. And this will allow us to see how, and how well, some of the many attempts to provide a normative solution to this problem work. Normative reasons explanations are explanations and norms at the same time: they have a dual character. If the normative and the explanatory (causal or explanatory but non-normative, depending on how one chooses to understand action explanation) aspects are separable, for example by the device of treating the belief as a cause or reason rather than the fact pointed to by the belief—a belief in Nixon's corruption rather than the fact of corruption itself—the normativist argument fails. The normative element adds nothing to the explanation. So there must be some intrinsic, inherent, logical, conceptual, or other bond between the normative and the explanatory parts of the duality that prevents this from happening. One solution, which Raz tries and which, as we will shortly see, is tried by others in different ways, is to cut off the use of the "belief" device at the next level. Raz tries to do this by saying that normative reason explanations, meaning in the case of Nixon's corruption those that cite the fact of corruption rather than the belief, are better and more comprehensive explanations, and fit better with our interests. He simply dismisses the explanatory interest of the social sciences in the origin and acquisition of these normative beliefs, though it is a mysterious and unanswered question as to why this is too much and unnecessary, and who it is too much and unnecessary for, other than the promoters of a particular moral position. The overt point, however, is that normative reasons explanations are explanatory regress stoppers, with respect to both the normative (or justificatory) and the explanatory regresses, and that only an explanation in which the dual aspects are not separated (namely, genuine normative reasons) are explanatory regress stoppers. These reasons, moreover, are motivators, and motivators as such, that require no additional motivational theory: A normative reason is sufficient in itself to explain and motivate.

THE NORMATIVE REASON REGRESS PROBLEM

It is easy to see what conclusion Raz wants to reach. In a phrase, Raz wants the goodness of a good reason to make it explanatory. Moreover, he wants goodness to be a dead end of explanation: the place where both the normative and the explanatory regresses end. But it is typical of these kinds of cases that the two regresses split and go in different directions. If we want to know why something is a law, for example, why the possession of firearms is a right in the United States and not in Europe, one needs to work one's way back to the historical differences that led to the enactment of various laws. For the normativist, in contrast, what makes a law a law is the fact of its enactment according to norms: one regresses along the chain of normative justification to the norms governing the creation of norms. To be sure, this is part of the causal story too, but not the *end* to the causal story.

Raz simply fails to give a reason for stopping the regress where he does. There is a large difference between an explanation that says "people believed Nixon was corrupt" and "Nixon was corrupt." Explanations involving beliefs invite and require further explanations of the beliefs; explanations that cite the "fact" of Nixon's corruption do not. By saying that the latter is more comprehensive and better, Raz wants to end the regress with it and to ignore the regress of explaining beliefs by how they were produced.

There are a number of possible normativist responses to the problem of how to make the regress end with normativity. One we will consider shortly: Motivated Judgment Internalism. But a somewhat different response to the problem of stopping regresses that appeal to beliefs, beliefs about beliefs, and so forth, comes from Christine Korsgaard. She claims that her argument

> …is essentially the same as a now-familiar argument to the effect that the standards of logic cannot enter into reasoning as premises. Suppose George does not reason in accordance with modus ponens. He does not see how you get from "If A then B" and "A" to the conclusion that "B." As is often pointed out, it does not help to add modus ponens as a premise, that is to say, to add "if A and B, and also A, then B." For you still need to reason in accordance with modus ponens in order to get any conclusion from these premises, and this is what George does not do.
>
> (2009, 67)

Because they are not premises, the things that compel one to reason in accordance with modus ponens must be something other than more premises, meaning more beliefs. And without this something other, Korsgaard claims, George will not have a mind at all.

> For it is important to notice that if George lacks logic, his mind will be a disunified jumble of unrelated atomistic beliefs, unable to function as a mind at all. It will be a *mere heap* of premises. And that is where the normativity comes in. What obligates George to believe B in these circumstances is not merely his belief that "if A then B" and also that "A," but rather modus ponens itself. And it is not his *belief* in modus ponens that obligates him to believe B, for that, as the argument we have just looked at shows, is irrelevant. What obligates him to believe B is that, if he does not reason in accordance with modus ponens, he will not have a mind at all.
>
> (2009, 67; emphasis in the original)

Modus ponens is unmistakably "normative"; so the argument is that normativity is a binding, motivating force in the mind, which forces us to reason in accordance with modus ponens, is the "something other" that is missing, and allows George to have not merely a jumble of beliefs, if indeed he can properly be said to have beliefs, but a mind.

Does this stop the regress at something normative? No. The property of "normativity" of modus ponens is borrowed from its role as a normative rule in a formal system. To "reason in accordance with modus ponens" is something else entirely. The idea that George "will not have a mind at all" if he fails to reason in accordance with it does not mean that we do not need a further explanation of why George reasons in this way. And it does not mean that this further explanation will not be a naturalistic, psychological one. The argument fails the squirrel test: They reason in accordance with modus ponens when they are thinking ahead several steps in defeating the anti-squirrel defenses of a bird feeder. But they are "bound" only by pragmatic considerations. Modus ponens may be a rule, within a formal system, and thus normative. Reasoning in accordance with it no more requires a binding force of normativity than falling in accordance with Galilean laws requires one.

The structure of the problem can be seen in the notion of "normative practice." The term practice means something like skill, in both a minimal and a more elaborate sense. Learning when to use the word "cat" is learning a skill of sorts. So is the very complex skill of arguing a case before a particular tribunal governed by a set of legal traditions, laws, and accepted modes of argument. And here we see a characteristic pattern. Learning is a natural fact: Whatever is learned goes through a natural psychological process to be learned. If we break down the notion of practices into its elements we get a characteristic structure: Practices are psychological facts, such as dispositions that take the form of habits and have been learned, perhaps material objects that are part of the activity, and beliefs about the activity, about what is the right and wrong way to do something. These beliefs do the explanatory work that "normativity" is supposed to do.

THE "POSSESSION" SOLUTION

The default position of rationalistic normativists, well encapsulated by Korsgaard, who rejects it, is that

> normativity—in particular, rightness—is an objective property grasped by reason. On such views, the rightness of an action, or for that matter the logical force of an argument, is an objective fact about the external world, which the rational mind as such grasps, and to which it then conforms its beliefs and actions.

(2009, 6)

The oddity is evident here in the language: The properties are not observed, nor do they push people around in a causal way. They are rather "grasped" by something, "the rational mind," which is itself described in such a way that it has unusual properties, such as a faculty of "reason" that enables it to "grasp" normative facts, which, once grasped, are conformed to.

Call this the epistemic form of the naturalistic moment problem. The classical form of this problem arises with Platonic forms: if they exist, how do they relate to us as ordinary human beings? The question is usually answered in terms of novel concepts, such as "participation." And one can identify the places in which forms of normative idealism arise when one stumbles on these words. In this case, one finds them in the writings of Levy-Bruhl on the primitive mind ([1922] 1923), among other places. "Participation" is distinctive, and with enough unusual historical associations to stand out. Some of these terms are so commonplace that they no longer seem as odd as they should.

The idea of "possessing a concept" is a particularly strange member of this family, but ubiquitous. All the talk about acquiring and possessing is metaphor. Learning is what actually happens. The metaphors are redescriptions that allow for the introduction of usages that can be claimed to be normative: Once one gets the notion of concepts, one can claim that the concepts have conceptual linkages, that is to say linkages that can only be understood normatively. But what is the analogy here? That a concept is a kind of collective piece of property that multiple people can possess, but which some people do not possess? That it is acquired through some mysterious process that is like learning but cannot exactly be learning because it is not the kind of thing that can be "learned"? But this "acquisition" language is analogical, and it is unclear what the analogy is to. Similarly for the equally ubiquitous term "grasp." It is a physical metaphor for a person's engagement with a nonphysical thing, such as a rule or a concept. These metaphors stand in for something in the natural world. The problem is to figure out what this something is.

But even if we dispense with these metaphors, the regresses can be claimed to end in the normative. Suppose we are to say that the skills in question, using the word "cat," for example, are simply learned, and that beliefs about the rightness of the usage are also learned, and therefore as skills are wholly in the domain of the natural. The normativist can reply that the term "belief" implies rationality, because to attribute a belief requires us to attribute the believer as having reasons for the belief, and "reason" is a term that depends on a normative notion of rationality. "Rationality" is a normative concept. The regress thus ends in a norm, and the practice is thus normative after all.

Yet the same issues with the dualistic structure of "normative reasons" reappear in this case. With "rationality," there is the psychological stuff of actual reasoning, complete with its biases and errors, and the reconstructed purified stuff of decision theory and logic. If we are explaining actual behavior, it is the unreconstructed raw material that needs to be explained and to do the explaining. The reconstruction is a conscious attempt at representing reasoning, but one that cleans it up and simplifies it in order to meet other criteria, such as formal simplicity and adequacy, consistency, and so forth. By importing these notions into actual reasoning we substitute an explanation of an artificial structure for the things that need explaining and do the explaining, things that are not "normative" except by analogy: They fail the squirrel test. There is a direct social science parallel to this problem, in Weber. He treats the model of rationality employed in economics as an ideal-type. It does not explain the actual rational actions of people, but models them—as a model of the *Titanic* hitting the iceberg might be used to model the actual event. The actual causes in each case are to be found in the course of the events to be explained, not in the model. To imagine that something happening with the model caused the actual events would be voodoo.

Mistaking the properties of a reconstruction with the thing reconstructed, as I noted in relation to Carnap, is a characteristic problem, not limited to Korsgaard. One of the most influential texts on normativity is Ralph Wedgwood's attempt to account for the normativity of intention in terms of the normativity of language, under the slogan that "the intentional is normative" Wedgwood (2007), and to account for the normativity of language in the form of conceptual role semantics. This argument is intended to account for motivation as well. As Stephen Finlay explains Wedgwood's argument,

> normative and motivational concepts are interdefined, and that the characteristic conceptual role of normative concepts is to be specified in terms of certain dispositions of thought and intention. So, for example, the conceptual role of "ought" is tied to a disposition to form intentions to act.
> (2010, 337)

This amounts to the claim that a reconstruction, namely the reconstruction called conceptual role semantics, with its definitions and interdefinitions, has causal powers, or is at least "tied" to them. But the explanatory work goes on with the things it is tied to, not the definitions and interdefinitions, which are reconstructions. And these things, dispositions, learned patterns of inference, and the like, are not "normative."

One need not turn to social science for criticism of the whole project of turning concepts into motivators. As Finlay notes,

> . . . easily the most popular response to motivation-based objections today is simply to deny that there is any interestingly close relationship between normative facts/properties and motivation. Nobody argues this point more determinedly than Derek Parfit (2006), who suggests that support for MJI (motivational judgment internalism) is simply a result of conflating normative authority with motivational force.
> (Finlay 2010, 337)

As Finlay explains, Parfit thinks that

> in trying to fill out the blank in the equation, normativity = _____, phi-
> losophers have reached for psychological notions because they couldn't
> imagine what else normativity could be. But Parfit contends that the
> very project is misconceived: normativity is just normativity.
>
> (Finlay 2010, 337)

For Parfit, there is no need for the connection to the normal world—the
naturalistic moment—to be made via motivation. He would be happy dis-
missing Ihering's concern entirely.

One apparently compelling defense of the attempt to make concepts into
motivators that would respond to the approach I have taken here to abstrac-
tion and the dual character of normative reasons would be this: There is
something to the idea that "possessing a concept" motivates action, and
because concepts are normative, there is something to the idea that normativity motivates. But once we strip away the metaphors and set aside
the metaphysics of the concept of concept, and consider a level of explanation that deals with the actual psychological processes and social interaction that the idea of "possessing a concept" metaphorically represents,
we have the following: dispositions, learned inference patterns, long-term
memories perhaps organized into prototypical images as the natural facts
corresponding to "concepts" (Machery 2009), and so forth. There is more
than enough material here to account for any of the motivations in question,
and thus nothing left for the thesis that concepts or semantics are motivators
to explain.

Does this apply generally? Consider one more example, again from
Korsgaard:

> . . . the normativity of obligation is, among other things, a psychological
> force. Let me give this phenomenon a name, borrowed from Immanuel
> Kant. Since normativity is a form of necessity, Kant calls its operation
> within us—its manifestation as a psychological force—necessitation.
>
> (2009, 3)

Is Korsgaard explaining motivation, a plainly psychological phenomenon,
by non-psychological, normative facts? Does she know something psychology doesn't? More generally, how do we decide claims like this where there
are conflicting explanations of apparent psychological facts, one of which
appeals to "normativity," the other of which does not? This issue is clarified
by the formula for the standard theory of intentional action in psychology
provided by Icek Azjen (1991, 2002, 2009). What he calls the "theory of
planned behavior" holds that

> . . . human behavior is guided by three kinds of considerations: beliefs
> about the likely consequences or other attributes of the behavior

(behavioral beliefs), beliefs about the normative expectations of other people (normative beliefs), and beliefs about the presence of factors that may further or hinder performance of the behavior (control beliefs).

(Azjen 2002, 665)

Does Korsgaard add to this list? Not exactly. This would require some sort of evidence that the motivational force she alludes to actually has some sort of effect, and some explanation of what effect it has, where it is effective, and so forth. Needless to say, this is not her concern. The argument presupposes necessitation, and asserts that it is a motivating force, rather than providing, or even allowing, evidence for it. She locates specifically normative motivation in something prior, the human project of self-constitution: "Necessitation, [Kant] thinks, reveals something important about human nature, about the constitution of the human soul. What it reveals—that the source of normativity lies in the human project of self-constitution—is my subject" (2009, 4).

The appeal to self-constitution raises a simple question: is there is a social science doppelganger of the notion of self-constitution that is *not* "normative"? Stripped of the theological language and the hint of the teleological in the notion of "the human project," the claim that people construct or "constitute" a self doesn't seem "normative" at all: one can find a long history of non-normative accounts of the same phenomenon in thinkers like C.H. Cooley (1902), with his influential notion of the looking-glass self, G.H. Mead (1913), with his notion of the "I" and the "me," Erving Goffman, with his account of the presentation of self (1959), and in psychology itself with Kenneth Gergen (1993). Perhaps not surprisingly, these accounts problematize the very notion of the self that Korsgaard (2014) claims is essential to the concept of action, and turn her conception into an *explanandum*. And this, of course, is precisely what the quest for a regress-stopper is supposed to avoid. Moreover, they treat her notion of the self as an illusion generated by more fundamental processes, an illusion sustained by the obscuring implications of the notion of a genuine self. This raises the question of whether her account of the self, which is purpose-built to support her normative account of action, is even the right kind of theory of the self. For her purposes, it cannot merely be an ideology supporting her moral doctrine. But unless it can compete with these theories as an explanation, it cannot be anything more.

NOTE

1 Elster adds many qualifications and variations to this to cover apparent exceptions, but this core definition, which fits well with the ways norms appear in psychological explanatory models of intentional action, will suffice for what follows.

REFERENCES

Ajzen, Icek. 1991. The Theory of Planned Behavior. *Organizational Behavior and Human Decision Processes* 50: 179–211.

———. 2002. Perceived Behavioral Control, Self-Efficacy, Locus of Control, and the Theory of Planned Behavior. *Journal of Applied Social Psychology* 32: 665–683.

Ajzen, Icek, Cornelia Czasch and Michael G. Flood. 2009. From Intentions to Behavior: Implementation Intention, Commitment, and Conscientiousness. *Journal of Applied Social Psychology* 39(6): 1356–1372.

Audi, Robert. 1993. Mental Causation: Sustaining Dynamic. In *Mental Causation,* edited by J. Heil and A. Mele, 53–74. Oxford: Clarendon Press.

Carnap, Rudolf. 1992. Empiricism, Semantics, and Ontology. In *The Linguistic Turn: Essays in Philosophical Method,* edited by R. Rorty, 72–84. Chicago: The University of Chicago Press. Original edition, 1950.

Cooley, Charles H. 1902. *Human Nature and the Social Order.* New York: Scribner's Sons.

Elster, Jon. 1989. *The Cement of Society: A Study of Social Order.* Cambridge: Cambridge University Press.

Finlay, Stephen. 2010. Recent Work on Normativity. *Analysis Reviews* 70(2): 331–346.

Gergen, Kenneth. 1993. *Refiguring Self and Psychology.* Dartmouth, NH: Dartmouth Publishing Company.

Goffman, Erving. 1959. *The Presentation of Self in Everyday Life.* New York: Anchor Books.

Ihering, Rudolph von. 1913. *Law as a Means to an End,* volume 1. 4th edition. Translated by I. Husik. New York: Macmillan. Original edition, 1877.

Korsgaard, Christine. 2009. *Self Constitution: Agency, Identity, and Integrity.* Oxford: Oxford University Press.

———. 2014. The Normative Constitution of Agency. In *Rational and Social Agency: The Philosophy of Michael Bratman,* edited by M. Vargas and G. Yaffe, 190–214. Oxford: Oxford University Press.

Levy-Bruhl, Lucien. 1923. *Primitive Mentality.* Translated by Lilian Clare. London: George Allen & Unwin Ltd. Original edition, 1922.

Machery, Edouard. 2009. *Doing without Concepts.* Oxford: Oxford University Press.

Mead, George H. 1913. The Social Self. *Journal of Philosophy, Psychology and Scientific Methods* 10(14): 374–380.

Parfit, Derek. 2006. Normativity. In *Oxford Studies in Metaethics,* volume 1, edited by Russ Shafer-Landau, 325–380. Oxford: Clarendon Press.

Raz, Joseph. 2009. Reasons: Explanatory and Normative. In *New Essays on the Explanation of Action,* edited by C. Sandis, 184–202. New York: Palgrave/McMillan.

Turner, Stephen. 1991. Two Theorists of Action: Ihering and Weber. *Analyse & Kritik* 13: 46–60.

Weber, Max. 1946. The Social Psychology of the World Religions. In *From Max Weber: Essays in Sociology,* translated by H. H. Gerth and C. W. Mills, 267–301. New York: Oxford University Press. Original edition, 1915.

———. 1958. *The Protestant Ethic and the Spirit of Capitalism.* Translated by Talcott Parsons. New York: Scribner's Sons. Original edition, 1904–1905.

Wedgewood, Ralph. 2007. *The Nature of Normativity.* Oxford: Clarendon Press.

3 Toward a New Naturalism
Niche Construction, Conceptual Normativity, and Scientific Practice

Joseph Rouse

SETTING THE PROBLEM

Wilfrid Sellars (2007, ch. 14) framed contemporary philosophical debates over naturalism by recognizing tensions between two alternative conceptions of human beings in the world. Within the "manifest image" we are *persons*, who encounter our surroundings through sentient experience, conceptual understanding, and rationally reflective agency. The "scientific image" instead characterizes us in theoretical terms drawn primarily from the natural sciences. These two images each purport to completeness and autonomy. Sellars thought both conceptions make legitimate claims upon us. Yet each is also comprehensive, leaving no space for the other. Sellars's primary challenge to naturalists is to accommodate the legitimate claims of both conceptions, while still giving explanatory priority to science. Sellars has rightly characterized the challenge but understated its difficulty. Our received philosophical conceptions of scientific understanding and of normativity block any reconciliation of the two images, or so I argued in *How Scientific Practices Matter* (Rouse 2002).

The difficulty of accommodating conceptual normativity and rationality within a thorough-going naturalism has often seemed especially acute for the social sciences, as sciences *of* the manifest image. I think the challenge confronting naturalistic social science instead merges seamlessly with the challenge for naturalism more generally. The philosophical tradition's dualistic conception of nature and normativity seems to undermine the intelligibility of any comprehensively naturalistic understanding. The authority of the scientific image depends upon our capacities for conceptual understanding and rational accountability. These very conceptual capacities nevertheless seem hard to assimilate within a narrowly scientific understanding of nature. The most crucial philosophical task for naturalists is then to comprehend how that very capacity to understand the world scientifically fits within the bounds of nature, scientifically conceived. Once we have an adequately naturalistic account of scientific practice and understanding, other aspects of social life should fall into place.

The book from which this paper is adapted (Rouse 2015) proposes a constructive response to this challenge. This paper briefly sketches the mutually reinforcing convergence of two of its central revisions to our received conceptions of scientific understanding and conceptual normativity. First, I argue that we need to relocate "the scientific image" within the ongoing practice of scientific research rather than as a body of knowledge extracted from that practice. Second, we also need to recognize how recent developments within evolutionary biology and related fields offer a better way to recognize conceptual normativity as a natural phenomenon: specifically, as a distinctively human form of "niche construction." These two revisions converge in the recognition of the conceptual articulation achieved through scientific research as ongoing material and behavioral niche construction.

SCIENTIFIC RESEARCH ARTICULATES THE WORLD

We naturalists seek to align philosophy with a scientific conception of the world. We also recognize the fallibility of the best current science, and perhaps even more so the fallibility of prevailing conceptions of science. The Vienna Circle Manifesto (Neurath 1973) for a "scientific conception of the world" exemplifies the danger of mistaking a philosophical prescription for deference to scientific inquiry. For Sellars, the Vienna Circle's anti-metaphysical, empiricist, and formalist program was not a "scientific conception" at all, but a sophisticated version of the "manifest image" of ourselves as rational, sentient concept-users. Some recent work on scientific practice in turn challenges Sellars's "scientific image" by denying that science produces, or even aims to produce, a single, unified conception of the world. The disunifiers present scientific understanding as a patchwork that need not even aspire to the Sellarsian image as what Paul Teller (2001) calls a " 'Perfect Model' Model." Their criticism doubly misses its mark, however. First, the disunifiers still mistakenly share Sellars's aspiration to identify the shape or form of scientific knowledge as a whole, whether as unified "image" or patchwork. Second, a more adequate account of scientific understanding must still do justice both to its disunified practices and achievements, and their mutual accountability within discursive practice.

Sellars himself helps point us in a better direction. In a justly famous passage from "Empiricism and the Philosophy of Mind," he argued that "in characterizing an episode or a state as that of knowing, we are not giving an empirical description of that episode or state; we are placing it in the logical space of reasons, of justifying and being able to justify what one says" (Sellars 1997, 76). We usually identify scientific understanding with some position *within* the space of reasons, that is, as a body of knowledge. I think scientific understanding should instead be conceived as the ongoing reconfiguration of the entire conceptual "space." Scientific research brings aspects of the world into the space of reasons by articulating them conceptually. This achievement allows them to be recognized, discussed, understood, and responded to in ways open to reasoned assessment. The sciences also revise the terms and inferential relations through which we understand the world, which aspects of the world are salient and significant within that understanding, and how they matter to that overall understanding. Such revision is ongoing and built into how we articulate the world conceptually, so that scientific conceptualization is open-ended in already pointing beyond any current formulations.

This ongoing reconfiguration of the "space of reasons" underlies the acquisition and refinement of knowledge through scientific inquiry. Scientific knowledge is possible only because of ongoing practical work within the sciences and a broadly scientific culture, which lets relevant aspects of the world show up intelligibly. Being able to say what others cannot, and to talk about things not within their ken, is not just a matter of learning new words; it requires being able to *tell* what you are talking about with those words.[1] As John Haugeland once noted,

> telling [in the sense of telling what something is, telling things apart, or telling the differences between them] can often be expressed in words, but is not in itself essentially verbal. . . . People can tell things for which they have no words, including things that are hard to tell.
>
> (1998, 313)

The sciences allow us to talk about an extraordinary range of things, by enabling us to tell about them, and tell them apart. To pick a small sample of exemplary cases, people can now tell and talk about mitochondria, the Precambrian Era, subatomic particles, tectonic plates, retroviruses, spiral galaxies, and chemical kinetics. One need not go back very far historically to find not error but silence on these and so many more scientific topics.

Quine's (1953) famous image of scientific theory as a self-enclosed fabric or field that only encounters experience at its periphery encapsulates the widespread but mistaken presumption that conceptual articulation is intralinguistic. Experience can provide occasions for conceptual reconfiguration on this view, but the work of doing so is a matter of intralinguistic theory construction. My reconception of "the scientific image" emphasizes instead that conceptual articulation extends beyond theory-building. Philosophical work on scientific theories nowadays often emphasizes the need for models to articulate their content. Morgan and Morrison (1999) influentially describe models as partially autonomous *mediators* between theories and the world. Theories do not confront the world directly, but instead apply to models as relatively independent, abstract representations. Discussions of models as mediators have been one-sided, however, concerned with relations between theories and models while largely ignoring those between models and the world. Recent work on experimental practice shows that theoretical understanding is *doubly* mediated. Ian Hacking (1983) on "phenomena creation," Hans-Jörg Rheinberger (1997) on experimental systems, Hasok Chang (2004) on the experimental "invention" of the concept of temperature, my own work, and Marc Wilson's (2006) extraordinary studies of conceptual development in applied mechanics and materials science display an indispensable experimental contribution to conceptual understanding. The articulation and refinement of salient patterns in the world together with related capacities for pattern recognition are integral to conceptual understanding. Only in the interplay between "well-behaved" experimental systems, and theoretical modeling with its inferential refinement, do further aspects of the world become conceptually articulated or reconfigured. Only thereby does theoretical talk become more than "frictionless spinning in a void," in McDowell's (1994) picturesque phrase.

Wilson's work also highlights the ways in which scientific concepts are never fully articulated, but always open to further intensive and extensive articulation. Wilson treats empirical concepts as only loosely unified patchworks of "facades" bound together into atlases. Even in a well-understood domain such as that exemplified by "the popular categorization of classical physics as *billiard ball mechanics, . . .* one is usually provided with accounts that work approximately well in a limited range of cases, coupled with a footnote of the 'for more details, see . . .' type. . . . [That] does not simply 'add more details' to Newton, but commonly overturns the underpinnings of the older treatments altogether" (Wilson 2006, 180–181). After reviewing a long sequence of incompatible models of billiard ball collisions, Wilson concludes that, "to the best I know, this lengthy chain of billiard ball declination never reaches bottom" (2006, 181).

Alongside these *intensifying* sequences of conceptually articulative models, we also need to accommodate the *extensive* articulation that adapts familiar concepts to unfamiliar circumstances. Wilson objects here to what he calls "tropospheric complacency":

> We readily fancy that we already "know what it is like" to be red or solid or icy *everywhere,* even in alien circumstances subject to violent gravitational tides or unimaginable temperatures, deep within the ground under extreme pressures, or at size scales much smaller or grander than our own, and so forth.
>
> (2006, 55)

Scientific concepts thereby commit us to more than we know how to say or do. Nancy Cartwright (1999) has sought to accommodate the complexity of our "dappled world" by treating scientific concepts such as "force" or "gene" as uniformly projectible but only with limited scope. I respond that the concepts that figure in scientific laws and reasoning are "dappled concepts," with unlimited scope but only patchy and promissory application. Brandom (1994, 583) suggests a relevant analogy between conceptual understanding and grasping a stick. We may only firmly grasp a concept in one part of its domain, but we take hold of the entire concept from there. We are thereby accountable for the unanticipated consequences of its use at the other end and in between. The same is true for the pattern recognition displayed in experimental work. These patterns can be inductively salient far beyond what we know how to say or act upon.

That is why I talk about conceptual normativity in terms of what is at issue and at stake in concept use. "Issues" and "stakes" are fundamentally anaphoric concepts. They allow us to refer to the scope and significance of an extant pattern, concept, or practice (what is at stake there), and what it would be for them to go on in the same way under other circumstances or more stringent demands (what is at issue), even though those issues and stakes might be contested or unknown. This approach converges with Marc Lange's (2000a, 2000b, 2004, 2007) important reconception of the role of laws and nomological necessity in scientific reasoning throughout the sciences (biological and social sciences included). Laws express reliable inference rules for the best inductive strategies to pursue in various contexts, that is, for how their concepts are projectible. Importantly, they play this role not individually, but as sets of laws whose *collective* counterfactual invariance marks a conceptually articulated domain. In practice, of course, scientific reasoning proceeds without anything like a full extensional determination of the relevant laws. The most important scientific consideration is therefore not what the laws *are,* but what we are committed to in *taking* a hypothesis as among the relevant set of laws. Scientific reasoning occurs within ongoing inquiry, directed beyond itself towards an as-yet-indeterminate outcome. Recognizing the anaphoric character of conceptual normativity then clarifies Lange's account of how scientific disciplines shape coherent domains of inquiry. He says that

> a discipline's concerns affect what it takes for an inference rule to qualify as "reliable" there. They limit the error that can be tolerated in a certain prediction . . . as well as deem certain facts to be entirely outside the field's range of interests. . . . With regard to a fact with which a discipline is *not* concerned, *any* inference rule is *trivially* accurate enough for that discipline's purposes.
>
> (2000a, 228)

What matters is not a discipline's *de facto* interests, however, but what is at stake in its practices and achievements. Its members can be wrong about what is at stake in their own work, which also shifts over time as the discipline develops.

Perhaps the clearest indication of divergence between scientific understanding and anything like a composite "scientific image" is provided by the work of the Intergovernmental Panel on Climate Change. The IPPC has actually tried to identify the current state of knowledge in the multidisciplinary domain of climate science with extraordinary care and thoroughness, but that is not how sciences normally proceed. Moreover, the conservatism of this process of consensus-formation strongly suggests that most researchers' understanding of climate diverges from the IPCC conclusions, even when they endorse the process and its outcome as expressing scientific consensus. That claim is not a criticism of the IPCC, but instead shows the divergence between scientific understanding and any composite "scientific image." Scientific understanding both configures a field of reasonable disagreement, and outruns any current formulation in its constitutive openness to further intensive and extensive conceptual refinement.

I have been arguing that a scientific conception of the world is neither a unified nor disunified representation of the world from *within* the space of reasons, but is embedded within scientific practice through an ongoing expansion, reconfiguration, and refinement of the space of reasons itself. In the second part of the paper, I further indicate why this "space of reasons" is not something ethereal or non-natural, but is the natural world itself as our environmental niche, discursively articulated from within.

NICHE CONSTRUCTION AND CONCEPTUAL NORMATIVITY

Recent work in evolutionary biology and the philosophy of biology resonates in important ways with a conception of discursive practice as sustaining a "space of reasons." Earlier work on the evolution of cognitive capacities tended first to focus upon "intelligence" as a general cognitive capacity, and more recently upon the functional and adaptive role of mental representations within the behavioral economy of an organism's way of life. Sometimes that role has been described as modular, exemplified by hypothesized modules for grasping syntactic structures as recursive. In each of these approaches, the cognitive capacities of animals (including human animals) were construed in terms of self-contained abilities for perceiving, representing, and responding to an "external" world.

This entrenched way of thinking about cognition as self-contained has become increasingly problematic biologically, through closer attention to the developmental, physiological, and evolutionary entanglement of organisms with their environments. The resulting reconceptions challenge traditional cognitive internalism from two different directions. First, understanding how organisms' sensory systems are closely intertwined with their repertoires for behavioral and physiological responsiveness allows us to see them as closely coupled with their selective environments. An environment in this sense is not a physical region, but is instead configured and bounded by how its ongoing way of life takes up aspects of its surroundings. Understanding organism and environment as closely coupled shows how organisms can track and flexibly respond to multiple environmental cues, without needing representational intermediaries. Such perceptual and practical capacities are adaptively *directed* toward and *responsive* to a selective configuration of the organism's physical environment without being intensional: One cannot differentiate how the organism *takes* its surroundings to be from an "extensional" determination of life-relevant aspects of its physical surroundings.[2] This recognition may seem initially to sever the connection between non-human organisms' perceptual/practical capacities and our own conceptually articulated intentionality, and thus conflict with a naturalistic understanding of us as animals.

The second challenge to internalism restores this connection. The application of niche construction theory (Odling-Smee, Laland, and Feldman 2003) to the evolution of language and symbolic-conceptual understanding treats it as public discursive practice rather than internal neurological structure.[3] Niche construction is the transformation of organisms' developmental and selective environment by their ongoing and cumulative interactions with that environment; an organism's biological environment is not something given, but is instead dynamically shaped by its ongoing intra-action with the organism. Such transformations are not limited to enduring physical effects. Persistent forms of behavioral niche construction require only the reliable reproduction of selectively significant behavioral patterns.[4] The coevolution of language and human conceptual capacities is then a preeminent example of behavioral niche construction. Human beings normally develop in an environment in which spoken language is both pervasive and salient; languages in turn only exist via this developmental uptake and reproduction. The evolutionary emergence of this capacity, its ontogenetic reconstruction in each generation, and selection pressures for more rapid learning and extended abilities rely on the same kinds of closely coupled capacities for perceptual and practical responsiveness to one's environment that are characteristic of other social animals. There is nothing mysterious or even discontinuous about the gradual development of the linguistic capacities and performances that enable conceptual understanding.

Language thus emerges biologically as a flexible, self-reproducing and self-differentiating responsiveness to cumulatively constructed aspects of our selective environment. Language only exists in being continuously reproduced via the consequent coevolution of human cognitive capacities within this inherited developmental niche. As Millikan notes about her conception of language as similarly public,

> the phenomenon of public language emerges not as a set of abstract objects, but as a real sort of stuff in the real world, neither abstract nor arbitrarily constructed by the theorist. It consists of actual utterances and scripts, forming crisscrossing lineages.
>
> (2005, 38)

These lineages are themselves partially constitutive of the practice, in the sense that participants make and understand utterances as iterable iterations of ongoing patterns. To use a *word,* as Kaplan (1990); Millikan (2005); Ebbs (2009) and I (Rouse 2002, 2014) have each argued, is to use recognizably the same expression that others have used and can use again, *as* they have used it. Such patterns of practice, I have long argued, are neither a *de facto* regularity in what people do, nor a definite rule governing its constitutive performances. The "sameness" of iterative performances of a practice, thus, is reflexively constituted by the practical/perceptual ability to perform and track them *as* iterations. Practices are constituted as such by the mutual accountability of their performances, but there are no determinate norms *to* which they hold one another to account, for those are not yet settled, but are instead at issue within the practice. To say these norms are "at issue" is to say not merely that what performances are accountable *to* or *for* changes over time. These changes result in significant part from the ongoing effort to sustain a common practice, even though what the practice is, is partly "up for grabs." That is part of why it matters to understand language as a *social* and *material* practice. Semantic significance arises from the mutual accountability of language "practitioners" to one another's performances as situated in and responsive to a partially shared setting.

Conceptual normativity then arises from the *partial autonomy* of linguistic practices. This partial autonomy has at least three aspects. First, linguistic expressions are iterative of and iterated by other linguistic expressions. Second, the vocative and recognitive character of linguistic practice makes token expressions proximally responsive to other linguistic tokens, such that utterances typically make sense within a mostly intralinguistic context.[5] Third, these "conversational" exchanges are also situated within and responsive to other aspects of perceptual and practical response to an environment. The result is a *dual* practical/perceptual tracking of the environment: tracking vocal expressions in relation to their conversational and expressive contexts (i.e., to other recent utterances and to other uses of the same expressions), and tracking these larger patterns of "intralinguistic" expression in relation to one's broader perceptual and practical responsiveness to circumstances. This dual capacity accounts for the emergent ability to distinguish between meaningful performances (responsive to their intralinguistic contexts, or their place within some other partially autonomous expressive repertoire) and correct or truthful performances (responsive to broader perceptual/practical involvement in the world).

I spoke of performances rather than utterances, because the decisive evolutionary novelty was not just language itself, but a capacity for symbolic displacement and conceptual understanding that comes to extend far beyond language narrowly construed. This extension of conceptual capacities occurs in three mutually reinforcing ways. First, once vocal expressiveness became integral to human social life as significant and accountable beyond their surrounding circumstances, nonlinguistic forms of expression such as music, dance, drawings/diagrams/maps, bodily adornment, or games could also be undertaken and taken up in comparably transcendent ways.[6] Second and more strikingly, however, these also include the making and use of *equipment*: not just the kinds of individual tool use common to many organisms, but interrelated complexes of equipment understood as available and appropriate *for* some tasks and not others, within differentiated social roles.[7] That equipmental complexes are heritable forms of niche construction that are conceptually articulated has been nicely displayed by John Haugeland:

> [Much] of what a culture has learned about life and its environment is "encoded" in its paraphernalia and practices. Consider, for example, agriculture. . . . Crucial elements of that heritage are embodied in the shapes and strengths of the plow, the yoke, and the harness, as well as the practices for building and using them. The farmer's learned skills are essential too; but these are nonsense apart from the specific tools they involve, and *vice versa*. . . . Hence, they constitute an essential unity—a unity that incorporates overall a considerable expertise about the workability of the earth, the needs of young plants, water retention, weed control, root development, and so on.
>
> (1998, 235)

Third, the resulting capacities for symbolic displacement also feed back to incorporate a broader practical-perceptual responsiveness. Language is first and foremost a specialized, partially autonomous practical/perceptual capacity, and to that extent is continuous with our evolutionary heritage as animals and primates. As languages are sufficiently articulated and centralized within what thereby became a human way of life, other perceptual and practical capacities could acquire a broadly conceptual significance. Everything we perceive and do can have further discursive significance, as trackable in relation to their broader discursive/symbolic context as the Sellarsian "space of reasons." Our perceptual and practical capacities are not themselves initially different in kind from those of other organisms, but they are transformed by their uptake within discursive practice in ways prominently characterized by McDowell (1994) as "the unboundedness of the conceptual."

Any form of niche construction introduces a kind of non-linearity to the evolutionary process, as selective environments do not merely change over time but coevolve with organisms. Behavioral niche construction, and especially the emergence of discursive practices, nevertheless introduces a fundamentally different kind of flexibility into the human lineage. For other organisms, the constitutive goal of their physiology and behavior is the ongoing maintenance and reproduction of the life pattern that is their lineage.[8] That goal is irreducibly deictic, since the goal is to sustain *this* temporally extended pattern, *this* way of making a living in this environment, even if doing so introduces drastic changes into its present configuration. Discursive niche construction and conceptually articulated understanding then add a second level of goal-directedness to this teleological dimension of any living lineage. Human behavior is not merely directed toward the goal *that* its life pattern continue, but also toward *what* that life pattern will be.

Consider first how discursive niche construction works. Human organisms began to evolve capacities for conceptual understanding when they developed a partially autonomous expressive/responsive repertoire that eventually became recognizable as language. This repertoire was proximally responsive to its local conversational and broader intralinguistic contexts. Its autonomy was only partial to the extent that extended chains and patterns of linguistic exchange were then accountable to broader practical/perceptual engagement with the world. The ability to track both the intralinguistic and the broader practical/perceptual significance of linguistic utterances opened the possibility of a gap between how one takes things to be and how they show themselves.

This partial autonomy of conceptually articulated performances is then writ large by the emergence of differentiated but interconnected domains of social practice. Practices are not social regularities: They do not consist of various agents performing in similar ways, or sharing background beliefs or presuppositions. They are instead composed of performances that are mutually interactive in partially shared circumstances. The intelligibility of various performances within a practice normally depends upon the anticipation and achievement of appropriate alignment with others' performances and their circumstances, toward some "end." Ends in this sense, however, are not something external to a practice for which its performances are merely instrumental. Practices, like the biological lineage to which they belong, are instead typically what Aristotle called *energeia,* that is, "ends present in the [practice]" itself. Through discursive niche construction human beings have built up patterns of mutually responsive activity. These patterns open possibilities for newly intelligible ways of living, acting, and understanding ourselves within this discursively articulated "niche."

Although practices are constituted as Aristotelian ends through the ongoing mutual alignment of various performances and circumstances, performers and circumstances are usually only partly accommodating. One person's performances only make sense if others act appropriately, and the equipment, materials, and circumstances "cooperate." In response to various misalignments, agents adjust what they do. They change their own performances and try to affect what others do, or they rearrange the circumstances. These patterns of mutual responsiveness and recalcitrance typically focus a practice on specific issues. Issues arise wherever some adjustment of performances or circumstances is called for to allow the practice to proceed intelligibly; what is *at* issue is what adjustments are needed to sustain the practice. Moreover, as discursively articulate beings, we often try to respond to those issues in part by *saying* what the issues are, with what inferential and practical consequences. These efforts to talk through what is at issue, including responses to divergent interpretations of the issues, are themselves further performances within the practice. Through these ongoing interactions, or intra-actions in Karen Barad's (2007) more perspicuous term, practices evolve and articulate themselves. The normative "force" that binds us to one another in patterns of practice, and makes us responsive to these issues, comes from their contested "ends," these very possibilities for intelligible ways to understand and enact ourselves in the world.

What is at stake in a practice, and in the issues that divide its practitioners, are the very possibilities for who and what we might be through involvement in and submission to the practice, that is, their character as "ends" or *energeia*. Talk of "norms" is then misleading: Ends are not already determinate standards to which performances are accountable, but are instead temporally extended patterns that encompass how we have already been living our lives in relation to its apparently open possibilities. Just what this pattern of practice is (what we are up to, and who we are in our participation) is always partly ahead of us, as that toward which the various performances of a practice are intra-actively, but not always fully compatibly, directed.

This understanding of conceptually articulated practices as subpatterns within the human lineage belongs to the Davidsonian-Sellarsian tradition that emphasizes the "objectivity" of conceptual understanding. The "objects" to which our performances must be held accountable are not something "outside" our discursive niche, however. Discursive practice cannot be understood as an intralinguistic structure or activity that then somehow "reaches out" to incorporate or accord to objects. The relevant "objects" are the ends at issue and at stake within the practice itself. "The practice itself," however, already incorporates the material circumstances in and through which it is enacted. Practices are forms of niche construction, in which human organism and discursively articulated environment are formed together through an ongoing, mutually intra-active reconfiguration.

Practices are ways of life that might or might not continue, and within which an individual organism might or might not continue to participate. Consequently, in working out various issues that arise in their ongoing reproduction, what is *at* issue in the alignments or misalignments of performances within the practice is not only *whether* those forms of interaction will continue, but *what* they will be, and what place they have in the larger patterns of life-activity of the organism and the lineage. Diverse practices (including languages, sciences, and other forms of conceptually articulated understanding and responsiveness) are integral parts of a human being's niche-constructed environment, the "space" within which we develop into organisms with specific capacities and possibilities. What is at issue and at stake in such practices is what, or better who, we are thereby becoming. Moreover, these issues cannot be localized into the "ends" preferred or chosen by particular individuals. One cannot live a conceptually articulated way of life except as other agents and one's material surroundings accommodate it. How we can live and who we can be depends upon the mutually interactive configuration of a space of intelligible possibilities.

We should then not think of "intelligibility" or "rationality" as overarching, ahistorical ideals that are constitutive of conceptual understanding as it has emerged within human evolution. What defines a *conceptually* articulated niche is its modal character, such that an organism's life activities are directed not only in response to its actual setting, but in response to *possible* ways it might be, and how things *ought* to be in accord with those possibilities.[9] Whether things are as they ought or need to be for a practice to continue, and whether others will take up the enabling roles that would sustain the working out of that practice, are parts of what is at issue in its ongoing development. What is at stake in a practice is whether and how those issues are to be resolved, and thus whether and how the practice can continue as a possible way for human beings to live, and to understand themselves and their surroundings.

CONCLUDING REMARKS

As a naturalist, I am committed to understanding the normativity of scientific practice from within the horizons of the natural world disclosed within scientific research. One manifestation of this commitment has been the recognition of conceptual understanding in science as niche construction, a material transformation of the world that allows it to show itself in new ways. Conceptual understanding of nature does not and cannot take place from an imaginary standpoint outside the world that would allow us to represent it as a whole in an intralinguistically articulated image. Scientific understanding is intraworldly, and cannot transcend its own worldly involvement. That involvement extends outward from scientific practices in the narrowest sense to encompass the place of scientific understanding within human life more generally. Conceptually articulated niche construction extends throughout the entirety of human life. The sciences are important to us because of their integration within that larger set of issues rather than being separate from it and relatively self-contained. In this respect, scientific understanding has to be understood within the contingencies of human history and culture. I thus take naturalism to be opposed to what we might call "essentialist" conceptions of science or scientific understanding. Scientific understanding is not a perennial possibility always available throughout human history, or even available to rational or intelligent beings of different species or planetary ecologies. Sciences are historically specific sets of practices emerging within the human lineage. Moreover, that historical specificity reflects the biological specificity of language and conceptual understanding more generally.

Recognizing the bio-historical specificity of scientific understanding may seem to challenge its authority and significance. Philosophical understanding of science has often been supposed to answer to rational norms that transcend the local and the human, precisely in order to account for their normative authority. This aspiration to transcend our historical and ecological embeddedness has been erroneous, and is in any case at odds with a naturalistic standpoint. *Articulating the World* therefore concludes with a discussion of the contingency and locality of conceptual articulation generally, and of scientific understanding specifically. My aspiration is to show

how science matters, and makes authoritative claims upon us, *because* of rather than *despite* its historical and cultural specificity. Science, as a powerful but historically specific extension of the conceptually articulated way of life that is our biological heritage, is not a possibility perennially available to any entities with sufficient intellect and social support. It is instead a precarious and risky possibility that only emerged in specific circumstances, and could disappear.[10]

There are nevertheless important insights to be found in transcendent conceptions of the normative authority of the sciences, even though their underlying aspiration is mistaken. Such conceptions focus and help articulate what is at issue in specific conflicts or tensions over the maintenance of a scientific way of life and the intelligibility of a scientific culture as we know it. They should thereby be understood to be important to a scientific way of life, as a reflective effort to articulate who we are, how we live, and why it matters to sustain that way of life, from within its historically contingent horizons. In doing so, they help sustain and to some extent transform that way of life, by bringing its normative claims and their authority to reflective attention. The contingency of conceptual understanding generally and scientific understanding specifically thus does not undercut the authority or significance of the sciences, but instead calls attention to how much is at stake in whether and how those practices continue and develop. The contingent historical emergence and open-ended future possibilities for the subsequent development of scientific understanding is after all not just one historical possibility among many, whose fate might be a matter of arbitrary indifference from the standpoint of the universe. We do not and cannot occupy such a standpoint. In our living in the midst of that history, these possibilities are the horizons for our lives and our possibilities. Who we are and shall be—what the world is like and how it might further reveal itself—what possibilities it thereby opens or closes off to us and our descendants—these are all at stake in the subsequent unfolding of our social-discursive way of life and its conceptually articulated disclosure of the world. Nothing could matter more, or be less arbitrary from a naturalistic standpoint, within the world we inhabit and aspire to understand.

NOTES

1 Strictly speaking, as Putnam (1975) prominently called to philosophical attention, the division of linguistic labor allows people to talk intelligibly about all sorts of things that they are not themselves capable of telling about in this sense, or telling apart. Yet someone must be able to tell what is being talked about in some domain of discourse, if such talk is not to become a "frictionless spinning in a void" (McDowell 1994). Enabling and sustaining such conceptual engagement with the world is a central part of what the sciences accomplish.

2 "Extensional" is in scare quotes, because the notion of an extension is linked to that of intensions. An organism's way of life evolves and develops in closely coupled

responsiveness to its environment, in ways that are often flexible and reflexively transformed by past encounters, but that invokes no semantic intermediaries that would have intensions or extensions.

3 Price (2011) develops an alternative way to undertake a naturalistic version of this shift away from representationalist accounts of language and conceptual understanding. I will not here attempt to identify and justify the ways my approach differs from his.

4 The level of "reliability" of reproduction need not match the evolved replicative fidelity of cellular transcription, translation, and expression of DNA sequences. So long as there is sufficient stability to produce cumulative selective pressures on the organism's developmental patterns, niche construction can have a significant evolutionary effect, often on more rapid time scales than is possible for evolution that is directly driven by genetic mutations.

5 Declarative sentences typically have what Kukla and Lance (2009) call agent-neutral inputs and outputs: What is claimed in uttering that sentence is expressible by anyone who has appropriate warrants, and the claim, if warranted, ought to be taken into account by anyone. Focusing upon declarative assertions with this normative structure has encouraged most philosophers to put the pragmatics of utterances into the background of how they think about conceptual articulation and contentfulness. Yet even the most agent-neutral and decontextualized content only actually makes a claim on anyone through having been uttered to them in some specific context. In such contexts, moreover, claims are interpreted and assessed not merely as context-free truth claims, but for their relevance to the conversational context: If the contextual relevance of the claim isn't clear, we often find ourselves asking what the speaker meant by interjecting that claim into the conversation (where it would not be sufficient to identify what was meant with what was said).

6 My account remains agnostic concerning whether proto-languages arose first, paving the way for other forms of conceptual expression and uptake, or arose in concert with other two-dimensionally normative conceptually expressive repertoires such as music or equipmental complexes.

7 The locus classicus for the recognition of integrated complexes of equipment and social roles as distinctively human forms of intentional directedness is Heidegger ([1927], 1962, div. I, ch. 3).

8 Okrent (2007) develops compelling arguments for why a naturalistic account of organismic behavior needs to understand it as goal-directed rather than as teleonomically functional.

9 Neither alethic nor normative modalities involved can be understood independently. The possibilities in question are only articulated and sustained through patterns of intra-active responsiveness toward them as projected "ends" internal to the pattern itself. For more detailed discussion and argument for this interdependence, see Rouse (2015, ch. 8).

10 There is no necessary tension between essentialist conceptions of science as a perennial possibility within human life, and a recognition of the vulnerability of a scientific ethos and the way of life it sustains. One might think of the conceptual and epistemic norms of the sciences as always making claims upon us, even though recognition and uptake of those claims is at risk. I nevertheless make a stronger claim: The normative authority of scientific practices, concepts, and claims only emerges within an historically and biologically specific context, such that maintaining that authority requires also sustaining the way of life within which those practices, concepts, and claims could be authoritative for us. Recognizing the contingency of scientific practices and norms does not undercut their authority, I shall argue, but instead intensifies the significance of what is at stake in sustaining a scientific way of life.

REFERENCES

Barad, Karen. 2007. *Meeting the Universe Halfway*. Durham: Duke University Press.
Brandom, Robert. 1994. *Making It Explicit*. Cambridge: Harvard University Press.
Cartwright, Nancy. 1999. *The Dappled World*. Oxford: Oxford University Press.
Chang, Hasok. 2004. *Inventing Temperature*. Oxford: Oxford University Press.
Ebbs, Gary. 2009. *Truth and Words*. Oxford: Oxford University Press.
Hacking, Ian. 1983. *Representing and Intervening*. Cambridge: Cambridge University Press.
Haugeland, John. 1998. *Having Thought*. Cambridge: Harvard University Press.
Heidegger, Martin. 1962. *Being and Time*. Translated by E. MacQuarrie and J. Robinson. New York: Harper & Row. Original edition, 1927.
Kaplan, David. 1990. Words. *Proceedings of the Aristotelian Society,* Supplementary 64: 93–119.
Kukla, Rebecca and Mark Lance. 2009. *Yo! And Lo!*. Cambridge: Harvard University Press.
Lange, Marc. 2000a. *Natural Laws in Scientific Practice*. Oxford: Oxford University Press.
———. 2000b. Salience, Supervenience and Layer Cakes. *Philosophical Studies* 101: 213–251.
———. 2004. Who's Afraid of Ceteris Paribus Laws? Or How I Learned to Stop Worrying and Love Them. *Erkenntnis* 57: 407–423.
———. 2007. Laws and Theories. In *A Companion to the Philosophy of Biology,* edited by S. Sarkar and A. Plutynski, 489–505. New York: Wiley.
McDowell, John. 1994. *Mind and World*. Cambridge: Harvard University Press.
Millikan, Ruth. 2005. *Language: A Biological Model*. Oxford: Clarendon Press.
Morgan, Mary and Margaret Morrison. 1999. *Models as Mediators*. Cambridge: Cambridge University Press.
Neurath, Otto. 1973. The Vienna Circle, or the Scientific Conception of the World. In *Empiricism and Sociology,* edited by M. Neurath and R. S. Cohen, 301–318. Dordrecht: Reidel.
Odling-Smee, F. John, Kevin Laland and Marcus Feldman. 2003. *Niche Construction*. Princeton: Princeton University Press.
Okrent, Mark. 2007. *Rational Animals*. Athens: Ohio University Press.
Price, Huw. 2011. *Naturalism without Mirrors*. Oxford: Oxford University Press.
Putnam, Hilary. 1975. The Meaning of 'Meaning'. In *Mind, Language and Reality,* edited by H. Putnam, 215–271. Cambridge: Cambridge University Press.
Quine, Willard V. O. 1953. *From a Logical Point of View*. Cambridge: Harvard University Press.
Rheinberger, Hans-Jörg. 1997. *Toward a History of Epistemic Things*. Stanford: Stanford University Press.
Rouse, Joseph. 2002. *How Scientific Practices Matter*. Chicago: University of Chicago Press.
———. 2014. Temporal Externalism and the Normativity of Linguistic Practice. *Journal of the Philosophy of History* 8: 20–38.
———. 2015. *Articulating the World*. Chicago: University of Chicago Press.
Sellars, Wilfrid. 1997. *Empiricism and the Philosophy of Mind*. Cambridge: Harvard University Press.
———. 2007. *In the Space of Reasons,* edited by K. Scharp and R. Brandom. Cambridge: Harvard University Press.
Teller, Paul. 2001. Twilight of the 'Perfect Model' Model. *Erkenntnis* 55: 393–415.
Wilson, Mark. 2006. *Wandering Significance*. Oxford: Oxford University Press.

4   What Would It Be to Be a Norm?

Paul A. Roth

> Though philosophy is carried on as a coercive activity, the penalty
> philosophers wield is, after all, rather weak. If the other person is
> willing to bear the label of 'irrational' or 'having the worse argu-
> ments', he can skip away happily maintaining his previous belief. . . .
> Perhaps philosophers need arguments so powerful they set up rever-
> berations in the brain: if the person refuses to accept the conclusion,
> he *dies*.
>
> (Nozick 1981, 4)

REDUCTIVE NATURALISM OR NORMATIVE ESSENTIALISM? ROUSE'S WAY OUT

A philosophical controversy regarding norms concerns whether or not there exist features cognizers *qua* cognizers recognize in a sense yet to be specified as having justificatory *and* motivational imprimatur.[1] An ability to perceive normatively relevant aspects of situations—to operate in a Sellarsian "space of reasons"—assumes *philosophical* importance by virtue of this linking of norms and agency. Kant famously sought a rationale that would dress us in a dignity that encroaching science threatens to strip away. Kant's answer envisions moral agents as having an ability to apprehend and act for reasons apart from accidents of context or instinct.

Preserving some Kantian sense of freedom and dignity requires however imagining agents as authors of their world. For insofar as standards dis-covered reflect structures imposed by agents, this bestows on beings like us a status beyond that had by other bits of stuff. Put another way, whatever normative structures collectively bind do so on this account by way of our being, at least in part, their joint author. On such an account, creatures like us stand in some special, not fully determined relation to norms. It would threaten to short-circuit this happy story should a full explanation of all putatively normative features, including any proclivity to make norma-tive judgments, come to rest only on mundane facts about people and their environment.

I distinguish in what follows between what I shall term 'Turnerized' and 'non-Turnerized' explanations.[2] Turnerized accounts consist of just those explanations of things social about which no special philosophical assumptions regarding norms or normativity need be made. When Turnerized, explanations invoke no irreducibly normative language, for example, no appeals to the chiming of the will to reason's special call. Indeed, normative status represents something to be explained by appropriately naturalistic means—for example, sociologically, historically, neurologically. (Roth 2006) Only when normative talk in some form or other must be taken as brute or non-Turnerizable does one confront normative essentialism, that is, a position that maintains "inexplicability is of the very essence of normativity" (Finlay 2010, 333).

Joseph Rouse has sought to develop a naturalistic yet non-Turnerized account. What makes Rouse's view of particular interest resides in his focus on the notion of practices, a term that whether despite or because of its elusiveness has enjoyed considerable cachet in contemporary social theory. "Practices range from ephemeral doings to stable long-term patterns of activity" (Rouse 2007a, 639). A key to understanding philosophical uses of the term 'practice' resides in its assimilation to a type of intentionally guided behavior. This makes 'practice' by definition normative. Rouse deems his account *naturalistic* because he proposes explaining norms in a broadly ecological sense, as part of a process of niche-construction. On this view, organisms 'jointly author' their developmental and selective environments. An 'environment' as Rouse understands it consists not just of physical surroundings, but also includes those features of one's surroundings that are relevant to an organism's way of life, which in turn are only definable in relation to the environment thereby demarcated.[3]

What makes it a *non-Turnerized* account resides in the fact that for Rouse calling any account explanatory *presupposes* a stance from which one discerns a need for making a normative assessment. On a rough analogy with a Tarskian definition of truth, making a normative assessment takes place within a perspective from which candidates for assessment can be identified as such. One could not apply normative predicates absent a type of 'meta-perspective' that identifies the assessable units and interprets them. In this sense, normative notions can never be fully explicated in non-normative terms.[4] "Normativity is an interactive orientation towards a future encompassing present circumstances within its past. . . . On such a conception, the [norm involving] performances that contribute to a practice at least implicitly *already express* an interpretation of what is at issue and at stake in the practice" (Rouse 2007a, 673, emphasis mine). Interpreting 'object-language' normative notions requires a type of regress to an already existing normative stance.

The interpretative assignments nonetheless depend on environment (broadly construed), time, and place. "Such a conception of normativity is especially suitable for naturalists, since it deliberately eschews any determination of norms from a standpoint outside of nature and history, yet it is also non-reductive" (Rouse 2007a, 673; see also Rouse 2007a, 670). *The sense in which Rouse's account resists being fully Turnerized—"non-reductive" as Rouse puts it—invokes the necessity of a regress to an always already present facility to make normative assessments of certain performances.* Indeed, Rouse takes himself to be a more thorough-going naturalist than a thinker such as Turner, since Rouse contends that Turner's account presumes but does not account for such "meta-level" stances.[5]

Rouse initially develops his distinctive notion of normativity through a focus on scientific practices. Scientific practice, as understood by Rouse, must utilize some notion of constraint by norms (or 'normativity', as he prefers, for reasons that will be clearer as we proceed) in any philosophical accounting of it. As he puts it,

> I need to show how we can understand causality and normativity without reducing them to regularities or rules, and how we can understand *the* world without tacitly splitting it into a meaningful "social world" and an anormative "natural world." Once a conceptual space has been cleared within which such claims are concretely conceivable, it is comparatively straightforward to argue for the constitutive normativity of scientific practices and the world they disclose.
>
> (Rouse 2002, 13)

And just how does Rouse plan to unify into a single account of "normativity" the natural and the social? His discussion of Neurath's and Heidegger's respective critiques of Carnap and Husserl on the normativity of science foreshadows his more general strategy in this regard. Rouse understands both lines of critique as making the

> locus of the normativity of such concrete, historical-material activity . . . their contingently situated futural temporality. Unified science was conceived as a historically situated task oriented toward making predictions; authentically resolute Dasein was a thrown project of being-toward-death. Normativity was then to be located not in a structure outside the concrete historical-material world, but *in medias res*.
>
> (Rouse 2002, 72–3)

Yet nothing that Rouse says about the normativity of scientific practices proves unique or exclusive to science. A focus on the case of science rather shows how practices in Rouse's sense exist even in an area where one might least expect them, that is, in the case where authority may be taken to result from laws that bind us but which we do not author. But if practices matter even in science, then the mark of the normative will be revealed to inhere in all that appears to us.

In order to avoid well-known philosophical dead ends, Rouse requires a strategy that identifies "the *shared* normative accountability of its constituent performances" (Rouse 2002, 19) and yet does so *without* appealing to rules or behavioral regularities. Whatever normative element practices involve as Rouse positions them *cannot* reduce the right-making features to rules (regulism)—something fixed 'in the head'—or determinate patterns of behavior (regularism)—something specifiable 'in advance' and open to perception. Appeals to rules generate regresses of explanation, for rules in turn need interpretation. Behavioral regularities presuppose but do not explain perception of meaningful patterns.

But it would also be a mistake to imagine that how the normative element of a practice exercises its hold on us is due to a self-imposition of constraints. That is, Rouse rejects what he terms "voluntaristic" conceptions of normativity. "My arguments show that voluntarist conceptions of normativity cannot succeed. Such accounts presume that there is no normative force except to the extent that subjects impose it upon themselves, but the intractable difficulty is to understand how such self-imposed commitments could ever be binding" (Rouse 2002, 21). Moreover, on the Rousean account, both practices and the stuff to which practices respond remain in a historical flux.

In his review of Rouse's *How Scientific Practices Matter,* Stephen Turner concludes (with just a hint of exasperation), "The pressing question, which is never answered, is 'what is normativity?'" (Turner 2005, 428). On the one hand, in an important respect already noted Rouse takes the question as misposed insofar as it might be taken to imply that his (Rouse's) account makes recourse to any particular *norms* as unexplained explainers. On the other hand, Rouse invokes an unavoidable regress in the use of normative distinctions; any application of norms already presupposes and employs a special capacity for normative judgments.

HOW PRACTICES EXPLAIN

Has Rouse managed to turn the Sellarsian trick, that is, to demonstrate why and how intentional language grafts onto the scientific image? Practices (including language use as a type of practice) involve two core normative components—intentionality and sociality.[6] A *social* sense of normativity comes in by virtue of a presumably mutually orienting teleological aspect of a practice. "'Practices' thus constitute the background that *replaces* what earlier wholist theorists would have described as 'culture' or 'social structure'" (Rouse 2007a, 645, emphasis mine). Practices "replace" on Rouse's account what other social theories seek to explain as an irreducibly (at least not reducible to talk of *mere* individuals) social element that makes people part of this or that society, culture, or related collective. Participating in practices manifests whatever sense of the social people possess. Social life for humans on this account consists in a predisposition *ab initio* to jointly recognize and respond to open-ended situations, that is, ones that allow for a mutually intelligible sense of assessment. Rouse, in this respect, provides a 'condition of the possibility' argument for *social* interaction without, he maintains, positing anything 'ontologically strange' to account for what constitutes the social.

Specifically, Rouse contends that there exist "at least three crucial aspects to the explication of a normative conception of practices" (Rouse 2007a, 670). The first consists of the way in which practices relate to one another in a specifically normative dimension; for example, they can be subject to reward, sanction, correction, inference, etc. As a characterization of normativity, this can be read as a truism.

The second aspect that Rouse posits introduces a teleological dimension: "practices point ahead of themselves toward something essentially contestable" (Rouse 2007a, 672). For example, what it means to be a "good enough" parent ties to how what happens at a moment integrates and coheres over time with a general pattern of activity, and yet where the evaluations, outcomes, and even the goals cannot be viewed as settled at the moment or even in the indefinite future.[7] The relevant point, I take it, concerns the fact that it makes sense to speak of actions as oriented to an end, even if an end remains vague and indeterminate. Yet a hint of mystery emerges here. For why assume some engine drives matters in a particular direction?

Complicating this question is the third Rousean mark of the normative, which takes the ends as themselves "perspectivally variant" (Rouse 2007a, 672). This means at least that there exists no "sovereign perspective" as Rouse sometimes puts it. This effectively divests Rouse's accounts of any hint of any metaphysical givens working behind the backs of the people involved. Meaningfulness remains an ongoing and indeterminate project that involves us in acting and reacting in ways deemed significant by others and us.

This brings us back to a feature central to Rouse's particular view: an ability to recognize an intentional act for what it is—its meaningfulness—must be a non-eliminable feature of our communicative capacities. On Rouse's conception of scientific practices, particularly through experiment, those participating in that activity become accountable because they interpret what has been disclosed and so alter their conduct in light of such results. "We are accountable to what is at stake in our belonging (causally *and* normatively) to the material-discursive world: our fate is bound up with what is at issue and at stake in our practices, although those stakes are not yet definitely settled—indeed, that is part of what it is for them to be 'at stake'" (Rouse 2002, 25). I take it that for Rouse what a science identifies as laws of nature must also count as norms of its practice, as encounters with the world that we ignore only at our own risk. In this fashion, the norms of scientific practices become built in to and partly imposed by the objects we take to be described by that science. This neatly accounts simultaneously for both the sharing and the authority of such practices.

Rouse then seeks to weave into his more general vision of normativity an analogous notion of something being at stake, something that matters.

> *The intelligibility of anyone's participation in a practice turns on there being something at stake for everyone in getting it right.* That does not mean that the intelligibility of practices depends upon the possibility of ultimate agreement about and conformity to what those stakes are. *Rather, it depends upon a recognition of and by those to whom these practices matters, such that they (ought to) hold themselves responsible for their different interpretations and accountable to one another.*
> (Rouse 2002, 342, emphasis mine)

A key point to note with regard to what Rouse says here concerns how he configures practices as deeply social and not just a strategic or biologically guided bumping together of individuals.

> On this conception, a practice is not a regularity underlying its constituent performances, but a pattern of interaction among them that expresses their *mutual normative accountability*. On this 'normative' conception of practices, a performance belongs to a practice if it is *appropriate* to hold it countable as a correct or incorrect performance of that practice. Such holding to account is itself integral to the practice, and can likewise be done correctly or incorrectly.
> (Rouse 2007a, 669–70, emphasis mine; see also bottom 670)

Invoking "appropriate" and "getting it right" inserts normativity; implicating "everyone" makes it social. But what licenses the necessity of the assumption of a stance that makes us "accountable to one another"?

Rouse does away with any metaphysical element that determines what it is to individually or collectively "get things right," for example, an appeal to a mind-independent or 'real' nature of things as accounting for their structure and appearance to us. "What is *authoritative over and constitutive of human agency and meaning,* I will argue, is not the independent objective natures of things, but the emergent configuration of a situation as having something at stake in its outcome" (Rouse 2002, 257; emphasis mine). "Emergent configuration" signals the interdependence of our performances and how the world accommodates or resists them.[8] References to an "emergent configuration" emphasizes that what shapes responses to a performance depends upon situations as encountered (Rouse 2009, 27 fn. 25).

Yet he cannot do without orientation towards one another and a future. For without that assumed joint orientation, there could just as well be as many practices as there are individuals. But that would be a *reductio* of any assumption invoking a social shared normative orientation—a *mutual* concern for "getting it right." Rouse makes normativity explanatorily necessary by essentializing the social, by having no other way to account for how performances coalesce into practices and how people assess them in mutually intelligible ways. *Absent a mutual orientation that cannot be otherwise explained, an appeal to an ineliminable normativity becomes explanatorily superfluous.*

For the moment, this observation simply serves to highlight how basic a role a teleological assumption plays for Rouse. Normativity resides in a *recognition* of socially significant patterns that can be assessed. A focus on performances externalizes and so makes naturalistically accessible and tractable the objects of assessment. Yet what normatively binds performances to a practice must be an already present orienting stance that engenders and allows for joint recognition and mutual assessment.[9] Yet these "mutually constitutive interrelations" (Rouse 2002, 270) must satisfy two very different conditions. First, they must 'show up' for—be recognized by—other skilled practitioners. But, second, they only serve Rouse's purpose if recognition also *constrains* in a mutually recognizable, even if open-ended, fashion. The term 'appropriate' signals that a normative stance constrains *qua* normative stance.[10] These conditions jointly establish a performance as *socially* meaningful.

A problem with the particular conception of normativity as Rouse develops it connects to a case that Rouse himself develops at some length, *viz.*, conversation. Following his readings of Quine and Davidson about what language need not be, there exist no "semantic facts" that anchor meaning (Rouse 2002, 112, fn. 5; see also Rouse 2002, 161, fn. 1; see also 172, fn. 20). Yet at the same time, Rouse characterizes conversational practices in much the same way that he characterizes scientific practices, and likewise for his account of what keeps conversations "on track" (Rouse 2014, 36–7). But a 'history of uses' cannot devolve into a form of regularism, for language constitutes a dynamic practice, one that seemingly defies predictions about how use will evolve over time, "the commitment, that is, to continuity with other uses rather than to some specific explication of that continuity" (Rouse 2014, 34; see also Rouse 2014, 32). But how then to cash out this quoted aside that speaks of a "commitment" to "continuity" that does not consist in "some specific explication of that continuity"? For this would appear to be just the sort of case Rouse must capture by his invocation of an 'appropriate' response. Again, 'continuity' and 'built-in' cannot devolve to 'just anything'.

Rouse distinguishes between what he terms "descriptive" as opposed to "normative" accounts of conceptual content. Descriptive accounts are so-called because such views "take conceptual content to be something actually present or operative in specific performances by concept users. . . . To use a concept is to have something in mind, or something causally implicated in what one does" (Rouse 2013, 250). Normative accounts, by contrast, reject the presence of any such posit; no rule or other sort of representation determines in advance what falls in or out of any putative concept.

Rather, the determinative factor concerns the normative/rational assessablity of performance in question. "Normative approaches to conceptual articulation, by contrast, identify the conceptual domain with those performances and capacities that are *appropriately* assessed according to rational norms" (Rouse 2013, 250–1; emphasis mine). Put another way, what makes a performance an appropriate sort of candidate involves the possibility of error being present in that performance. And the presence or absence of this possibility is not fated *at the moment* of the performance (Rouse 2013, 255). Rousean conceptual understanding manifests practical-perceptual skills. Normative assessment manifests as a characteristic human activity. Norms 'exist' by virtue of their ongoing application by people and in no other way.

Rouse notes how in conversations one often responds to and applies assessments in a way that seemingly defies appeal to reflection or prior representation. "Rapid, fluent conversation is not explicitly 'mindful' of the concepts it expresses. Speakers can respond fluently and smoothly to the solicitations of the conversational situation, and often discover what they have to say only when they say it. Such talk is not thereby preconceptual or nonconceptual" (Rouse 2013, 256). Rouse looks to demonstrate how his articulation of conceptual content accounts as well for another key feature of concept use, *viz.*, "the maintenance of its normative force or authority" (Rouse 2013, 257).

Rouse's resolution to this problem as with that of content articulation reiterates the move that he takes to make norms explicable. "The intractable problem has been to secure both the causal and normative roles of these interrelations" (Rouse 2013, 258). Rouse's answer draws upon his basic premise that postulates the ineliminability of the normative because of the regress it generates; any judgment about acceptability or unacceptability invokes the very normative stance it seeks to explain. Although speaking here of Dreyfus and Todes, I take the following to apply to Rouse's own view as well: "practical-perceptual involvement with the world is already normative and reflective teleological" (Rouse 2013, 258). And in parallel with his view that applying normative predicates presumes a normative stance as a type of 'meta-language', so too the authority and force of all norms can be explained naturalistically in parallel with the scientific practices case. That is, just as the results of laboratory life constrain but do not dictate how scientists respond, Rouse extends this picture to human organisms in relation to their general social environment.

Rouse sketches how he imagines this unfolds in line with his naturalism conjoined with creatures always already predisposed to judge and reflect.

> The first is to understand organisms teleologically, as directed toward the goal of maintaining and reproducing their characteristic life-cyclical pattern under changing circumstances. Second, that life-cyclical pattern does not distinguish the organism's form of life from its environmental

niche, but is instead a unified phenomenon. . . . Neither an organism's environment, nor its characteristic ways of "being-in" it, can be adequately characterized independently. Third, . . . practical–perceptual activity has a reflective rather than determinative teleology. . . .

(Rouse 2013, 259)

A worry that arises here involves how one moves from a biologically based notion of teleology to a conceptual one, and so from one where 'normal' means just what these organisms do in these conditions to the open-textured notion of conceptual content that Rouse also endorses.

RECONSIDERING ROUSE'S WAY OUT

But just here Rouse's exposition grows uncharacteristically dark. The reason, as hinted earlier, involves his posited teleological element. Without this, Rouse loses the distinctively social and yet open-ended purposiveness that separates biological programming and human behavior.

[H]uman behavior is not merely instrumentally intelligible in its directedness toward a determinate way of 'making a living' as an organism. It is expressively intelligible in its collective, interactive, and reflexive directedness towards what Heidegger called a 'for-the-sake-of-which.' It is this reflexively open-ended teleology of our discursive practical-perceptual capacities that allows us to hold one another and ourselves accountable to conceptually articulated possibilities, rather than just to normal patterns of response to surroundings.

(Rouse 2013, 266)

But does imputing a teleology represent anything beyond our own imaginings? Without it, talk of an already present *mutual* accountability and stakes proves spurious. Teleology supposedly makes normativity something other than a phantom limb of social life. It putatively names that which guides and authorizes an assessment of practices as well as orients individual performances to a joint but ineffable end.

Two examples help illustrate problems with such imputations of teleology. One comes from the neurologist Oliver Sacks (Sacks 1970). He recounts a case of twin brothers who had long been confined to mental institutions when Sacks first met them, because "variously diagnosed as autistic, psychotic or severely retarded" (Sacks 1970, 195). However, these twins were also the subject of intense study and scrutiny prior to Sacks. For, on the one hand, they possessed an incredible ability to remember numbers of literally any length or to calculate dates within an 80,000-year span. But, on the other hand, these very abilities proved paradoxical. For with regard to any test for an ability to calculate, "they do astonishingly badly, as badly as their IQs of sixty might lead one to think. They cannot do simple addition or subtraction with any accuracy, and cannot even comprehend what multiplication or division means" (Sacks 1970, 197). Yet, given known hard problems for which the algorithms are either unknown or extremely complex, for example, identifying the date of Easter in random years in the past or in the future, the twins provide amazingly swift and accurate answers.

What I take to be of particular interest for our purposes concerns a conversation that Sacks encounters the twins having. Sacks describes it as follows:

> They seemed to be locked in a singular, purely numerical, converse. John would say a number—a six-figure number. Michael would catch the number, nod, smile and seem to savor it. Then he, in turn, would say another six-figure number, and now it was John who received, and appreciated it richly. . . .
>
> *What* were they doing? What on earth was going on? I could make nothing of it. . . .
>
> As soon as I got home I pulled out tables of powers, factors, logarithms and primes—mementos and relics of an odd, isolated period in my own childhood, when I too was something of a number brooder, a number 'see-er', and had a peculiar passion for numbers. I already had a hunch—and now I confirmed it. *All the numbers, the six-figure numbers, which the twins had exchanged were primes.* . . . [Yet] Certainly they could not be *calculating* them—they could calculate nothing.
>
> (Sacks 1970, 201)

Sacks returned the next day, equipped with his table of primes.

> After a few minutes I decided to join in, and ventured a number, an eight-figure prime. They both turned towards me, then suddenly became still, with a look of intense concentration and perhaps wonder on their faces. There was a long pause—the longest I had ever known them to make, it must have lasted a half-minute or more—and then suddenly, simultaneously, they both broke into smiles. They had, after some unimaginable internal process of testing, suddenly seen my own eight-digit number as a prime—and this was manifestly a great joy. . . .
>
> (Sacks 1970, 202)

The new, longer prime was not just appreciated by the twins. It became the basis for an extension of the game.

> They drew apart slightly, making room for me, a new number playmate, a third in their world. Then John, who always took the lead, thought for a very long time—it must have been at least five minutes, though I dared not move, and scarcely breathed—and brought out a nine-figure

number; and after a similar time his twin, Michael, responded with a similar one. And then I, in my turn, after a surreptitious look in my book, added my own rather dishonest contribution, a ten-figure prime I found in my book. There was again, and for even longer, a wondering, still silence; and then John, after a prodigious internal contemplation, brought out a twelve-figure number. I had no way of checking this, and could not respond, because my own book—which, as far as I knew, was unique of its kind—did not go beyond ten-figure primes. But Michael was up to it, though it took him five minutes—and an hour later the twins were swapping twenty-figure primes, at least I assume this was so, for I had no way of checking it.

Nor was there any easy way, in 1966, unless one had the use of a sophisticated computer. . . . *There is no simple method, for primes of this order—and yet the twins were doing it.*

(Sacks 1970, 203)

Now, what were the *twins* doing in this 'game of primes'? One cannot say of them that they were identifying or calculating prime numbers. Neither had a capacity to know what counts as a prime number, much less how to calculate primes.

Too many hypotheses can be made to fit the situation, including the hypothesis that whatever the twins respond to, it has *for them* nothing at all to do with the primeness of the numbers. Nothing deep or shared in any philosophically substantive sense then need be invoked to account for what goes on. Validating claims to 'appropriateness' comes to no more than forming a behaviorally based hypothesis about how to play a conversational game. Why invoke anything *joint,* and so a need for normativity at all?[11]

Rouse's notion of an inherent and mutually orienting teleology thus threatens to become yet another ersatz for bad old notions of understanding and meaning. The most plausible assumption to make would be that the twins and Sacks share nothing. He has no clue of how they orient themselves, or they of him.

But can this case be taken to be at all representative? Might not this situation be too odd to count against what Rouse takes to be paradigmatic of practices and their performances? Consider then a seemingly different but I shall suggest ultimately intimately related example. Stanley Fish—a noted postmodern theorist—recounts an incident (Fish 1980) that took place when he taught two seminars back-to-back, one on literary criticism and linguistics and the other on English religious poetry of the seventeenth century. The classes had no students in common.

Fish tells of listing on a blackboard the names of people that he wanted those students in the literary criticism class to read. Fish then writes, "In the time between the two classes I made only one change. I drew a frame around the assignment and wrote on the top of that frame 'p. 43.' When the members of the second class filed in I told them that what they saw on the blackboard was a religious poem of the kind they had been studying and I asked them to interpret it. Immediately they began to perform in a manner that . . . was more or less predictable" (Fish 1980, 323–4). That is to say, the students came up with multiple, learned, clever readings of the names on the board that interpreted them as if a seventeenth-century English religious poem.

Fish takes the reaction of the students to demonstrate that "acts of recognition, rather than begin triggered by formal characteristics, are their source. It is not that the presence of poetic qualities compels a certain kind of attention but that the paying of a certain kind of attention results in the emergence of poetic qualities" (Fish 1980, 326). I take Fish's anecdote to show that people can easily read into situations literally whatever they anticipate, as cognitive dissonance theory teaches.

The Fish case suggests that understanding what people interpretatively project onto situations requires no special *philosophical* notions regarding normativity. For the observed behavior proves easily explicable in a mundane way. The specter of the regress argument raises its ugly head only on the assumption that explanations must be grounded in an appeal to a *predilection* for mutually oriented normative judgments. But if this very assumption proves to be implausible (as per Sacks) or a sociological artifact (as per Fish), then no philosophical regress threatens. Put another way, Rouse needs to show that there exists for typical cases something more than the *appearance* of a shared orientation.

Indeed, given the previously noted Quinean and Davidsonian scruples against appeals to meaning, my suggestion would be that the twins case and the Fish case in fact exemplify what linguistic practices come to, that is, as instantiating a type of ongoing experiment. But there exists no need to invoke some special philosophical pre-recognition of right or wrong here. In the business of surviving in the world around us, sometimes it helps to posit that others orient themselves as we do. Sometimes this works to our advantage, and sometimes not. But nothing deeper than hypothesis formation and testing need be assumed to account for the process. Even with those with whom with one imagines that one has communicated successfully, time often reveals (something like Kripke's 'plus' and 'quus') that at some point understandings diverge, sometimes radically so. All one observes consists of conversations continuing or not.

NATURALISM REDUX

I want to conclude by sketching a principled reason for rejecting this assumption of an inherent teleology by assimilating it to John McDowell's worry about how to understand Sellars's criticism of the 'Myth of the Given'. McDowell's accepts the Sellarsian critique of givenness but worries that it does not yet reveal how experience enters in as a rational and not just a causal constraint. "A genuine escape would require that we avoid the

Myth of the Given without renouncing the claim that experience is a rational constraint on thinking" (McDowell 1996, 18). In parallel with McDowell, Rouse wants the social to enter in as rational constraint on thinking, but does not want to hypostatize the social.

McDowell worries that holism positions our mental life as a "frictionless spinning in a void" (McDowell 1996, 11) absent some more substantive account of how mind and world connect. So too Rouse worries that we face a social analog of such a frictionless spin, that is, no account of how more than just the appearance of human interaction actually takes place. How could we succeed in responding intelligibly to one another absent a *shared* perception of situations requiring assessment? Rouse assumes interrelatedness authentic and so needing explanation. By arguing for such a normative relation between human organisms and their environment, he makes mind and social world one. Normative responsiveness to the world *and* others becomes Rousean 'second nature'.

A basic move in the larger argument of "Empiricism and the Philosophy of Mind" occurs when Sellars presses the question of how to recognize any statement as epistemically *authoritative*. In the case of empirical knowledge Sellars argues that authority flows from sentence token to type. Sellars here has in mind instances of tokening sentences in a particular 'appropriate' context, for example, "This is green" in the presence of that color in good light, etc. Tokens of this sort when appropriately tokened have authority; they signal the presence of a relevant epistemic kind.

But, Sellars observes, such tokenings must themselves not depend on any other knowledge in order to be authoritative *qua* given. Otherwise they would not function as advertised. For if a supposed regress stopper itself depends upon some additional empirical knowledge, then the threatened regress of justification reappears. To have the epistemic authority to which 'the given' lays claim, certain sentences must token the presence of the given and yet presuppose no other additional premises about what must be known. The token must be non-inferentially known, and so *self-authorizing* in this key respect. But a demand for statements to play this authoritative role engenders an epistemic paradox: In order for tokens to be authoritative, they cannot presuppose other knowledge, but tokens can be authoritative only by presupposing other knowledge.

Consider in this light Rouse's account of practices. In order for any performance to *token* a practice—and so be a candidate for normative assessment—it must already be mutually recognizable as being of a type. But talk of tokening however indeterminate becomes something other than an individual's act of creative imagination only on the *assumption* of a teleologically guided orientation. Otherwise, there simply exists nothing type-like, no linking assessment to a collective standard. A teleological orientation constitutes that collective; no mutual orientation, no collective. Yet the examples indicate why there exists no need to posit a mysterious normative invisible hand that somehow constrains and directs interpersonal interactions. Experimentation or empirical sociology provides all that explanation requires.

No ineffable something remains on the scene in need of explanation unless what makes for coordinated activity has no other possible explanation. No doubt people assess what others do; but this fails to demonstrate that behaviors actually token any practice type. *With respect to generating normativity, nothing collective can serve just as well as that of something.* (Recall Millikan 2010; see also Roth 2003.) Rouse's account of normativity proves to be a solution to a problem he creates. Practices become inescapably normative only by surreptitiously inserting a mysterious teleological element. But explanations of things social just do not require that practices be construed as Rouse imagines.

In a recent essay, Michael Williams urges a similar moral. "As naturalists, we should be pragmatists about norms. We should see norms as entering the world by way of our taking up normative attitudes." One can agree as well with Williams when he adds that this view "is not objectionably 'subjectivist': norms are instituted by evaluative practices that are socially shared. They are not subject to anyone's whims" (Williams 2012, 328). Williams also points to what remains unsettled with respect to arguments about the role of normativity, and so returns to where Rouse's argument began.

> My argument does not complete the case for pragmatism's being a fully naturalistic outlook. As Sellars stresses, there is still the question of how we ever got into the normative dimension in the first place. . . . [But] the question concerning the emergence of normative attitude-taking is the *only* question that a pragmatist, as a naturalist, needs to answer. And second, the social-practice view of norms indicates where to look for the required explanation: in the evolution of co-operative behaviour.
> (Williams 2012, 328–9)

Rouse deploys a threat of regress to argue that the evolution of cooperative behavior must presuppose a normative stance. Rouse takes it that his version of the regress is not vicious since for any particular actual norm an explanation can be found relating it to its environment. But only a teleological assumption that fashions a version of a token-type relationship allows such stance-taking to slip a naturalist net. For that takes as prior to and necessary for any actual assessment a collective orientation that engenders a joint perception of stakes and assessments that is also mutually intelligible. Collectivity cannot emerge for Rouse via a prudential invisible hand guiding individuals. Mutual orientation must come prior to anything individually strategic in order to have Rousean normativity.

Rouse posits that an elusive teleology generated by humans in their environments puts us in a shared space of reasons. An already present mutual orientation allows this space to be constituted and accounts for why reasons can have a hold on us. This preordained inclination to look for collective and creative responsiveness to an environment explains why we have a joint stake in assessments we make, and so why the dance we do does not represent the social equivalent of a frictionless spinning in a void. To play on Alasdair MacIntyre's *bon mot* regarding Paul Feyerabend, Rouse fears Turner to be the Emerson of social theory, one who threatens to make "every man his own Jesus" (MacIntyre 2006, 16). Yet Rouse has no argument that motivates and makes compelling his teleological assumption.

Clinging to a story that locates a capacity for action as emanating just from within attracts insofar as it promises to preserve some vestige of Kant's attempt to salvage human agency. But as Rouse's heroic efforts to sustain it reveal, attempts to preserve agency by imagining that the space of reasons must somehow be immune from full naturalistic explication have becomes hopelessly thin. Rouse's teleological assumption offers no real hope of gain in explanatory power. Rather than settling for fig leaf Kantianism, some small way of avoiding being fully exposed to scientific scrutiny, best just to accept a bare naturalism.[12]

NOTES

1 "As rules of obligation, social norms come with a normative expectation to conform, and there are sanctions against those who deviate. Norms are also deemed more important . . . than other rules" (Peter 2011, 218).

2 See, in particular, (Turner 1994, 2010) and this volume. Turner himself explicitly sees the current normativist craze as symptomatic of a reaction against the disenchantment of the social world (Turner 2010, 5). I agree.

3 I owe these two sentences to Joe Rouse. "I'm a naturalist. We always find ourselves already in an environment, which is of course partially the outcome of generations of niche construction, and which is partially transformed by our own activities in turn, but it is never MADE by us. We are 'made' (i.e., we develop biologically as organisms) within it, and in the course of doing so, also transform it." (J. Rouse, personal correspondence)

4 As Rouse also notes, these sorts of regress arguments take a variety of forms (Rouse 2007a, 668). I do not wish to overplay the analogy with Tarskian semantic theory. However, the analogy makes vivid a point that resides at the philosophical heart of Rouse's view, *viz.*, that any account of norms presumes some already made normative distinctions.

5 I owe this way of putting the matter to comments made to me by Rouse.

6 In shifting the focus to practices, the explananda become the constitution of various types of socially coordinated behaviors. What allows these to be objects for us in this context relies crucially on a notion of recognition that also must be taken, or so the claim goes, as intractably normative. For an ontology of practices presupposes a notion of recognition, one that "unlike response, is a normative notion; it is possible to *misrecognize* something, to get it *wrong.* . . . [O]nly insofar as something determinate is supposed to be recognized, can there be an issue of recognizing *it* rightly or wrongly; and it is only as that which determines rightness or wrongness that the object of recognition is determinate" (Haugeland 1993, 57). The italicized 'it' refers, as I read this passage, to activities such as what will be discussed under the rubric of practices below. Focusing on norms as what 'calls into being' certain types of objects, for example, games, signals a specifically

Heideggerian orientation taken by Haugeland and by Rouse. Haugeland puts the matter in the following way. "Here lies the true import of the phrase 'you know one when you see one': recognition is essentially a *skill*. . . . more generally, if a larger arrangement pattern is constitutive for the domain of its elements, and is as such insisted upon by skillful practitioners, it can induce norms by which those elements can themselves be cognition patterns. That is, the elements can be *criterial* for the correctness of their own recognition, and in that sense objects" (ibid., 62). Patterns become patterns of objects in the hands of skillful practitioners; but pattern *recognition* remains an ineluctably normative element that belongs in part to the skill of practitioners, although the practice of that skill relies on perceiving patterns in the world.

7   Recall that Rouse's characterization of scientific activity discussed above specifically incorporates a teleological element by virtue of its "futural" orientation.

8   I owe this way of putting it to Joe Rouse.

9   As Davidson famously argues using the example of malapropisms, meaning prevails even in the absence of a shared structure. See especially (Rouse 2002, Ch. 3).

10   'Appropriate' I take to be Rouse's favored normative term. See, for example, his remark that "On this conception, a practice is maintained by interactions among its constitutive performances that express their mutual accountability. On this normative conception of practices, a performance belongs to a practice if it is appropriate to hold it accountable as a correct or incorrect performance of that practice" (Rouse 2007b, 3). Rouse also uses the term to characterize Brandom's conception of certain discursive norms (e.g., Rouse 2002, 195), and he later explicitly endorses this aspect of Brandom's account (e.g., Rouse 2002, 260). Indeed, if Rouse's own frequent use of terms such as 'accountability' and 'responsibility' do not tie to, or function as rough synonyms for, whatever 'appropriateness' means to connote, I find it impossible to grasp what 'normativity' supposedly comes to if just anything can count as 'being responsible' or 'acting appropriately' or 'being accountable'.

11   Millikan (2010) argues powerfully against the view that anything like Rouse's social sense of teleology or appropriateness must be invoked to account for a common language. "Basic empirical terms are learned in a way that does not pass on to the learner any particular manner of thinking of or identifying their extensions, but only some kind of grip or other, perhaps completely idiosyncratic, on a naturally bonded extension having multiple handles" (Millikan 2010, 44). Or again: "In sum, agreement in applications and hence in the judgments expressed with many property and kind terms, agreement both with oneself and with others, . . . is an empirical matter, resting on natural law and on clumping and humping and peaks in nature. . . . It is because of the clotting that enough agreement occurs in practice to coordinate speakers and hearers of these terms in projects of common interest, hence to keep these terms in circulation" (Millikan 2010, 63–4).

12   My appreciation and thanks to Maks Del Mar, Michael Hicks, Matthew Margulis, Mark Risjord, Joe Rouse, and Stephen Turner for their comments on earlier drafts of the paper.

REFERENCES

Finlay, Stephen. 2010. Recent Work on Normativity. *Analysis* 70: 331–346.

Fish, Stanley. 1980. How to Recognize a Poem When You See One. In *Is There A Text in This Class ?* 322–337. Cambridge, MA: Harvard University Press.

Haugeland, John. 1993. Pattern and Being. In *Dennett and His Critics*, edited by Bo Dahlbom, 53–69. Cambridge, MA: Blackwell.

MacIntyre, Alasdair. 2006. Epistemological Crises, Dramatic Narrative, and the Philosophy of Science. In *The Tasks of Philosophy: Selected Essays, volume. 1*, 3–23. Cambridge: Cambridge University Press.

McDowell, John. 1996. *Mind and World*. Cambridge, MA: Harvard University Press.

Millikan, Ruth Garrett. 2010. On Knowing the Meaning, with a Coda on Swampman. *Mind* 119: 43–81.

Nozick, Robert. 1981. *Philosophical Explanations*. Cambridge, MA: Harvard University Press.

Peter, Fabienne and Kai Spiekermann. 2011. Rules, Norms, and Commitments. In *The Sage Handbook of The Philosophy of Social Sciences*, edited by I. Jarvie and J. Zamora-Bonilla, 217–239. Thousand Oaks, CA: Sage.

Roth, Paul A. 2003. Why There Is Nothing Rather Than Something: Quine on Behaviorism, Meaning, and Indeterminacy. In *Philosophy, Psychology, and Psychologism*, edited by D. Jacquette, 263–287. Dordrecht, The Netherlands: Kluwer.

———. 2006. Naturalism without Fears. In *Philosophy of Anthropology and Sociology*, edited by S. Turner and M. Risjord, 683–708. Amsterdam: Elsevier.

Rouse, Joseph. 2002. *How Scientific Practices Matter: Reclaiming Philosophical Naturalism*. Chicago: The University of Chicago Press.

———. 2007a. Practice Theory. In *Philosophy of Anthropology and Sociology*, edited by S. Turner and M. Risjord, 639–681. Boston: Elsevier.

———. 2007b. Social Practices and Normativity. *Philosophy of the Social Sciences* 37: 1–11.

———. 2009. *Haugeland on Biological and Social Conceptions of Intentionality*. Unpublished paper presented to the International Society for Phenomenological Studies, Pacific Grove, CA. Cited with permission of the author.

———. 2013. What Is Conceptually Articulated Understanding? In *Mind, Reason, and Being-in-the-Word: The McDowell-Dreyfus Debate*, edited by J. K. Schear, 250–271. Oxon: Routledge.

———. 2014. Temporal Externalism and the Normativity of Linguistic Practice. *Journal of the Philosophy of History* 8: 20–38.

Sacks, Oliver. 1970. *The Man Who Mistook His Wife for a Hat and Other Clinical Tales*. New York: HarperCollins.

Turner, Stephen. 1994. *The Social Theory of Practices*. Chicago: The University of Chicago Press.

———. 2005. Normative All the Way Down. *Studies in History and Philosophy of Science* 36: 419–429.

———. 2010. *Explaining the Normative*. Malden, MA: Polity Press.

Williams, Michael. 2012. Pragmatism, Minimalism, Expressivism. *International Journal of Philosophical Studies* 18: 317–330.

5 Social Normativism

Jaroslav Peregrin

DO WE NEED NORMS TO ACCOUNT FOR A HUMAN SOCIETY?

Normativity is one of the keywords of contemporary philosophical discussions. It is clear that philosophy has to do not only with facts, but also with norms (especially in ethics); but more and more current philosophers are busy arguing that, in addition, those parts of philosophy where norms are *prima facie* not in high focus, such as philosophy of language or philosophy of mind, have kinds of 'normative dimensions'.

However, not everybody subscribes to this enthusiasm for normativity. Within philosophy of language, there is, for example, an ongoing fierce discussion between 'normativists' and 'anti-normativists' about the normativity of meaning.[1] A similar, though I think both much broader and much deeper, discussion concerning normativity has been launched within the context of philosophical and scientific accounts for human societies. Should we, explaining how a society works, merely state the facts concerning the behavior of the members of the society in the way natural scientists describe the behavior of ants in an anthill, or how they describe the behavior of particles in an atom, or do we, over and above this, need to take a recourse to some 'normative facts'?

Stephen Turner, one of the leading figures of contemporary philosophy of social sciences, in his recent book (Turner 2010) nicely summarized the anti-normativist claims and arguments. His central claim is that to account for human societies we need not go beyond the ordinary social science revealing ordinary causal interconnections and ordinary facts. He denies that we would need any extra-scientific means of disclosing normative facts that would exist over and above the causal ones. Hence the whole normativist movement, according to him, is nothing more than a storm in a teacup. "Normative facts," Turner claims in his book, "constitute a rupture in the world of ordinary fact" (2010, 9). They do not fit into "the ordinary stream of explanation." In short, "normativity is a name for a non-natural, non-empirical stuff that is claimed to be necessarily, intrinsically there and to in some sense account for the actual" (2010, 5).

The worries that the recent preoccupation of philosophers with normativity might lead philosophical accounts for society into muddy waters, treating 'the normative' as an occult realm, are understandable. However, I do not think that everybody who stresses the importance of 'the normative' (i.e., rules or norms) for 'the social' is an occultist. Thus, though I whole-heartedly agree that when explaining social (or, for that matter, whatever) phenomena we should avoid any occult facts and that we should avoid ruptures within ordinary streams of explanations, and I also agree that some of the philosophers whose views Turner discusses in his book may be guilty of at least flirting with trafficking facts of a suspicious nature, I think that he underestimates the role normativity is capable of playing in accounting for human societies and humans as social animals.

In what follows I start from the discussion of Turner's criticism of normativism, to reach a positive account of what I call *social* normativism. I will claim that this stance not only does not clash with scientific accounts of human societies, but, ultimately, it is indispensable. To be able to reach this conclusion, I will start from approaching the views of the normativists that Turner presents as a single position in a more discriminative way; and I will try to show not all such views are guilty of the sins Turner accuses them of having.

NORMATIVISM DECONSTRUCTED?

Turner characterizes the ways in which normativity is claimed to enter the explanation of human and social phenomena and points out how this might conflict with the ordinary scientific explanation as follows[2]:

> The background to normative facts is ordinary, involving the kinds of facts that are parts of the ordinary stream of explanation. There is nothing binding, compelling or constraining about these facts. So these new normative facts constitute a rupture in the world of ordinary fact. The normative, however, arises out of ordinary facts: meanings, obligations, rationality and so forth, come into existence through actions, learning, and the like, but have the special added properties of norms: of binding, constraining and the rest. Once the norms are established, they have consequences for behavior. They do not directly cause behavior, but they regulate it normatively, by specifying what is the right way to say something, what obligations one has, what one owes to others as a result of one's meaningful actions, and what is justified for others to do in response to your actions.
>
> (2010, 9)

In this way the 'normativists' (= those who claim the indispensability of normativity for explaining social phenomena) may readily get into conflict with the 'scientists' (= those who propose that ordinary science with its causal explanations is enough). Turner contends that social scientists are able to describe the variety of human societies and human affairs in its multiversity;

but he assumes that the normativists will claim that all of this still falls short of truly describing normative phenomena, because these are transcendent to any description of contingent affairs. However, Turner argues that the very concept of normativity (not to speak about the concepts such as truth, rationality, etc.) is itself largely a product of our particular society, and as such it is not reasonably seen as 'transcendent' to the social.

Various human communities, Turner claims, have their various ways of organizing their affairs, ways that often include directions concerning what should or should not be done, what is permitted or what is prohibited or what kind of consequences some doings can have; and this is a fact social science can account for very well. In particular, Turner claims, we can usually see alien communities as following some kinds of "Good Bad Theories"—"meaning that they are good theories for a particular, unspecified set of purposes in a particular setting, but bad theories if we are thinking of them as adequate explanations of anything, or proto-explanations that can be turned into genuine explanations with a little empirical vetting and some minor revision" (2010, 43). (Hence such a theory, though it is not true by our scientific standards and hence it is "bad," serves the purpose of organizing or coordinating the society, and hence it is useful—"good.") There is no need for any notion of normativity, Turner claims, over and above this; especially no need for any normativity that would transcend human communities and that would ground 'absolute' correctness.

Let me just note in passing a problem concerning the concepts of "causal mechanism" and "ordinary stream of explanation" as used by Turner. It does not seem that what Turner can have in mind when using them can be explanations that are causal in a narrow sense of the word—*viz.* simple explanations in terms of the causal laws of natural science. In particular, even Turner's favorite example of "good" explanation in social sciences, explanation in terms of his "Good Bad Theories," does not seem to quite live up to this standard. For what is the causal connection between a theory held in a society and the behavior of its members?[3] And what, indeed, does it mean to say, in causal terms, that a society *has* a theory? (It seems that the only characterization of such a state of a society in purely *causal* terms would be in terms of the brain states of the members of the community; and obviously any nontrivial characterization of this kind is beyond our ken.)[4]

Turner then considers what he calls the "fundamentalism" of some of the normativists, which "involves the claim that all views other than our own are wrong, and justifies this claim on the basis of our own preferred grounds, such as reflective, self-validating analysis of our own views" (2010, 47). He dismisses it, claiming that it "relies on a set of devices, such as the ideas of eyes opening to the dictates of reason, that are basically fictional" and that it "fails to produce the results it promises, namely, objective normative conclusions" (2010, 59).

In general, Turner is convinced that current normativism in fact continues the legacy of sociologists postulating various kinds of collective objects (collective will, group intention, objective mind, etc.), which he finds mythical. In contrast to this, Turner thinks that

> collective claims are not based . . . on a "group sense" in some sort of raw, preconceptual mode, but on a fully developed set of ideas about the group—a theory, if you wish, about the existence of nations, races, and so on. These ideas are Good Bad Theories.
>
> (2010, 136)

It is, I think, not too controversial to say that an integrated social group has something as its 'own mind'; that there is a sense in which we can say that the community 'has' certain views, 'desires' certain things or cherishes certain 'norms'. It is also plausible to say that newbies born into such community (or being integrated into it from outside), to become its truly integral members, must come to be attuned to this 'group mind', must somehow adopt their individual minds to it. The term some philosophers have recently adopted from psychology is *social cognition*[5] (but in many contexts the good old term *culture* would do).

What is controversial is the status of such a social cognition and the question of how it relates to the cognitions of individual members of the society. On the one extreme, the view is that talking about 'social cognition', 'group sense', etc. can be nothing more than a *façon de parler,* reducible to talking about individual minds: that any movement on the social level is only an aggregate of movements on individual ones. On the other extreme, the idea is that 'social cognition' or 'culture' is something totally independent of the individual level: far from being determined by it, the social level determines the individual ones. (Between the two extremes, there is a land of intermediary views willing to grant the social level *some* kind of autonomy, thought not an utter independence; here we find landmarks such as 'supervenience', 'emergence', etc.)

It is the last extreme view that was, long ago, sharply criticized by Tooby and Cosmides (1992) and that has been target of similar kinds of criticism ever since; and it is also essentially this view that is the target of Turner's criticism. What these social scientists consider as essentially misguided is seeing ordinary reality (consisting of things, people, and their properties and relations) as overlain by a layer of some social, cultural, or collective reality, floating free of the bustle of the underlying layer, but wielding influence on it. It is understandable why such a picture is repulsive for a scientifically minded theoretician; and it is true that some philosophers treating of norms do not shun it.

However, what I would like to point out in this chapter is that stressing the role of normativity in human affairs may be not only a way of falling with this picture (which I agree we should resist), but also a means of elucidating the intricate relationship between the individual and social levels of social reality and cognition. I think, and I am going to argue, that it is certain 'social' normativism that may help us get a grip on this relationship allowing us to explain it as a nontrivial, though a nonmysterious affair.

VARIETIES OF NORMATIVISM

Turner's most basic worry, we saw, is that normativity may smuggle some kind of occultism into science. This worry is understandable. However, the spectrum of those whom Turner sees as defending views of this kind and whom he calls *normativists* is much too wide: It includes Korsgaard, O'Neill, Kripke, David Lewis, Boghossian, Sellars, McDowell, Brandom, Haugeland, Rouse, etc.; and this inclusiveness necessarily drives him to see 'normativism' as a generic doctrine which far from coincides with the views of many of the scholars on his list. Indeed, as he himself claims, "the sheer variety of normativism mocks any attempt to defeat them or even make them consistent with one another" (2010, 67). But this, I think, only points to the fact that to summon all the thinkers under a common banner is problematic. The most straightforward target of Turner's criticism are those whom he calls "fundamentalists," that is, those who claim the existence of "absolute" normativity—*viz.* normativity that is independent of any contingent facts about human communities.

Fundamentalism, then, can be seen as advocating the existence of some non-causal, but causally effective forces. Characterized in this way, it may well look like a doctrine nobody would want to subscribe to, but as Turner documents in his book, this view is, as a matter of fact, implicit to the views of at least some philosophers. It is possible to agree with Turner that this is not a view we should embrace; my aim, however, is to indicate that there are versions of normativism that are not fundamentalist in this sense and that might be worth being taken seriously.

Hence the viable version of normativism we are going to defend concurs with Turner in rejecting that there would be any normative force transcendent to the social forces of human communities, and agrees that if we can talk about a normative force, normative facts, or normative explanations, then all of this must be grounded in the social facts, which are in turn grounded in the causal facts regarding the individuals forming the societies. However, the societies are such complicated entities, held together by such complex and feedback-driven interactions of their members, that we can expect that the very organizations of these entities will provide us with specific problems, not to be encountered elsewhere.

To begin with, consider the following two scenarios.

> *Scenario* 1. A bunch of individuals kicks a ball around a playground. There are no rules.
> *Scenario* 2. As before, but now the individuals are playing according to some rules; either the usual rules of football, or some kind of rules which

they have made up during some previous games. (The rules need not be written down and may be somewhat open-ended—there may be situations that they do not cover and that are to be negotiated when they occur.)

Taking part in the game from Scenario 1 does not appear very appealing; in contrast to this, taking part in the one from Scenario 2 is much more attractive. It is only in the latter case that you can score a goal, develop strategies to do so, win a game or, indeed, lose one. All of this makes this enterprise into something quite enjoyable for many of us. And all of this is made possible by the fact that in this case, unlike in the other one, the game is rule-governed—we can say that this enterprise, in contrast to that of Scenario 1, has a *normative dimension*.

Now the claim a normativist may urge is that most of what we humans do has this kind of normative dimension; indeed most of what is specific to our species somehow presuppose various normative dimensions of our lives. In particular, it is already meaningful talk and our distinctively human way of thinking (which is usually called *rational* or *conceptual*) that is constituted by certain normative frameworks—just like you can score a goal only within a framework of rules, you can assert that something is thus and so, or you can have a belief to this effect, only within a certain framework of rules.

Needless to say that normative frameworks laying the foundations of our talk or our rational thought cannot be explicit like the rules of football. Therefore the claim of the normativist involves the claim we can establish implicit normative frameworks—frameworks, that is, which are not a matter of explicitly agreed-upon and written-down rules, but rather rules that are implicit to our conduct. (Remember that the rules making the difference between Scenario 1 and Scenario 2 need not have been codified, and even need not be explicitly agreed upon—they may be based merely on the habitual concurrence of treating certain ways of playing as faulty and behaving in accordance with this.)

Nobody would probably want to deny that rules play some nontrivial roles in human affairs; hence this very fact is not likely to be a point of quarrel between a normativist and an anti-normativist. The anti-normativist may dispute especially two points:

1. that the normative dimension of human affairs is all-pervasive;
2. that its existence would compromise naturalism.

Let us consider (1) first. Here the anti-normativist's claim would be that the role of rules within human affairs is not really central. She might deny that belief and language are normative. Norms, from this viewpoint, are a relatively recent sprout of human social organization, they come into being in that members of a society agree upon them (explicitly or implicitly), and they are, hence, rather higher-level social constructs that do not have more than a superficial importance from the viewpoint of the human communities and us humans as their members.

Why would the normativist insist that even assertion or belief require a normative framework and hence that a normative dimension does not concern only some superstructure of human social life, but rather its very foundations? An exhaustive answer to this question would be quite complex and it would go far beyond the limits of the current paper (a very detailed version is given by Brandom 1994; I have discussed the foundations of normativist semantics on a number of places—see esp. Peregrin 2012b, 2012c, 2014). However, in essence the answer is that the normativist sees no viable alternative way of accounting for the phenomena of meaning and content, which are essential both to human language and human thought—in particular she sees no alternative *naturalistic* answer.

The normativist is convinced that the traditional accounts of meaning and meaningfulness based on relations such as *standing for* or *representing* are bound to fail to give a satisfactory explanation of these fundamental relations (such that they would avoid "ruptures in the ordinary stream of explanation"). Instead of this, she proposes that the mechanism that makes the type of sound into a meaningful expression is of the same nature as that which makes a piece of wood into a piece of chess (a knight, say)—it is subordination to a certain bundle of rules that furnishes the piece of wood with a certain *role;* and similarly it is subordination to a certain bundle of rules that furnished the type of sound with a *role* that we have come to call its meaning. And in view of the fact that hardly anybody would want to challenge the existence of chess pieces as something non-naturalistic, and thus illusory, the analogous construal of meaningful expressions also seems to be unproblematic in this respect.

WEAK SOCIAL NORMATIVISM

Let me call the version of normativism that assumes no other kind of normativity save that resulting from the society, and hence from the interactions of the individuals within the society, *social normativism*. Hence social normativism is not fundamentalist in Turner's sense; it does not assume any causally effective non-causal forces and no normative facts independent of the causal ones.

Let us now turn to the above point (2), that is, to the question of how far is social normativism reconcilable with naturalism. The anti-normativist would claim that the existence of norms, just like existence of any other higher-level social constructs, such as rituals, sport, music, or financial markets, is of course in no such conflict, for none of these phenomena is more than a product of intersections of various individual intentions, beliefs, and interests, whose analysis in a language of natural science may be difficult, but it simply cannot be impossible.

I do not think that the reducibility of the level of description on which we talk about rules to a level of a more directly scientific talk (perhaps language of physics?) can be taken for granted. Imagine that somebody wants you to explain what football is: You will probably start with spelling out (some of the) rules of football (continuing talking about the social role of the sport, players and their roles in the game, strategies to win a match, etc.). Can we replace the talk about the rules with a talk about some physical reality (perhaps about the neurophysiology and brains of the players and/or the brains of other relevant people)? Surely not, really. Consider the rule *that no player with the exception of the goalkeeper can touch the ball with a hand.*[6] What would it amount to in physicalistic terms? We might perhaps try: *Whoever touches the ball will get a penalty.* But this is (i) not true (the referee may fail to notice), and (ii) a far cry from the desired reduction (it contains the word *penalty,* which would have to be further reduced). The anti-normativist may admit that though it is hardly imaginable that we do really carry out the reduction, it is surely possible *in principle.*

The normativist's response here might be that this 'in principle' is suspicious and using it is dangerously close to a vicious circle. For how do we know that it is 'in principle' possible if we are in no way able to carry out the reduction? Well, an 'answer' may come to mind: how could it *not* be possible? But of course this 'answer' rests on the very same claim that we want to establish, namely on a non-empirical (metaphysical?) principle that everything that there is must be so describable.

But let us not dispute this 'in principle possibility' (though the normativist might want to take note, for the record, of the fact that although we do not deny it, that does not mean that it is established)—what I call *weak social normativism* urges merely the *de facto* irreducibility.[7] In particular, it is based on the claim that

a. rules and what we called the normative dimension are crucial for so many things we humans do that to analyze humans as social beings is not really possible without paying due attention to them;[8] and
b. though there may be no reason to reject the claim that any talk of rules and of what is correct is in principle reducible, no such reduction is realistic and hence rules must figure in many essential explanations of human social life.

Weak social normativism might well declare a truce with the (Turnerian) anti-normativism. The anti-normativist may keep claiming that all social phenomena are at bottom causal, whereas the weak social normativist would hasten to add that though this might be in some sense true, no reduction is practically feasible and hence we need an intermediary language with the (practically) irreducible concepts like that of rule. The elaboration of this truce might then call for such words as "emergence," "supervenience," etc.

Hence the weak social normativist claims that we humans have developed into tremendously complex mechanisms whose functioning is so multifaceted and inter-individually interlocked that it is no longer feasible to try to describe and understand us as mechanisms. (Compare trying to understand a chess program by contemplating the patterns of 1's and 0's in the memory of a computer on which the program runs. And note that even the phrases 'the program runs', or 'patterns of 1's and 0's' may be deemed non-naturalistic descriptions—after all, the only thing that happens is a swarming of electrical potentials . . .) This makes it, I think, necessary to investigate *some* aspects of the social reality in terms that are not useful for the description of other facets of our world.

STRONG SOCIAL NORMATIVISM

Aside from weak social normativism, however, we can also think of its stronger version, according to which normativism claims more substantial irreducibility than the merely *de facto,* practical one. The strong normativist insists that there is a sense in which some normative claims that we need to provide for adequate explanations of some social phenomena are irreducible to non-normative ones as a matter of principle. To elucidate this sense, let us consider the following example:

Imagine that while watching a football game, I notice that a forward, who could have run to the opponent's goal and perhaps scored, simply stops. I ask my co-spectator: "Why did he not go for the goal?" and he answers, "It would have been an offside!" This is, no doubt, a reasonable explanation of what happened. Now this explanation can be considered as normative, and not only in one sense.

What are the senses? First, 'offside' is a purely normative matter, in the sense that it does not exist other than within the rules of football. It is a status conferred on a player in a certain position by the rules. Hence it is not like the player being fat, or quick, or running. Second, it explains the player's behavior by citing his *reason* for doing what he did (instead of pointing out the cause of his behavior). Third, it might be the case that what my colleague said not only invokes rules and the player's reason, but also reminds me that we are in the 'world of football': hence that the rules are in force for us and we must take them for granted—that what the player did was not only intelligible, but *correct.*

For example, Brandom, whom I take to be a social normativist in my sense, insists that the normative idiom is not reducible to the declarative one. To say that *killing is not correct* (or that *one ought not to kill people*) cannot be translated as *in our community we have a rule that prohibits killing people,* or *if you kill somebody, you will be punished,* or anything of this kind. Hence insofar as we need to use this idiom in our explanations, this renders them irreducibly normative in the sense mentioned above. Do we need to use it?

Take the first case first. Do we, in referring to an offside, need to use some normative claim? Not obviously. But what if somebody asks what an offside *is*? We would probably describe the situation to which the term 'offside' refers (a player of a team receives a pass from his teammate, while in the moment the pass was sent he was closer to the opponent's goal line than the ball and also the second-to-last defender . . .). Is this not a purely 'naturalistic' description of a situation? Notice that our explanation must be framed by the assumption that all of this happens within a *football game,* that is, that the rules of football are in force. And to say (or presuppose) this is to say (or presuppose) that many things are *correct* or *incorrect,* hence they *should* or *should not* be done (i.e. that, for instance, the field players *should not* touch the ball with their hands, etc.). Notice that if the very same situation, perhaps even on the very same field and with the very same persons occurs without this framework (say, after the match is already over, but the players are still on the field and one of them kicks the ball aimlessly away), it is *not* an offside.

Hence does this description of what an offside is, then, involve the normative idiom *essentially*? The anti-normativist might object that though in this case it might be necessary or at least reasonable to mention rules and the proprieties governed by them, we can do this in purely non-normative terms. It is enough to *refer to the fact* that a community follows such or another rules. Hence if we disregard the problem of specifying, in causal terms, what exactly it means to say that a community follows specific rules, or that the rules are in force for its members, it seems that we merely state a fact.

What about the second normative dimension of the above explanation, namely the fact that we give a *reason*? The concept of reason is normative in that it cites a fact or a belief that *should* be compelling for a *rational* being. Here everything hangs on the possibility of explaining away this *should* (perhaps as an instrumental one that could be reduced to an *if not, then an undesired outcome is probable*). And again the anti-normativist might want to insist that saying that somebody does something for a reason might be seen as a shortcut for some much longer causal explanation.

This leaves us with the third of the normative dimensions of the explanation listed above as the crucial point; and indeed I think it is crucial because, in a sense, the relevance of the previous two dimensions boils down to their implicitly involving what is explicit in the third—an element of endorsement that goes beyond mere statement. (If we can make do with merely stating that members of a society follow [what they call] rules, that some parts of what they perceive as reality is instituted by their holding to their rules, that they decide what to do on the basis of [what they call] reasons—all of this staying wholly neutral with respect to the validity of any kind of rules of the society, then perhaps the anti-normativism can be vindicated.)

Now what I call strong social normativism, is characterized, in addition to (a) and (b) above, also by

c.   talk about what is correct or what should be done is not reducible—not even 'in principle'—to non-normative talk.

THE NORMATIVE IDIOM

Typically, an explanation consists of declaratives stating some facts. Why was the magician able to pull the rabbit out of his hat? Because the rabbit was hidden in his habit and he moved it into the hat while he distracted the attention of the audience with his magic wand. Hence if an explanation were to be irreducibly normative, that is, consist, aside of ordinary declaratives, also of some 'normatives' irreducible to declaratives, we would seem to be driven back into the assumption that there must be some 'normative facts' irreducible to causal facts. This, I think, is in one sense true; however, in another sense it is not. To see why, we must look more closely at the normatives.

There is one imaginable explanation of the failure of reducibility of the normative idiom to the declarative one, which may render the irreducibility almost trivial. Perhaps the normative pronouncements constitute a different kind of speech act than declaratives, and hence their intranslatability into a declarative idiom is straightforward—after all, who would wonder that interrogatives and imperatives are not translatable into declaratives?

And indeed what I think is that sentences claiming that something *ought to be done* or that something *should be done* can be used in a mode different from the purely declarative one, that they can be used to carry out a kind of speech act different from (though somewhat similar to) assertion. Issuing such a 'normative', for example, saying that killing is wrong, may not (only) mean to state a fact, but it involves also voicing a (dis)approval and perhaps making a kind of a proposal. This, in my view, explains why such normatives are similar to ordinary declaratives, they are as it were, 'would be' declaratives: They spell out what there is *on the condition that others support it*. If I say *killing is wrong,* then I propose to establish that killing is wrong and if others concur with their normative attitudes, then killing is, indeed, wrong. If I, as a football player, claim that a player should not touch the ball with their hands, then if the attitudes of other football players resonate with mine, then touching the ball becomes, indeed, wrong.

Thus, normatives used in this mode constitute specific speech acts designed to project and extend our human affairs into the future. But no single speaker is able to *establish* the course of such an extension; it is a *communal* matter. Therefore, a single normative represents a kind of proposal that is submitted and is pending until it either resonates with acts of enough other members of the society to qualify it as accepted, or else fades away in the absence of such a resonance. (Why do we use normatives and this oblique way of accepting/rejecting proposals instead of doing all of it explicitly in terms of explicit proposals, evaluations, and acceptances/rejections? Explicit proposing, evaluating, and accepting already *presuppose* a framework of norms and thus cannot be generally used to establish it.)

Hence normatives are what I would call *cooperative performatives*. They are like Austinian performatives, in that they can become true by just being proclaimed, but unlike Austinian performatives, they can become true only when endorsed by a nontrivial number of members of a community. Purely theoretically, we could imagine that all the supporters first meet and agree on the support and nominate a representative who then does one (Austinian) proclamation for all of them; but as this is not feasible, the mechanism is such that the individual contributions are often put forward as the cooperative declaratives looking as stating a fact that, however, may still be merely *in spe*.

This results in the situation that we see even the normatives as close enough to declaratives to be true or false. This sets them apart from interrogatives or imperatives, and makes them more like some specific kind of declaratives, say subjunctive conditionals. While the truth value of a sentence such as *People in Prague are polite* may be seen as a straightforward matter of correspondence between the sentence and the world, the truth value of *If people in Prague were polite, there would be many more tourists there* is a more intricate matter. And the truth value of *People in Prague should be more polite* is a still less straightforward matter (so much less that we had better exempt sentences of this kind from our *declarative* box altogether); yet sentences of this kind are nevertheless still felt as 'truth-apt'. This is also the reason we are tempted, and may, in a sense, even be substantiated, in talking about *normative facts*.

I should add that besides the reading I have just been discussing, normatives also may have a reading that is *purely* descriptive. The two readings correspond to assuming the respective standpoints which we can call, using an apt metaphor, as 'inside' and 'outside' the rule involved with the normative. Being outside a rule means describing it as a fact, in a 'disengaged' manner; being inside means being engaged, accepting and upholding the rule.[9]

Now the anti-normativist may say that it is only describing rules from the outer perspective that should interest a theoretician of society, and anyway that it is only this perspective that is available to science. What complicates the situation is the fact that human thinking, speaking, and acting presupposes a framework of rules. This inevitably compromises the requirement of dealing with all rules merely from outside. One thing is that even if it were possible to move outside of *any* particular system of rules, it would be hardly possible to move outside of *all* such systems at once (at least without regressing to a level of an inhuman being).[10] And it is even not clear that we can really move outside of every one of the systems of rules we, as a matter of fact, inhabit.

And we should add that even if it were unproblematic to move outside of all systems of rules, there would still be a reason for being interested in how they look 'from inside': we normally do live inside them, and hence to understand our human predicament, this 'inside' should not be beyond the scope of our interest.

NORMATIVISM RECONSTRUCTED

Willfrid Sellars, one of the ur-normativists (if not *the* ur-normativist), has famously declared that "in the dimension of describing and explaining the world, science is the measure of all things, of what is that it is, and of what is not that it is not" (1956, IX.41). Insofar as this goes, Sellars was a devoted 'scientist'. However, he believed that besides the "scientific image" of the world (*viz.* the image consisting of spatiotemporal, causally interacting objects) there is something that he called the "manifest image" and which is both irreducible to the scientific image and indispensable. The manifest image contains "normatively constituted" objects. Thus, whereas within the scientific image I exist as an organism behaving in a certain way and interacting with the environment, it is only within the manifest image that I, moreover, exist as a person carrying out actions that are intentional and for which I am responsible. It is only this world that contains meanings, thoughts, reasons, etc.[11]

I urge that to be able to understand some parts of our human reality we must assume the 'internal viewpoint', but this must not be misunderstood. What I urge is *not* any kind of a collective 'first-person perspective' analogous to the first-person perspective urged by the exponents of introspective philosophy of mind (though I certainly do not want to deny that studying the psychology of rule-followers may be interesting!). Looking at rules from inside means, first and foremost, taking the correctness they institute at face value; and also taking the 'normative reality' instituted by systems of rules as a reality without a proviso.

Consider studying a ritual of an alien community, which involves something that we would tend to consider morally wrong (such as humiliating, or even torturing children). Of course that we *can* study it wholly suppressing our moral judgments, that is, take the behavior of the natives as being wholly beyond any correctness or incorrectness (similarly as we do when we study non-human animal species). But that just seems *wrong*: Unless we are ready to believe that the natives do not deserve to be seen as persons, that is, as somebody morally accountable for what they do (as we believe in case of elephants or lions), denying them the status seems to be degrading them, *viz.* doing them harm. Hence it seems that assuming that their norms have no overlap with our moral norms is acceptable only when there is no way to interpret them otherwise.

Or consider some practices of the natives that would resemble our argumentation and reasoning. Again, we can completely disregard this similarity and study these practices as we study the regularities of ants running around their anthill. But it would be much more natural—at it would seem much more appropriate—to take it, at least tentatively, as the natives' version of reasoning, which hence may be considered in some respects correct and in others incorrect. And again, not to do this would seem to be a kind of ostracizing the natives—to deny them the status of persons, fully fledged human beings, which rightfully belongs to them.

This indicates that staying outside of some rules is *not* unproblematic. And what holds of individual rules, holds also for systems of rules and for the institutions they constitute—*viz.* about the 'normative reality' that forms the niche of us, normative beings. And this 'normative reality' is wholly constituted by rules in the sense that it exists only insofar as we endorse the rules that establish it. Thus, for example, as long as we do not accept the rules of chess, the wooden pieces the players use can be said merely to be held for (what they call) *pawns, rooks, bishops,* etc. by the players; it is only when we come to accept them that we can say that they *are* pawns, rooks, or bishops.[12]

Our human life is inextricably trapped within many systems of rules, and many things we tend to see as constituting the reality in which we live are normative in the sense that they are constituted by normatives rather than declaratives. This, in one sense, does not make these things not enough thingish— for example, I think that from certain perspectives numbers are almost prototypical things (in that we do not hesitate to ascribe them properties, speak about relationships between them, etc.). However, in another sense, they do have a deficit in their thingishness (measured by the thingishness of our middle-size dry goods): they stand or fall with our holding to our normatives, with our normative attitudes.

The objects and facts of this kind are *institutional* ones—they exist in terms of certain attitudes of people. It is not too controversial to say that a great deal of our social reality is of this kind. However, what, precisely, is the link between *institutional* and *normative*? As we humans are 'goal-directed' animals (i.e., we operate in terms of our complicated feedback loops that make it possible for us to *pursue goals* and constantly evaluate our means in terms of the ends to which they lead), we build the reality in which we live—insofar as this reality has an institutional character—so that it is in a sense always provisional and open to revision.[13]

Moreover, it is provisional in a different sense from that in which anything we build is—anything such is liable to being rebuilt, upgraded, or modified. However, the upgrading of our normative reality brings about a certain retroactivity: Changing the view on what is correct brings about the view that it has always been correct. Though what we do looks, to an outside observer, as a kind of *building,* we ourselves cannot but see it as a kind of *discovery.* In this way, our social reality, insofar as it has a normative dimension, is of a peculiar character.

A realm where this is clearly illustrated is mathematics. *Groups,* for instance, as mathematical objects, were introduced into mathematics in the nineteenth century (by Galois and others). Hence in one sense we can say that this was when groups came into existence. However, a group is not a kind of entity that can 'come into existence'—its mode of existence is eternal, or better, atemporal. Therefore we have introduced groups together with the assumption that a group is not something that can have an origin—so from this viewpoint their introduction immediately starts to look more like a discovery. And my point is that this affects—more or less—any kind of normative reality: We do the introducing, but in such a way that we are obliged to see what is introduced as discoveries of certain forms of pre-existent correctness. And hence we can also apply these correctnesses retroactively: We can use them to measure also historical events prior to the introduction of these measures.

A lot of ink has been spilled about the "social construction of reality."[14] Some of the normativists can now be seen as anatomizing what such a construction is: how the kind of reality that can be called *institutional* (and that constitutes such an important part of what we perceive as reality today) comes into being, how it is sustained, and in what sense it is aligned with our tangible reality. It is clear that it is a matter of a 'social consensus', but how exactly does such a 'consensus' work? The answer that, I think, emerges out of the normativists' considerations is that the consensus is a matter of intersections among the members of the society holding each other responsible for what they do and answerable to the rules implicitly governing the society's functioning (and later perhaps made explicit in the form of written or spoken codes).

CONCLUSION

'Normativism' is a rather blurry notion: Philosophies holding norms to be crucial come in very different varieties. One variety suggests that the realm of the normative is an independent stratum of reality to be recognized in addition to that of the factual—this is the variety Turner and other philosophers of social sciences reject, and I think justly. But there is also another variety, which does not suggest anything like this, but holds norms as the key to understanding the tremendously complex social practices that lay the foundations to institutional reality and to the interplay between the social cognition and cognitions of individual people. I think that this variety is not only viable, but inevitable. It stems from the fact that when accounting for human societies, we cannot always approach all their norms 'from without':

we are embedded within some of them to such an extent that the demand to restrict ourselves to the 'view from without' would compromise our ability to account for our societies and for the place of us humans within them. It does not mean that norms constitute a layer of reality elusive of scientific understanding; it does mean, however, that scientific understanding needs to be complemented by an understanding of our societies' normative scaffolds as seen from within.

In particular, what I call *normativism* is the view that norms are essential for human societies and that we cannot understand or explain the societies without scrutinizing the way that norms alter the way in which we humans inhabit our world. What I call *social normativism* is normativism based on the conviction that all sources of normativity are ultimately social, that is, there are no norms that would transcend human societies (though we cannot but *take* the most basic norms of our society as transcending the society). What I call *weak social normativism* is the conviction that social normativism is consistent with naturalism in the sense that the normative dimension of any society that can be—in principle, though not necessarily in fact—expressed in the descriptive mode. What I call *strong social normativism* is the conviction that to account for the normative dimension we sometimes need the normative mode irreducibly. And in this paper I have tried to marshal some evidence in favor of strong social normativism.[15]

NOTES

1 See, for example, Lance and O'Leary-Hawthorne (1997); Whitting (2008) or Peregrin (2012a) for the normativist side and Wikforss (2001); Hattiangadi (2006, 2007) or Glüer and Wikforss (2009) for the anti-normativist one.

2 For a more detailed discussion of Turner's book see my review—Peregrin (2011).

3 We may certainly say that such a theory supplies members of the society with *reasons,* which tend to lead the members to behave in the way they do. But even if we waive the fact that thus we still gloss over causally quite complex problems, we can hardly waive the fact that reasons are not yet obviously causes. For the ongoing discussion about the relationship between reasons and causes, see Davidson (1963); von Wright (1971); Risjord (2005); or Setiya (2011).

4 Something similar can be said about the naturalistic attitude of Henderson (this volume): For example, his basic characterization of participation in a social group involves "sets of similar and (nearly enough) coordinated understandings." But what, speaking naturalistically, is "understanding"?

5 See, for example, Fiske and Taylor (2008) or De Jaegher and Froese (2009).

6 Mind you: What I mean is *football,* not *American* football.

7 Henderson (this volume) urges the distinction between supervenience and what he calls "superdupervenience," where to "superdupervene" on some natural properties is to "supervene on those natural properties, and, for the supervenience relationship itself to be naturalistically explicable." It seems to me that here *one more* distinction is vital. To say that a "supervenience relationship is naturalistically explicable" may mean either that we are able to specify the relationship in naturalistic terms, or merely that there is no reason to think that this cannot be—"in principle"—done. In the latter case, the only thing that underlies the reducibility

claim is the bias towards naturalism, which makes us consider everything as naturalistically explicable until we have a proof of the contrary. (I do not mean to say that such preconception is unreasonable—I think it *is* reasonable in view of the fact how successful natural sciences are in describing and explaining our world. However, when what is at issue are *foundational* questions, then this preconception can easily lead us to take the absence of the proof to the contrary as the proof of naturalism.)

8   Okrent (this volume) stresses that what is distinctive of us, contemporary humans, is that we are not only sensitive to the "shoulds" of instrumental rationality (we are able to choose suitable means for our ends), but that we are also sensitive to the "oughts" of social norms. And what is urged by Rouse (this volume) is that the environment of norms such as these brings about new ends, thus completely altering the ways in which we live our lives.

9   The metaphor of an inside of a system of rules has been employed by Hart. Note that, as Hart stresses, we must not misunderstand the internal aspect of rules as a matter of mere subjective experience of the rules, that "feelings are neither necessary nor sufficient for the existence of 'binding' rules" and that "there should be a critical reflective attitude to certain patterns of behaviour as a common standard, and that this should display itself in criticism (including self-criticism), demands for conformity, and in acknowledgements that such criticism and demands are justified" (1961, 57).

10   The situation is reminiscent of the post-Tarskian view of the languages of logic: We can treat *any* such language as an object language, but only because we can always recruit another language as a *meta*language.

11   See Rosenberg (2007) for more details.

12   Zahle (this volume) argues, very persuasively, that it is not the case that "social scientists make indispensable use of a distinct method when studying norms by way of participant observation." I think this is correct. I think that any kind of *description*—independently of whether it is carried out from an "outside" or from an "inside"—has to rely of the same kind of well-known methods. What it takes to be "inside" of rules is not a matter of different methods of description, but rather of something beyond description, of an element of endorsement that is present when we consider a human being as a *person*.

13   This is our specifically human way of *niche construction*—see footnote 12.

14   From the classical Berger and Luckmann (1966), via Searle (1995) or Hacking (1999), up to contemporary discussions.

15   Work on this paper was supported by the grant No. 13-20785S of the Czech Science Foundation.

REFERENCES

Berger, L. B. and Luckmann, T. 1966. *The Social Construction of Reality (A Treatise in the Sociology of Knowledge)*. New York: Doubleday.
Brandom, R. 1994. *Making it Explicit*. Cambridge, MA: Harvard University Press.
Davidson, D. 1963. Actions, Reasons and Causes. *Journal of Philosophy* 60: 685–700.
De Jaegher, H. and T. Froese. 2009. On the Role of Social Interaction in Individual Agency. *Adaptive Behavior* 17: 444–460.
Fiske, S. T. and S. E. Taylor. 2008. *Social Cognition: From Brains to Culture*. New York: McGraw-Hill.
Glüer, K. and A. Wikforss. 2009. Against Content Normativity. *Mind* 118: 31–70.
Hacking, I. 1999. *The Social Construction of What?* Cambridge, MA: Harvard University Press.

Hart, H. L. A. 1961. *The Concept of Law.* Oxford: Oxford University Press.

Hattiangadi, A. 2006. Is Meaning Normative? *Mind & Language* 21: 220–240.

———. 2007. *Oughts and Thoughts (Rule-Following and the Normativity of Content).* Oxford: Clarendon Press.

Lance, M. N. and J. O'Leary-Hawthorne. 1997. *The Grammar of Meaning.* Cambridge: Cambridge University Press.

Peregrin, J. 2010. The Enigma of Rules. *International Journal of Philosophical Studies* 18: 377–394.

———. 2011. Review of S. Turner: Explaining the Normative. *ORGANON F* 18: 405–411.

———. 2012a. The Normative Dimension of Discourse. In *The Cambridge Handbook of Pragmatics,* edited by K. Allan and K. Jasczolt, 209–225. Cambridge: Cambridge University Press.

———. 2012b. Inferentialism and the Normativity of Meaning. *Philosophia* 40: 75–77.

———. 2012c. Semantics without Meaning ? In *Prospects of Meaning,* edited by R. Schantz, 479–502. Berlin: de Gruyter.

———. 2014. *Inferentialism: Why Rules Matter.* Basingstoke: Palgrave.

Risjord, M. 2005. Reasons, Causes, and Action Explanation. *Philosophy of the Social Sciences* 35: 294–306.

Rosenberg, J. F. 2007. *Wilfrid Sellars: Fusing the Images.* Oxford: Oxford University Press.

Searle, J. 1995. *The Construction of Social Reality.* New York: The Free Press.

Sellars, W. 1956. The Myth of the Given: Three Lectures on Empiricism and the Philosophy of Mind. In *The Foundations of Science and the Concepts of Psychology and Psychoanalysis (Minnesota Studies in the Philosophy of Science 1),* edited by H. Feigl and M. Scriven, 253–329. Minneapolis: University of Minnesota Press.

Setiya, K. 2011. Reasons and Causes. *European Journal of Philosophy* 19: 129–157.

Tooby, J. and L. Cosmides 1992. The Psychological Foundations of Culture. In *The Adapted Mind: Evolutionary Psychology and the Generation of Culture,* edited by J. Barkow, L. Cosmides and J. Tooby, 19–136. New York: Oxford University Press.

Turner, S. 2010. *Explaining the Normative.* Cambridge: Polity Press.

von Wright, G. H. 1971. *Explanation and Understanding.* London: Routledge.

Whitting, D. 2008. On Epistemic Conceptions of Meaning: Use, Meaning and Normativity. *European Journal of Philosophy* 17: 416–434.

Wikforss, A. M. 2001. Semantic Normativity. *Philosophical Studies* 102: 203–226.

6 Methodological Anti-naturalism, Norms, and Participant Observation

Julie Zahle

INTRODUCTION

The methodological naturalism debate revolves around two key questions:

> *May* social scientists always make use of the same methods as those used within the natural sciences?
>
> *Should* social scientists always make use of the same methods as those used within the natural sciences?

There are two main positions within the debate. The naturalist stresses that social scientists should always make use of the same methods as those used within the natural sciences. This demand is reasonable, she argues, in the sense that social scientific research may perfectly well be carried out while relying exclusively on natural scientific methods. In contrast, the anti-naturalist insists that social scientists sometimes have to make use of methods that are distinct to the social sciences: These methods alone make it possible to generate knowledge about certain aspects of social reality. Natural scientific methods are simply not up to this task. The anti-naturalist continues that since the study of these aspects is crucial for an adequate understanding of social reality, social scientists should sometimes make use of methods that are not used within the natural sciences.

Within the methodological naturalism debate, there are different ways in which to spell out the notion of method. Sometimes, methods are understood as the standardized procedures that researchers use when constructing and justifying hypotheses. Other times, methods are taken to include the upshot or product of applying various research procedures. And so on. In the foregoing characterization of the naturalist and anti-naturalist positions, I had the procedural specification of methods in mind and I continue to understand methods in this procedural sense in the following. I am concerned with the question of whether the anti-naturalist is right to hold that social scientists sometimes have to make use of distinct methods, that is, ones not employed within the natural sciences. More precisely, this paper is a discussion of a specific version or subversion of this claim to the effect that social scientists make indispensable use of a distinct method when studying norms by way of participant observation. Anti-naturalists frequently stress that the study of norms necessitates the use of a distinct method (Braybrooke 1987, 12; Kincaid 1996, 217). Further, they often favor the use of participant observation as a research technique: They regard participant observation as one main way in which to gather data (Williams 2000, 90). Consequently, by focusing on the use of participant observation to find out about norms, I stack the cards in favor of the anti-naturalist: If social scientists sometimes have to make use of distinct methods, this is likely to be brought out by a discussion of the study of norms by way of participant observation.

Whatever their exact focus, contributions to the methodological naturalism debate tend to disregard social scientific practice. Discussions are rarely, if ever, based on detailed analyses of the manner in which social scientists actually go about the study of various aspects of social reality. I part from this tradition by providing an explication of the manner in which social scientists make use of participant observation when studying norms. In the first part of this paper, I offer this analysis after a brief presentation of the research technique of participant observation. Then, in the second part, I use this analysis as basis for a discussion of the correctness of the specific version of the anti-naturalist claim. I argue that, on diverse understandings of 'method', social scientists do not make indispensable use of a distinct method when studying norms by way of participant observation.

Before embarking on this task, however, let me say a few words about the spirit in which my discussion is carried out. One main motivation for engaging in the methodological naturalism debate has been a concern with the scientific status of the social sciences (Little 1991, 225). Thus, many theorists have defended the naturalist stance out of the conviction that unless social scientists make use of natural scientific methods, the social sciences will fail to qualify as sciences or as good sciences at least. These theorists have been opposed by defenders of the anti-naturalist stance who have insisted that the social sciences are perfectly respectable scientifically speaking. My motivation for entering the naturalism debate is quite different and hence unrelated to any worries about the scientific status of the social sciences. I take up the discussion out of a general interest in social scientific methods. I believe that reflection on the two key questions of the debate, or on subversions thereof, is worthwhile simply because this is conducive to a better grasp of the methods that are, may be, and should be employed within the social sciences.

This view has consequences for the significance assigned to the methodological naturalism debate. The debate used to be a central one within the philosophy of the social sciences. Lately, though, the issue has received rather little attention. As the editors of a recent anthology observe, "the old 'is there a fundamental cleavage between social and natural science' question that was once so prevalent in philosophical debates on interpretation has become increasingly peripheral" (Steel and Guala 2011, 144).

In response to this situation, it may be wondered whether we should completely abandon the methodological naturalism debate. In light of the above considerations, the answer is no: There is something to be learned about the social sciences methodology-wise from reflection on its two key questions. At the same time, however, it has to be acknowledged that if the aim is to get a better grasp of social scientific methods, then there are other questions whose examination may likewise serve this purpose. For example, there is also a lot to be learned, methodologically speaking, from pondering whether so-called quantitative methods are more reliable than qualitative ones and whether there are important differences with respect to the data that may be obtained by using participant observation and unstructured interviews respectively. For this reason, the concern with social scientific methodology does not provide any basis for holding that the methodological naturalism debate should be restored to its former centrality within the philosophy of the social sciences. It only provides grounds for a partial rehabilitation of the methodological naturalism debate, as it may be put. The following discussion, I hope, will illustrate that there are indeed methodological insights to be gained from engaging in the methodological naturalism debate.

THE STUDY OF NORMS BY WAY OF PARTICIPANT OBSERVATION

The research technique of participant observation is employed within a wide range of sciences including anthropology, sociology, history, and cultural studies. In this section, I begin by presenting the research technique. Then I examine how social scientists use participant observation to study norms. I should stress that I disregard a number of issues and complications pertaining to the use of participant observation to find out about norms. My aim is solely to say enough for the analysis to serve as basis for a discussion of whether social scientists make indispensable use of a distinct method when employing this research technique to study norms.

There are two aspects to the research technique of participant observation.[1,2] The participatory component has it that, over an extended period of time, the social scientist should participate in the ways of life she studies while trying to intervene as little as possible. There are different extents to which the social scientist may take part in the ways of life under study. For instance, she may participate in the sense of simply hanging around or in the stronger sense of engaging actively in the activities she studies. Irrespective of her degree of participation, the social scientist may, in virtue of her sheer presence or by accident, cause a change in business as usual. Still, she should try to interfere as little as possible since her aim is not to alter, but to find out about, the ways of life she studies. Finally, the social scientist should participate in the ways of life under study for a longer period of time. Earlier on within anthropology, this was taken to mean that the social scientist should stay with the individuals she studied for at least a year. Today, studies of a shorter duration are also regarded as perfectly acceptable.

Turning to the observational component, the participating social scientist should observe, in the broad sense of taking notice of, what goes on. Above all, the social scientist should register how the people she studies go about living their lives. In addition, she should make observations of herself to the extent that these observations provide her with insights into the ways of life that she studies. For example, insofar as the social scientist has become deeply immersed into certain ways of life, she may use her own acquired ways of experiencing situations as a source of insight into the ways of life under study.

The whole point of carrying out participant observation is famously described by Bronislaw Malinowski who is regarded as one of, if not *the,* main founder of the research technique. Participant observation, he states, allows the social scientist "to grasp the native's point of view, his relation to life, to realize *his* vision of *his* world" (Malinowski 1922, 25 italics in original).

One aspect of individuals' point of view that participant observation may be used to study is what they take to be appropriate or inappropriate ways of acting, that is, their norms of behavior. Examples of these norms are to greet somebody by way of shaking their hand, to stand in line in the supermarket in order to pay, not to leave the table before everybody has finished eating, to cover one's shoulders before entering a Catholic church, and to hold the door for the person immediately behind one. There is, of course, much to be said on the topic of norms. For the present purposes, it is important to stress one feature, namely that norms are often tacit: Individuals are often unable to state, on the spot, under what circumstances they take it to be appropriate or inappropriate for certain individuals to act in certain ways. This feature of norms is one of the main reasons why participant observation is useful when it comes to their study. As sometimes noted in the literature, participant observation may be used to grasp individuals' tacit knowledge (see, e.g., Spradley 1980, 11; Hastrup and Hervik 1994, 3; DeWalt and DeWalt 2002, 1). By implication, it may also be employed to find out about individuals' tacit knowledge of norms. But how? Unfortunately, this is never spelled out in any systematic fashion. I want to make up for this lack. Based on various scattered comments and examples offered by social scientists, it is possible to distinguish four types of observation that are suggestive of the norms individuals follow. I go through these four types of observation one by one.

Type 1 Observations: The social scientist makes observations of individuals' actions as these are met with approval or disapproval by competent assessors. An action met with approval is suggestive as to how it is appropriate to act while an action met with disapproval is suggestive as to how it is inappropriate to act.

The idea here is that by attending to the manner in which competent assessors evaluate actions, the social scientist is pointed to instances of appropriate or inappropriate ways of acting. Depending on the behavior in question, all, some, or only a few of the adult members of a community may be competent assessors. Also, note that there are numerous ways in which competent assessors may show their appraisal of an action. For example, competent assessors may express their approval by smiling, nodding, or clapping their hands, just as they may display their disapproval by giggling, hitting the wrongdoer, or yelling "you idiot."

In a paper on Candomblé, an Afro-Brazilian religious cult, Inger Sjørslev offers an example of a type 1 observation (Sjørslev 1987). As part of the cult, rituals are conducted in which mediums invite an Orixa Ogum, that is, a God, to possess them. One day, Sjørslev attended a ritual in the company of a young man called Milton. The ritual had not been going on for very long before Milton showed signs of being possessed by a God. Normally, Sjørslev tells, "the drummers would respect the presence of an Orixa, and start drumming the rhythm to accompany his dance. The drummers looked at each other, but they did not start drumming. The dancing women walked aside and stood there giggling and not quite knowing what to do. 'What kind of Ogum is this?' I heard somebody whisper and there was more giggling" (Sjørslev 1987, 11). These reactions pointed Sjørslev to the fact that the timing of the arrival of a God during a ritual is important: Milton becoming possessed by a God so early during the ritual was inappropriate.

> *Type 2 Observations:* The social scientist makes observations of competent performers' actions. An action carried out by a competent performer is suggestive as to how it is appropriate to act.

By taking note of the manner in which competent performers act, the social scientist is provided with examples of appropriate actions. Similarly to above, when it comes to certain ways of acting, more or less all adult members of a community are competent, whereas other ways of acting are only mastered by some or a few individuals. An illustration of a type 2 observation is provided by Karin Ask as part of her discussion of how it is appropriate for Pakistani women of honor to behave: "A group of women and girls and I went to take a bath after a long day's work. The place chosen was situated under a steep bank overhanging the riverside. On the top of the embankment ran a road going into the town centre, the bazaar area. . . . The women and girls took off all their clothes and ran stark naked into the river, leaving me behind, embarrassed in my bathing suit" (Ask 1994,69). Ask was highly surprised by the women's behavior since they could be seen from the road by men. Still, she makes it clear, she does not at any point doubt that they act in a manner that is suitable for women of honor. She regards the women and girls as competent regarding the extent to which women of honor should cover their bodies in different contexts.

> *Type 3 Observations:* The social scientist makes observations of her own actions as met with approval or disapproval. Her action being met

with approval is suggestive as to how it is appropriate to act; it being met with disapproval is suggestive as to how it is inappropriate to act.

In order to make this type of observation, the social scientist's action must fall within the scope of the norms of the individuals she studies. In that case, her own actions as assessed by competent individuals may serve as instances of appropriate or inappropriate ways of acting. Judith Okely has commented on the use of type 3 observations while using an example from her fieldwork among Gypsies (Okely 1992). She writes that "ignorance and unfamiliarity with the group's rules and rhythms brings key crises. These are also informative. After noticing a young Gypsy woman in trousers, I gladly wore some to avoid the cold. But I was reprimanded and told that trousers were permitted as long as I wore a dress to cover my hips" (Okely 1992, 17). In this fashion, Okely's own way of dressing provided her with an example of how it is inappropriate for Gypsy women to dress.

> *Type 4 Observations*: The social scientist makes observations of actions—others' as well as her own—that she herself, as a competent assessor, meets with approval or disapproval. An action that she meets with approval or disapproval is suggestive of how it is appropriate or inappropriate, respectively, to act. Also, she makes observations of actions that she, as a competent performer, carries out. An action of this sort is suggestive of how it is appropriate to behave.

Observations of this sort may only be made by a social scientist who possesses the competence to assess actions in terms of their appropriateness and/or who possesses the competence to act appropriately. As an illustration of the basic idea of type 4 observations, consider the following remark by Maurice Bloch: "As a result of fieldwork I too can judge quickly whether a bit of forest in Madagascar would make a good swidden. Indeed, I find as I walk through the forest I am continually and involuntarily carrying out this sort of evaluation. Once this level of participation has been reached we can attempt to understand . . . [this kind of] knowledge through introspection" (Bloch 1991,194). To this end, Bloch might simply provide himself with examples of good and bad swiddens by registering his own judgments of bits of forests in Madagascar. Though this is not a case of finding out about norms, it is obvious that a social scientist may use the exact same approach to find out about norms: She may note actions that she regards as appropriate or inappropriate or that she performs appropriately.

The four types of observations provide the social scientist with instances of appropriate and inappropriate actions. On their basis, she constructs, tests, and adjusts her norm hypotheses.[3] These hypotheses may be seen as variations over the following basic scheme: Ceteris paribus, individuals, I, take way of acting, a, to be appropriate or inappropriate for individuals, n, in circumstances, c.[4] It should be stressed that social scientists rarely present their findings in this manner: They leave out the ceteris paribus clause, they do not explicitly state who considers a certain way of acting appropriate since this is already clear from the context, and so on. Moreover, social scientists should not be taken to hold that the individuals they study necessarily harbor corresponding beliefs as to how it is appropriate or inappropriate to act. The formulation that individuals *take* a certain way to act to be appropriate or inappropriate is meant to convey this point.

These considerations suffice as an explication of the manner in which social scientists make use of participant observation to find out about norms. They make it possible to examine the anti-naturalist claim that social scientists make indispensable use of a distinct method when studying norms by way of participant observation. A few words are in order as to how I approach the discussion of this contention.

SETTING THE SCENE OF DISCUSSION

Within the methodological naturalism debate, two groupings of sciences are in focus: the social sciences and the natural sciences. The distinction between these two categories of sciences is taken to be fixed prior to, and independently of, the discussion of whether the social sciences may, and should, always make use of the same methods as those employed within the natural sciences. Moreover, it is standard to subscribe to some variation of the view that the social sciences are those studying the social world or social reality, whereas the natural sciences examine the natural world or natural reality (see Gorton 2010). For the present purposes, I adopt this view too and, in line with the participants in the debate, I leave it at that: I do not go into how, more precisely, to sort specific sciences according to this criterion.

There has been considerably less agreement on the use of the notion of method: Participants in the debate may have a different method in mind when claiming that social scientists sometimes make indispensable use of a distinct method. This feature of the debate is reflected in the following discussion: Here, I examine various proposals as to how the anti-naturalist may specify the notion of method when defending her position. There are three main schools of anti-naturalism, the *verstehen* or empathy tradition, the phenomenological tradition, and the Wittgensteinian tradition (see Skinner 1988, 79). I make no attempt to cover all the ways in which 'method' has been cashed out within these schools of anti-naturalism. Rather, I examine various understandings of 'method'—and corresponding ways in which to defend the anti-naturalist position—that I think are natural to consider both in light of my analysis of the study of norms by way of participant observation and in view of the current debate on methodological naturalism.

This clarified, imagine that the anti-naturalist has spelled out what exact method she has in mind when maintaining that social scientists make indispensable use of a distinct method while studying norms by way of participant observation. There are several strategies that may be adopted in the attempt to challenge her stance.

First, it may be argued that social scientists do not make use of the distinct method in question when studying norms by way of participant observation. Accordingly, the anti-naturalist claim that the method is indispensable is belied by the way in which social scientists actually go about their business: They seem to be doing just fine without it. Second, it may be maintained that though the method is used by social scientists and qualifies as a distinct method, it is not indispensable: An alternative method that is also used within the natural sciences may as well be employed. Third, it may be shown that the method in question is also used within the natural sciences; it is not distinct to the social sciences. Fourth, it may be held that the method proposed by the anti-naturalist is not really an adequate example of a method: If this understanding of a method is adopted, the debate is trivialized or in some other way rendered uninteresting. Fifth, it may be contended that the method proposed by the anti-naturalist is in some way deficient so that it is not conducive to the generation of knowledge about social reality. It goes without saying that the last two approaches need to be further motivated to reject the anti-naturalist's assertion in a satisfying manner.

Within the more recent debate, particularly the third strategy has been popular: Anti-naturalists have been accused of relying on incorrect accounts of the methods used within the natural sciences with the result that many methods have wrongly appeared as being distinct to the social sciences.[5] As Russell Keat puts it, "many arguments opposing the methodological unity of the natural and social sciences rest upon a view of the former which has been increasingly, and successfully challenged" (Keat 1983, 271). In the following discussion I make use of a mixture of the second, third, and fourth strategy. I argue that, on various understandings of methods, the anti-naturalist does not succeed in showing that social scientists make indispensable use of a distinct method when studying norms by way of participant observation.

DEFENSES OF THE ANTI-NATURALIST THESIS

The Data Gathering Method of Participant Observation

The analysis of the study of norms by way of participant observation may, in a very straightforward way, serve as the starting point for a defense of the anti-naturalist thesis. The anti-naturalist could simply point out that participant observation may not only be described as a research technique but also as a data gathering *method*. Accordingly, she may venture, when social scientists study norms by way of participant observation, their use of this method exemplifies the use of a method that is both indispensable and distinct to the social sciences.

But is participant observation really a method that is distinct to the social sciences? Above it was presented as applied to human beings. However, it seems perfectly possible to apply the research technique to animals too. Consider the ethologist who studies gorillas in their natural habitat.

The ethologist comes every day to watch them and slowly they get used to her to the point where she can sit close to them and interact a little bit with them. It is reasonable to describe this ethologist as carrying out participant observation. Admittedly, her participation in their way of life is quite limited but this does not disqualify her as employing the method: It is generally recognized that its use is compatible with different—including very limited—degrees of participation.[6] Since ethology is a natural science concerned with the study of the natural world, it follows that participant observation is not a method that is distinct to the social sciences.

One possible response to this conclusion is to look for a way in which to differentiate the use of participant observation as applied to humans and animals respectively: If it were possible to specify a version of participant observation that is only applicable to human beings, then the anti-naturalist thesis could be saved by recasting it by appeal to this specific version of the method. While this may well be feasible, the proposal runs into another problem, namely that the debate is thereby trivialized. Little observes that it "is obvious enough that the techniques of research, empirical procedures, quantitative methods, and the like differ substantially from one discipline to another—even among the natural sciences" (Little 1991, 223). Or at least, it may be specified, this is likely the case if these techniques are described in a sufficiently detailed manner. As such, it is generally recognized that if the anti-naturalist appeals to methods of this concrete sort, then she is obviously correct but also making a rather uninteresting point. The methodological naturalism debate has revolved around methods at a higher level of generality where the methods cut across, or encompass, various specialized data-gathering methods.

The Method of Reenactive Empathy

The anti-naturalist may look to the anti-naturalist tradition for help. One important strand of anti-naturalism appeals to the method of empathy or *verstehen*. Karsten Stueber is an influential contemporary defender of this tradition by holding that social scientists sometimes have to make use of the distinct method of reenactive empathy (Stueber 2012).[7] The anti-naturalist may draw on Stueber's account: Perhaps it may be shown that social scientists who study norms by way of participant observation make indispensable use of the distinct method of reenactive empathy.

Stueber's focus is rational actions. A satisfactory explanation of an individual's rational action, Stueber contends, points to her beliefs, desires, and the like, that caused the action. Moreover, it shows that the individual had reasons to act as she did: In light of her beliefs, desires, and the like, the action was a rational response to her situation. But how does a social scientist determine whether certain beliefs, desires, and the like make it rational for an individual to act in a given manner? According to Stueber, it is implausible to maintain that the social scientist relies on an implicit theory to this effect. Instead, he states, "[o]ur only option is to activate what I refer to as our capacity for reenactive empathy: We grasp another person's action as a rationally compelling one because we can grasp his thoughts as reasons for acting by putting ourselves in his shoes, by imagining the situation that he faces and trying to reenact his thought processes in our mind" (Stueber 2012, 28). In this fashion, the method of reenactive empathy is indispensable when explaining rational actions. Moreover, it is distinct since the social sciences, but not the natural sciences, have as one of their tasks to explain rational actions.

At first sight, it is not obvious how these considerations may be brought to bear on the participating social scientist who makes type 1–4 observations in order to construct and test her hypotheses about norms. However, consider this comment by Stueber: It is "legitimate to wonder how it is possible to interpret a certain behaviour such as an agent waving his hand as that agent's trying to warn another person unless we can also grasp that the agent has *reasons* to warn the other person. And if my considerations . . . are right so far, to grasp such reasons involves our empathetic abilities" (Stueber 2010, 199). Stueber does not further pursue this idea but, in light of his views more generally, here is how it may be elaborated: In order to be justified in her interpretation of an individual's action as having a certain meaning, the social scientist must grasp the individual's reasons to perform an action with that meaning and this requires her, among other things, to make use of the distinct method of reenactive empathy.

With this point in mind, return to the participating social scientist who makes type 1–4 observations. Clearly, making these observations goes together with the interpretation of actions as having certain meanings: When making type 1 and 3 observations, she interprets actions as being expressions of approval or disapproval, and when making all four types of observation, she interprets actions with a certain meaning as being instances of appropriate or inappropriate actions. As an illustration of the suggestion that individuals' reasons to perform actions with certain meanings must be grasped, consider the situation in which the social scientist observes Amy doing something whereupon Ben hits her. The social scientist is inclined to think that she has just made a type 1 observation: Ben is a competent assessor whose hitting of Amy is an expression of his *disapproval* of Amy's action rather than, say, an attempt to swat a fly sitting on Amy's chin. The social scientist now asks herself whether Ben had reasons to disapprove of Amy's action. To determine this she must, on various grounds, ascribe certain beliefs and desires to Ben while also putting herself in his shoes to make sure that these beliefs and desires gave him reasons to disapprove of Amy's doing. If these reasons make it rational for Ben to disapprove of Amy's action, then she may regard herself as justified in holding that Ben's hitting of Amy was indeed an expression of disapproval and hence she is partly justified in maintaining that she has made a type 1 observation.[8] If all this is right, then the anti-naturalist has a case: The social scientist who studies norms by way of participant observation makes indispensable use of the distinct method of reenactive empathy when making her type 1–4 observations.

I want to challenge this claim while focusing on the interpretation of actions as being expressions of approval or disapproval. With this aim in mind, it is instructive to begin by contemplating Taylor's observation that "[p]utting a cross beside someone's name on a slip of paper and putting it in a box counts in the right context as voting for that person" (Taylor 1985c, 32). The example is an illustration of the more general idea that, in certain situations, making certain bodily movements, as Taylor puts it, counts, as a matter of convention, as performing an action with a certain meaning. This idea carries over to actions that are expressions of approval or disapproval. In certain situations, shaking one's head from side to side or holding up one's index finger say, counts, as a matter of convention, as expressions of disapproval, just as nodding or clapping counts, as a matter of convention, as expressions of approval.[9] This being the case, the social scientist does not need to bother about individuals' reasons and hence she does not have to make use of the method of reenactive empathy when interpreting their actions as being expressions of approval or disapproval. She may simply pay attention to their bodily movements and the situations in which their actions take place while drawing on her knowledge of the relevant conventions. On this basis, she is in a position to grasp their actions as being expressions of approval or disapproval. Furthermore, by proceeding in this manner, she does not make use of a method that is distinct to the social sciences: Natural scientists, too, classify or interpret various events in accordance with the relevant conventions in this respect. Thus, the use of reenactive empathy is not indispensable: An alternative way of proceeding, used within the natural sciences too, is available.

On its own, this argument will not do. The reason is that the procedure just outlined cannot be used in cases where the social scientist is not familiar with the conventions for expressing approval and disapproval, nor in situations where an individual expresses approval or disapproval in ways that are not conventional. In these two situations, it may be argued, the social scientist needs to grasp individuals' reasons when interpreting their actions and, by implication, she must make use of the method of reenactive empathy. Accordingly, it may be continued, the preceding considerations show at most that the use of this method is limited to these two situations—not that its employment is superfluous.

In response to this line of reasoning, note a point stressed by Stueber, namely that in order to make use of reenactive empathy, the social scientist must have quite a lot of knowledge about the acting individuals, the sort of situations in which the actions takes place, and so on (see Stueber 2010, 195ff). I think that insofar as the social scientist has this much knowledge, there are ways in which she may grasp actions as being an expression of approval or disapproval that does not require her to figure out the underlying reasons. To see this, return to the social scientist who hypothesizes that Ben's hitting of Amy is an expression of disapproval. To support this interpretation, the social scientist may consider how it coheres with her understanding of other observed events. For instance, assume that she hears witnesses to the hitting incident make comments along the lines of "Ben thought Amy crossed the line there" and "Amy shouldn't have done that"; that she notes that Amy responds to Ben's hitting her by discontinuing her action and looking remorseful; that she registers that Ben's hitting is accompanied by what she regards as alternative expressions of disapproval such as foot stamping and frowning; and that she has made other observations of hitting that she has likewise taken to be expressions of disapproval. On the basis of these sorts of observations, the social scientists may reasonably conclude that Ben's hitting was an expression of disapproval.

The social scientist may make similar kinds of observations in situations where she thinks that an individual expresses approval or disapproval in an unconventional way. For example, if she hypothesizes that Susan expresses her approval of Emily's action by clenching and unclenching her hands, then she may examine how this interpretation coheres with, say, her observations of Susan's friends as they react to Susan's hand movements, of Emily's response to Susan's hand movements, of how Susan has acted in other situations where she was likely to express approval, and so on. To the extent that these observations cohere with her understanding of Susan as expressing approval, then the social scientist may reasonably hold on to this interpretation. It may now be noted that this alternative way of proceeding is sometimes used by natural scientists too: At times, they also support their interpretation of some event by noting how it coheres with their understanding of other events. For instance, an ethologist may interpret a gorilla's behavior as being aggressive and justify this proposal by showing how it fits in with her understanding of other observed events.

In light of these considerations, it may be concluded that when the social scientist interprets actions, as part of making her type 1–4 observations, she does not also have to grasp the individuals' reasons for their actions. By implication, she does not need to make use of the distinct method of reenactive empathy. In other words, the proposal that social scientists make *indispensable* use of the distinct method of reenactive empathy when studying norms by way of participant observation may be discarded.[10]

The Method of Introspection

Staying with the focus on the observations made by the social scientist, the anti-naturalist may propose that there is something special about type 4 observations: When the social scientist makes observations that require her to take notice of herself as a competent assessor or performer, she has sometimes to employ the method of introspection. For example, she may make an observation of an action that she is competent to assess. Insofar as she does not outwardly express her evaluation of the action, she has to use introspection to determine whether she approves or disapproves of it. Further add that the use of introspection is distinct to the social sciences and the anti-naturalist has provided a defense of her thesis.

The problem with this proposal is that if this is really all there is to the employment of introspection, the natural scientist uses it too. For example, the natural scientist may carry out an experiment where only those samples of liquid that turn out to have the right color should continue to form part of the study. Here, the natural scientist may well introspect her assessment of the color of the liquids and on this basis decide which samples to throw out.

The Method of Normative Deliberation

The last claim to be examined is based on Wolfgang Spohn's recent defense of the view that the method of normative deliberation, as I shall call it, is a distinct and indispensable method when studying norms in a diachronic perspective (Spohn 2011). The anti-naturalist may argue that Spohn's considerations sometimes apply to the social scientist who makes use of participant observation to study norms.

In his (2011), Spohn distinguishes between two perspectives which may be adopted towards norms (2011, 244). One the one hand, it is possible to consider them from a third-person external perspective. Thus approached, norms are the object of empirical investigation. On the other hand, norms may be viewed from a first-person internal perspective. Here, the norms are evaluated by asking whether they should be adopted and to answer this question it is necessary to engage in normative deliberation. Spohn's claim is that sometimes when social scientists study norms, they have to take on not only an external, but also an internal, perspective. More specifically, he thinks, this is the case, when social scientists take an interest in how the norms or normative conceptions within a community have changed over time.

Spohn's argument may be reconstructed as follows. When considering norms in a diachronic perspective, their development may sometimes be explained as due to changes in fashion or as a result of historical contingencies (2011, 247–8). In addition, the changes in norms over time sometimes have to be seen as a result of individuals aiming "to find out and do what *is* right" (2011, 248 italics in original). In the latter case, an idealized theory must be adopted to the effect that, as a result of their efforts, individuals get closer and closer to a certain ideal situation in which they have found out and are doing what *is* right. In actuality, there are always aberrations from this ideal development and hence it is necessary to supplement the idealized theory with error theories that explain moves away from the ideal state. These reflections may be summarized by saying that the change of norms over time must sometimes be conceived of as "a history of errors and approximations to" a given ideal (2011, 248).

But how is the social scientist to determine the ideal whose implementation a community ideally moves towards? Spohn makes it clear that the ideal is not reachable; it is "a normative fiction" (2011). For this reason, he concurs, it may not be posited from a third-person external perspective: Empirical investigation may not be used to uncover something that has not been realized. Instead a first-person internal perspective must be adopted: In order to specify the ideal, the social scientist must engage in normative deliberation. Since this sort of normative deliberation is never called for within the natural sciences, its use is not only indispensable, but also distinct to the social sciences.

These points may be applied to the social scientist who studies norms by way of participant observation. Inspired by Spohn, the anti-naturalist may state that so far the analysis in this paper exemplifies a third-person external approach to norms: It shows how a social scientist empirically investigates norms actually followed by the individuals she studies. On occasion, the anti-naturalist may continue, a social scientist may also want to understand these norms in a diachronic perspective. When the social scientist has collected data about the past norms within a community, she may sometimes come to realize that the employment of an idealized theory is called for: She must represent the norms as changing, over time, in the direction of an ideal state in which *the* right norms are implemented. In order to posit *the* right norms, the social scientist has to make use of the distinct method of normative deliberation.

There are at least two problems with this line of reasoning. One is that there are different ways in which to go about the task of specifying an unreachable ideal. To see this, imagine that a social scientist is interested in the development of norms that concern the relationship between the sexes. She discovers that, over time, the norms within the community she studies have largely changed in the direction of favoring a more equal relationship between the sexes. This being the case, she posits an ideal by simply exaggerating, or extrapolating from, this trend: The ideal is one in which individuals implement norms reflecting the view that the relationship between the sexes should be one of complete equality. Insofar as this alternative way of proceeding is available, it follows that the employment of normative deliberation is not indispensable when the social scientist hypothesizes an unreachable ideal.

The objection just considered grants that the social scientist has to offer an idealized theory. Spohn takes this to flow from, or go together with, the observation that the development of norms must sometimes be seen as a result of individuals aiming "to find out and do what *is* right" (2011, 248). I take it that this last point is most plausibly read as suggesting that, sometimes, changes in norms have to be seen as a result of individuals having reflected on these matters while reaching, and implementing, new conclusions as to what is right. However, this observation is perfectly compatible with the social scientist registering the changes and trying to reconstruct the considerations that motivated them. There is no need to regard some changes as approximations to an ideal while considering other changes as aberrations that must be accounted for by way of error theories. In other words, the social scientist may well refrain from offering idealized theories and, by implication, the situation in which it might be claimed that normative deliberation is called for, does not arise.[11]

The upshot of these reflections is that the social scientist who studies the norms within a community by way of participant observation and who wants to consider these norms in a historical perspective does not have to employ the distinct method of normative deliberation. This last attempt to defend the anti-naturalist's thesis may be dismissed.

CONCLUDING CONSIDERATIONS

In the first part of this paper, I presented the research technique of participant observation and the manner in which social scientists make use of participant observation to study norms. In the second part, I argued that, on diverse specifications of 'method', the anti-naturalist is wrong to contend that social scientists have to make use of a distinct method when studying norms by way of participant observation. By way of ending, let me briefly consider the question of how the anti-naturalist may respond to this conclusion.

Most obviously, perhaps, the anti-naturalist may try to come up with an additional understanding of methods, that is, one I have not considered. She may then argue that, thus specified, it appears that social scientists make indispensable use of a distinct method when finding out about norms by way of participant observation. Another option is that the anti-naturalist leaves behind the concern with norms or participant observation. Thus, she may instead attempt to establish that when it comes to other aspects of social reality than norms, and/or the employment of other research techniques than participant observation, there are methods distinct from natural scientific ones that social scientists have to use. Lastly, the anti-naturalist may change her focus and consider whether social scientists *should,* rather than *may,* employ the same methods as those used within the natural sciences: In situations where it is equally possible to use a distinct method and a method that is also employed within the natural sciences, she may try to show that the distinct method should be utilized.

The fact that the discussion leaves open these ways in which the anti-naturalist may attempt to defend her position does not in any way detract from its significance. Anti-naturalists tend to hold that the study of norms necessitates the use of a distinct method just as they tend to be very favorably disposed towards the employment of participant observation. Accordingly, it is food for thought that, on diverse specifications of 'method', the anti-naturalist claim is incorrect: No distinct method has to be employed when studying norms by carrying out participant observation. More importantly, in the process of reaching this conclusion, various methods were examined in considerable detail and from various perspectives. As a result a better grasp of these methods has been gained and this means that the discussion is a step in the direction of a better understanding of the social sciences with respect to the methods they use, may use, and should use. As I suggested in the introduction to this paper, it is exactly with this aim in mind that we should engage in the methodological naturalism debate.[12]

NOTES

1 The following characterization draws on various handbooks about the use of participant observation. Guides of this sort largely began to appear in the 1980s and are still being widely published. Examples of handbooks of this sort are Agar (1980); Spradley (1980); Jorgensen (1989); Bailey (1996); Davies (1999); DeWalt and DeWalt (2002) and Hammersley and Atkinson (2003).
2 This section draws on Zahle (2012, 2013).
3 It should be acknowledged that it is no easy matter to make the four types of observations. For example, when making type 1 and type 3 observations, the social scientist must determine that an assessor is indeed competent; when making a type 2 observation she must determine that a performer is actually competent; when making a type 4 observation, she must have good grounds for holding that she is a competent assessor or performer; and so on. I discuss some of these difficulties in my (2012).
4 Clearly, there are complications pertaining to the testing of ceteris paribus generalizations. For a discussion of this issue in a social science context, see, for example, Kincaid (1996, 63ff).
5 It should be specified that the third strategy has been applied to methods broadly understood, that is, not only to methods in the procedural sense. An example of this sort of criticism is Geertz's discussion in his (2000) of Taylor's portrayal of the natural sciences as part of his, *viz.* Taylor's, defense of the anti-naturalist position in (Taylor 1985a, 1985b).
6 Within the literature on participant observation, it is common to differentiate between different degrees of participation. Three commonly mentioned classifications are Gold (1969); Spradley (1980, 59ff) and Nelson (1986, 8).
7 To be precise, Stueber claims in his (2012) that the method of reenactive empathy is indispensably used within the human sciences. Spohn too, in his (2011) to be discussed below, is concerned with the human sciences. In the following, I present their points as applied to the social sciences; this makes no difference to the critical discussion of their views.
8 She is only partly justified in thinking so since she must also make sure that Ben is indeed a competent assessor and that his action was an expression of disapproval due to the inappropriateness rather than the ineffectiveness of Amy's doing.
9 Similarly, in certain situations, saying certain things counts as expressions of approval and disapproval. For the sake of simplicity, I disregard these verbal ways of expressing approval and disapproval in the following discussion.
10 Note that I have not taken a stance on whether the method of reenactive empathy needs to be used in other contexts. As such, I am also not engaging in the debate between, on the one hand, defenders of the use of reenactive empathy or simulation and, on the other hand, defenders of the theory-theory.

11　Perhaps it may objected that I am misreading Spohn: The claim that, sometimes, changes in norms have to be seen as a result of individuals aiming to discover and do what *is* right should be taken to state that individuals must sometimes be understood as aiming to discover and do what *is* right *as specified by the social scientist*. This proposal may be rejected too: As already illustrated above, it is always possible to understand the changes of norms without considering them from the perspective of whether they approximate or deviate from some ideal.

12　I would like to thank Jan Faye, David Henderson, Mark Risjord, and Karsten Stueber for helpful comments. Also, I have benefitted from suggestions by the audiences when presenting versions of this paper at the conference on Naturalism and Normativity in the Social Sciences at University of Hradec Kralowe in 2012; at the Finnish Centre of Excellence in the Philosophy of the Social Sciences, University of Helsinki in 2012; and at the University of Vienna in 2013.

REFERENCES

Agar, Michael H. 1980. *The Professional Stranger. An Informal Introduction to Ethnography*. Orlando: Academic Press.

Ask, Karin. 1994. Veiled Experiences: Exploring Female Practices of Seclusion. In *Social Experience and Anthropological Knowledge,* edited by K. Hastrup and P. Hervik, 65–77. London: Routledge.

Bailey, Carol A. 1996. *A Guide to Field Research*. Thousand Oaks: Pine Forge Press.

Bloch, Maurice. 1991. Language, Anthropology, and Cognitive Science. *Man* 26(2): 183–198.

Braybrooke, David. 1987. *Philosophy of Social Science*. Englewood Cliffs: Prentice Hall.

Davies, Charlotte A. 1999. *Reflexive Ethnography*. London: Routledge.

DeWalt, Kathleen M. and DeWalt, Billie R. 2002. *Participant Observation. A Guide for Fieldworkers*. Lanham: Altamira Press.

Geertz, Clifford. 2000. The Strange Estrangement: Charles Taylor and the Natural Sciences. In *Available Light,*, 143–159. Princeton: Princeton University Press.

Gold, Raymond L. 1969. Roles in Sociological Field Observation. In *Issues in Participant Observation,* edited by G. J. McCall and J. L. Simmons, 30–39. Reading, MA: Addison-Wesley Publishing Company.

Gorton, William A. 2010. The Philosophy of Social Science. In *The Internet Encyclopedia of Philosophy,* edited by J. Fieser and B. Dowden. ISSN 2161–0002, http://www.iep.utm.edu/.

Hammersley, Martyn and Paul Atkinson. 2003. *Ethnography*. London: Routledge.

Hastrup, Kirsten and Peter Hervik. 1994. Introduction. In *Social Experience and Anthropological Knowledge*, edited by K. Hastrup and P. Hervik, 1–13. London: Routledge.

Jorgensen, Danny L. 1989. *Participant Observation*. Newbury Park, CA: Sage Publications.

Keat, Russell. 1983. Positivism, Naturalism, and Anti-naturalism in the Social Sciences. *Journal for the Theory of Social Behavior* 1(1): 3–17.

Kincaid, Harold. 1996. *Philosophical Foundations of the Social Sciences*. Cambridge: Cambridge University Press.

Little, Daniel. 1991. *Varieties of Social Explanation*. Boulder: Westview Press.

Malinowski, Bronislaw. 1922. *Argonauts of the Western Pacific*. London: George Routledge and Sons.

Nelson, Richard K. 1986. *Hunters of the Northern Forest*. Chicago: University of Chicago Press.

Okely, Judith. 1992. Anthropology and Autobiography. Participatory Experience and Embodied Knowledge. In *Anthropology and Autobiography,* edited by J. Okely and H. Callaway, 1–29. London: Routledge.

Sjørslev, Inger. 1987. Untimely Gods and French Perfume. Ritual, Rules, and Deviance in the Brazilian Candomblé. *Folk* 29: 5–23.

Skinner, Quentin. 1988. Social Meaning and the Explanation of Social Action. In *Meaning and Context: Quentin Skinner and His Critics,* edited by J. Tully, 79–96. Princeton: Princeton University Press.

Spohn, Wolfgang. 2011. Normativity Is the Key to the Difference between the Human and the Natural Sciences. In *Explanation, Prediction, and Confirmation, The Philosophy of Science in a European Perspective,* vol. 2, edited by D. Dieks, W. J. Gonzales, S. Hartmann, Th. Uebel and M. Weber, 241–251. Dordrecht: Springer.

Spradley, James P. 1980. *Participant Observation.* Fort Worth: Harcourt Brace Jovanovich College Publishers.

Steel, Daniel and Francesco Guala. 2011. Interpretation. In *The Philosophy of Social Science Reader,* edited by D. Steel and F. Guala, 143–147. London: Routledge.

Stueber, Karsten R. 2010. *Rediscovering Empathy.* Cambridge, MA: The MIT Press.

———. 2012. Understanding Versus Explanation? How to Think About the Distinction between the Human and the Natural Sciences. *Inquiry* 55(1): 17–32.

Taylor, Charles. 1985a. *Human Agency and Language.* Cambridge: Cambridge University Press.

———. 1985b. *Philosophy and the Human Sciences.* Cambridge: Cambridge University Press.

———. 1985c. Interpretation and the Sciences of Man. In *Philosophy and the Human Sciences,,* 15–57. Cambridge: Cambridge University Press.

Williams, Malcolm. 2000. *Science and Social Science.* London: Routledge.

Zahle, Julie. 2012. Practical Knowledge and Participant Observation. *Inquiry* 5(1): 50–65.

———. 2013. Participant Observation and Objectivity in Anthropology. In *New Challenges to Philosophy of Science. The Philosophy of Science in a European Perspective,* vol. 4, edited by H. Andersen, D. Dieks, W. J. Gonzales, T. Uebel and G. Wheeler, 365–376. Dordrecht: Springer.

7 Agents, Reasons, and the Nature of Normativity

Karsten R. Stueber

Introduction

Prima facie the social realm is a domain that is thoroughly permeated by various kinds of rules and norms. We seem implicitly and explicitly to appeal to them on a daily basis in teaching our children of how to behave and in recommending appropriate courses of actions to our colleagues, friends, and significant others. More generally, rules and norms are involved in evaluating behavior as appropriate and inappropriate, rational and irrational, legal and illegal, decent and indecent, just and unjust, or courageous and cowardly, to just name a few normative distinctions commonly referred to. Even so-called moral emotions such as feeling guilty, ashamed, resentful, or insulted or feeling admiration or pride can be made sense of only in light of normative standards to which we are in some sense emotionally attuned. For that very reason we commonly talk about behavior in the social realm as being guided by rules and by norms and advise social scientists who study the social domain to properly explicate and understand the ruling norms of the society under investigation.

More importantly, the realm of norms and rules seems also to be discursively structured, that is, opinions and beliefs about norms and our normative evaluations of particular behavior in light of them are regarded to be similar to beliefs about the natural world in that we can argue about them and demand intersubjectively accessible reasons and justifications for accepting them as objectively true and false. We certainly acknowledge a continuum of normative notions and distinguish between social norms and conventions that have validity merely within a rather circumscribed social and cultural practice and norms that we regard to have almost universal scope of validity such as the norms of rationality and morality (Southwood 2010; Southwood and Eriksson 2011). But regardless of this issue, we regard all normative questions to have a very different epistemic status than questions of subjective taste about which one cannot intelligibly argue but can only politely exchange one's opinion. But if this is so, then it seems as if we should also accept normative facts as truth-makers of our normative opinions, since it is only in light of such truth-makers that we can fully make sense of normative objectivity. Given the variety in the scope of normative statements, some of those facts would have to be regarded as specifically social facts limited only to particular environments while others would have a more universal presence.

Yet modern science has taught us that our ordinary folk scheme of making sense of things cannot be trusted as being indicative of the underlying ontological structure of the world unless our ordinary categories of thinking about the world are in some sense validated with the help of categories that play an explanatory role in the context of scientific theories that have survived rigorous empirical testing. More specifically, it has been argued (most recently very powerfully by Turner 2010) that appeal to irreducible normative facts does not play any explanatory role within the context of a scientific exploration of the social realm. Rather, that explanatory task can be completely fulfilled by appealing to complex dispositions of individuals or social groups. One certainly can continue to use the language of social norms even within this context but only if one is aware of the fact that such talk is merely a shorthand for referring to states of affairs such as patterns of complex dispositions that are naturalistically acceptable (see Henderson 2005) or if it can be shown that our talk of social norms can be redefined in light of such naturalized terminology (for an attempt in this respect see Bicchieri 2006).[1] The world is just "everything that is the case" and nothing that is the case in a sense to be further determined intrinsically demands anything from us.

And yet a world devoid of normativity seems to be a world that is completely different from the world that rational agents, who have to make up their minds of how to act, encounter in very specific circumstances. Normativity always seems to reassert itself from the first-person and deliberative perspective where we have to choose between alternative courses of actions and where we have to justify our choices to ourselves and to others (see particularly Korsgaard 1996). From this perspective, the world does seem to put demands on us, and there do seem to be ways of getting things objectively right or objectively wrong. Indeed it seems the very essence of what we are doing can be made sense of only in light of normative distinctions and the rules of the games we are playing. In the history of the philosophy of social science, such intuitions have often been expressed by suggesting that merely adopting the third-person explanatory perspective of the natural sciences fundamentally falls short of even allowing us in the first place to delineate the social reality that we want to explain naturalistically in terms of non-normative dispositions (see paradigmatically Taylor 1985). Within the social realm there is nothing to explain unless one has first articulated the norms and rules in light of which agents make sense of their agency and understand themselves as playing chess, as being law-abiding citizens of a country, or as moral agents in the world. Accordingly, the social world is a world that has to be primarily approached using the methodology of understanding. Wittgensteinians have emphasized similar points by emphasizing the analogy of understanding a language (Winch 1958) and by stressing that the very reality of the social world requires us to immerse ourselves in social practices in order to get a real feel for the social game and its rule-bound complexity. Such practices are to be conceived of in an "irreducibly, but not inexplicable manner" as normative, a normativity that is accessible only from the perspective of a practice's participants who hold each other accountable (See Rouse 2007, following Brandom 1994 in this regard).[2]

In some sense, the above considerations express a typical philosophical conundrum. On the one hand we can't fully dismiss the reality of normativity in light of the inescapability of the first-person perspective; on the other hand, as good philosophical naturalists who are disposed to believe in the ontological primacy of the explanatory scientific point of view, it seems we can do so only with a guilty conscience. We have, therefore, either to show that and explain why the first-person perspective is illusory or we have to provide a better philosophical account that makes sense of the reality of norms vis-à-vis the natural world as it is revealed from the third-person scientific perspective. Turner opts for the first route in his recent attempt to explain or rather explain away normativity. He however moves beyond this philosophical stalemate by arguing in light of new insights from the cognitive sciences that the very notion of understanding, particularly empathic understanding, used by hermeneutic philosophers to defend the inescapability of normativity in the social realm can be conceived of completely in non-normative terms (Turner 2010, particularly 175–185).

As will become clear in the following, I part company with Turner in this very respect. While I do think that the Wittgensteinian spade trying to account for normativity does not dig deep enough or turns too soon (See Wittgenstein 1953, § 217), I also think that Turner's conception of empathic understanding does not account for the complexity of interpersonal understanding in the social realm and in actual social scientific research, particularly anthropology. I will argue that while normativity, in a sense to be further explained, itself does not appeal to causal explanatory properties, it is a notion that is inseparably linked to our causal explanatory practice of explaining actions in terms of agents' reasons for acting. As I see it, facts are not in any sense intrinsically normative. Rather, facts become normatively relevant and normative reasons for acting only from the perspective of agents trying to mutually make sense of each other by simulating each other's thoughts as reasons for acting. In negotiating the intersubjective intelligibility of one's agency in this manner, we are committed to something like an impartial spectator perspective and thus committed to the idea that there are normative reasons whose validity is independent from one's merely subjective perspective.

I regard my account of normativity as being sympathetic to the constructivist project in metaethics (see Korsgaard 1996) in that I regard it to be philosophically necessary to further elucidate the nature and reality of normative reasons, even if such elucidation falls short of a reductive analysis.[3] Moreover, my elucidation and defense of the reality of normativity will appeal to considerations that I see at least implicit in Adam Smith's *Theory of Moral Sentiment* rather than in Kant. In this manner, I will reveal objective normativity as a genuine feature of the stance that human agents, given their empirical psychology, naturally take towards each other. Accordingly, we can acknowledge the reality of normative properties without requiring them to be causal explanatory properties.

How to Conceive of the Reality of Normative Reasons

Before I begin my constructive account of normativity, it is helpful to explicate in a bit more detail the conceptual framework I will use to approach the topic of normativity. Since I regard the notion of agency and normativity to be intimately linked, I will approach the question of normativity, as it is quite common in the meta-ethical literature, in terms of the notion of normative reasons. Accordingly, normative facts are those facts that provide agents with objective considerations for or against certain kinds of actions (see in this respect also Scanlon 2014). The moral fact that killing is wrong, if you allow me for a moment that terminology, is a normative fact because it provides us with a moral consideration that objectively speaks against killing, and the social norm of eating food with knives and forks is a norm because it provides us in certain circumstances with considerations that speaks for eating with knives and forks. In the same manner we can speak of prudential norms, logical norms, legal norms, and so on. However, we have to be careful in this context. Normative reasons are not necessarily those reasons that agents recognize subjectively as considerations that speak for their actions. Agents, for example, might not know that the ice on a frozen pond is rather thin and they might therefore fail to recognize that the thinness of the ice objectively speaks against them walking on the ice. For that very reason one commonly distinguishes between an agent's motivating reasons for acting and his normative reasons. Whereas motivating reasons are identified with agents' psychological states (beliefs, desires, intentions, and so on), normative reasons are conceived of as objective features of the world in light of which their action can be objectively validated, criticized, or corrected.

Nothing that I have said so far should be regarded as being philosophically particularly controversial. The notion of a normative reason seems to be implied by our ordinary experiences that we can stand corrected, that we did not act as we normatively ought to have acted, or that there actually were considerations that spoke against our actions and that we had overlooked or misconceived. Problems, though, arise immediately the moment we want to provide our intuitions with an ontological grounding that attempts to conceive of the truth-makers of our normative claims realistically and as intrinsic features of reality. Reality would then come endowed with rather queer features or facts (Mackie 1977), which provide us intrinsically with normative reasons in light of which our behavior can be evaluated as being appropriate or inappropriate and so on. Or to follow a suggestion and analogy of Stevenson (1937), to understand normative properties realistically means to think of them in analogy to magnets. Like magnets, which produce magnetic fields and attract certain metals because of it, normative facts have the intrinsic capacity to produce objective orientations for agents within their normative fields. For example, cruelty provides agents with normative reasons not to engage in cruel behavior. Rational agents who fail to respond to such features of the world are objectively mistaken or, if one is inclined to view reason-responsiveness as an essential capacity of rational agency, they are clearly irrational.[4]

To a certain extent, I have nothing against this way of talking. It is a way of talking that I regard as the only manner in which we can make sense of our intersubjective manner of deliberation and holding each other accountable for our actions (see also Enoch 2011). I also think it is a mistake to argue against a realist understanding of normativity primarily by pointing to the fact that normative properties are not appealed to in providing a causal explanatory account of the world, especially the social world, and that we at most need to appeal to normative attitudes (or psychological dispositions) for this purpose. Normative properties are indeed not helpful for such purposes, but as it has traditionally been pointed out by realists, in this respect normative properties are not worse off than logical or mathematical properties.[5] For instance, the property of validity is a genuine property that arguments possess. An argument has this property if and only if it is impossible for its premises to be true and its conclusion to be false. Moreover it possesses this property independent of any of our attitudes; whether or not we wish it were valid, believe it to be valid, and so on. Similar remarks apply to the central logical categories like the consistency of a set, whether or not two statements are contradictory, or even whether or not a particular statement is true or false. Merely to deny the existence of such properties because they do not describe causal powers (validity indeed does not move any mountains, can't be perceived with our sensory organs or kicked around with our feet), seems to indicate a questionable and mistaken reliance—at least implicitly—on the so-called Eleatic principle. According to that principle we should accept the reality of an entity, fact, or property if and only if it "makes some sort of contribution to the causal/nomic order of the world" (Armstrong 2004, 37) or if it is directly appealed to in our causal-explanatory account of various phenomena. Yet, even if mathematical properties do not have any causal powers in this sense, we could not provide scientific causal explanatory accounts of the natural world without mathematics (see particularly Colyvan 1998, who also argues for special kinds of mathematical explanations). Similar remarks apply to logical properties, which characterize in an abstract and non-causal manner aspects of the very activities involved in our providing causal and explanatory accounts. It is therefore a mistake to insist that only those properties are real that science appeals to in order to explain how the world and the heavens move. There are indeed properties that exist and that do not necessarily move anything. The acceptance of their existence is not merely an article of blind faith. Rather their existence is validated since they reflect features of the structures of activities that are intimately and intrinsically tied to our providing a causal explanatory account of the world.

The above remarks are not sufficient for establishing the reality of facts that intrinsically provide normative reasons for rational agents. They merely show that the Eleatic principle cannot be the only criterion according to which facts and properties gain some ontological respect. Take, for example, the property of being valid or being consistent. The fact that an assertion that an argument is valid or that a belief set is consistent can be objectively true or false alone does not establish validity or consistency as normative properties, which provides us intrinsically with reasons for constructing valid arguments. Indeed, to insist on constructing only valid arguments or forming only consistent belief sets seems to be a bit pedantic and to be indicative of a boring personality. Maybe it even expresses an unhealthy commitment to logical puritanism or fetishism. More importantly, as the debate about human rationality and inferential shortcomings has shown, it is not even clear why creatures like us with rather limited cognitive abilities should regard consistency or validity, for example, as a normative reason (See Stueber 2006, Chapter 2). Ultimately, normative reasons are considerations in light of which the agent's subjective considerations can be criticized or ultimately validated. Normative reasons are thus considerations that have to address the agent's perspective and that challenge or validate the intelligibility of the agent's action in a manner that he could also potentially recognize. Otherwise it seems the relation between normative reasons and agents would have to be conceived of in analogy to the relation in which the rules of baseball stand to the action of a soccer player. The rules of baseball just are not the appropriate standards for the evaluation of soccer players. Appealing to them in this context would constitute an external imposition on the soccer player, an imposition that could rightfully be rejected from the perspective of the soccer player.

Accordingly, any philosophical account of normative reasons has to explicate or say something interesting about the conditions under which agents *own* them as normative standards. Only in this manner are we also able to philosophically account for the central role of normativity in our lives. It is for that very reason that Platonist realism regarding rules and norms has in the last few decades never been a real-life option in the philosophy of social science. Merely postulating that rules and norms reside in a third realm fails to address the question of why we should be normatively judged according to such entities residing in a realm that seems not to have anything to do with our human practices.[6] Instead one has generally followed Wittgenstein in conceiving of normativity as being an internal and irreducible feature of our linguistic and social practices. The reality of normativity has to be acknowledged because there are practices in which agents, on reflection, acknowledge norms and rules as standards according to which they can be evaluated and in light of which they can stand corrected (see Stueber 1994, 2005 in this respect). Ultimately, norms have to be regarded as having objective status in light of our attitudes towards each other. For Brandom, more specifically, we have to conceive of them as attitudes of "treating ourselves and each other as having commitments" and of holding each other accountable according to such commitments: a practice that we can philosophically and reflectively make sense of only in terms of norms and rules that have intersubjective validity (Brandom 1994, 626).

And yet, the above argument is too quick in trying to establish the objectivity of normativity. While normative realists and Platonists seem to be happy to regard the centrality of normativity for our lives as merely a contingent psychological fact, which is irrelevant for accounting for the nature of facts as normative reasons, Wittgensteinians seem to think that they have avoided the pitfalls of Platonic realism by merely asserting the centrality of normativity in our social practice without fully accounting for the reasons of why that is so. In light of the plurality of social practices one also wonders whether the notion of an objectively normative reason is more than a mere imposition of one point of view or practice onto another. Take, for example, the following statement from Brandom according to which "contradiction, correct inference, correct judgment are all normative notions, not natural ones" (Brandom 1994, 12). I do not want to comment on the notion of correctness in this context, but it does not seem to be true to say that contradiction is intrinsically a normative notion. Rather it is primarily a logical one and describes the relationship between two statements such that they cannot be true together. Whether or not the principle of non-contradiction is in addition an objective standard that can provide normative reasons for the evaluation of a person's inferential behavior is something that needs to be argued for.

The Wittgensteinian practice account of normativity does not sufficiently calm the worries of the nihilist and eliminativist for whom appeal to objective normative standards within a practice is nothing more than a way of talking since ultimately social reality and social interaction can be fully explained in terms of patterns of individual dispositions. While I have rejected the Eleatic principle as sole criterion for conferring ontological respect, I still hold on to the idea that ontological respect can be given only to properties that are in some sense connected to our explanatory practices. And none of the positions so far have shown that the very fact of holding each other accountable from the first-person perspective is also essentially tied to the explanatory stance we adopt towards each other. In the following I will show that this is the case by arguing that the notion of objective normativity is an emergent feature of agents who fundamentally are conceiving of each other as being like-minded and who try to make sense of each other by simulating another person's point of view.

Situating the Normative Domain from Within Our Explanatory Folk-Psychological Practice

In order to develop my account, it is may be best to start with acknowledging Turner's recent challenge to the very strategy that I am proposing in order to avoid the accusation that I am trying to ride a dead horse. Turner acknowledges that in understanding other agents we have to find their actions to be intelligible, that is, we have to understand them as rational agents acting for reasons. Yet Turner suggests that such insight about the nature of interpretation, as being guided by standards of intelligibility and rationality, should not be cashed out in terms of an irreducible normative aspect of reality; an aspect that is moreover not part of its "causal order" as Brandom suggests (Brandom 1994, 626).[7] Rather intelligibility can be accounted for from the "disenchanted" and naturalized perspective favored by Turner as the ability to follow the thoughts of others, "a capacity of beings with brains with particular kinds of neurons, perhaps, in this case mirror neuron or mirroring systems, rather than souls participating in forms, or slates being inscribed on" (Turner 2010, 168).

Like Stephen Stich (1990, 1994), Turner does not regard norms of rationality as constraining our interpretation of others. Rather it is our ability to see the other person as being similar to ourselves and to simulate their thoughts that allows us to find them intelligible. In contrast to Stich, who is also known for his defense of a hybrid theory-theory position and who bases his rejection of rationality as an interpretive constraint primarily on insights about widespread inferential shortcomings among humans, Turner aligns himself in this context squarely with simulation theory and more specifically seems to conceive of the discovery of mirror neurons as evidence for simulation being the default method of understanding other agents. Of course, as a proponent of simulation and empathy as the default method of interpersonal understanding (see Stueber 2006), I am quite sympathetic to Turner's stance. Yet, as I will argue, recognizing simulation as being central in interpersonal understanding does not lead to a dismissal of normativity. Rather it allows us to conceive of the proper source of objective normative reasons in a manner that at the same time enables us to understand why they are objective reasons that agents own.

So why is it that one can draw such different conclusions from the centrality of simulation in interpersonal understanding? First it is important to understand that the range of understanding supported by mirror neurons is rather limited. In the recent literature in philosophy and cognitive science, there also has been a rather intense debate about the question of whether mirror neurons can be at all understood as a form of simulation or whether the primary function of mirror neurons is a cognitive one enabling us to gain some understanding about what the other person is doing. The fact that I might automatically resonate with you on the neurobiological level when I observe your action does not seem to be an instance of perspective taking and it does not automatically imply that I also understand what you are doing or what you are feeling. It could just mean that whenever I observe you feeling sad I also feel something, without necessarily knowing on a conceptual level that it is a feeling of sadness that you and I are feeling. The stimulation of a particular area in the amygdala just causes us to feel fear but it does not cause us self-reflectively and conceptually to become aware of the fact that we are feeling fear. Otherwise we would have to assume that every creature (animals and infants) that is able to feel fear, also has the concept of fear.

Nevertheless, I am happy to agree that mirror neuron research validates the claim made by very many philosophers—as different from each other as Wittgenstein and Husserl—that the primary and also developmentally basic stance that human beings have towards each other is very different from the theoretical and detached stance that they have towards other inanimate objects. More specifically, mirror neurons can be understood as allowing us to grasp in a non-conceptual manner other persons' bodily movements as being goal-directed like my own bodily movements and as expressing inner states or emotions that I am familiar in feeling (for more detail see Stueber 2012a and 2012b). Agents are, however, not merely bodies whose movements are caused by inner events and whose movements are goal-directed towards objects in the external world. Rather agents are persons who, in light of their conception of the situation and their goals, develop and deliberate about plans of action and act for reasons that from their own subjective perspective speak for the chosen course of action. For that very reason, the intelligibility of other agents provided by systems of mirror neurons is rather limited; at most it concerns the domain of skilled bodily movements and the recognition of emotions expressed in our facial expressions and bodily stances.[8] It is for this reason that some simulation theorists distinguish between low-level and high-level simulation, mirroring and constructive empathy, or between basic and reenactive empathy (Goldman 2006; Stueber 2006). For them, only a cognitively more advanced form of imaginative perspective taking, which is independent of mirror neuron systems, allows us to grasp another agent's reasons for acting by simulating his beliefs and desires with the help of our own cognitive system. Moreover, it is only as long as we can understand another person's attributed belief and desires as his reasons for acting (through forms of reenactive empathy) that we are also putting any trust in the folk-psychological explanations of his behavior.

All of the above assertions can certainly be challenged in a variety of ways.[9] But even if one agrees with them so far, one should acknowledge that the above account of how we grasp the intelligibility of another person's actions does not involve any normativity in the sense we are looking for. It seems to be dealing with considerations that count as reasons from a subjective point of view, but those considerations are not necessarily objective normative reasons. Yet, things become a bit more complicated when we consider cases where it seems initially not possible, at least without some imaginative effort, to grasp the action of the other person as an intelligible one. We might, for example, not fully understand and be genuinely puzzled (given that we experience the other person otherwise as being like-minded) why somebody flies off the handle given that the insult he suffered was only slight or why somebody's urgent desire to know how many blades of grass are in his backyard could be a consideration that would count under any circumstances as a reason for counting the blades of grass. From the interpreter's perspective, these puzzlements constitute explanatory problems that call out for interpretive solutions. For the purpose of this essay, it is also important to realize that such puzzlements are more than interpretive problems. We have to remind ourselves of insights from philosophers such as David Hume, and particularly Adam Smith, who understood the fact that "the minds of men are mirrors to one another" (Hume [1739] 1978, 365) as psychologically central for creating social cohesion among human beings and as being foundational for our self-conceptions as rational agents. To be understood in an empathic and reenactive manner by people whom we experience as like-minded and whose thoughts and feelings we ourselves empathize with, does have repercussions for how we ourselves think of our own thoughts and emotions.

Adam Smith also links our ability to empathize with each other and to be able to reenact another person's thoughts and sentiments to our propensity to approve of another person's behavior or emotions. Smith puts a particular sentimentalist spin on this insight by claiming that we regard a consideration or feeling as appropriate not only when we are "affected in the same manner as he is [by actively sympathizing with him], but we must [also] perceive this harmony and correspondence of sentiments between him and ourselves" (Smith [1759] 1982, 78). The perception of such harmony is supposedly tied to an "agreeable and delightful emotion" and it is this emotion "in which the sentiment of approbation properly consists" (Smith [1759] 1982, 46). Smith aligns himself throughout the *Theory of Moral Sentiments* with the position of moral sentimentalism and views sentiments associated with sympathy (rather than reason) as the source of our moral judgments and moral concepts. Yet ultimately it is not even so clear in Smith how important he regards the enjoyment of the perception of correspondence between our mental states for evaluating the moral quality of another person's behavior. In the context of discussing the notion of merit, for example, Smith is quite definite that what bestows merit on an action is my ability to put myself in the other person's shoes and consider whether an agent's action towards that person would make me feel gratitude toward him (or, as I would say, constitutes a reason for me to feel gratitude), regardless of whether that person himself would feel gratitude.[10] More importantly, it is not even clear why the expression of such enjoyment based on the perception of a mental correspondence has any normative force, that is, why we should conceive of it as a relevant standard for the evaluation of our behavior. We certainly might be psychologically prone to be influenced by the expression of such sentiments, but that alone would not endow such sentiments with a normative status.

In light of my conception of reenactment being primarily concerned with reasons, I would like to suggest a slightly different take on the importance of mutual understanding for our self-conceptions of agents. Being rational and self-reflective agents does mean that we are persons who are able to say something in favor of our actions and who can situate our actions vis-à-vis our environment in light of considerations that, from our perspective, speak for them. It is in this sense that we can take ownership of our actions, they become actions that are not merely caused by us but are our doing. I would regard such feature as one of the constitutive features of agency (see also Velleman 2009). Moreover, in experiencing others as being like-minded and in interacting with them in this manner on a daily basis we do experience them as creatures that act for considerations similar to our own. A fortiori we view our considerations as thoughts that somebody who is like-minded could reenact and could, at least in his or her imagination, regard as reasons for acting. In that sense the intelligibility of our actions (which is so central for our self-conceptions as agents) is not merely a subjective or solipsistic notion. It is ordinarily an intersubjective one in that the intelligibility of our actions itself can be mirrored in other minds. And it is exactly those expectations about the intersubjective and mutual accessibility of our considerations for actions that are disappointed when mutual understanding breaks down.

Accordingly, an interpreter's puzzlement of the form "I just don't get you, why do (or did) you do it?" potentially challenges the intelligibility of another person by suggesting that there is no reason for him (even from his subjective point of view) to take ownership of his actions. In this manner, our failed attempt to reenact other persons' reasons challenges and weakens the very foundations of their agency, a challenge that can, however, be rejected by claiming that the perspective of the interpreter is inadequate or that it is biased. Both the interpreter and his or her subject thus have a reason to overcome their mutual puzzlements. From the interpreter's perspective, it would allow him or her to restore an epistemic equilibrium and from the agent's perspective it would allow him or her to restore the expectation central to his or her own sense of agency. Most often the reason why an interpreter fails to reenact the considerations of the other person as his or her reasons for acting has to do with the fact that the attempt to do so was subjectively biased in that he projected all of his or her beliefs, desires, or values onto the other person. Quite often then an interpreter will be able to reenact another person's considerations for acting and understand them as his or her reasons by taking into account the relevant differences between him and the other person. Here I do not want to dwell on the difficulties involved in this project (particularly in cases of great cultural differences).

For my purposes it is sufficient to note that I will be able to reenact your reasons successfully if I am able to locate the differences in our psychological attitudes, imaginatively take up the attitudes that I do not share with you, and quarantine the attitudes that you do not share with me while simulating your thoughts and deliberating about the situation that you encounter from your perspective. Under no circumstances, though, is it required that I fully become you or any other person I am trying to understand. Rather empathic understanding proceeds in that other persons' thoughts are, to quote Collingwood, "*incapsulated* in a context of present thoughts which, by contradicting it, confine it to a plane different from theirs" (Collingwood 1939, 114). In reenacting another person's thoughts, and by being sensitive to the relevant differences between us, I am simultaneously aware of the fact that I myself would have deliberated differently.

Nevertheless, insofar as I reenact considerations as reasons for acting, those thoughts have at least the status of my considerations and deliberations when I hypothetically reflect on various courses of actions and decide which action to pursue. I might, for example, wonder what would be the best present to buy for my wife or children and in deliberating about the various options I make assumptions about their various interests, preferences, and needs. In the end, I have to settle on one option by recognizing that various considerations that I have entertained seem overall to favor it. They are in some sense 'stronger' than the considerations that favor other options; they are for some reason the considerations I should adopt. The considerations that I adopt as my reasons for settling on one option, therefore, gain their status as such a reasons in light of considerations that allow me to prefer them to other reasons for acting. Reasons of another person, which I grasp in a reenactive mode, put a similar pressure on my own manner of making sense of my actions. It seems that if I adopt imaginatively the different background assumption of the other person his considerations can be perfectly understood as reasons for acting, that is, as my reasons for acting in those circumstances. But such reenactment potentially raises the question of whether the attitudes that I quarantined in the reenactment (a quarantine that allowed me to grasp his reasons) need to be reconsidered and should be given up, a question that requires a rational response. Insofar as I am in this case negotiating among considerations of at least two different persons, the considerations I appeal to in that context have to be conceived of as having more than mere subjective validity or strength. Moreover the perspective within which those reasons are accessible has to be regarded to be more than my own subjective perspective. It has to be regarded as an impartial perspective, since it is a perspective within which both of us struggle to get our reasons for acting validated as the intersubjective appropriate reasons for acting.

The commitment to something like an impartial spectator perspective is thus closely tied to the challenges that arise to our own preferred way of looking at the world from within our simulative practices of finding each other's action intelligible. The perspective of the other person challenges me (internally so to speak) to appeal to considerations that settle the questions of what are the reasons for acting in a particular situation in an objective and unbiased manner.[11] Indeed the question of whether the perspective adopted is an impartial and unbiased one is intrinsically linked to the questions of whether the reasons appealed to are genuinely normative reasons that are reasons for acting for every rational and like-minded agent. Asking whether the claimed reasons are genuinely objective is always asking whether the adopted perspective is genuinely unbiased. It is in this very context that questions about biases in our empathic capacities or other shortcomings of our cognitive capacities are of central importance for the impartial spectator perspective. As Adam Smith has in my opinion already emphasized, reflection on the nature of the impartial perspective has to be seen as being an integral part of the impartial spectator perspective itself.

The above considerations on the nature and source of our commitment to the notion of the impartial perspective constitute more than philosophical armchair reflection. They also reflect the nature of the discourse about primitive rationality so fervently discussed in the philosophy of the social sciences in the 1970s (see also Risjord 2000). For that very reason, the above philosophical reflection should be appealing to philosophers regarding themselves as naturalists in that it is a perspective that reflects the actual practices of the social sciences. Specifically the discussion about the witchcraft practices of the Azande show how reenactment of another person's reasons can compel one to adopt a more 'objective stance' in order to validate one's own perspective. In addition, this debate illustrates how the adoption of such a more supposedly impartial stance can itself be challenged as being biased. As it is well known, Evans-Pritchard (1937) found the witchcraft practice of the Azande in some sense perfectly intelligible. Yet insofar as he was able to make sense of them he felt also compelled to evaluate the Azande's perspective more objectively as a practice for which there are no objective normative reasons. It is exactly at this stage that Winch interfered and argued the Western scientific perspective is not the appropriate perspective for the evaluation of the Azande reasons for acting (for the debate see Wilson 1970 and Winch 1964). Regardless of how one is inclined to view this particular debate, what should be clear is that the notion of a normative reason is not a philosophical invention. Rather it reflects a central feature of our interpretive practices, which depend on our reenactive and empathic ability to find each other intelligible. They force us to become more self-reflective and for that very reason they are practices that we cannot make sense of without commitment to something like the notion of an impartial spectator perspective allowing us to conceive of normative reasons that we own.

Conclusion

My defense of normativity as objective normative reasons that agents own proceeded not by showing that the notion of normative reasons itself is a causal explanatory notion. Indeed I would think this is a hopeless enterprise and I do not wholeheartedly accept the Eleatic principle as a necessary criterion for ontological respectability. Nevertheless, I tried to locate the source of normativity by showing that it is tied to our explanatory folk-psychological practice of trying to make sense of agents in terms of considerations that speak for their actions from their respective perspectives. Such explanatory practice involves our empathetic and reenactive capacities and is thus essentially tied to the deliberative first-person perspective. It is also committed, or so I have argued, to the idea of an impartial spectator perspective. It is a dimension within which reasons for acting proposed from different points of view have to be negotiated as part of our attempt to protect the intelligibility of our agency in light of the challenges encountered in reenacting other persons' points of view.

Accordingly, normative reasons are not queer facts or queer properties. Rather they are rather ordinary facts and properties (in a variety of shapes and sizes) that are grasped from within the impartial spectator perspective as considerations that speak for adopting certain attitudes. It is also in this context that we can understand properties such as truth, contradiction, or validity as normative ones insofar as they can be appealed to considerations for adopting certain beliefs and so on. Since the main purpose of my essay has been to safeguard a notion of objective normativity and locate its source, I have not distinguished between various degrees of normativity and different kinds of normative reasons. This has to be the topic of another paper. Let me say, however, that if one agrees with the argument so far then it also appears very likely that we have to distinguish between normative reasons that have universal validity and normative reasons that have a more localized validity. From my perspective, norms traditionally regarded as norms of rationality and moral norms have universal validity because the idea of an impartial spectator perspective as the dimension within we negotiate different points of view commits us also to certain kinds of behavior, inferential and otherwise, and it requires us to respect in some sense our like-mindedness. The normative force of more localized social norms however can be understood as the fact that patterns of disposition that exist in a certain society are considerations that speak from the perspective of the impartial spectator as considerations in favor of acting, choosing, desiring, and so on.

But as I have said, this is a complex topic that needs to be explicated in much more detail elsewhere. Let me just end by emphasizing that on my account the reality of normativity is in a sense stance dependent. It is constitutive for a fact being an objective normative reason that it can be grasped from the impartial spectator perspective as a consideration that speaks for an action or adoption of certain attitudes towards the world. Being stance dependent, however, does not mean that normativity is less real. It means only that it is as real and natural as the stance on which it depends. But the stance that agents (as natural organisms with a certain organization of their brains) take towards each other in order to make sense of their behavior as intelligible agents is not something that can be explained away or that we are free to negotiate about. The stance is part of the natural world, even if it is a stance that does not have its equivalent in the natural sciences. But if naturalism were to claim that something is real only if it can be reduced to the vocabulary of the natural sciences, that would be just too bad for naturalism.[12]

NOTES

1   Similar argumentative strategies have been used to argue against moral or ethical realism within the context of contemporary meta-ethics. See for example Blackburn (1993) and more recently Street (2006).
2   I have been generally quite sympathetic to these Wittgensteinian considerations. See for example (Stueber 1994). In (Stueber 2005), I analyze rule-following in terms of complex sets of self-monitoring dispositions. However, as I argue in this article, in order to safeguard normativity against Turner's eliminativist challenge one has to dig a bit deeper. For a discussion of whether the notion of understanding is suitable to distinguish between the natural and the human sciences see (Stueber 2012c).
3   In this essay, I will mainly address the challenge to the reality of normativity as it is posed within the context of the philosophy of the social sciences. For my take on the notion of normativity within the meta-ethical context see my forthcoming article on 'Smithian Constructivism'.
4   In this respect see Parfit and Scanlon, who are both realist about normative reasons. Parfit opts for the latter manner of expressing our failure to recognize normative reasons, Scanlon for the former. See (Scanlon 1998) and (Parfit 2011, vol. 1, particularly 119–125).
5   See for example Ross: "The moral order expressed in this proposition is just as much part of the universal nature of the universe (and, we may add, of any possible universe in which there were moral agents at all) as is the spatial or numerical structure expressed in the axioms of geometry or arithmetic" (Ross [1930] 2002, 29–30). For an interesting critique of the analogy to mathematics popular among moral realist and rationalists see (McGrath 2014).
6   It is, in my opinion, generally puzzling that within the context of the revival of contemporary meta-ethical realism proponents of realism do not feel the need to address this topic (See, for example, Shafer-Landau 2003, 212). Such realist conception of normative facts appears akin to pointing to the famous beetle in the box that Wittgenstein talks about (Wittgenstein 1953, § 293). It is revealed as an ontological reification of a grammatical illusion since the postulated object does not play any role in making sense of our concerns for normative reasons (a point forcefully made by Christine Korsgaard 1996 in the meta-ethical context). Admittedly, within the contemporary context, there are also attempts to reduce normative facts to naturalistically less objectionable entities. While I do not have the space to argue for this claim here, ultimately I am doubtful whether such naturalistic reduction is able to preserve the normative feature of such facts.
7   Turner also suggests that his position is compatible with Davidson's conception of interpretation. Here is not the place to engage in Davidson exegesis. Let it just be noted that I do not fully agree with Turner in this respect. Alternatively, if this were indeed what Davidson had in mind, then I would respectfully disagree with both Turner and Davidson.
8   For a survey of mirror neuron research see (Rizzolatti and Sinigaglia 2008). While I agree with their claim that mirror neurons do provide us with non-conceptual

understanding, I tend to be skeptical about their claim that mirror neurons also provide us with understanding of more extended action sequences.

9   Admittedly, within the so-called theory of mind debate the epistemic centrality of reenactive empathy for grasping the intelligibility of agency is contested territory. Since I am however not in disagreement with Turner in this respect, I take it in this context for granted. For my positive arguments see however (Stueber 2006, 2008). Here I am interested in drawing out the implication for philosophical elucidation of the notion of a normative reason.

10 "When I hear of a benefit that has been bestowed upon another person, let him who has received it be affected in what manner he pleases, if, by bringing the case home to myself, I feel gratitude arise in my own breast, I necessarily approve of the conduct of his benefactor, and regard it as meritorious. . . . No actual correspondence of sentiments, therefore, is here required" (Smith [1759] 1982, 78).

11 The impartial spectator perspective is indeed, as Adam Smith calls it, the "man within the breast." It is not a perspective that speaks to us *sub specie aeternitatis*. Rather it is appealed to internally in order to resolve internal tensions after reenacting the thoughts of others.

12 The paper has benefitted from the discussion of a first draft among the majority of the contributors to this volume at a workshop organized by Mark Risjord at Amicalola Falls State Park. Many thanks for their comments. Workshops in such relaxed surroundings are indeed the best ways of doing philosophy. In addition, I would like to thank Julie Zahle (who could not participate in the workshop) for her comments.

REFERENCES

Armstrong, D. M. 2004. *Truth and Truthmakers*. Cambridge: Cambridge University Press.
Bicchieri, C. 2006. *The Grammar of Society: The Nature and Dynamics of Social Norms*. New York: Cambridge University Press.
Blackburn, S. 1993. *Essays on Quasi-Realism*. Oxford: Oxford University Press.
Brandom, R. 1994. *Making It Explicit: Reasoning, Representing, and Discursive Commitment*. Cambridge, MA: Harvard University Press.
Collingwood, R. G. 1939. *An Autobiography*. Oxford: Oxford University Press.
Colyvan, M. 1998. Can the Eleatic Principle Be Justified? *Canadian Journal of Philosophy* 28: 313–336.
Enoch, D. 2011. *Taking Morality Seriously*. New York: Oxford University Press.
Evans-Pritchard, E. 1937. *Witchcraft, Oracles, and Magic among the Azande*. Oxford: Oxford University Press.
Goldman, A. 2006. *Simulating Minds: The Philosophy, Psychology, and Neuroscience of Mindreading*. Oxford. Oxford University Press.
Henderson, D. 2005. Norms, Invariance, and Explanatory Relevance. *Philosophy of the Social Sciences* 40: 30–58.
Hume, D. 1978. *A Treatise of Human Nature*. Oxford: Clarendon Press. Original edition, 1739.
Korsgaard, C. 1996. *The Sources of Normativity*. Cambridge: Cambridge University Press.
Mackie, J. L. 1977. *Ethics: Inventing Right and Wrong*. London: Penguin Books.
McGrath, S. 2014. Relax? Don't Do It! Why Moral Realism Won't Come Cheap. In *Oxford Studies in Metaethics,* volume 9, edited by R. Shafer-Landau, 186–214. Oxford: Oxford University Press.
Parfit, D. 2011. *On What Matters,* 2 volumes. Oxford: Oxford University Press.

Risjord, M. 2000. *Woodcutters and Witchcraft*. Albany, NY: SUNY Press.

Rizzolatti, G. and C. Sinigaglia. 2008. *Mirrors in the Brain? How our Minds Share Actions and Emotions*. Oxford: Oxford University Press.

Ross, W. D. 2002. *The Right and the Good*. Oxford: Clarendon Press. Original edition, 1930.

Rouse, J. 2007. Social Practices and the Normative. *Philosophy of the Social Sciences* 37: 46–56.

Scanlon, T. 1998. *What We Owe To Each Other*. Cambridge, Mass.: Harvard University Press.

Scanlon, T. M. 2014. *Being Realistic about Reasons*. Oxford: Oxford University Press.

Shafer-Landau, R. 2003. *Moral Realism: A Defense*. Oxford: Oxford University Press.

Smith, A. 1982. *The Theory of Moral Sentiments*. Indianapolis: Liberty Classics. Original edition, 1759.

Southwood, N. 2010. The Authority of Social Norms. In *New Waves in Meta-Ethics*, edited by M. Brady, 234–248. New York: Palgrave MacMillan.

———. 2011. The Moral/Conventional Distinction. *Mind* 120: 761–802.

Southwood, N. and L. Eriksson. 2011. Norms and Conventions. *Philosophical Explorations* 14: 195–217.

Stevenson, C. L. 1937. The Emotive Meaning of Ethical Terms. *Mind* 46: 14–31.

Stich, S. 1990. *The Fragmentation of Reason*. Cambridge, MA: MIT Press.

———. 1994. Could Man Be an Irrational Animal? Some Notes on the Epistemology of Rationality. In *Naturalizing Epistemology*, edited by H. Kornblith, 337–357. Cambridge, MA: MIT Press.

Street, S. 2006. A Darwinian Dilemma for Realist Theories of Value. *Philosophical Studies* 127: 109–166.

Stueber, K. 1994. Practice, Indeterminacy, and Private Language: Wittgenstein's Dissolution of Scepticism. *Philosophical Investigations* 17: 14–36.

———. 2005. How to Think about Rules and Rule-Following. *Philosophy of the Social Sciences* 35: 307–323.

———. 2006. *Rediscovering Empathy: Agency, Folk psychology, and the Human Sciences*. Cambridge, MA: MIT Press.

———. 2008. Reasons, Generalizations, Empathy, and Narratives: The Epistemic Structure of Action Explanation. *History and Theory* 47: 31–43.

———. 2012a. Varieties of Empathy, Neuroscience, and the Narrativist Challenge to the Contemporary Theory of Mind Debate. *Emotion Review* 4: 55–63.

———. 2012c. Understanding vs. Explanation? How to Think about the Difference between the Human and the Natural Sciences. *Inquiry* 55: 17–32.

Taylor, C. 1985. Interpretation and the Sciences of Man. In *Philosophical Papers*, volume 2,, 15–57. Cambridge: Cambridge University Press.

Turner, S. 2010. *Explaining the Normative*. Oxford: Polity Press.

Velleman, D. 2009. *How We Get Along*. Cambridge: Cambridge University Press.

Wilson, B. (ed.) 1970. *Rationality*. New York: Harper and Row.

Winch, P. 1958. *The Idea of a Social Science and Its Relation to Philosophy*. London: Routledge and Kegan Paul.

———. 1964. Understanding a Primitive Society. *American Philosophical Quarterly* 1: 307–324.

Wittgenstein, L. 1953. *Philosophical Investigations*. Translated by G. E. M. Anscombe. New York: Macmillan Publishing Company.

8 Empathy, Like-mindedness, and Autism

Janette Dinishak

INTRODUCTION

In many contexts of inquiry and in many traditions in the study of interpersonal understanding, one encounters the idea that the extent, and even the very possibility, of understanding, explanation, and normative evaluation of human behavior depends on a degree of like-mindedness. The idea is found not only among philosophers (e.g., Davidson and Wittgenstein) but in the two dominant approaches to understanding the nature of social cognition: theory-theory, and simulation theory. Although theories vary on a number of dimensions in the kinds of likenesses and degrees of likeness required for interpersonal understanding, like-mindedness is often characterized in terms of shared beliefs, desires, values, and commitments between individuals or groups. In this paper I explain how recent work on affective, sensory, perceptual, and cognitive atypicalities in people with autism[1] underscores forms of like-mindedness (e.g., commonalities in behavioral expression, sensitivity to external stimuli, and perceptual processing) that are largely neglected in contemporary discussions of interpersonal understanding. Autists and non-autists may have sensory, perceptual, and movement differences that make for pervasive differences in their perspectives on and ways of being in both the physical and social world. Central to the paper is the idea that the forms of *un*like-mindedness among autists and non-autists revealed by this research present the very live possibility that individuals without autism are unable to understand some autistic subjects as acting for reasons, or that if such understanding is available, it is available only through means other than those standardly emphasized in dominant theories of interpersonal understanding.

This idea has critical importance in a variety of ways. It has significance for the case of autism itself as we will see, both for our understanding of autists, and for methodology in scientific and philosophical investigations of autism. It also calls us to redress a systemic problem of theoretical and practical importance: the tendency of philosophers and other theorists to conceptualize and investigate barriers to interpersonal understanding between autists and non-autists almost exclusively in terms of autists' limitations.

Scant attention is paid to identifying and articulating limits on non-autists' abilities to understand autists.[2] My investigative focus, by contrast, is *non-autists'* limitations. The forms of unlike-mindedness among autists and non-autists revealed by autism research also raise more general questions. Do the conclusions from the case of autism apply more widely, to other forms of human variation? What are the practical and theoretical dangers of limits on understanding unlike-minded others? And how should the issues brought to light by reflection on the autism case affect future inquiry into other sorts of unlike-mindedness and suitable notions of like-mindedness?

Here is the structure of the paper. In Section 2, I briefly elucidate the influential idea that interpersonal understanding depends on like-mindedness. In Section 3, I present recent empirical work concerning some potentially crucial differences between autists and non-autists. In Section 4, I investigate the possibility that there are greater limitations than many have realized for a non-autist understanding an autist. I use simulation theory as a lens to explore these potential challenges and focus in particular on the understanding of reasons for action. In Sections 5 and 6, I examine the implications of this possibility. In Section 5 I raise some pressing questions about methodology in the study of autism as well as issues that our culture more broadly needs to confront in rethinking its engagement with autists. Finally, in Section 6, I briefly reflect on some wider issues brought out by our discussion concerning suitable notions of like-mindedness, theories of interpersonal understanding more generally, and the value of epistemic humility.

INTERPERSONAL UNDERSTANDING AND LIKE-MINDEDNESS

Interpersonal understanding admits of kinds, senses, levels, degrees, and stages. People have a host of context-sensitive capacities to achieve both basic and sophisticated forms of interpersonal understanding. Some of these capacities are available to introspective awareness and some are not. Some are exercised automatically and without conscious effort while others involve conscious, effortful construction. A central component of interpersonal understanding is "mentalizing" or "mindreading," the ability to attribute mental states to others. The two dominant approaches to explaining mindreading are called "theory-theory" (Churchland 1979; Dennett 1987; Gopnik and Meltzoff 1997) and "simulation theory" (Gordon 1986; Davies 1994; Heal 1998; Goldman 2006).[3] Both turn on the idea that some kind and degree of like-mindedness is needed to successfully exercise one's mindreading capacities.

Theory-theorists explain the human capacity to attribute mental states in terms of the possession and use of a "theory of mind" that captures generalizations about how humans' mental states and behaviors are usually connected. This theory allows one to infer mental states from observable behavior. For example, if one observes an individual hopping around, clutching her or his foot, and yelling, "Ow!" one can use one's behavioral observations of the individual and generalizations about human behavior, including relevant psycho-behavioral correlations, to infer that the individual one is observing is in pain.

Like-mindedness plays a more explicit central role in simulation theory. Simulation is an egocentric method. One uses one's own mind as a model in the simulation of the other's mind. To elaborate on the role of like-mindedness in simulation theory, I will focus on Stueber's (2006) and Goldman's (2011) accounts of empathy or simulation.[4] Both Goldman and Stueber distinguish two kinds of empathy or simulation. Stueber (2006) characterizes basic empathy as a non-reflective form of understanding supported by mirror neurons that enables understanding of others' goal-directed behavior and emotional states. Basic empathy is a low-level intelligibility of others' feelings and actions. Reenactive empathy, the second kind of empathy, is a cognitively complex form of "inner imitation" that enables a more sophisticated understanding of the intelligibility of other agents' actions in complex social contexts. In reenactive empathy, "[w]e are trying to understand agents as being engaged with and as responding to demands of an environment-as-they-conceive-of-it" (Stueber 2006, 201). When reenactive empathy is successful one comes to understand others' reasons for action and feeling, their conceptions of situations and stances toward the environment. This form of empathy is reenactive in that it requires imaginative perspective-taking. The interpreter simulates the mind of the interpretee. That is, one takes an "as-if" stance towards the interpretee and recreates the interpretee's thought processes by imagining that one has the same desires, beliefs, goals, conception of the situation, and so forth that the interpretee has and then reasons about what one would do and how one would feel in that situation. Similarly, Goldman (2011) distinguishes two "routes" to empathy. The mirroring route is a low-level, largely automatic form of "mental mimicry" of action-planning, sensations (e.g., of touch and pain), and emotions (e.g., disgust) that is prompted by observation. Typically this form of mirroring occurs below the threshold of conscious experience. Reconstructive empathy is a high-level, conscious, and more effortful route. One adopts the perspective of the empathetic target and reflects on the person's situation, imaginatively constructs how things are, were, or will be "playing out" for the person, and imagines how one would feel and what one would do if one were in that person's shoes.

Though reenactment may be effortful in some cases, ordinarily, in a great many cases, it is relatively effortless. We do not hesitate to accept the explanation of why someone stopped at a bar in terms of his desire to drink a beer and his belief that bars sell beer as perfectly intelligible reasons for his behavior. We understand how those considerations can be reenacted in our own minds and how they speak in favor of his actions. The ease with which we accept this explanation as rendering his action intelligible may obscure the fact that our finding the behavior intelligible relies on an implicit assumption of like-mindedness. That is, we assume that he shares relevant beliefs, desires, values, and commitments. If we instead assume, for example, that be believes that drinking one beer has severe negative consequences for one's health, we would not be able to make sense of his action. Rather, we would think that if one has such a belief, visiting a bar is not the thing to do.

In short, like-mindedness enables and constrains empathy and simulation.[5] High-level simulation involves using oneself as a model to explain, predict, and understand others' mental states and how these states and other aspects of their psychology contribute to their actions (past, present, and future). Matching between the empathizer's and the target's cognitive systems is required for successful simulation. The more like-minded the empathizer and the target, the more successful empathy is as a method of achieving interpersonal understanding. Being like-minded and *seeing* the other person *as* like-minded facilitates successful simulation. Recognition of like-mindedness helps us determine which of our beliefs, desires, commitments, values, and so forth to include in the simulation and which to quarantine. When the empathizer and the target are like-minded and the empathizer perceives them to be such, the empathizer can rely more on egocentric defaults in the initial stage of simulation. Fewer adjustments (i.e., supplementing individuating information and quarantining one's own genuine states) to the egocentric starting point need to be made for successful simulation.

UNLIKE-MINDEDNESS: RECENT WORK ON AUTISTS AND NON-AUTISTS

Empirical findings on and firsthand descriptions of atypical sensory, movement, and perceptual features associated with autism show significant ways in which autists and typical individuals are not like-minded. The notion of like-mindedness used in recent discussions of simulation (i.e., shared beliefs, values, and commitments) does not take into account these more fundamental forms of unlike-mindedness although, as we will see in Section 4, they are relevant to assessing whether and how simulation is a route to interpersonal understanding between those who are unlike-minded in these ways.

Sensory, Perceptual, and Movement Differences Associated with Autism

Autism is characterized as a neuro-developmental condition and is diagnosed via behavioral criteria for identifying symptoms listed in the *DSM-V (Diagnostic and Statistical Manual of Mental Disorders)* entry for autism spectrum disorder: difficulties with social interaction (e.g., little or no eye contact), linguistic challenges (e.g., misunderstanding pragmatic uses of language), and restrictive, repetitive, or stereotyped activities (e.g., spinning objects). Research on autism has exploded in recent decades, but there are few uncontested facts about the condition. Although we have some clues about possible environmental triggers and the biological underpinnings of autism, its causes are unknown. Moreover, the cognitive and behavioral phenotypes of autism are still works in progress.

Data from autobiographical accounts of autists and empirical research studies suggest that many autists experience a wide range of sensory, movement, perceptual, and cognitive differences that are multifarious and sometimes idiosyncratic. Many autists use the notion of neurodiversity to capture fundamental differences in their ways of being in the world by comparison with "neurotypicals." Neurodiversity is the provocative idea that some forms of atypical neurological "wiring" in humans, such as autism, attention deficit hyperactivity disorder, Tourette's Syndrome, and schizophrenia, may be positive variations (Blume 1998). Proponents of the neurodiversity movement, as it applies to autism, advance the idea that autism (in at least some of its manifestations) is an ineliminable aspect of an autistic person's identity, a way of being that should be respected and supported, even celebrated, rather than eliminated.

Below I briefly describe some of the reported differences in sensory sensitivities, movement, perceptual processing, and proprioception. Before I do so a few cautions are in order. First, the kinds of differences I single out for discussion are only a sampling of those reported. Second, I am not claiming all and only people with autism experience these kinds of differences. A related third point is that autism is a highly heterogeneous condition that manifests in diverse ways across individuals and within the same individual. The heterogeneity of autism raises serious doubts about whether autism spectrum disorder is a valid, unitary diagnostic category. It is also unclear how far one can generalize from particular personal accounts and research studies of differences associated with autism. Third, the impact of these differences on autists' development and everyday social functioning are not well understood.

Sensory Sensitivities

Many autists experience either increased (hyper-) or decreased (hypo-) sensitivity to incoming stimuli. These sensitivities have been reported across sensory modalities (i.e., vision, touch, taste, hearing, smell), are often idiosyncratic, can vary from hypo- to hypersensitivity within the same individual (Baranek *et al.* 2014), and may result in reacting differently to the same stimuli. In the case of hypersensitivities, Bogdashina suggests that some autists are able to perceive stimuli that others cannot: "For example, a child might hear (and be disturbed by) the sound of a microwave oven working in the next room" (2010, 177). Matt, a person with autism, experiences pain and anxiety in reaction to certain sounds. He reports, "My mom took me through a drive-thru carwash once when I was in grade school and I was terrified. The brushes sounded to me like the sound of intense machine gunfire, but I could not communicate well enough to explain why I got so upset" (quoted in Robledo, Donnellan, and Strandt-Conroy 2012, 4). To take another example, for some autists a particular food smell, taste, or texture, or clothing texture can be experienced as intensely painful or pleasurable. A hyposensitivity that is especially troubling to parents of children with autism is that their children may experience a decreased sensitivity to pain, which can prove dangerous if the child is injured. One mother explains how her autistic daughter extracted four of her front teeth over the course of two weeks: "[I could] say with confidence that at least three of them were, at most, only slightly loose. . . . She wouldn't make a sound until she had excitedly announced what she had done" (Sheahan and DeOrnellas 2011, 92).

Proprioception

Proprioception is a form of body awareness that helps one determine the movement and position of one's body in space without the aid of sight. Autist Dawn Prince-Hughes reports that she would "walk through" or "look through" other people because of her "unawareness of where [her] body began and ended" (2004, 29). Compromised proprioception can lead to difficulties regulating movements that are typically automatic and effortless. For example, if autists with challenges in this area are asked to raise their hands, they may need to check that their hands are raised because they cannot simply feel that they are raised. Also, they may be physically unaware of their own facial expressions. An autist with proprioceptive difficulties may stand "too close" to another person, rock back and forth, or lean on furniture. Some autists report that flapping their hands helps them locate their bodies in space. Tito Mukhopadhyay, an autist with minimal speech who communicates through typing, observes that difficulties with body awareness contributed to his difficulty pointing: ". . . I had very little sensation of my body. So to learn the technique of moving my right hand needed control over the ball and socket joint of the shoulder and then the hinge joint of my elbow and finally fold the other fingers and keep the point finger out" (Quoted in Biklen 2005, 133). Some autists describe themselves as feeling alienated from their own bodies. Take Donna Williams, for example:

> I was somewhere between three and five when my body called to me . . . [I]t started to make its presence felt as though nagging me to listen to it and respond to it. At first, I tuned out this foreign invasion as was natural and instinctive to do with things that gave the feel of robbing one of control. Later, I tried to escape the sensed entrapment of physical connectedness, first spiritually by getting out of it and later physically

by trying to pull it off from its suffocation of the me inside, slapping at it, punching it and later trying—physically—to run from it but the damn thing just came after me. As far as I was concerned, my body was welcome as a sensory tool, but as a body with something of a competing will of its own, it was like a leech that happened to be there by coincidence but wouldn't take the hint and couldn't be got rid of. It was my first known enemy.

(Williams 1999, 53; quoted in McGeer 2001, 125)

Starting, Stopping, and Combining Movements

Some autists experience difficulties starting, stopping, switching, or combining motor movements that are not immediately recognizable to an observer. For example, they may walk away in the middle of a conversation, sit until prompted to get up, touch objects repeatedly, or turn away when they are called. Although these movements are often non-volitional, observers commonly interpret them as "autistic behaviors" that are both volitional and meaningless or as communicative acts that convey a desire to avoid interaction, or some combination of these interpretations (Donnellan, Hill, and Leary 2012). Charles Martel Hale Jr., an autistic adult, describes his frustration when he is unable to move or respond in an appropriate manner: ". . . [S]ometimes I know that I am not smiling but may be even frowning. This causes me a great deal of pain and makes me look as though I am not comprehending when, in fact, I am trying to respond in an appropriate manner" (Hale and Hale 1999, 32; quoted in Donnellan, Leary, and Robledo 2006).

Perceptual Processing

Many research studies have demonstrated that autists' performance in some perceptual domains is superior to comparison groups, especially when the perceptual task requires attention to details, parts, specific features, and local information. For example, autists consistently perform at a level superior to non-autists on visual search (Joseph *et al.* 2009), the Block Design test (Shah and Frith 1993), and Embedded Figures tasks (Mottron *et al.* 2006). Autists are also less susceptible to some kinds of visual illusions (Happé 1996). Autists' superior performance on these tasks is thought to be due to superior local processing. While typical individuals focus on global information by default, autists appear to focus on local information by default and do not automatically attend to and understand the gestalt or "gist" of what they perceive. It is unclear whether autists' strength in local processing comes at the cost of a weakness in global processing. Some theorists hypothesize that autists are just as capable of global processing as comparison groups, but that it is not their default or preferred processing style.[6]

The wide array of sensory, movement, and perceptual differences reported in autism suggest that how autists perceive and sense the world may differ, but also, even more fundamentally, *what* they perceive and sense may differ. What they look at, how they move, what they orient to and attend to, and how they respond to the same kinds of stimuli non-autists encounter make for experiences, perspectives, and ways of being in the world that are atypical and unfamiliar to those without these differences.

INTERPERSONAL UNDERSTANDING AND UNLIKE-MINDEDNESS

It is well known that social interaction between autists and non-autists is compromised. A guiding question of scientific and philosophical research on autists' social difficulties is how and to what extent autists understand others' mental states. Standard accounts of autism explain autists' difficulties in social interaction by attributing to autists deficiencies in social cognition. For example, theory-theorists hypothesize that autists have a deficit in "theory of mind." Simulationists hypothesize that autists have impairments in pretense, imagination, imitation, and perspective-taking. Both approaches present autism as an illustrative case of humans who lack the ability to empathize. Limits on interpersonal understanding between autists and non-autists has been conceptualized and investigated almost exclusively in terms of autists' limitations. Scant attention is paid to identifying and articulating limits on non-autists' abilities to understand autists. For example, although Myers, Baron-Cohen and Wheelwright (2004) concede that "[a]utistics may lack a non autistic theory of mind. Just as non autistics may lack an autistic theory of mind. Each is mindblind to the other" (57, footnote 17), this point is relegated to a footnote. Likewise, Kennett (2011) suggests in passing that failure of reenactive empathy between autists and non-autists "goes both ways" (191, footnote 10). My investigative focus, by contrast with standard accounts of compromised interpersonal understanding between autists and non-autists, is characterizing *non-autists'* limitations.

Here I investigate the possibility that there are greater limitations than many have realized for a non-autist understanding an autist. I claim that the forms of unlike-mindedness among autists and non-autists revealed by this research present the very live possibility that there are actions and reasons of autistic subjects that are unavailable to autists—that non-autists are unable to understand autistic subjects' reasons for acting or even to understand autists as acting for reasons at all. I look in particular at whether non-autists can grasp autists' individual agency by way of simulation, raising questions for the availability of autists' reasons and actions to non-autists. I leave open the possibility that there are other routes through which non-autists can grasp autists' individual agency.

Understanding an Agent's Reasons for Acting by Way of Simulation

Stueber (2006, 2012a, 2012b) argues that reenactive empathy plays an ineliminable epistemic role in understanding individual agency, which is holistic and context dependent. To grasp an individual's reasons for act-ing, one needs "inside" understanding of how the individual agent's specific beliefs and desires are part of the reasons that motivate that agent to act in that specific context, on that particular occasion. Simulation delivers this inside understanding. It renders another person's actions intelligible from an engaged, personal perspective. During simulation one imagines what one would believe, want, feel, and think in those circumstances, what one would do in that situation given those mental states. By putting oneself in the oth-er's shoes, imagining the particular situation the other faces, and reenact-ing her or his thoughts in one's own mind, with an eye to understanding how the other's desires and beliefs on that occasion "fit in with an agent's other beliefs, desires, plans of actions, values and rules of conduct to which the agent is committed" (Stueber 2012b, 69), one comes to appreciate how the agent's action is rationally compelling in that situation. Stueber (2006) illustrates understanding rational agents in their individuality by analyzing an example in Goldman ([1989]1995). Imagine that somebody just missed a train. It left a minute before she reached the platform. Compare this with somebody who misses a train by two hours. We intuitively understand that the person who misses the train by a minute is more annoyed and why this response is appropriate in the situation. Through reenactive empathy we grasp that the person who just missed the train has more reason to be annoyed because if she had just run a little faster or hadn't stopped to buy a newspaper on the way she probably would have made it on time.

Limits on Simulation Simulationists Discuss

Simulation theorists suggest that in ordinary circumstances even high-level simulation proceeds almost unnoticeably and automatically. However, high-level simulation can be effortful, deliberate, and challenging as an inter-pretive strategy in some cases. Attempts at reenactive empathy can fail. Stue-ber (2006) describes "twin dangers" that one encounters during the matching phase of simulation: projectionism and non-projectionism. Projectionism involves failing to recognize the relevant differences between oneself and the target, which leads one to see the target as too much like oneself and thus to quarantine failure, where one is "merely projecting one's own centrally held beliefs and attitudes onto the other person" (Stueber 2006, 205)[7]. For example, one may fail to disregard one's belief that drinking beer is morally wrong when interpreting an individual's beer-drinking behavior even though one knows that the individual one is trying to explain does not hold this belief. Non-projectionism is the opposite. It involves conceiving of the other person as not being sufficiently like oneself because one is influenced by pre-conceptions and prejudices about other people and cultures as foreign. For example, one conceives of the target as belonging to a more primitive culture and thereby incapable of certain ways of thinking (Stueber 2006, 205).

Although these obstacles to successful simulation might occur in every-day situations, we are much more susceptible to them when interpreting actions in unfamiliar contexts that are not sufficiently articulated, for example, in cases where there is great historical or cultural distance between the interpreter and the interpretee.[8] In such cases the interpreter must supplement the initial matching phase of simulation with knowledge of historical, cultural, and personal differences that influence the target's "inferential and argumentative practices, their values, their emotional attunement to the world, and so on" (Stueber 2011, 170). This information allows interpreters to determine which pretend-beliefs and desires to add and which of their own genuine states to quarantine from the simulation in order to successfully take the perspective of the target.

In addition to knowledge of historical, cultural, and personal differences, interpreters may need to draw on psychological research to supplement simulation, for example, when we are trying to understand individuals at different developmental stages. Stueber (2011) considers how this applies to understanding teenagers. Teenagers tend to find their parents' advice and commonly accepted rules of conduct less salient than their peers' opinions. To understand them, one must quarantine "considerations that normal adults would find salient" (171) and focus one's simulation on what we know teenagers might find salient (e.g., peer opinions).

The limits on empathy sketched here suggest that simulation becomes more difficult when the empathizer and target are not like-minded in the relevant ways. The more dissimilar the empathizer's and target's beliefs, values, commitments, and so forth, the more challenging and effortful the imaginative reconstruction, the less one is able to use one's own mind as a model without substantial "retooling" of one's own cognitive system, the more quarantining of one's own beliefs, desires, commitments, and values is required, and the more "opportunities" there are for error and bias during the simulation process.

Additional Potential Limits on Simulating Autists' Minds

The examples simulationists cite to illustrate impediments to successful simulation involve recognizing and adjusting for dissimilarities in beliefs, values, and commitments. However, as we saw in Section 3, reflection on sensory, movement, and perceptual differences associated with autism indicates that there are other forms of unlike-mindedness among autists and non-autists. What other limitations on non-autists' empathetic engagement with autists does this expanded notion of unlike-mindedness bring into view? I suggest here that there may be greater limitations on non-autists' capacity to simulate autists' minds than many have realized. In particular, I argue that there is the very live possibility that autists' reasons for acting may be unavailable to non-autists, by way of simulation. If unlike-mindedness between autists and non-autists means that non-autists cannot simulate autists' minds and simulation is required for understanding individual agency, then non-autists cannot see autists as acting for reasons. Non-autists may be unable to "see" autists as engaging in intentional action.

Being labeled autistic. I begin by describing a potential error in simulating autists that warrants further investigation, although I can only note it in passing here. It concerns the possibility that interpreting a person through the lens of a diagnostic label undermines that person's agency. As one woman diagnosed with borderline personality disorder remarked, "The minute I got that diagnosis people stopped treating me as though what I was doing had a reason" (Herman 1992, 128; quoted in Ussher 2011, 74). The kind of danger brought out by this woman's comment is that an individual's thinkings, sayings, doings, feelings, and experiences may be understood merely as meaningless symptoms of her psychiatric condition if viewed through the lens of a diagnosis. This danger is more general than those connected with specific stereotypes and stigmas about particular conditions and is not confined to contexts with non-expert interpreters. How medical professionals conceptualize the relation between bodily and mental illness impacts how they view the sayings, doings, feelings, and experiences of people with psychiatric diagnoses and how they intervene on mental illness. The anthropologist Tanya Luhrmann (2012) elucidates this idea in her reflections on the biomedical view of hearing voices (i.e., auditory hallucinations):

> In the new biological psychiatry . . . voices were symptoms of psychotic illness in the same way that a sore throat was a symptom of the flu. Sore throats didn't "mean": they were signs of a problem that had to be treated and resolved. So, too, voices. . . . In biomedical psychiatry, mental health professionals ask whether the patient hears voices, not what the voices say. The goal is to get rid of the voices, like getting rid of a fever.
>
> (52)

Turning back to autism, if an individual is already understood as autistic one may perceive her or his behaviors as mere meaningless symptoms of a disorder. This rendering of their behaviors would make it difficult to place autists in the "space of reasons" when one perceives and interprets them. For example, autists' hand-flapping is often interpreted as a meaningless symptom to be eliminated through behavioral interventions rather than as an action performed for a reason.

Köhler's phenomena and autism. The Gestalt psychologist Wolfgang Köhler provides an illuminating description of a basic feature of our relations with others that brings us closer to consideration of how forms of unlike-mindedness rooted in sensory, movement, and perceptual differences may threaten non-autists' capacities to "see" some features of autists' mentality or normativity: "[N]ot only the so-called expressive movements but also the practical behavior of human beings is a good picture of their inner life, in a great many cases" (Köhler 1929, 250). Ordinarily, in a variety of situations in everyday life, human behavior "pictures" human thoughts, feelings, and intentions such that one can perceive what another person is thinking, feeling, and intending by attending to the ways those aspects of the other's mental life are expressed in her or his facial expressions, bodily movements, postures, and gestures. Köhler called these phenomena of under-standing one another non-theoretically and non-inferentially the "common property and practice of mankind" (1929, 266). To illustrate this, Köhler describes a supervisor who is friendly with his subordinates but must deliver an unfriendly command. One can see the supervisor's hesitation to give the command in the supervisor's expressive behavior (1929, 234).

Importantly, as Hacking observes, Köhler's phenomena are *not* the com-mon property of and practice between some autists and non-autists:

> [M]ost people cannot see, *via* the behavior of severely autistic people, what they feel, want or are thinking. Even more disturbing is an inabil-ity to see what they are doing: their intentions make no sense. With the severely autistic, it may seem as if they do not even *have* many inten-tions. They are taken to be . . . thin children who grow up to be thin men and women, lacking a thick emotional life. Or so it has seemed to most people, including many parents and many clinicians.
>
> (Hacking 2009a, 1471)

The lack of Köhler's phenomena between autists and non-autists contrib-utes to a lack of common norms or standards for rendering autists' behavior intelligible to non-autists. As such, there are serious dangers of using a frame-work of interpretation that is built on the presence of Köhler's phenomena when trying to understand autists' behavior. Using behavioral norms of typical individuals as a standard by which to determine whether and how autists' behavior is meaningful, "makes sense," or is a reasonable response or intelligible expression may prompt one to interpret autists' behavior as meaningless, senseless, or unreasonable. This would be to interpret autists as if their movements and behavior are meaningful only when the meanings are readily understood by non-autists. As one autist aptly puts it:

> We move, we act . . . but our movements and acts have no recognizable goal, and thus people assume we lack intelligence, and lack all but the most rudimentary stages of consciousness. Our emotional responses are similarly discarded as meaningless, because we do not react in the same way most people do to the same things. Things in the environment that most people might not even notice scare us or irritate us, but because the stressors don't make it onto most people's radar, we are assumed to be throwing a fit for no reason. So our movements, our behaviors, and even our emotional responses and attempts to communicate are discarded as meaningless and we are believed not to be conscious or intelligent to the same degree that most people are.
>
> (Lindsay 2009, n.p.)

The meanings of autists' behaviors are often not apparent to non-autists, but from this fact it does not follow that their behaviors are meaningless.

Fixed limits on simulating autists' minds? In Section 4 we saw that to correct for dissimilarities in beliefs, desires, commitments, and values between the interpreter and interpretee, the interpret must 'retool' her cognitive system to better match that of the interpretee. But can quarantining one's own genuine mental states during simulation correct for forms of unlike-mindedness resulting from the sensory, perceptual, and movement differences described above? One aspect of the question is the extent to which non-autists can quarantine the relevant "parts" of their cognitive systems that clash with autists'. To better appreciate this aspect, consider the likely far-reaching effects of sensory, perceptual, and movement differences of the kind associated with autism. Possibilities for action in a particular physical or social environment depend on the information the individual picks up from her or his environment. And this, in turn, depends on the capacities and characteristics of the individual and her or his interactions with the environment (Hellendoorn 2014). As Donnellan, Hill, and Leary emphasize, those with sensory, perceptual, and movement atypicalities have a different developmental trajectory than typical individuals, which results in pervasive effects on the individual's experiences and interactions:

> In the course of development, if individuals move and respond in idiosyncratic ways from infancy, they will experience all interactions within a unique frame that most certainly differs from that which is called typical. The cumulative effect of such interactions will be one in which all aspects of relationships, including how to establish and maintain them, may be markedly skewed from the broader cultural consensus and expected rules of how relationships work.
>
> (Donnellan, Hill, and Leary 2012, 3)

On this line of thought, there are pervasive differences in how autists become minded over the course of their development by comparison with typically developing individuals. Suppose that one tries, through simulation, to understand the thoughts, feelings, and actions of an individual who has developed along this atypical trajectory. To achieve isomorphism during the matching phase of simulation one would have to somehow inhibit and suppress pervasive aspects of one's perspective on the world, including one's basic orientation towards one's physical and social environment and how one responds and moves in such environments. However, quarantining seems to be a meager tool for the task. It is doubtful that these forms of different-mindedness are the kinds that can be corrected for through the piecemeal addition and subtraction of particular beliefs, desires, commitments, and values. Even if these differences are the kinds that can be addressed by quarantining aspects of one's cognitive system that clash with theirs in relevant ways, one might still wonder whether enough or the right kind of like-mindedness is "left" after quarantining to use oneself as a model and imaginatively take the perspective of the unlike-minded other so that one's simulation renders an autist's actions intelligible and rationally compelling to oneself.

Now the following question arises: What would be the significance of the situation in which non-autists cannot understand autists' reasons for acting by way of simulation? That depends in part on whether there are other ways than by simulation that non-autists can grasp autists' individual agency.[9] What would simulationists say? Simulationists claim that simulation is our default method of understanding other minds, but, it would seem, on their understanding of "default method," simulation is not all there is to social cognition. It is neither an exhaustive nor an exclusive method. Rather, to call simulation the default is to say that it is typical individuals' go-to, spontaneous method (Goldman and Shanton in press). When it comes to understanding rational agents in their individuality, however, Stueber (2006, 2012a, 2012b) makes the strong claim that we can grasp individual agency *only* through reenactive empathy.

Suppose, then, that non-autists cannot understand autists' individual agency by way of simulation. Could other accounts of social cognition accommodate such understanding, given these forms of unlike-mindedness among autists and non-autists? Most theories of interpersonal understanding would seem to depend on the condition of like-mindedness. Think of Davidson's (1973) radical interpretation and principle of charity. Davidson claims that interpretation, of which mental state attribution is a part, is only possible when much is shared between ourselves and those we wish to interpret. For example, suppose that my friend believes that she has arthritis in her hands because they are swollen. To attribute this belief to her, she and I need to share many other beliefs, such as that arthritis is an ailment that occurs in humans, that swelling is a symptom of arthritis, that arthritis can develop in one's hands, and so on. Or recall Wittgenstein (1958, [1953], 2009) on a background of typical circumstances, shared reactions to training, and shared affinities and behaviors as preconditions for language-games. Still, it would be premature to say there are not or could not be other such accounts. But until we know more it would remain a live possibility that there may be mental features of autists that non-autists cannot understand.

METHODOLOGICAL CONSEQUENCES

What is the significance of the case in which there are some mental features of autists (e.g., their reasons for acting) that non-autists could not understand by any means? A wide variety of interrelated questions arise: How should this possibility affect how we proceed to understand autists? In particular, how should we regard the possibility that there is more mentality and normativity than we "see" in autists? What are some of the pernicious consequences of concluding there is no mentality/normativity when there is? What are some of the ways we could respond to limits on the understandability of autists' differences? What are some accompanying dangers of these possible responses? I cannot address all these questions here. I focus on characterizing some pertinent dangers regarding how we might respond to this possibility.

One response to the situation where there are some mental features of autists that non-autists could not understand by any means is to be *too* sensitive to their differences, to engage in pernicious forms of "othering" the Other. The concept of othering is used in different ways in a variety of contexts (e.g., anthropology, critical race studies, disability studies, feminist studies, education). I use "othering" to characterize a process involving an acknowledgement of an individual's or group's differences that differentiates those who are othered but mainly in harmful ways. Instead of embracing (or at least tolerating) those who are deemed different, othering is a strategy of amplifying or emphasizing the differences in representations of the individual or group to the exclusion of similarities and conceiving of the differences negatively—as deficiencies in features or traits deemed desirable or even essential to being human. The Other's differences are highly visible but are visible only as a problem. Othering, in this sense, can lead to a form of dehumanization whereby the Other is denied knowledge, rationality, intentionality, competence, subjectivity, and voice. For example, it is not uncommon for autists to be depicted in scientific and cultural representations as utterly strange, robotic or alien, or as people whose real selves are missing, hidden, or "kidnapped" by autism.[10]

Dehumanization has many pernicious consequences. It is used to justify the oppression, exclusion, and marginalization of those deemed the Other. We observe these harmful effects time and time again within and across cultures and historical eras. Recent research in social psychology (Epley, Schroeder, and Waytz 2013; Waytz, Schroeder, and Epley 2014) suggests that there are also more moderate, subtle, and passive forms of dehumanization with less obvious effects. Dehumanization may manifest at the bodily interaction level by, for example, by compromising one's ability to perceive dehumanized others' behavior as expressive of their affective states and one's ability to intuitively grasp their intentions and actions (Gallagher and Varga 2014). These failings may lead the interpreter to mistakenly conclude that there is no mentality or normativity when there is.

Another response to the situation where there are some mental features of autists that non-autists could not understand by any means is to ignore or to seek to obviate the differences associated with autists' forms of unlike-mindedness. Medina's (2013) reflections on meta-attitudes that contribute to the erasure of racial differences help characterize this phenomenon: "[B]lindness to differences is often rooted in a blinding meta-attitude according to which others appear under one's radar as one's peers only when their differences are erased or rendered inconsequential, that is, only when they are seen as being *like oneself*" (2013, 151). Simulation and other routes to interpersonal understanding whose success depends on the leveling of differences between the interpreter and interpretee run into this danger. Simulation, as we have seen, is an egocentric method that takes as one's starting point one's own first-person experience. One must identify relevant differences between oneself and the target, with the aim to "retool" one's cognitive system in ways that remove the differences between oneself and the target.

What are some of the dangers of seeking to understand the other by ignoring or obviating their differences? According to Medina (2013), it contributes to what Spelman calls boomerang perception: "I look at you and come right back to myself" (Spelman 1988, 12). The only way that I am able to see your humanity is by seeing you as a reflection of me. In other words, I do not see your humanity in its specificity. Medina argues that this attitude leads to a form of meta-ignorance:

> not simply a wrong-headed attitude toward specific others, but a restrictive overarching attitude that limits how others can appear to oneself, thus affecting one's attitudes toward specific others in negative ways, restricting one's sensitivity to differences and one's capacity to learn about this. This too (and not just the blatant denials of humanity) makes one blind to human differences and becomes an obstacle to the acquisition of social knowledge.
>
> (Medina 2013, 151)

To apply these considerations to the case of autism, there may be good intentions behind the attitude or recommendation to regard autists as "like us," but there are serious dangers of such an attitude, however well-meaning it may be in some cases. By seeking to erase differences we may inadvertently be promoting and sustaining a kind of ignorance whereby we fail to understand autists' thinkings, feelings, sayings, and doings in their specificity. We may even be restricting our capacity to learn about their differences. With regard to the particular issues of understanding individual agency and of treating autists as intentional agents in the "space of reasons" when we interpret them and interact with them, we should keep continually aware of the possibility that there is more mentality and normativity than we "see" in autists.

A closely related danger is to attempt to understand autists exclusively through the lens of our default framework of interpersonal interpretation. Modeling our understanding of autists' experience on typical human experience and conceptualizing autists' points of view simply as impoverished versions of "normal" ones can only go so far toward capturing the content of autists' experience of people, objects, environments, interactions, situations, and so forth. We need frameworks that make room for conceptualizing autists as having points of view on the world that are not simply a matter of missing things that typical individuals perceive. As proponents of the neurodiversity movement suggest, there are aspects of being autistic that involve unusual but not deficient ways of being in, experiencing, and knowing the world. As Amanda Baggs, an autistic adult, argues, "This is about what is, not what is missing. . . . It is about the fact that those of us who are viewed purely as having had things taken away—as being essentially barren wastelands—are not shut out of the richness of life by being who we are. The richness we experience is not some cheap romanticized copy of the richness others experience" (Baggs 2010, np; quoted in Nicolaidis 2012, 504).

CONCLUSION

I end with some brief reflections on how the issues raised in our discussion should affect future inquiry into autism specifically and understanding unlike-minded others more generally. First, in the light of the long history of stigmatization, exclusion, marginalization, oppression, dehumanization (aggressive and overt or passive and subtle), and silencing of unlike-minded others, it is imperative that we deepen our understanding of these and related dangers and how they influence social cognition.[11] Second, the dangers outlined above occur not only in the practical and social spheres but also in academic research and writing—in how researchers conceptualize and represent their subjects. Recognition of the differences in autism should encourage us to be more wary, more self-conscious, and more methodologically humble. We should be vigilantly attentive to whether and how our theories and practices make room for autistic personhood. Our science of autism depends on our keeping all this in mind, as does our theoretical understanding of social cognition, as do the lives of autists. Finally, autism is a case study, but the lessons from reflection on autists' forms of different-mindedness and on the neurodiversity movement's call for greater recognition of cognitive differences and human variation generalize. The questions raised about autism go for all sorts of different differences. And there may be additional relevant forms of difference in the range of human variations that have gone undetected. Thus, one may find oneself in a situation of interpreting an unlike-minded other even in one's own culture much more frequently than is commonly taken into account in our theorizing about social cognition and in our interactions with others in everyday life.[12]

NOTES

1 Some people with autism prefer "person with autism" because it puts the person before the autism. Others prefer "autistic person" to signal that autism is inseparable from the person (Sinclair 1999). I will use both kinds of language to acknowledge the different ways individuals may choose to talk about themselves. I will also use "non-autist" and "typical individual" interchangeably.
2 Hacking's essays (2009a, 2009b, 2009c) are important exceptions. See also Dinishak and Akhtar (2013) for a discussion of how the common uses of the metaphor "mindblindness" in portrayals of autism contribute to this one-sidedness.

3 The theory-theory and simulation theory were, for some time, considered the only two approaches and were treated as mutually exclusive. There is a growing consensus that some combination of theoretical approaches will be needed to explain mindreading since many now think mindreading better understood as a host of interrelated processes and capacities rather than a single thing. Likewise, hybrids of theory-theory and simulation theory and a variety of "third" alternatives to these dominant approaches are currently being developed. Accounts inspired by the phenomenological and hermeneutic traditions have been particularly generative. See Gallagher and Hutto (2008); Hutto (2008); Zahavi (2001, 2010); Zahavi and Overgaard (2012), for example.

4 "Empathy" and "simulation" are used in a great variety of ways in accounts of interpersonal understanding and social cognition. As Goldman observes, "the term 'empathy' . . . does not mean the same thing in every mouth. Nor does there seem to be a single, unified phenomenon that uniquely deserves the label" (2011, 31). One could say the same for "simulation." In contemporary philosophical discussions the two notions are often equated. For the purposes of this paper I follow Stueber and Goldman and use "empathy" and "simulation" interchangeably.

5 In addition, it may be that empathy is a mechanism that enables us to *become* more like-minded, in cases where empathizing results in the empathizer "feeling with" the target. See Sorensen (1998) for discussion.

6 See Koldewyn *et al.* (2013) for discussion. Similarly, while theory-theorists hypothesize that autists have deficits in reasoning about other minds, and simulationists hypothesize that autists have deficits in perspective-taking, imagination, and pretense, social motivation theorists hypothesize that autists' social difficulties arise from a lack of motivation to connect with the minds of others rather than from an inability to do so (Epley, Schroeder, and Waytz. 2013; Chevallier *et al.* 2012).

7 Goldman (2011) identifies two similar kinds of errors in high-level simulation: omission and commission.

8 Gallagher argues that simulationists face what he calls the diversity problem even in our own culture because simulation depends specifically and narrowly on one's own first-person experience: "If we depend on our own prior experience in order to sense what the other person may be thinking in a particular situation, the question is whether we really attain an understanding of the other or are merely projecting ourselves" (2012, 370).

9 A related issue is whether it follows from the impossibility of understanding some mental features of autists by way of simulation that non-autists could not acquire some kind or degree of experiential, "inside" understanding of said features by some other route. That would depend on whether simulationists would say that simulation is the only route to experiential, "inside" understanding. If so, then on this line of reasoning it seems that some mental features of autists would be un-understandable from an engaged, personal perspective, a perspective whose value (e.g., epistemic, pragmatic, affective) many theorists of social cognition take to differ from that of more detached stances, such as a third-person, observational stance.

10 See Smukler (2005), Broderick and Ne'eman (2008), Hacking (2009a, 2009b, 2009c), Duffy and Dorner (2011), and Sarrett (2011) for insightful analyses of these and other metaphors for autism.

11 Recent work in critical social epistemology could further our reflections on the causes and consequences of these harmful phenomena. Congdon characterizes critical social epistemology thus: "[It] offers analyses of unjust social formations by approaching them at a distinctly epistemological level, focusing on ways in which certain forms of knowledge are excluded from public exchange, and how the epistemic authority of certain would-be knowers is either denied

or diminished, not simply as the result of contingent epistemic failures, but in ways structurally connected with unjust conditions themselves" (Congdon 2015, 76).

12 I am greatly indebted to Jonathan Ellis, Rebekah Johnston, Kara Richardson, and Mark Risjord for helpful discussions and critical comments on earlier versions of this paper.

REFERENCES

Baggs, A. 2010. Cultural Commentary: Up in the Clouds and Down in the Valley: My Richness and Yours. *Disability Studies Quarterly* 30(1), http://dsq-sds.org/article/view/1052/1238.

Baranek, Grace, Lauren Little, Diane Parham, Karla Ausderau and Maura Sabatos-DeVito. 2014. Sensory Features in Autism Spectrum Disorders. In *Handbook of Autism and Pervasive Developmental Disorders,* 4th edition, 378–408.

Biklen, Douglas with Richard Attfield, Larry Bissonnette, Lucy Blackman, Jamie Burke, Alberto Frugone, Tito Rajarshi Mukhopadhyay and Sue Rubin. 2005. *Autism and the Myth of the Person Alone.* New York/London: New York University Press.

Blume, Harvey. September 30, 1998. Neurodiversity: On the Neurological Underpinnings of Geekdom. *The Atlantic.* Accessed June 30, 2015. http://www.theatlantic.com/magazine/archive/1998/09/neurodiversity/305909/.

Bogdashina, Olga. 2010. *Autism and the Edges of the Known World: Sensitivities, Language and Constructed Reality.* London: Jessica Kingsley Publishers.

Broderick, Alicia A. and Ari Ne'eman. 2008. Autism as Metaphor: Narrative and Counter-narrative. *International Journal of Inclusive Education* 12(5–6): 459–476.

Chevallier, Coralie, Gregor Kohls, Vanessa Troiani, Edward S. Brodkin and Robert T. Schultz. 2012. The Social Motivation Theory of Autism. *Trends in Cognitive Sciences* 16: 231–239.

Churchland, Paul. 1979. *Scientific Realism and the Plasticity of Mind.* Cambridge: Cambridge University Press.

Congdon, Matthew. 2015. Epistemic Injustice in the Space of Reasons. *Episteme* 12(1): 75–93.

Davidson, Donald. 1973. Radical Interpretation. *Dialectica* 27: 314–328.

Davies, Martin. 1994. The Mental Simulation Debate. In *Objectivity, Simulation and the Unity of Consciousness,* edited by Christopher Peacocke, 99–127. Oxford: Oxford University Press.

Dennett, Daniel. 1987. *The Intentional Stance.* Cambridge, MA: MIT Press.

Dinishak, Janette and Nameera Akhtar. 2013. A Critical Examination of Mindblindness as a Metaphor for Autism. *Child Development Perspectives* 7: 110–114.

Donnellan, Anne M., David A. Hill and Martha R. Leary. 2012. Rethinking Autism: Implications of Sensory and Movement Differences for Understanding and Support. *Frontiers in Integrative Neuroscience* 6 Article 124.

Donnellan, Anne M., Martha R. Leary and Jodi P. Robledo. 2006. I Can't Get Started: Stress and the Role of Movement Differences in People with Autism. In *Stress and Coping in Autism,* edited by M. Grace Baron, June Groden, Gerald. Groden, and Lewis P. Lipsitt, 204–245. New York: Oxford University Press.

Duffy, John and Rebecca Dorner. 2011. The Pathos of "Mindblindness": Autism, Science, and Sadness in "Theory of Mind" Narratives. *Journal of Literary & Cultural Disability Studies* 5: 201–216.

Epley, Nicholas, Juliana Schroeder and Adam Waytz. 2013. Motivated Mind Perception: Treating Pets as People and People as Animals. In *Objectification and (De)*

Humanization: 60th Nebraska Symposium on Motivation, edited by Sarah J. Gervais, 127–152. New York: Springer.

Gallagher, Shaun. 2012. Empathy, Simulation, and Narrative. *Science in Context* 25(3): 355–381.

Gallagher, Shaun and Daniel Hutto. 2008. Understanding Others through Primary Interaction and Narrative Practice. In *The Shared Mind: Perspectives on Inter-subjectivity*, edited by Jordan Zlatev, Timothy P. Racine, Chris Sinha and Esa Itkonen, 17–38. Amsterdam/Philadelphia: John Benjamins Publishing Company.

Gallagher, Shaun and Somogy Varga. 2014. Social Constraints on the Direct Perception of Emotions and Intentions. *Topoi* 33: 185–199.

Goldman, Alvin I. 1995. Interpretation Psychologized. In *Folk Psychology*, edited by Martin Davies and Tony Stone, 74–99. Oxford: Blackwell. (First published in *Mind and Language* 4 [1989]: 161–185.)

———. 2006. *Simulating Minds: The Philosophy, Psychology, and Neuroscience of Mindreading*. Oxford: Oxford University Press.

———. 2011. Two Routes to Empathy: Insights from Cognitive Neuroscience. In *Empathy: Philosophical and Psychological Perspectives*, edited by Amy Coplan and Peter Goldie, 31–44. Oxford: Oxford University Press.

Goldman, Alvin I. and Karen Shanton. (in press). The Case for Simulation Theory. In *Handbook of "Theory of Mind"*, edited by A. Leslie and T. German. New York: Psychology Press.

Gopnik, Alison and Andrew N. Meltzoff. 1997. *Words, Thoughts and Theories*. Cambridge, MA: MIT Press.

Gordon, Robert. 1986. Folk Psychology as Simulation. *Mind and Language* 1: 158–171.

Hacking, Ian. 2009a. Autistic Autobiography. *Philosophical Transactions of the Royal Society, Biological Sciences* 364(1522): 1467–1473.

———. 2009b. How We Have Been Learning to Talk About Autism: A Role for Stories. *Metaphilosophy* 40(3–4): 499–516.

———. 2009c. Humans, Aliens and Autism. *Daedalus* 138(3): 44–59.

Hale, Mary Jane and Charles M. Jr. Hale. 1999. *I Had No Means to Shout!* Bloomington, IN: 1st Books.

Happé, Francesca, G. E. 1996. Studying Weak Central Coherence at Low Levels: Children with Autism Do Not Succumb to Visual Illusions. A Research Note. *Journal of Child Psychology and Psychiatry* 37: 873–877.

Heal, Jane. 1998. Co-Cognition and Off-Line Simulation: Two Ways of Understanding the Simulation Approach. *Mind and Language* 13(4): 477–498.

Hellendoorn, Annika. 2014. Understanding Social Engagement in Autism: Being Different in Perceiving and Sharing Affordances. *Frontiers in Psychology* 5 Article 850.

Herman, Judith L. 1992. *Trauma and Recovery: The Aftermath of Violence—From Domestic Abuse to Political Terror*. New York: Basic Books.

Hutto, Daniel. 2008. *Folk Psychological Narratives: The Sociocultural Basis of Understanding Reasons*. Cambridge Mass.: MIT Press.

Joseph, Robert M., Brandon Keehn, Christine Connolly, Jeremy M. Wolfe and Todd S. Horowitz. 2009. Why is Visual Search Superior in Autism Spectrum Disorder? *Developmental Science* 12(6): 1083–1096.

Kennett, Jeanette. 2011. Imagining Reasons. *The Southern Journal of Philosophy*, Spindel Supplement 49: 181–192.

Köhler, Wolfgang. 1929. *Gestalt Psychology*. New York: Horace Liveright.

Koldewyn, Kami, Yuhong J. Jiang, Sarah Weigelt and Nancy Kanwisher. 2013. Global/Local Processing in Autism: Not a Disability, but a Disinclination. *Journal of Autism and Developmental Disorders* 43: 2329–2340.

Lindsay. February 7, 2009. Attributions of Consciousness. [Web log comment]. Accessed June 30, 2015. http://directionlessbones.wordpress.com/2009/02/06/attributions-of-consciousness/.

Luhrmann, Tanya. 2012. Living with Voices. *American Scholar* Summer: 49–60.

McGeer, Victoria. 2001. Psycho-practice, Psycho-theory and the Contrastive Case of Autism: How Practices of Mind Become Second-Nature. *Journal of Consciousness Studies* 8(5–7): 109–132.

Medina, José. 2013. *The Epistemology of Resistance: Gender and Racial Oppression, Epistemic Injustice, and Resistant Imaginations.* Oxford: Oxford University Press.

Mottron, Laurent, Michelle Dawson, Isabelle Souliéres, Benedicte Hubert and Jake Burack. 2006. Enhanced Perceptual Functioning in Autism: An Update, and Eight Principles of Perception. *Journal of Autism and Developmental Disorders* 36: 27–43.

Myers, Peter with Simon Baron-Cohen and Sally Wheelwright. 2004. *An Exact Mind: An Artist with Asperger Syndrome.* London: Jessica Kingsley Publishers.

Nicolaidis, Christina. 2012. What Can Physicians Learn From the Neurodiversity Movement? Virtual Mentor: American Medical Association. *Journal of Ethics* 14(6): 503–510.

Prince-Hughes, Dawn. 2004. *Songs of the Gorilla Nation: My Journey through Autism.* New York: Three Rivers Press.

Robledo, Jodi P., Anne M. Donnellan and Karen Strandt-Conroy. 2012. An Exploration of Sensory and Movement Differences from the Perspective of Individuals with Autism. *Frontiers in Integrative Neuroscience* 6: Article 107.

Sarrett, Jennifer C. 2011. Trapped Children: Popular Images of Children with Autism in the 1960s and 2000s. *Journal of Medical Humanities* 32: 141–153.

Shah, Amitta and Uta Frith. 1993. Why Do Autistic Individuals Show Superior Performance on the Block Design Task? *Journal of Child Psychology* 34(8): 1351–1364.

Sheahan, Bobbi and Kathy DeOrnellas. 2011. *What I Wish I'd Known about Raising a Child with Autism: A Mom and a Psychologist Offer Heartfelt Guidance for the First Five Years.* Arlington, TX: Future Horizons.

Sinclair, Jim .1999. *Why I Dislike "Person-First" Language.* Accessed June 30, 2015. http://autismmythbusters.com/general-public/autistic-vs-peoplewith-autism/jim-sinclair-why-i-dislike-person-first-language/.

Smukler, David. 2005. Unauthorized Minds: How 'Theory of Mind' Theory Misrepresents Autism. *Mental Retardation* 43(1): 11–24.

Sorensen, Roy A. 1998. Self-Strengthening Empathy. *Philosophy and Phenomenological Research* 58(1): 75–98.

Spelman, Elizabeth. 1988. *Inessential Woman: Problems of Exclusion in Feminist Thought.* Boston: Beacon Press.

Stueber, Karsten R. 2006. *Rediscovering Empathy: Agency, Folk Psychology, and the Human Sciences.* Cambridge, MA: MIT Press.

———. 2011. Imagination, Empathy, and Moral Deliberation: The Case of Imaginative Resistance. *The Southern Journal of Philosophy,* Spindel Supplement 49: 156–180.

———. 2012a. Varieties of Empathy, Neuroscience and the Narrativist Challenge to the Contemporary Theory of Mind Debate. *Emotion Review* 4: 55–63.

———. 2012b. Empathy Versus Narrative: What Exactly Is the Debate About? Response to My Critics. *Emotion Review* 4: 68–69.

Ussher, Jane M. 2011. *The Madness of Women: Myth and Experience.* New York: Routledge.

Waytz, Adam, Juliana Schroeder and Nicholas Epley. 2014. The Lesser Minds Problem. In *Humanness and Dehumanization,* edited by Paul G. Bain, Jeroen Vaes and Jacques Phillippe Leyens, 49–67. New York: Psychology Press.

Williams, Donna. 1999. *Autism and Sensing: The Unlost Instinct.* London: Jessica Kingsley Publishers.

Wittgenstein, Ludwig. 1958. *The Blue and Brown Books.* New York: Harper & Row.

134   *Janette Dinishak*

———. 2009. *Philosophical Investigations,* 4th edition. Translated by G. E. M. Anscombe, P.M. S. Hacker and J. Schulte. Oxford: Wiley-Blackwell. Original edition, 1953.

Zahavi, Daniel. 2001. Beyond Empathy: Phenomenological Approaches to Intersubjectivity. *Journal of Consciousness Studies* 8: 151–167.

———. 2010. Empathy, Embodiment and Interpersonal Understanding: From Lipps to Schutz. *Inquiry* 53: 285–306.

Zahavi, Daniel and Soren Overgaard. 2012. Empathy without Isomorphism: A Phenomenological Account. In *Empathy: From Bench to Bedside,* edited by J. Decety, 3–20. Cambridge, MA: MIT Press.

9   Responsiveness to Norms

Mark Okrent

INTRODUCTION

It is a central tenet of modern naturalism that in principle every event can be explained by reference to its physical causes. But it is also obvious that in a variety of different ways we explain what agents do by mentioning what the agent *ought* to do in the situation and suggesting that the agent does what she does because she is responding to the fact that she ought to do it. That is, we treat some agents as if they actually respond to norms. We treat agents in this way not only when we attempt to understand their behavior in social scientific terms, but also in ordinary life when we treat what an agent does as essentially evaluable in light of a norm, an act as successful or unsuccessful, or an inference as rational or irrational. But that some event satisfies a norm is no physical fact about that event, and no event so described can be an instance of either the antecedent or the consequent of any physical causal law. So it is something of a puzzle to see how norms, or the response to norms, could ever play an explanatory role in nature.

In this paper I approach this problem from what I hope is a somewhat novel direction. I look at three different classes of entities that can be thought to be responsive in different but related ways to distinct but related kinds of norms. When we describe an entity as living, or when we describe an agent as instrumentally rational, or when we describe an agent as a functioning member of a cultural community, we describe that entity as responsive to the norms of life, or the norms of instrumental rationality, or the norms acknowledged in the practices of a community of agents. In each of these cases, we treat what the agent does as explicable by appeal to a norm; we treat the agent's acts as happening *because* the agent in some sense responds to the fact that this is the right way to behave. The problem is to make explicit how the entities in question can properly be thought to be responsive to these norms, and how such responsiveness can both explain what the entities in question do and be compatible with explanations that appeal to physical causality. I suggest that a certain way of understanding the manner in which evolutionary explanations work in the explanation of the behavior of living organisms provides us with an unproblematic model that can be extended to the other two cases. That is, my suggestion is the vaguely Aristotelian thought that the key to giving a naturalistically acceptable account of normativity is to recognize that to classify an entity as a living organism already involves an implicit and naturalistically innocuous invocation of normativity and the responsiveness to norms on the part of that entity.

LIFE

Life is all about making distinctions. This is true not only of human life, but all life. Living things always live in some environment or other, and that environment is always liable to changes. Whether an organism lives or dies in some particular environment crucially depends upon whether or not its response to that environment varies in an instrumentally appropriate way to changes in its circumstances. While every natural entity, both living and non-living, responds differentially to its surroundings, living things are distinctive in that their existence is fragile, self-maintaining, self-replicating, and dependent for that self-maintenance and self-replication on the appropriately instrumental variability of their responsiveness to the environment. For this reason, living things, insofar as they continue to live, must in their responsive behavior to the environment distinguish between classes of situations by doing just those things that in the actual situation keep them alive. Thus a plant that fails to distinguish water and ammonia by responding differentially in an instrumentally self-maintaining way to the presence of water and ammonia will die in an environment that includes both, and an antelope that fails to distinguish giraffes and lions in its environment by responding differentially to their presence in an instrumentally appropriate manner will cease to exist in an environment that includes both lions and giraffes. The physical mechanisms through which the first discrimination is made are more apparent to us than the physical mechanisms through which the second discrimination is made, but irrespective of this the fact remains that unless such appropriate distinctions are made in the behavior of the living thing there is no life.

With distinction comes classification. Insofar as a living thing responds to two numerically different environmental situations with the same response, but to a third situation with a different response, the organism implicitly classifies the first two as similar and the third as different from the other two. And the similarity in question here need not be a physical similarity. Just as we humans in fact respond in similar ways to physically quite different sounds, and thereby classify them as being instances of the same phoneme, when a cat has learned to avoid shrews, having eaten one, while still chasing and eating other small mammals, that cat is implicitly treating shrews as belonging to a different class from the other mammals, and implicitly treating those other mammals as belonging together in the same class. Whether or not the organism in any sense 'represents' this difference as a difference of a certain type, or 'represents' the individuals in different classes in any way at all, is strictly irrelevant to the implicitly classificatory character of this behavior. And *we* can identify the implicit, instrumental, kinds into which the organism is categorizing the individuals with which it deals. The hypothetical animal that systematically avoids eating all and only those things that can physically harm her has spectacularly successfully distinguished, in and through her practice, the class of things that count as poisons for that animal. And this class is completely objective in that it picks out the instrumentally relational property of an object being poisonous for this organism, regardless of the fact that the things that are poisons share little else in common physically.

The fact that life only continues when the organism responds to its environment as it should in order to stay alive introduces error into the world. If it is possible for the organism to do the instrumentally right thing for itself, it is also possible for it to do the wrong thing. That is, the actions of all living things stand under success conditions; the organism does the right thing relative to its environment to keep itself alive, or it does not. Since doing the right thing involves implicitly correctly discriminating in its behavior among instrumentally important differences in its environment, correct behavior by an organism entails correctly sorting elements of environments into classes defined in terms of differences and similarities that are instrumentally important for the organism, and incorrect behavior entails incorrectly sorting environments along those same parameters. These standards of correct action and correct ways of sorting the environment are grounded in what it is to be the individual organism, and they obtain regardless of whether or not the organism in any way acknowledges or responds to those standards. Though, of course, since an organism only survives insofar as it does the right thing in its actual environment, insofar as it continues to live, all *living* organisms, as such, sufficiently satisfy the norms that they stand under in their environments. To be alive is to satisfy a primitive form of the principle of charity; organisms, as such, mostly do the right thing and mesh with, categorize, and *reveal* their world, as they should.

In both ordinary and philosophical contexts, the English word 'norm' is said in many ways. In one sense, 'norm' is a statistical concept: A norm for a group is what is statistically typical for members of that group. That is not the sense that is relevant here. 'Norm' is also used as 'a required standard; a level to be complied with or reached'. This is how I will use the word. Life imposes standards of action and discrimination, and those standards are to be complied with by the organism on pain of death. Insofar as the organism continues to live it satisfies those norms. In and through its behavior the organism distinguishes features of its environment into instrumental kinds and does so, in general, as it should distinguish those features. Organisms that continue to live do what they should on most occasions. The actions of organisms are, in general, in accord with the norms under which they stand. That is, in general the actual behaviors of organisms covary with the norms of correct behavior and discrimination. But in what sense, if any, do simple organisms *respond* to those norms; in what sense, if any, are they responsive to norms?

The language of 'response' and 'responsiveness' carries with it more than a hint of a certain kind of etiology. To 'respond' involves 'replying', or 'reacting', so for A to do B *in response* to 'C' is for A to do B *because* of some property or action of C. Responsiveness is essentially an *explanatory* concept. For the behavior of an agent to be responsive to some feature it is not enough for variations in that behavior to be correlated with variations in that feature. In addition these behavioral variations must occur *because of* the variations in the environment. So, for an agent to be responsive to a *norm* the agent must do what she does because of the *correctness* of that behavior. Norm responsiveness is behavior that responds variably to whether or not a certain type of action is correct in actual circumstances and does so because of the correctness of that type of action.

Since we have good biochemical explanations for what simple organisms do, and these explanations make no reference to the correctness of the agent's response, it seems otiose to suggest that such organisms do what they do because of their norm responsiveness. Nevertheless, it seems to me that there are two reasons that this consideration, while clearly having some force, is less compelling than it might first appear to be. First, it is always good to remember that *every* event in nature has a physical cause that makes no reference to norms. Every event has a cause. The fact that we happen to know more about the physical causal laws that operate at the level of single cells than we do at the level of human beings makes no difference to the ontological facts in the area. Whatever it means to say that some agent is responding to some norm, it just can't mean that there is no physical cause for what the agent does. If it did, then there would be no norm responsiveness in the world, human or non-human, at all. So the fact that simple organisms act in accordance with physical law does not imply that they are not norm responsive unless it also implies that we ourselves are not norm responsive.

The second consideration in this area has to do with *why* it is that the behavior of simple organisms varies in accordance with the norms of correct action and discrimination that cover their situations. While the fact that that behavior varies in accordance with differences in the environment, physically described, is sufficient for explaining the behavior of simple organisms, *physically described,* to explain that in general such organisms do the instrumentally right thing in their environment to secure their continued existence one must appeal to natural selection. Explanation is intensional; which explanations correctly explain an event varies as a function of how the event is described. When on an occasion a wasp performs a particular act in a particular environment that results in her killing and eating another animal she is doing something that has a physical description, say moving from point A to point B at some average velocity and through some trajectory. That such an event so described, that is, described as a physical event, occurs when it does has, presumably, some explanation that appeals to some physical law of which this event so described is an instance of the consequent of that law. But that the wasp's behavior will always or for the most part vary in subtly changing circumstances in the ways that it needs to so that the wasp continues to do *something* that tends to result in it killing and eating other animals, and thus performs this particular instrumentally successful act, described in terms of its instrumentally salient goal, when it does, requires a different kind of explanation. Living things come equipped by evolution with instinctive reactions to various environmental factors, and are caused to have the reactions that they do to those factors, *because* those kinds of reactions have in the past proved successful, that is, instrumentally appropriate, for the ancestors of the individual organism. That a simple organism exists that acts successfully in a particular kind of environment is the result of the fact that that way of acting was the instrumentally right way for the organism's ancestors to have acted in the past, that is, it was the kind of act that resulted in the ancestor surviving and reproducing. And in that sense, the simple organism is responsive to the norms of correct action and correct discrimination and categorization of features in its environment. It does what it does in environmental circumstance C because in the past that way of behaving was correct for organisms of its type, that is, it was the way of behaving that was conducive to the survival and reproduction of this type of organism.

The hypothetical animal that perfectly avoids eating anything that is poisonous for her engages in a set of behaviors that together can be correctly described as shunning all and only poisonous material. That fact, so described, has an explanation, an explanation that appeals to the fact that ancestors of this animal include only organisms that tended to avoid poison, that is, who for a certain range of behaviors did what they should have done relative to eating. So the explanation for the fact that our current animal avoids eating poison appeals to the fact that her ancestors did what they should have done; the current animal has the disposition to act so as to shun all the things that are poisonous *because* all those things are poison (for her), and she acts as she does because those things have that property. If carrots, for example, are poisonous for this kind of organism, then our particular critter avoids eating carrots *because* carrots are poisonous for organisms of its type. That is, this animal is responsive to the organic norms that govern eating behavior, it avoids eating things that are poisonous for her because they are poisonous, and this fact is entirely compatible with there being perfectly ordinary physical causes for the animal severally shunning each of the things that happen to be poisonous for her. *That* the organism is so constituted so as to shun eating carrots, that it has *some* physical constitution that provides a mechanism that results in her avoiding eating carrots, rather than having some alternative physical constitution, is *itself* a function of the fact that ancestors of this individual who had this variant constitution survived and reproduced and other potential ancestors with different variants did not. That is, the existing individual has this particular physical constitution precisely *because* it is good for organisms of its type to have it, and in that sense it is responsive to the instrumental norms of organic life.

Having said this, it is now time to take it back, via qualification. The tenses here are important. Environments are complex and subject to change, and there is no guarantee that the kinds of responses that evolution has given to an organism because they have proven in the past to be the correct thing for that kind of organism to do will be the correct responses now. And, in the case of the simplest organisms, on those occasions when they are doing the wrong thing, they will simply continue to do it, even though it is wrong, and even if it leads to catastrophe for the organism in question. Because this is the case it seems more wrong than right to say that what such organisms do, they do because it is the right thing to do. The possibility of correct behavior implies the possibility of wrong behavior, of course, and in fact there are no real organisms that don't actually make mistakes, or fall into error. When error occurs the simple organism cannot vary its behavior to compensate for that error. It is oblivious to the actual correctness or incorrectness of what it is doing *now*. And for that reason, one can't say that such agents are norm responsive in anything but a very limited, though real, sense.

INSTRUMENTALLY RATIONAL AGENTS

This result, however, points us in the right direction. Full responsiveness to norms depends crucially on responsiveness to error. An organism that cannot revise its behavior in response to doing the wrong thing can be said to be responsive to standards of correctness in only the most limited sense. On the other hand, when they make mistakes, some organisms *are* capable of revising what they do. To have this ability is to be capable of learning. And the organism that learns has become responsive to the gap between the norms that are relevant to the explanation of the organism's actual behavior and the norms that the agent should be responsive to, and has become capable of closing that gap.

Consider the case that I alluded to previously. Young cats indiscriminately chase, capture, and ingest a wide variety of small mammals, but of course do not engage in the same behavior relative to many other kinds of mammals. In acting in this way the kittens implicitly distinguish the kinds 'small prey mammals' and 'other animals'. That the cat discriminates in this manner is itself partially explained by the fact that in the past its ancestors that discriminated in this way survived and reproduced, as many such small mammals are in fact both edible by and present no predatory threat to cats. And in that minimal way what the cat currently does is the result of this instrumentally normative fact about its ancestors' relationship with past environments. In that sense, what the present kitten does is explicable by appealing to its responsiveness to the set of norms or standards that it inherited from its successful ancestors. But, as it turns out, while in a very general sense shrews belong to the same morphological class as many other small mammals that are edible by cats, they lack what from the cat's-eye perspective is the single most important property of those other animals; they are inedible by cats. From the standpoint that I have been developing here, this fact amounts to a difference between the norms, derived from her ancestors, that actually inform our kitten's behavior by helping to explain that behavior (the norm that it's good to eat small mammals that look substantially similar to mice, and because it is I should eat them!) and the norms to which she should be responsive (the norm that it's good to eat small mammals, except for shrews, and because of that I should eat non-shrew small mammals, but not shrews!). In this regard what distinguishes the kitten from simpler forms, such as a wasp, is that the kitten, but not the wasp, can respond to this difference between the norms it has been following and the norms it should follow by altering the first to accord with the second. Having experienced the inedibility of shrews by eating one and getting sick, in the future the kitten distinguishes, as she should, between shrews and non-shrewish small mammals. And she makes this alteration in her behavior and her discriminations *because* it is the right thing for her to do. Whatever physical mechanism drives learning in cats is there precisely *because* that mechanism has operated successfully in the evolutionary past so as to correct mistakes. So the kitten who is capable of learning by responding to her own mistakes by learning to do something else is responsive to the correctness or incorrectness of the *norms* that it is now proper to say she is attempting to satisfy. This is clearly a higher level of responsiveness to norms than is displayed by a non-learning capable organism such as a wasp.

In an important respect, animals that are capable of learning come to be unique. Since the ways in which such agents classify things in their environment varies as a function of their unique learning histories, conspecifics come to be responsive to different sets of norms. The cat that has learned to distinguish inedible shrews from edible small prey animals is sensitive to a difference, and a norm, that is invisible to her unlearned cousins. When she acts so as to shun shrews, this particular cat is motivated by factors that are unique to herself, rather than by some general feature of her evolutionary heritage. She is motivated to shun animals that she recognizes as shrews, whereas her untutored sisters, failing to distinguish shrews from other little furry things, entirely lack this form of motivation. For that reason, the normative explanations of the behavior of animals that are capable of learning allude to these variable distinctive factors. The learned cat *wants* to avoid eating shrews, and *believes* that the animal before her is a shrew, so she avoids eating this animal. By their nature, beliefs and desires are motivational factors that are unique to individuals and can arise out of a process of the individual coming to learn new instrumentally effective ways of coping with their current environments.

In its simplest forms, the capacity to learn from experience is relatively common among animals. I'm told that when exposed to slightly toxic potential food sources even sea anemones can learn to avoid that kind of ingestible in the future. And, even though learned anemones differ in their abilities to respond appropriately to different environmental stimuli from their unlearned cousins, many of us share the intuition that there is something distinctly odd about attributing beliefs and desires to anemones. And this intuition is not mistaken. For cats, but not anemones, have a further ability to respond to norms that is a second necessary condition on truly having beliefs and desires. On the basis of their experience of instrumental linkages, some animals, including cats, can learn to construct relatively long chains of activity that use intermediate proximate steps to reach instrumentally distant goals. That is, in the course of learning how better to cope with the world such animals have learned appropriate ways to respond to a host of instrumentally important properties of various objects and actions, and such animals can come to be motivated to bring about proximate ends to distal goals by recognizing the presence and potential importance of these various instrumental properties. Such animal agents can, in effect, not only acquire new beliefs from direct experience of the results of their actions on the world, but also *infer* new beliefs from old beliefs. This capacity to create inferentially related webs of belief inevitably carries with it the ability to develop desires for the achievement of proximate ends that are instrumental for the achievement of ultimate ends. When this occurs it is possible to explain each of these intermediate actions by appealing to the uniquely acquired motivations that the agent has developed, that is, by appealing to the inferentially interwoven complex of beliefs and desires. Any animal for whose behavior there is in principle such an explanation that appeals to the multiplicity of the agent's beliefs and desires, that is, that appeals to the agent's reasons, is an instrumentally rational animal.

Where there is the possibility of success there is the possibility of failure. Since the unique motivational factors that are represented by talk of beliefs and desires depend upon the peculiar experience that a particular individual contingently undergoes, agents can derive lessons that do not project to future environments, as well as learn the lessons that they should learn in order to continue coping with their world. Just as there is a gap in principle between the norms that a simple organism responds to on the basis of its evolutionary endowment and the norms that it should respond to, there is a similar gap in principle between the beliefs and desires that an agent actually has and the beliefs and desires that the agent should have. That is, not all beliefs are true, and not all desires are instrumentally appropriate. Instrumentally rational agents can act for their own reasons and still not do what they should.

Instrumentally rational agents can be more or less rational, of course, depending upon how good the agent is at learning what it is good for it to do, inferring new beliefs and desires from old ones, and planning and executing instrumentally appropriate acts. And, observing the squirrels in my yard overcome my attempts to keep them from eating birdseed, I sometimes think that they are far more instrumentally rational than I am. There is another respect in which humans are more instrumentally rational than even super-squirrels, however. We humans, but no squirrel, have the ability to explain, predict, and influence the behavior of other instrumentally rational agents by correctly ascribing beliefs and desires to them, and to use this ability to generate instrumentally appropriate action in response to those other agents' own agency. In order to use this explanatory strategy an observer, of course, needs to have access to the agent's beliefs and desires, which is a decidedly nontrivial difficulty. And, as far as we know only human beings in fact have the ability to use this 'intentional stance' in an explanatorily successful manner. The trick to recognizing beliefs and desires in other agents, and thus acquiring the capacity to use this mode of intentional explanation, prediction, and control, turns on being able to recognize that, because beliefs and desires are grounded in learning how to successfully cope with an objective world, the set of an agent's desires and beliefs is, in general, both internally rationally coherent and explanatory of the entire set of the agent's behaviors taken as a whole. While any individual belief might be in error, any individual desire might be counterproductive, and any belief or desire might be incoherent with the agent's other beliefs and desires, insofar as the agent remains an instrumentally rational agent, most of the agent's beliefs must be true, most of the agent's desires must not be counterproductive, and the set of beliefs and desires must be mostly internally coherent and explanatory of the agent's mostly instrumentally successful behavior.

Taking all of these points together, a picture emerges of a certain class of highly instrumentally rational agents. As organisms, such agents stand under a group of organically instrumental norms, and these agents are adept at satisfying these organic norms because they are capable of responding to the difference between their actual motivations and the motivations that they should be responsive to; that is, they can learn from their mistakes. And, as opposed to their simpler relatives, these special organisms have the additional advantage of being instrumentally rational. That is, they are able to learn how they should act to achieve their organic ends, how they should act in order to satisfy the norms of organic life, without always needing to first make potentially dangerous mistakes. To be instrumentally rational in this way is to be responsive to instrumental reasons. In virtue of this, what these interesting agents do can be explained by reference to their beliefs and desires, and since most of their beliefs must be true and most of their desires must be instrumentally appropriate, these instrumentally rational agents in general do what they do *because* they should do so. As we saw above in the discussion of simple organisms, the fact that in principle this same behavior, physically described, is also explicable through appeal to causal law is irrelevant to whether or not an agent is an instrumentally rational agent, as to be such an agent is to be an agent whose behavior, described in instrumentally relevant terms, can be explained in this way. But organisms that are instrumentally rational to the highest degree have an additional ability, the ability to explain and predict the behavior of *other* agents that are instrumentally rational by treating those agents *as* instrumentally rational. That is, these peculiar highly instrumentally rational agents, because they have the capacity to understand the unique motivations of other instrumentally rational agents (they ascribe beliefs and desires to other agents and thus have a 'theory of the mind' of those agents), are able to predict and explain the actions of those agents and thus also able to learn how to respond instrumentally appropriately to the changing behavior of other instrumentally rational agents.

One phrase that is sometimes used to pick out this extraordinary class of agents is 'social scientists that employ rational decision theory'. As far as I can tell, all normal adult human beings, but no squirrels, belong to this class.

PRACTICALLY RATIONAL AGENTS

In one important respect human beings belong to the same class of organisms as cats. Both the felines and we are instrumentally rational agents, even if, partially because of our superior ability to plan and to employ rational decision theory, we are so to a higher degree than are cats. But we humans think that there is another respect in which we differ qualitatively in respect to norm responsiveness from felines, non-human primates, canines, and cetaceans. Philosophers in the Kantian tradition have attempted to articulate this supposed difference in terms of the distinctive *way* in which we are responsive to norms. For example, it has been said that we, but not the felines *et al.*, act *in light of* norms, or out of a *recognition* of norms, or that for us, but not our animal cousins, the norms themselves are at stake because we can become aware of the norms we follow *as* norms. On other occasions I have addressed this strategy. Here I would like to approach this difference in a different way, from the perspective supplied by another distinctive fact about humans. Instead of focusing on the *way* in which we are responsive to norms I want to focus on a difference in the character of the norms to which we are responsive. In short, we can do what we do because we *ought* to do it, as well as doing what we do because we *should* do it.

Although the terminology that I am going to employ is perhaps somewhat novel, the distinction that this terminology is marking is familiar. It is widely and correctly held that not all norms are directly reflective of success conditions that follow from instrumental utility. Even when one can successfully cheat on a test, and thereby act in an instrumentally effective way to realize one's goals, we feel that there is another sense in which this is the wrong way to act. When in an Ethiopian restaurant, one ought to eat with one's hands, even if it is more efficient for most North American patrons to eat with a fork; one ought not to use someone else's 'property' even if such use is the only way for one to achieve one's goals; one ought to eat one's salad with the smaller fork; one ought to believe what is true, even if false beliefs are sometimes instrumentally more valuable.

What is at first sight distinctive about this second class of norms is the fact that they are not in any obvious way grounded in instrumental utility and efficiency. Although there is little warrant in either current usage or etymology for a clean distinction, I propose to mark this difference between the teleological-instrumental and *prima facie* non-instrumental kinds of norms by consistently using 'should' for the instrumental style of normative evaluation and 'ought' for the non-teleological. When an agent can achieve her goal only by acting in some way, that is, when the agent stands under a norm of instrumental utility to act in a certain way, I will say that the agent 'should' act in that way. On the other hand, when an agent stands under a norm of behavior that is not immediately grounded in conditions under which the action is required to achieve some goal, I will say that the agent 'ought' to act in that way.

From the standpoint of life there are two striking things about the non-instrumental norms that are specified in 'oughts'. First, 'oughts' appear capable of conflicting with 'shoulds' in such a way as to be incompatible with them. Trivially, if it is more efficient for me to eat with a fork, and I am engaged in eating, then I *should* eat with a fork. Nevertheless, in the actual situation in the restaurant we take it that we *ought* to eat with our fingers. If I am in a situation in which I can cheat without anyone knowing it, and I can get what I am aiming for by successfully cheating, then, in my terminology, I *should* cheat. Nevertheless, most of us believe that one still *ought* not to cheat. These potential and actual conflicts between 'shoulds' and 'oughts' point to the second odd thing about 'oughts'. Since what we ought to do can contradict what we should do, from the perspective of life the norms codified in 'oughts' appear to hang in mid-air, without support. If I should eat with a fork or cheat, in order to attain my goal, then what can it so much as mean to say that, nevertheless, one ought to eat with one's fingers and one ought not to cheat? Norms are standards that are *to be* complied with. But what is it about the standard embodied in an 'ought' that makes it the case that *it* is *to be* complied with? In the case of the norms of instrumental effectiveness, of the norms embodied in 'shoulds', from the perspective of life the answer to this question is obvious. An organic agent should do what will help keep it alive and refrain from doing what will result in its death. The norm is anchored in the sanction of obliteration and the reward of survival. But the whole point of an 'ought' is that none of that seems relevant. So what makes it the case that an 'ought' is to be complied with? On what authority can there be non-instrumental norms at all?

Non-instrumental norms thus occupy an odd intellectual status. Our self-interpretation assumes that they are ubiquitous. One ought to be honest, regardless of the outcome for me; I ought to grade my students' papers fairly and expeditiously, because that is part of what it is to be a teacher, regardless of the fact that I am a tenured full professor, and thus relatively immune from punishment, although the activity of grading is painful and carries serious opportunity costs; I ought to believe what is true, even if it is more useful to me to believe what is false. On the other hand, what makes it the case that such norms are to be complied with is anything but obvious. This is the question of the 'normativity' of non-instrumental norms. As the most obvious cases of these non-instrumental norms appear in the regulation of social interactions among humans, it has seemed natural to approach this question by way of the contemplation of such interactions, and I will approach this question from this angle here.[1]

Consider the case of the norms of professorial behavior. The problem is to account for the 65-year-old who grades her students' papers quickly and fairly (to the best of her ability), *because* she ought to do so, even though she recognizes that doing so is of no utility in achieving her goals. To understand this responsiveness to this non-instrumental norm, we look at the manner in which the professor came to be a professor, that is, was accepted as such within her community. And here we see an application of what appears to be a general principle: If one ignores the non-instrumental norms the others in the society will tend to penalize one instrumentally; if one complies with the norms the others will tend to treat one in such a way that certain instrumental benefits accrue. Because this is the case, the young human animal will be trained in such a way as to learn to respond to situations as the others would have one respond. Further, the learner will ultimately become the teacher, because part of what it is to be responsive to this socially instituted type of norm is to approve and disapprove of others' performances, as one ought to approve and disapprove, according to the norm. In the case of the aged professor, her predecessor time-slice, the young teacher, was instrumentally rewarded for grading papers quickly and fairly, instrumentally punished for not doing so. Because she is a highly instrumentally rational animal, and is capable of learning and inference, the fledgling professor is disposed to come to act in the ways that solicit instrumental advantage and to avoid acting in the ways that indirectly cause her instrumental harm. That is, she is capable of being trained by other members of her community to act in ways of which they approve. Either this training stuck or it didn't. If it didn't she would have been denied tenure and would no longer be subject to the norms, nor in a position to enforce them. If it did stick, she has learned to respond to a set of papers, as she ought, according to the norm, independently of any future rewards and punishment.

Since the explanation for our professor grading her current papers turns on the fact that she is currently disposed to act in accordance with the norms of appropriate social behavior for professors, and she has come to have this disposition because these norms are accepted and enforced as obligatory by the community of professors, she acts as she does *because* it is, or is considered to be, the right way to act. Our professor is responsive to the norms of professorial behavior and what she does is explicable by appeal to this responsiveness. So, from this perspective, 'oughts' enter the world through the attitudes of social agents towards the behavior of others and the social ability to reproduce those attitudes in others. Non-instrumental normative 'oughts' are grounded in the attitudes of those who are responsive to them, and nothing else. As Robert Brandom sums up this view: ". . . one way to demystify norms is to understand them as *instituted* by the practical attitudes of those who acknowledge them in their practice. Apart from such practical acknowledgment—taking or treating performances as correct or incorrect by responding to them as such in practice—performances have natural properties, but not normative proprieties; they cannot be understood as correct or incorrect without reference to their assessment or acknowledgment as such by those in whose practice the norms are implicit" (Brandom 1994, 63).

When trying to understand the institution and grounding of non-instrumental norms, it is natural to combine some version of the above conditioning account with the notion of a system of 'practices'. In the words of John Rawls, a practice is "any form of activity specified by a system of rules which define offices, roles, moves, penalties, defenses, and so on, and which gives the activity its structure" (Rawls 1955, 3). (While Rawls uses 'rules' in his definition, I will continue to use 'norm'; a rule is one definite type of norm, and not all norms to which an agent is responsive are rules.) The 'offices' and 'roles' that are defined within such a system of practices are the social roles that social agents can occupy that are established by the structure of penalties and rewards. If one is a professor, but only if one is a professor, one is both authorized to and obliged to grade college student papers; to be a college professor is in part to stand under the grading norms. One comes to occupy such an office only if one is accepted by the others as an occupant of the office, in and through being assessed in terms of the requirements of the office instituted by the practice, and this acceptance itself is conditional on prior assessments of whether or not the prerequisites for attaining the office have been satisfied by the agent. Similarly, the system of practices establishes systems of instrumentalities through which the various social roles are to be realized by agents in the community; the small fork comes to be the tool that is to be used to eat the salad through the system of rewards and penalties that go in to the teaching of the practice of correct dining behavior within the community.

This way of understanding non-instrumental norms gives us a third distinct sense in which an agent can be responsive to norms. There is the limited sense in which all organisms that continue to live respond to the norms of survival-securing action in their actual environment. There is the less limited sense in which certain organisms, the highly instrumentally rational ones, can respond to instrumental mistakes as mistakes, learn from their failures, correct their behavior in light of what they should have done, construct elaborate strategies for attaining distant goals, and thereby respond to the norms of instrumental reason. Some of these highly instrumentally rational agents, the social scientists who use rational choice theory, are even capable of learning how to respond instrumentally rationally appropriately to the instrumentally rational behavior of other agents. And then there are the agents who can learn to be responsive to the non-instrumental norms of social propriety, and come to act as they ought to act, given the attitudes that they have come to share with their fellows in a community. Such agents have become capable of responsiveness to a different kind of norm, the norms specified in practices, and in this way are responsive to different norms than merely instrumentally rational agents. Not every animal that is responsive to instrumental norms is capable of responsiveness to *practical* norms, the norms that institute and are instituted by social practices. The class of agents who are responsive to the non-instrumental norms of social proprieties, the class of agents that on occasion do what they do because they ought to do so given their role within their society, comprises the class of *practically rational agents,* that is, agents who are responsive to the norms that establish and are established by the practices in their communities.

In being responsive to the non-instrumental norms of social proprieties, in responding, as one ought to respond, to elements of the environment because one ought to respond in that way, agents who are norm responsive in this third way succeed in differentiating classes of entities that are invisible as classes to merely instrumentally responsive agents. Just as organisms as organisms differentiate in their behavior among types of entities that differ in their instrumental properties relative to the organism, animals that are responsive to 'oughts' are capable of differentiating among kinds of entities that, in virtue of their social significance instituted within the practices in their communities, ought to be responded to differently. As what it is correct for the social agent to do in a situation is a function of how that action is assessed in terms of the norms instituted within her community, the classes of environmental entities differentiated by these actions also depend for their contours on these norms of assessment, rather than upon their physical properties. What counts as an instance of a given phoneme depends upon the norms current around here: Two sounds that instantiate different physical types can count as instances of the distinct phonemes 'l' and 'r' for us English speakers, but count as instances of the same phoneme for Japanese speakers; two sounds that instantiate the same physical type can, depending on phonetic context, count as instantiating different phonemic types even in the same language.

The opening of the possibility of responsiveness to non-instrumental oughts brings with it the possibility of new kinds of conflict and new kinds of 'implication' among norms. And these possibilities implicitly carry with them the further possibility for the development of yet a fourth type of norm and a fourth type of responsiveness to norms. Since social proprieties are instituted by patterns of responsiveness among the members of groups, rather than by instrumental facts about the environment, the conditions under which an action ought to be performed can include that some other action ought to be performed. This fact, combined with the relative independence of what one ought to do from what one should do, allows for the development of chains of conditional proprieties that are different in kind from the chains of conditional instrumentalities operative in the organic world. If one's goal is to eat at some point in the future, and one can eat the ripe fruit of a blackberry plant, then one should pull out plants rooted close to any given blackberry plant (thereby creating the kind 'weed'), because doing so is instrumental to the health of the blackberry plant, which is instrumental to the ripening of fruit, which is instrumental to one's eating in the future, even though no instrumental benefit accrues directly from the activity of weeding itself. Similarly, but in a radically new key, the norms embodied in practices institute chains of conditional oughts, chains that can be separate from the environmental instrumentalities. To return to the professorial example, if an individual has attained the status of a professor in an institution, then that individual ought to be deferred to by other individuals who in a similar way have attained the status of student in that institution, and the professor ought to fairly and expeditiously grade the students' papers, (where of course what counts as a 'paper' and 'grading' is similarly instituted by a chain of proprietary 'oughts').

Since such chains of conditional proprieties can float relatively free from any connection with the non-social environment, there is nothing to prevent such chains from forming in such a way that a particular action is both demanded and prohibited by different chains of social proprieties. Particular agents on particular occasions can and do find themselves in the situation in which they both ought to do something and ought not to do that very same thing. The same individual can occupy the role of physician and the role of parent, and in a situation a physician ought to be at the hospital treating patients and the parent ought to be at home caring for a sick child. As agents can only in fact do one thing at a time in a situation, this conflict will be resolved in one way or another in the agent's actual action. But this leaves open the separate question of what the agent ought to do in the situation. Whether or not there is an answer to this question depends upon whether or not there are norms within the group for the resolution of such conflicts, and whether or not the members of the group are capable of responsiveness to any potential norms of conflict resolution among the set of first-order norms. (Norms for resolving conflicts among norms come in several possible forms, including norms that prioritize among the force of norms and norms for revising norms, and for each of these different types it is possible for agents either to be or to fail to be responsive to these kinds of norms.) As is the case with socially instituted practical norms in general, such second-order norms find their grounds for objectivity in the pattern of acceptance and rejection of action that is operative within the community. So whether or not there *is* a right way to resolve such normative conflicts within a given community itself depends on the ability of the members of the group to be responsive to the second-order norms of conflict resolution. Here, if anywhere, Brandom's dictum that actions "cannot be understood as correct or incorrect without reference to their assessment or acknowledgment as such by those in whose practice the norms are implicit" holds true. As it is possible for agents who are responsive to social norms to fail to be capable of responding to the full range of second-order practices for resolving conflicts among norms, those social agents who have such an ability stand at a fourth distinct level of responsiveness to norms. In my terminology, these are the agents who are capable of being responsive to *theoretical* as well as *practical* reasons. These agents comprise the class of practically theoretical rational agents.

Practically rational agents are responsive to norms that have their origin in the pattern of implicit assessment embodied in the behavior of a social group to which the agent belongs. To say that there are such practically rational agents is to say that there are agents who in part do what they do *because* they ought to do so given the norms operative in their society. Once again, this is a claim regarding the applicability of a certain style of explanation of the agents' behavior. It is interesting that it is possible for an agent to *be* practically rational without that agent being capable of *using* practically rational modes of explanation to predict and explain the behavior of practically rational agents. Just as it is possible for an agent to stand at a certain distance from another person without recognizing that she is doing so because it is socially appropriate in her society to do so, it is possible for an agent to be in general responsive to social practical norms, and to live in a community of agents who are similarly responsive to those norms, without in any way recognizing that this is so or being capable of using this fact to explain and predict any of the behavior of any of the members of her community. It is even possible for theoretically rational agents to be oblivious to the fact that they are theoretically, or even practically, rational and oblivious to the fact that the response of an agent in a situation can be inferred from that agent's position in her society and the norms governing that position. On the other hand, some practically and theoretically rational agents are cognizant of these facts. Such agents comprise the class of social scientists who study the ways in which social cultural norms help to determine behavior within a community. As far as I can tell, and as opposed to the class of social scientist who can apply rational decision theory, not all normal adult human beings belong to this class of social scientists.

Just as, in effect, the explanation of the behavior of instrumentally rational agents in terms of their beliefs and desires is an extension of the evolutionary mode of explanation to organisms that are capable of learning and inference, in effect the explanation of the behavior of socially cultural agents in terms of their training to occupy a position defined by the practices instituted in an articulated cultural community is an elaboration of modes of explanation that appeal to learning regimes to organisms that are capable of being trained within a society. And, just as evolutionary explanations are compatible with physical explanations, and instrumentally rational explanations that are grounded in the capacity of certain organic agents to learn and infer are compatible with evolutionary explanations, social scientific explanations that appeal to cultural facts are compatible with explanations that appeal to the instrumental rationality of individual agents. What explains the actions of our professor, described as acts that satisfy certain requirements of the socially instituted role of 'professor', such as 'grading papers', is that she is responsive to the culturally instituted norms of professorial behavior. Since this explanation is fully compatible with there being a perfectly adequate physical explanation of the same event, when that event is described as 'the movement of the human being's right hand through a certain arc while the hand is holding a pen', explanations that appeal to an agent's responsiveness to cultural norms are naturalistically fully kosher.

NOTE

1 It is not always noted that an important problem in evolutionary theory is exactly analogous to the problem of normativity. If behaviors are naturally selected to enhance the reproductive fitness of individuals, then how can 'altruistic' behavior ever evolve? In fact, 'altruism' is a somewhat misleading term in this context. What needs to be explained is how behavior that seems non-instrumentally valuable to the agent could ever evolve in a population. One answer to this evolutionary problem, that I favor, is to appeal to natural selection over groups. It seems to me that this same move is also valuable in articulating the problem of normativity.

REFERENCES

Brandom, Robert. 1994. *Making It Explicit*. Cambridge: Harvard University Press.
Rawls, John. 1955. Two Concepts of Rules. *The Philosophical Review* 64(1): 3–32.

10 Explaining by Reference to Norms Is Only Natural (or Should Be)

David Henderson

THE ISSUE

I have elsewhere expressed misgivings regarding the idea that one explains the thought or action of agents by showing that so doing or thinking was rational, given what else the agent believes (Henderson 1987, 1991, 1993). Instead, explanations turn on recognizing that the agent's actions or thoughts were of sorts that would be generated by the kinds of cognitive processes in play in that agent. Such cognitive processes may vary with training, or with elements of the agent's setting that activate certain acquired models that the agent has learned. But, in all this, the connection with normative rationality (how the agent ought to reason rather than the agent's learned models of normative rationality) is tenuous. Here, it is important to emphasize this general idea: rationality supposedly is a real normative property—one that is distinct both from the character of folk's innate or acquired cognitive processes and from the normative models that folk happen to possess at a time. Explanation turns on these more descriptive, factual, matters and is thus disassociated from real normativity. What matters are the processes in play—explanations ultimately depend on one's understandings of agents' cognitive processes and states, not on the rationality or irrationality of those processes. Of course, an agent's processes may depend to some extent on the agent's normative understandings or models. But the fact that the agent has such understandings then carries the explanatory load, and does so whether or not the understanding is correct. In sum, the character of agents' cognitive processes, commonly including the agents' normative models for thinking, explains what agents think or do, and this screens off any rational normativity of explanatory relevance.

Now, some believe that there are social phenomena that give rise to oughts—not just to folk being coordinated in thinking that they ought to think or act in certain ways, but to normative facts to the effect that the folk ought to so think or act. Social norms or rules, and related phenomena such as shared or joint intentions, are commonly mentioned here. The norms are thought to constitute a social phenomena that itself has a distinctive normative dimension—a kind of oughtness. It is thought that this obtains for some simple everyday social matters; it is thought that our joint intention to take a walk makes it wrong for you to strike off on your own without special reason. Such normativity is also said to be intrinsic to relatively fancy social matters; a more extended "we" might have the joint intention to empower only certain social groups to make certain classes of decisions for "us." Forms of norm-based real normativity are posited in Gilbert's writings—the walk example is her familiar starting point (Gilbert 1989) and her ideas are readily extended. The philosophy of law is one of many applications she pursues (Gilbert 2000). One can find similar ideas in Brandom (1994) and in Rouse (2006; see also this volume). On such views, there are a plethora of both everyday and 'highfalutin' acts of individuals and groups that are normatively infused—the normativity being part of what they are.

In this paper, I focus on the suggestion that some forms of normativity arise from at least some social norms, and I critique the idea that there is an explanatory role for real normativity associated with norms. In parallel with the above points, I distinguish the real normativity (if any) arising out of social norms from the sociological norms themselves, understood as factual matters of folk having coordinated normative/evaluative stances. I argue that explanation turns on the latter, not the former.

I here understand social norms, as a broad family of social/psychological phenomena in the neighborhood of what is characterized in Boyd and Richerson (1985), J. Henrich *et al.* (2004), Skyrms (2004), Bicchieri (2006), N. Henrich and J. Henrich (2007), Tomasello (2009), and Bicchieri and Chavez (2010). Such norms are a matter of more or less coordinated cognitive and conative states obtaining among a set of interacting agents—notably human agents. Agents come to be coordinated in some of their standing evaluative stances, and these standing states make for a responsiveness to significant ranges of information (or putative information) that those same agents might come also to episodically possess. When agents having such standing evaluative states do come to have (contentfully related) episodically occurrent (apparently) informative states, they then typically generate occurrent episodic evaluations (although these may be inarticulate and not fully conscious). In such cases, the agents typically undertake actions—more or less coordinated actions. In broad outlines, having such more or less coordinated standing evaluative stances or states is what constitutes the norms among the group of agents. The coordinated actions that result constitute conformity to norms among the relevant folk. Coming to participate in a social group or coming to form a social group involves agents coming to have sets of similar and (nearly enough) coordinated understandings. These understandings characterize such things as actions, action-possibilities, and contextually appropriate actions or responses. Among the relevant descriptive understandings may be understandings to the effect that the members of the group are depending on each other in some joint project. Among the relevant evaluative stances may be evaluations of various harms, benefits, and some sense for commitments or obligations that have been incurred.

(Of course, the 'understandings' and 'senses for' alluded to here do not require veridicality.)

It is important here to distinguish sociological norms from what I call 'norms-*qua*-normative'. Sociological norms obtain when, as a matter of fact, the descriptive and evaluative thinking on some matter among some folk comes to be coordinated as above. To characterize a sociological norm, one represents the character and content of the relevant folk's thinking. One can characterize this coordinated thinking without any commitment to what folk ought (or ought not) to do or think. In contrast, one cannot espouse or hold a norm-*qua*-normative without thinking that what it prescribes or proscribes actually has the relevant rightness of wrongness (goodness or badness). To express a norm-*qua*-normative, one evaluates certain states of affairs, actions, or the like—one does not merely report someone or some folk's evaluation of that matter. The difference is that between saying that "the *P*s think eating horses is wrong" (a mundane matter of fact regarding the thought of *P*s) versus saying that "among the *P*s, eating horses is (really) wrong."

Suppose that the *P*s do have a norm against eating horses. Then, in their own thinking, many of them embrace the content that eating horses is in some sense wrong or bad—that it is not to be done. But, in characterizing their thinking and action, in characterizing their sociological norms, one needs not think in this way oneself—the content, notably the evaluative content, is attributed to them and is not thereby embraced oneself. That they hold it is a fact about their more or less coordinated cognition.

There is a big difference between thinking that sociological norms are explanatory and thinking that norms-*qua*-normative are explanatory.[1] If there is a sociological norm, then folk within the relevant population are more or less coordinated in their thinking, some of which has normative content. But this can be so, and one's description of these norms can be true, without the norms-*qua*-normative being correct—perhaps even without real normativity being a feature of the world. Central in the difference insisted on here is an idea that seems common coin in much writings on norms and normativity: the idea that there is always a distinction between something being right or correct, or good, and some folk at a time thinking that it is right or good. The idea is expressed in the early chapters of (Brandom 1994), who drives home this idea that there must be some distinction between the judgments of some individual or group and the correctness of those judgments.

According to what I will call *explanatory naturalism*, folk's thinking (and how such thinking is occasioned by their surroundings) explains all that there is to explain in the social sciences. Folk's *evaluative thinking* (their *thinking* something good, or bad, or *thinking* some things right or wrong, or perhaps just *preferring* something to something else), together with their descriptive thinking (what they broadly *believe* about their world, including about their fellows), the character of their *cognitive processes,* and what they then *intend* to do, explain all that there is to explain in the social sciences.[2]

Those who I will call *explanatory normativists* insist that there is an explanatory resource somehow left out of the naturalist's approved explanatory toolbox: real normativity. What is left out is a matter of something *being good or right—rather than merely being thought so.* The normativist insists that an explanatorily adequate social science will have to appeal to norms-*qua*-normative in their explanations.

Norms look fully naturalistically respectable, and explanatorily powerful—so they look promising to the explanatory naturalist. Yet, they are tempting to the normativist, who may see them as making for real normativity. Normativists suspect that at least some norms somehow bring in their train a form of real normativity and that this normativity is explanatorily important. I here argue that the naturalistic base of norms—the coordinated thinking of folk—screens off from being explanatory any related normative feature.

CLARIFYING THE ISSUES: CHARACTERIZING A SPACE OF POSSIBLE POSITIONS

There are several ways in which normativity might be thought to be significant for the explanatory portfolio for which the social sciences are responsible. First, if there are normatively infused acts or events, these might plausibly be among the explananda of the social sciences—for example, the act of passing legislation (which supposedly entails a legitimate governmental setting and a legally binding result). Call this *the normative explananda thesis.* Second, and relatedly, it might be thought that investigators need to explain the normative statuses themselves—those with which such explananda are supposedly intrinsically infused. Call this *the normativity as explananda thesis.* Third, it might be thought that such normative statuses and relations serve as explanans for explananda that that are likewise normative in character. Call this *the normativity as explanans thesis.*[3]

These theses make for a rather tidy package. The social sciences commonly deal with social or sociological norms of various stripes, so it might seem reasonable that the social sciences be responsible for accounting for the associated normatively laden phenomena. It then might be insisted, explanatorily adequate social sciences should be up to explaining the social and cognitive phenomena by which the normativity-constituting norms come about, and by which the various normatively laden actions come to be undertaken (both the conforming and violating actions). It should, in short, preside over a normatively laden world. If you think that norms have real normative powers, and do not merely cast normative shadows,[4] and if you think that social norms are at least important phenomena for the social sciences to explain and understand, then it will seem to you that the social sciences should explain social phenomena and their real normative properties.

Various forms of *normativism* embrace combinations of these theses. *Weak normativists* embrace the normative explananda thesis. *Metaphysically ambitious normativists* embrace the normativity as explananda thesis in addition. *Full* (or shameless) normativists embrace all three, including the normativity as explanans thesis.

Remember, I am focusing on issues of the explanatory role of normativity insofar as this normativity is thought to arise out of social norms. We may say that the coordinated ways of thinking involving the patterns of evaluative stances had or internalized by agents within an interacting population constitutes the mundane descriptive basis of norms. What I will call *basic explanatory naturalism* supposes that this is all the social scientist needs—that sociological norms as matters of coordinated thinking, including evaluative stance-taking, is all that the social sciences need by way of explanans—it repudiates the normativity as explanans thesis—and thus repudiates full normativism. This is the form of explanatory naturalism that I seek to unambiguously support here. This is the focus of my final section. As with normativism, naturalisms come in strengths. Stronger forms of explanatory naturalism would repudiate normative acts and normativity as explananda.

The fitting naturalist stance with respect to the normativity as explananda thesis and the normative explananda thesis is a delicate matter. Issues of meta-normativity intrude. (Meta-normativity is the generalization of meta-ethical positions into positions regarding normativity in general—positions regarding the metaphysical status of forms of normativity including, but not limited to, moral normativity.) How, if at all, do normative properties fit in a natural world? The standard catalog of options includes the following four general positions. First, there is anti-realism about the normative—either non-cognitivism (including, for our purposes, the quasi-realist approaches advanced by Blackburn 1993; and by Gibbard 1990, 2003; Gibbard and Stroud 2008), or error theory (such as that recently advocated by Joyce 2006). Secondly, one might think that normative properties are strictly reducible to (perhaps complex disjunctions of) natural factive states (including the kinds of cognitive and conative stances that make for sociological norms).[5] This would allow the naturalist to embrace these theses. Prinz, for example, argues that the normative property of *having an obligation* is naturalistically reducible.[6] Third, one might hold

Table 10.1 Forms of normativism

	Normative explananda thesis	Normativity as explananda thesis	Normativity as explanans thesis
Weak normativism	Accepts		
Metaphysically ambitious normativism	Accepts	Accepts	
Full normativism	Accepts	Accepts	Accepts

that normative properties superdupervene on natural/factive properties. This would be for real normativity to supervene on those natural properties, and, for the supervenience relationship itself to be naturalistically explicable (Horgan 1993). For comparison, simple functional properties as understood by Cummins (1975, 1983) clearly superdupervene on the underlying physical properties within a system—as the structured input-output states within the system and their causal relationships are clearly explicable physically or naturalistically. Finally, one might hold that normative properties supervene, but do not superdupervene on some natural basis.

These alternatives have very different implications for the issues pursued here. If, for example, anti-realism is correct, if there are no real normative properties in the world, then naturalism wins by default. No events or states are really normatively infused; there is no normativity to be explained, and no normativity to serve as explanans. On the other hand, if one thought that real normative properties (properties with a to-be-done-edness) were strictly reducible (without remainder) to the natural stuff of (at least some) sociological norms, then one is a meta-normative naturalist of a strong form, and this would render the normativity as explananda and the normative explanans theses congenial to explanatory naturalism. But, note, on this view, the normative properties are simply a matter of being thought of in a certain coordinated way—nothing more. This would be to eliminate any difference between being correct and being thought of as correct (in the way constituting the naturalistic basis of norms). Alternatively, suppose that some form of real normativity supervened on the naturalistic stuff of norms, and that this supervenience was itself naturalistically explicable. Then the explanatory naturalist could happily conclude that such normativity was a proper explanandum for the social sciences. The naturalist again could embrace the normativity as explananda thesis and the normative explananda thesis. Finally, the idea that some form of normativity supervenes on the natural, but does so in a naturalistically inexplicable way, would be a problem for explanatory naturalism. As this shows, depending on what views of meta-normativity one supposes, explanatory naturalism might be compatible or even congenial to the normative explananda and normativity as explananda theses.

However these four meta-normative alternatives also vary dramatically in their plausibility, and I will only pursue the more plausible alternatives here. Insofar as it requires normativity to be identified with some finite set of natural features (some finite disjunction of finite conjunctions of natural features) reductive normative realism is not really plausible, and will not be pursued further.[7]

To my mind, supervenient normative realism that envisions supervenient but not superdupervenient normative properties is also not plausible. However, in fairness to the explanatory normativist, I should (under protest) keep it under discussion. At the same time, I can enter my protest by explaining why I find this view untenable. Explanatory naturalism is best understood as rooted in the attempt to work out a naturalistic understanding of the world and humans' place in it. Naturalism is here understood as an empirically informed hypothesis. Since we have found at various levels of analysis that the properties important in the working of systems are explained by the underlying natural properties (ultimately properties at many levels have proved to depend on arrangements of the underlying physical properties), we have reason to generalize—thinking that such dependency relationships is very likely a general feature of the world. This general naturalistic understanding suggests more than mere supervenience of properties on more basic natural properties. After all, the dependency relationships—the specific supervenience relationships obtaining in classes of organized systems—are themselves features of the world. So, the presumption of naturalism is that these dependency relationships should themselves be explicable in terms of the naturalistic bases (including their histories, including selection processes). The reason for thinking that features of the world should supervene on natural properties is thus also a reason for thinking that the supervenience relationships should depend on natural properties, and thus be naturalistically explicable. Thus, the initially plausible explanatory naturalist possibilities are these:

Table 10.2 Initially plausible forms of explanatory naturalism

	Sweeping explanatory naturalism	Embracing explanatory naturalism
	Anti-realism about normativity	Real superdupervenient normativity
Normative explananda thesis	Reject	Accept
Normativity as explananda thesis	Reject	Accept
Normativity as explanans	Reject	Reject

Basic Naturalism—shared by both the above—rejects normativity as explanans.

While explanatory naturalism would seem to be open to just these two variants, many explanatory normativists would at least want to hold that the normative supervenes on the natural—as the vast majority of moral and normative realists seem to recognize the plausibility of the general idea that what is real supervenes on the natural. Thus, the explanatory normativist who insists that the naturalist cannot do what is required by the normative explananda and normativity as explananda theses would seem to call for a naturalistically *inexplicable* supervenience of normative properties on natural properties—for supervenience without superdupervenience. To represent the dialectic at this juncture, the three options can be listed in three columns below. Table 3 represents the apparent results for explanatory naturalists

Table 10.3 A space of alternative positions with respect to the normativity as explananda and the normative explananda theses

	Normative anti-realism	Normative realism with normative properties that SDV on the natural stuff of norms	Normative realism with normative properties that SV but not SDV on the natural stuff of norms
Explanatory naturalism	Wins by default	Apparently acceptable: as the natural properties can explain all.	Clear loser
Explanatory normativism	Non-starter	Apparently acceptable: as normativity and normative explananda are manageable (albeit naturalistically)	Clear winner

and normativists. The final column is here retained under general naturalist protest. Similarly, the anti-realist column would doubtless draw normativist objection.

Insofar as we are trying to sort out these matters with regard to the normativity supposed to arise out of sociological norms, an important question should be: how plausible is it that there is a normativity arising out of at least some sociological norms that is superdupervenient on flatly natural facts? If this is implausible, then both naturalists and normativists should look to their more radical opposing columns.

PURSUING A CENTRAL QUESTION

Do forms of real normativity superdupervene on just the naturalistic bases that constitute (at least some) sociological norms? Is there a richness to the "stuff" of some sociological norms that affords a naturalistic explanation of the real normativity with which they are supposed to be associated? If yes, then the middle way identified above seems correct. It would amount to a moderate naturalist result—one in which there is nothing (no explananda, no explanan) that is strictly missing from naturalistic social science. While this would be a broadly naturalistic result, it might perhaps satisfy some normativist sensibilities. It at least allows one to honor the normative explananda and normativity as explananda thesis. However, if no, then the choices are starker: either an explanatory naturalism alloyed with an anti-realism regarding normative properties, or normativism alloyed with an anti-reductionist normative realism that posits mysterious (inexplicable) normative properties.

The present section begins with a quick survey of the plausible richness of contents of the coordinated thinking involved in many sociological norms. This is to provide an understanding of what plausibly might be the richness of the material of these norms. One common thought is that coordinated thinking with such rich contents brings in its train real normativity. Such proposals are discussed in this section. In the final pages of this section, I argue that the forms of normativity associated with norms do not super-dupervene on the naturalistic stuff of norms. Rather, normative notions of rich rationality (for example) are found already deployed in the envisioned accounts of how normativity supposedly arises out of the stuff of sociological norms.

Naturalistically Respectable Materials

Social norms are matters of the coordinated thinking that some things are right, correct, or good. Here, I intend the phrase "thinking something is right" in a rather inclusive way. Thinking something is right or good is not limited to *believing* something is right or good—unless believing is understood more broadly than would be philosophically paradigmatic.[8] (There are norms for conversational distance, and discomfort when someone violates these norms, but this need not turn on having paradigmatic beliefs regarding conversational distance.)

The relevant thought or thinking can be understood as follows. Agents come to be coordinated in some of their standing evaluative stances, and these standing states make for a responsiveness to significant ranges of information (or putative information) that those same agents might come also to episodically possess. When agents having such standing evaluative states do come to have (contentfully related) episodically occurrent descriptive states, they then typically generate occurrent episodic evaluations (although these may be inarticulate and not fully conscious). In such cases, the agents typically undertake actions—and these actions are themselves more or less coordinated. In broad outlines, having such more or less coordinated standing evaluative stances or states is what constitutes the possession of norms among the group of agents. The coordinated actions that result constitute conformity to norms among the relevant folk. Learning in a social group—coming to participate in a social group or coming to form a social group—requires agents to come to have sets of similar and (nearly enough) coordinated understandings. These understandings characterize such things as actions, action-possibilities, and contextually appropriate actions or responses. Among the relevant descriptive understandings may be understandings to the effect that the members of the group are depending on each other in some joint project. Among the relevant evaluative stances may be evaluations of various understood harms or benefits, and sense for commitments or obligations that have been incurred.

Of course, the 'understandings' and 'senses for' alluded to here do not require strict veridicality—agents could have a sense for commitments among their group, even were the coordinated stances not to make for any real normative obligation. First, supposing normative realism, it would be possible that the agents are mutually committed to do something for which there could be no obligation. (Perhaps they have coordinated in their commitments to exterminating all members of their neighboring tribe to get their land.) Second, supposing normative anti-realism in the form of an error theory, all sensed obligations might be fictive (although doubtless commonly adaptive).

In the previous paragraphs I seek to be neutral between various more committal accounts of the kinds of cognitive states constituting the evaluative stances and descriptive understandings making for norms. Are the relevant evaluative stances just preferences, or are they *contentfully* more rich and normative? I suspect that richer understandings have empirical advantages. I think that naturalists can be satisfied with whatever is empirically revealed about the character of the relevant psychological processes and states.

To orient ourselves, we can begin with accounts of norms that are austere in the contents attributed to norm holders. The accounts provided by Bicchieri (2006) and Skyrms (2004) are relatively austere. Bicchieri's account of norms turns on agents having "knowledge that a certain behavioral rule exists" in a group (a descriptive understanding) and "conditional preferences to conform, provided enough others do" (a standing evaluative stance of a sort). Actual conformity to norms then turns on agents having certain further descriptive understandings that connect with their conditional preferences to trigger conformity. On this account, contents of the relevant standing evaluative stances are characterized austerely—as individual preference structures. When there is a social norm, sufficiently many agents in a population prefer conforming to the rule (rather than defecting), provided that significantly many others conform. Call this conspicuously austere approach the *preference-approach* to evaluative stances.

On a less austere approach, the standing evaluative stances might be thought of as involving *more richly normative content*. Perhaps the evaluative stances are thought of as representing classes of actions as ones that 'ought to be undertaken', or as 'good', or as 'owed' to the others. Perhaps some of the evaluative stances involve social or moral emotions. The evaluative stance might respond to classes of cases as fair or unfair, pure or impure, harmful or benign, respectful or disrespectful, or loyal or disloyal.

Such basic dimensions of evaluative response (suggested by Haidt 2012, chapter 6) might be explanatorily relevant in understanding sociological norms—such content might make for an explanatorily relevant facet of some of the evaluative states that constitute certain classes of sociological norms. If so, a full understanding of the explanatory resources available to one characterizing various sociological norms would require one to register such facets of *normative content* within the relevant evaluative stances of agents. Call this the *rich-content-approach* to evaluative stances.

I do think that it is empirically plausible that a fully adequate account of social norms will feature a host of social emotions and empathetic states and that an empirically adequate understanding of these facets of human social-cognitive life will likely require the social scientist to register the contentful richness in the thinking of relevant agents. Much of what goes on in connection with human norms is best understood only with the recognition of normatively rich social (and sometimes moral) sentiments. An empirically successful account of norms will not flat-footedly talk of 'preferences', but will register the more complex cognitive dynamic turning on richly contentful evaluative states.

I see no reason for the explanatory naturalist to be threatened by such normative content in the thought of those holding social norms. Richly thinking something is good or right is still a form of thinking it is good or right. And richly thinking something is good or right does not make it right. Again, that much is central to normativist thought, as reflected in Brandom (1994). Characterization of such evaluative stance-taking is to be counted as comfortably within the naturalist's resources.

There are several respects in which one might think that an account of at least some norms requires more than is provided in the relatively austere baseline account advanced by (Bicchieri 2006). Here are two:

> First, for certain norms at least, it may be important that folk have states with 'we-contents', rather than merely having individual preferences or desires.
> Second, it might sometimes be important that norm holders have contents with distinctly normative contents (contents about what one, or we, 'ought to do', and contents about 'commitments' made and thus 'obligations' had).

One might prefer that 'we' do such and such because 'we have committed to so doing'—and thus 'are obligated' to so doing. It might be that the cognitive dynamics of such thoughts about 'us' and 'oughts' are crucial.

To make the concerns vivid start with Bicchieri's austere materials:

> **Norms—Austere:** there is a norm when sufficient agents in an interacting population have individual conditional preferences for conforming

to some behavioral rule, where these conditional preferences are keyed to expectations regarding others' behaviors.

What follows are three proposals for registering certain aspects of content that may underlie certain of the preferences that are significant in norms. An explanatory naturalist could accommodate and welcome each of these.

Norms—Rich Normative Content: there is a norm when sufficient agents in an interacting population have standing evaluative stances to the effect that A-ing is 'good' or 'right', given that enough others in that population will so act.

Here, the normative content of the relevant evaluative states represents acts conforming to the norm as having normative statuses. But, notice that what is at issue here (what an account of norms is trying to capture) is the content of the evaluative stance-taking around which the norm-holding agents are largely coordinated. The content is the content of *their* thought. The account of norms need only report this stance-taking. It need not adopt the same stance.

The normative content in play among the agents may involve ideas about the making of commitments to certain courses of action, and about the implications of being so committed. Now, commonly, one thinks of commitments in connection with the idea of reciprocity. I commit to you, looking for a reciprocal coordinated commitment from you. We thus come to be coordinated in our commitments—*we* are committed. Further, in light of being jointly committed, one thinks, we become a *we who are committed*. It is thus plausible that some norms involve agents who are coordinated in thinking that involves 'we-contents'. One might then think of elaborating Bicchieri's formulations. Perhaps folk think that "enough of *us*" see the application of some behavioral rule. Perhaps folk prefer to conform if "sufficiently many of us" conform. Perhaps they prefer that "*we* abstain from littering," or that "*we* divide product fairly." And such preferences may reflect normative contents keyed to their understood commitments: They prefer to do what they have committed to doing, provided sufficient coordination. The general approach can readily accommodate we-contents and related normative contents.

To do justice to such thinking, one would need to restructure the account somewhat. In some cases, the standing evaluative stances by which individuals are coordinated is not best understood as independent from, and thus antecedent to, the agent's understanding of themselves as a part of a jointly committed we. To do justice to these ideas would call for something like this:

Norms—Rich Normative Content involving 'We'-Intentions and Commitments: There is a norm when

1. There is sufficient coordination in some folk's descriptive and evaluative stances to make them a 'we'—which obtains when

    i.   sufficient agents in an interacting population (descriptively and evaluatively) understand themselves jointly as a 'we,' and
    ii. these agents have standing evaluative states to the effect that A-ing is good or right, given that 'we' are committed to so acting.

2. These descriptive and evaluative stances occasion conformity to the understood commitments—at least provided the agents also anticipate enough conforming from the others comprising the 'we'.

My own sense is that some norms are best understood in such terms (an empirical matter). This poses no problem for explanatory naturalism.[9]

Instead of merely *preferring* that "we do such-and-such," provided "enough of us are on-board," it may sometimes be causally important that folk think that "we *ought* to so act" provided "enough of us are (or have) so *committed*" and provided "enough of us will keep our commitments." But, again, there is a clear difference between so thinking and it being that they ought so to act. (A read of Browning 1992 should make this apparent.) Crucially, some folk's thinking in these ways is enough to explain how they act, regardless of the correctness of their putative oughts.

Thus, I allow that there are open empirical issues having to do with how to most adequately understand various forms of norms—these include questions about why exactly we ultimately cooperate to the extent that we do (for example, J. Henrich and Boyd 2001; J. Henrich *et al.* 2004; N. Henrich and Henrich 2007; Tomasello 2009), and what specifically is learned in becoming at home in a group or culture (for example, Bicchieri and Chavez 2010; Turner 1994, 2002). And, these matters of how to best describe the content of folk's cognitive states must be sorted out while also sorting out an account of the cognitive dynamics of human cognition—a matter of descriptive psychology. But, such open questions pose no threat to naturalism in the social sciences. Rather, they are of a piece with naturalism.

Regarding the Suggestion That Real Normative Properties at Least Supervene on Some Sociological Norms—It Is False.

Focus now on the suggestion that there is a form of normativity arising out of norms. Both the explanatory normativists and those explanatory naturalists who are also realists regarding normativity think that the relevant 'oughts' supervene on the coordinated thinking of some set of folk. But, as provisionally argued in section 2, the broadly naturalist reasons for thinking that normativity should supervene on the natural also indicate that this dependency relation should itself be naturalistically explicable—that normativity should be superdupervenient. There should be an explanation, appealing only to natural facts or states, and natural processes, of how it is that the natural supervenience bases constitute the relevant normative properties. This constraint, which I take from general metaphysical naturalism, already gives explanatory naturalism an apparent advantage. If the normative properties superdupervened on the natural bases, then they can be explained naturalistically, and we get a normativity-explaining form of explanatory naturalism. If the putative normative properties do not superdupervene on naturalistically respectable properties, there are no such properties—and normativity eliminating explanatory naturalism wins. Now, it will be instructive to look at several accounts of how a form of real normativity is supposed to arise out of sociological norms. This will show that the normativity envisioned does not superdupervene on the naturalistic base alone. Instead, antecedent forms of normativity must be supposed to get the norm-engendered normativity that is envisioned.

Gilbert (1989) focuses on what she calls conventions. These are clearly related to, but somewhat broader than what Lewis (1969) counts as conventions. Conventions are said to arise with a kind of coordinated thinking that she terms a "joint acceptance" of some "rule" as a "simple fiat" (Gilbert 1989, 373, see also 368–77). The collectivity constituting joint acceptance is said to present the members of the collective with a principle that has real normative force for them.

> [T]he 'ought' is understood to be based on the fact that together they jointly accept the principle, 'I ought to conform, insofar as I am one of us*, because it is our* principle'.
>
> (Gilbert 1989, 377)

Gilbert insists, "Conventions generate reasons for acting by their own force, so to speak, without appeal to considerations of intrinsic value" (Gilbert 1989, 394). Insofar as we accepted some rule or principle, we are rationally committed thereby to conforming in the indicated contexts" (Gilbert 1989, 394).

Thus, as understood by Gilbert, the reason and normative force, the ought, arises out of the intentional act of acceptance. Note, for this is crucial: The real normativity envisioned here seems to be a version of the normativity of rationality—it is a matter of what is entailed by what one is already committed to.

Michael Bratman develops a related view of joint action (Bratman 1999, see particularly, chapters 6 and 7). On his approach, the normativity posited for joint intentions provides a model for thinking about the normativity of sociological norms. On Bratman's account, this normativity is rooted in his systematic views on individual agency and planning (Bratman 1999, particularly chapters 2–4). Further, in an interesting wrinkle, the agency associated with planning does seem to be associated with moral normativity (1999, 6–7) as well as with rational normativity.

I cannot here develop the details of Gilbert's and Bratman's rich accounts, and must focus on general ideas. Out of this literature, one can distill four very general ideas about how the kinds of coordinated thinking that makes for norms might generate or give rise to real normativity of a sort that the normativist needs.

1. Internal/rational normativity: normativity that is a matter of what *rationally follows* from the content of the attitudes (the descriptive and evaluative stances) that constitute the coordinated thinking of the relevant folk. The sociological norm—the coordinated thinking—is thought of as giving folk a normative reason to do what rationally follows from their commitments. But this normativity arises only against a background of an antecedent form of normativity: rationality.
2. Practical rational normativity: a matter of benefits attained, or costs incurred, by agents who are coordinated, or who fail to be coordinated. Game theory provides an accounting of these costs and benefits. Here, the norm would not so much constitute the normativity as it would afford a coordinated way of attaining the goods extrinsic to the norm. In some cases, these goods will be public goods of some sort.
3. External moral normativity: The norm might afford a way of attaining moral goods or bads that are not strictly speaking constituted by the norm. For example, perhaps one should conform to a given norm because it affords a way of providing moral goods (for a utilitarian, for example, these might be matters of enhanced welfare or happiness), or of avoiding moral bads (such as highly unequal distributions, perhaps).
4. Internal moral normativity: The norm might constitute moral entitlements and responsibilities analogous to those arising out of promises.

Reflecting on this list, a very important point should immediately occur to the reader: In none of these suggested ways would the normative property that is supposedly associated with the sociological norm really supervene just on the naturalistically respectable bases of that norm. In each case, some normative matter seems presupposed as an aspect or component of the basis, and seems needed to provide the normative umph. In the first two pictures obviously a normative notion of rationality is deployed. The third and fourth suggested pictures each also invoke an additional normative notion that is not in the naturalistic base of the sociological norm (not in the thinking that constitutes the norm).

Let me then emphasize the central point: On the accounts of the normative force of norms that seem to be suggested in the normativist literature, one does not get the normativity there imagined without some form of root normativity in the background. I am inclined to say that this supposed normative background amounts to a component of their imagined supervenience base for the normativity they associate with norms. They hold that the normative does not supervene merely on the natural facts. One might also say that all the suggested accounts presuppose some antecedent form of normativity.

Because there is this common feature in normativists' account of the normativity of norms, it will be straightforward to generalize the argument to be provided in the next section. However, before moving to that argument, which focuses on the normativity as explanans thesis, we can draw out an implication regarding what flavors of either explanatory naturalism or normativism now look promising.

I have argued that normative properties that do not at least explicably supervene on a naturalistically kosher basis would make for trouble for an explanatory naturalist. For one thing, they accord poorly with a general naturalistic understanding of the natural world. They might be said to be supervenient, but the supervenience seems mysterious. Insofar as explanatory naturalists are naturalists, they should conclude that there are no such mysterious *sui generis* properties. I thus concluded the naturalist needs to embrace either explicable supervenient normative realism (superdupervenient realism) or normative anti-realism. I also suggested that explanatory normativism required some sort of metaphysical normative realism. Now we have observed that one thing seems common regarding suggested ways in which normativity might supposedly arise out of norms—they each seem to require some antecedent normativity that combines with the naturalistically respectable bases of sociological norms in order to generate norm-associated normativity. Until such background normativity is itself shown to be superdupervenient, it is reasonable to strongly suspect that the normativity purported to be associated with sociological norms would not superdupervene on the naturalistic basis provided by sociological norms. For the explanatory naturalist, the implications are pretty straightforward: The explanatory naturalist ought to be highly skeptical about normative properties, and should likely be a normative anti-realist.

What of the explanatory normativist? The normativist is committed to there being normative properties that neither reduce to nor superdupervene on these purely natural bases. As noted, this means that normativism cannot fit comfortably within a broadly naturalistic picture of the world. Since I think that we have good reason to hold such a picture, we already have good reason to embrace explanatory naturalism and normative anti-realism (see Table 10.4).

But, suppose that we hold off on drawing this inference. Suppose that we think that a form of normativity arises from social norms by way of some background normativity—such as rational normativity. The point of the next section is to argue that no such form of normativity will be explanatory—thus supporting the component of explanatory naturalism that I take to be shared across its varying versions: opposing the normative explanans thesis.

Table 10.4 A plausible forced choice: Sweeping Explanatory Naturalism or some form of Normativism with naturalistically mysterious normative properties.

	Normative anti-realism	~~Normative Realism with normative properties that SDV on the natural stuff of norms~~	Normative realism with normative properties that SV but not SDV on the natural stuff of norms
Explanatory naturalism	Wins by default	~~Apparently acceptable: as the natural properties can explain all.~~	Clear loser
Explanatory normativism	Non-starter	~~Apparently acceptable: as normativity and normative explananda are manageable (albeit naturalistically)~~	Clear winner

WHY NORMS PLUS THE NORMATIVE RATIONALITY DOES NOT HELP THE NORMATIVIST—RATIONALITY IS NOT EXPLANATORY—AND WHY THIS GENERALIZES TO OTHER SUPPOSED BACKGROUND NORMATIVITIES.

Suppose that there is a kind of internal rational normativity associated with norms—one along the lines suggested by Gilbert and by Bratman. Of course, *in the norm-holders there would be a range of actual cognitive processes that are like what would be so rationally prescribed in some ways, and that are unlike it in other ways.* One should wonder just what is the *explanatory role* of the kind of reasons and rationality that these writers posit—*what can reasons and rationality explain that the actual non-normative processes and states that constitute sociological norms cannot explain?* Recall that on Gilbert's account, we have a reason to so act in the relevant contexts because we have jointly accepted a principle that directs us to do so. On Bratman's account, I have a reason to so act insofar as we have a reason to so act, and we have a reason to so act because so acting coheres with extant information and with the planning and joint intention that rationally structures our practical reasoning. Suppose that, as per Gilbert, I am a party to this joint acceptance of some principle. The force of this reason/principle, this ought, is that it follows from my or our antecedent attitudes, so I have these rational reasons. Similarly, for Bratman, the ought is a matter of what rationally follows from the joint intentions of which I am a party. Thus, ultimately, what is envisioned in Gilbert and Bratman is some version of the ought of rationality. The normativist, as fan of the normativity as explanans thesis, then must claim that this ought—the ought of rationality—contributes to explanations that cannot be provided merely in terms of coordinated evaluative and descriptive attitudes had by agents. They must hold that something being rational (in light of commitments) is distinct from merely being thought so rational, and that there are phenomena—thoughts and actions—that *cannot be explained by the folk's* coordinated *thinking* or *judging* things to be rational (or normatively correct), but *can be explained by those things being rational* (or normatively correct).

We thus arrive at a recurrent issue in the philosophy of the social sciences: what is the explanatory role of rationality? The essential points have been made elsewhere (Henderson 1991, 1993, 2002, 2005, 2010), and I will gloss them here.

First, explanation in the sense of concern here has to do with understanding patterns of counterfactual dependency. Explanatory generalizations or principles must then characterize patterns of counterfactual dependency. For example, a characterization of the emission/absorption spectra of elements allows us to understand how the light emitted from luminous bodies depends on their chemical composition. We can appreciate that were the body to contain different elements (lacking some it contains, or having some it does not contain), it would emit light in systematically different wavelengths than it does. The explanatory generalization characterizes the features on which dependencies turn, and features are explanatory only if they feature in such explanatory generalizations.[10]

Second, patterns of counterfactual dependency in what is thought and done depend on the character of the processes within the relevant cognitive system. The smell of a female baboon in estrus provokes excitement in male baboons, and not in humans (I hope). One explains the excitement of certain baboons by mentioning the olfactory presence of female baboons in estrus—had such a scent not have been around, then no such excitement would have obtained in an episode (given other features of the environment are held constant).

In cases involving norms, the relevant cognitive systems are primarily us humans. So, characterization of our actual psychological dynamic would provide the fitting explanatory generalizations.[11] There seem to be certain rudimentary human cognitive processes, and generalizations characterizing these are relevant. But much of human cognition has been shaped by learning or training. The learning or training gives rise of modified cognitive processes in sets of humans, and to varying patterns of counterfactual dependencies. The characterization of these shaped processes, and the characteristics of states to which they are systematically responsive, are explanatory.

Third, one can see the learning of, or adoption of, norms as cases in which the cognitive processes of a set of humans come to be shaped in coordinating ways. The patterns of counterfactual dependencies then obtaining among that folk will depend on the character of the folk's shaped cognitive processes, including their more or less coordinated standing evaluative stances. Characterizations of these are explanatory generalizations concerning a specific range of folk. Characterizations of sociological norms would be a case of such explanation.

Fourth, there is always some divergence between the actual cognitive dynamic of any actual human or set of humans and what one might term the ideal cognitive dynamic. Let us term this ideal cognitive dynamic *rationality*. This is the normativity to which normativists now seem to appeal. There are, admittedly, various ways in which one might think of this ideal cognitive dynamic—this rationality—depending on just how much accommodation one makes for the in-principle limitations of the human species. But, however one settles such matters in detail, the rational pattern of thinking is supposedly different from the actual cognitive dynamic of the relevant norm-possessing folk or individuals, at least marginally (see Henderson 2010 for some discussion of details).

Fifth, the patterns of counterfactual dependency obtaining in a given case will then depend on the character of the shaped cognitive processes in the relevant set of humans. In the case in which the folk have some norm, they have more or less coordinated ways of thinking. And, as we have just noted, the cognitive processes of these folk will be marginally different from what is rational. Admittedly these cognitive processes commonly approximate what is rational to some degree. But, *the patterns of counterfactual dependency obtaining in the given case depend on the actual cognitive processes in play, not on what would be rational.* This is no less true when the cognitive processes in the instance make for cognitive transitions that are, in that particular case and situation, rational. The *pattern* of counterfactual dependencies reflects the facts about the actual cognitive processes, and diverges from full normative rationality.

Thus the actual, factual, character of the agents' cognitive processes explains what they think. It explains the descriptive and evaluative stances that they take as things unfold in the case. This explains what they do. (This seems no less true of their joint thinking and acting than it is of their individual thinking and acting.) This should be emphasized: Facts about the actual cognitive processes in play in agents (and in groups)—facts about the putative information to which these processes are sensitive, the descriptive character of the transitions that they yield, and the setting in which they are deployed—these are the facts that explain what is thought and done. There seems to be nothing left over for rationality as real normativity to explain. Even in those cases in which the transitions made by the agents are rational, the patterns of counterfactual dependencies between these states turns on the factual character of the cognitive processes, and these features (including the features of the cognitive states to which they are sensitive) leave nothing for rationality to explain. The descriptive characteristics of cognitive processes 'screens off' normative characteristics (if any) from explanatory relevance.

One might object that people are thinking about what is rational, or fitting, in light of their situations as they understand them. Exactly so. And, insofar as this is so, and that this thinking (broadly understood) makes a difference to the course of their thinking and acting, it is their understandings of what would be correct (thinking right rather than being right) that is explanatory. Further, what would seem explanatory would be how they think about what is right, rather than what is right or correct, that is explanatory.

The above serves as a direct response to the suggestion that there might be an explanatory role for the normative force of norms—when that is understood in terms of the rationality that should normatively govern, given the factual bases of the relevant sociological norms. The point applies equally, whatever form of ideal normative rationality is entertained—epistemic or practical. In fact, it applies with complete generality to whatever account of the normative force of norms one adopts as long as that account involves a form of normativity to which people's cognitive processes always imperfectly correspond. As long as folk are less than morally, or rationally, or normatively, perfect in their capacities, the problem for normativism remains: The explanatory role of the character of actual cognitive processes and the features to which they are sensitive, screens off normative features as explanatorily irrelevant. The counterfactual dependencies, and the explanation, are wedded to the character of the cognitive processes and states, and these would be at best roughly correlated to what is normatively correct.[12]

NOTES

1 Here I am continuing to use "norm qua normative" in the way I consistently have (Henderson 1991, 4)—thus, in the way I use it in the passages to which Risjord (this volume) responds. Since I believe that what Risjord proposes cannot not constitute real normativity, and that the social scientist need not embrace the purported normativity in explaining, I believe that he is mistaken in thinking that there is an explanatory role for norms-*qua*-normative. As I understand Risjord, he is proposing some form of expressivist account of the relevant normativity, and I would understand expressivism as a gentle deflationary account that constitutes a form of anti-realism about the normative (compare Gibbard's 1990, 2003). My disagreement with Risjord is thus at the level of meta-ethics—as he apparently believes that expressivism can amount to a kind of realism about normativity.

This should be emphasized here. Contrary to Risjord's understanding of my position, I do not hold that "all the explanatory work of the foregoing account is being done by the lower-level attunements, affordances, and meta-cognitions, not by the social norm." Rather, I hold that social norms, insofar as they super-dupervened on coordinated understandings in some group—including normative stance-takings—can explain what is done. What is argued is that any imagined real normativity does not superdupervene on the factual matters constitutive of social norms—and is thus screened off from being explanatory. It is the mundane factual matters making for social norms that is explanatory, and there remains nothing for real normativity—oughtness—to explain.

2 Of course, it is itself a subject of explanatory attention, as when one seeks to understand the relevant evaluative thinking in terms of some combination of genetic and cultural history. But, here, the point iterates, as such explanations themselves appeal to descriptive matters.

3 Okrent and Rouse (both in this volume) seem clearly to embrace all three—and both think that the relevant explananda and explanans normativity is common to both biological and sociological systems. Stueber (this volume) seems to embrace the normative explananda and normativity as explananda theses—envisioning some manner of transcendental account of the normative status arising out of the first-person perspective of folk with norms, and thinking that normativity is itself explicable. Risjord is a difficult case to classify, as the normativity that he would place in the role of explananda and explanans is of an expressivist sort. However, insofar as he thinks of this expressivist normativity as real normativity, he seems to embrace normative explananda and normative explanans. Turner and Roth each reject all three theses, and I ultimately would do so as well.

4 Tomasello gives us a formulation that is delightfully subject to either a naturalist or a normativist reading: "The upshot is that human beings live not only in the physical and social worlds of other apes, but also in an institutional cultural world of their own making, a world that is populated with all kinds of deontologically powerful entities" (Tomasello 2009, 59). Reflection on Tomasello's own explanatory practice suggests that his purposes would be served by a scrupulously naturalist reading.

5 Again, I am here concerned with how normative properties are thought to relate to natural properties. Thus, the reductivism of concern here holds that normative properties reduce to natural properties. There is a very different issue, call it content reductionism, that also is discussed as a conflict of reductionism versus anti-reductionism. The content reductionist holds that norms can be understood in terms of cognitive states none of which have normative content—perhaps they are just preference structures, or desires. Content reductionism is not my concern at this juncture. Ultimately, I am inclined to believe that content reductionism is false (see also Brennan, Eriksson, Goodin, and Southwood 2013).

6 He formulates the reduction simply: "The obligatory is that which we regard as obligatory" (Prinz 2007, 1). However, Prinz also allows that one can have an obligation to act in some way—while it is also the case that one ought not so act. It is not clear that the supposedly real normative property here—the ought—is strictly reducible to naturalistic states of affairs.

7 Rouse's and Okrent's positions are difficult to situate within the positions discussed here—for they seem to think that the natural world is suffused with normativity somehow arising out of selection processes. The most straightforward reading is that they would say that normativity is naturalistically reducible because the natural is always already normative (see also Rouse 2007). Social normativity then would superdupervene on the naturalistic base—because normativity is always already a part of that basis, because 'functions' are thought to be a part of the natural world. I believe this represents a deeply mistaken understanding of natural selection and of talk of functions in biology. In sections 3 and 4, I will explain why I believe that the normative does not superdupervene on the natural (and thus does not supervene either). My discussion will proceed on the common understanding that there are not really purposes in nature.

8 The sensitivity that agents acquire for such matters might be partially realized by way of what Horgan and Tienson (1996) term *morphological* content, see also Henderson and Horgan (2011).

9 I have written of 'we-intentions' as a matter of the content of the intentions of individual agents constituting a group. I have not written of them as the intentions had by a group. I doubt that intending is really something done by groups, rather than by individuals within a group. However, were there group intentions, the arguments given in this paper would apply mutatis mutandis.

10 Such a requirement should be understood as allowing for generalizations of limited scope or 'invariance'; see (Woodward 2000).

11 I have in mind work such as (J. P. Henrich 2004; N. Henrich and Henrich 2007; Tomasello 2009). Of course work comparing humans with their near primate relatives may be probative, such as that by Tomasello and his collaborators, or (Waal, Macedo, Ober, and Wright 2006)

12 I thank Joseph Mendola, Mark van Roojen, Jaakko Kuorikoski, Mark Risjord, Paul Roth, Karsten Stueber, Mark Timmons, and Stephen Turner for helpful comments. Notable also were participants at the 2013 European Network for the Philosophy of the Social Sciences discussion at the University of Stockholm.

REFERENCES

Bicchieri, Cristina. 2006. *The Grammar of Society: The Nature and Dynamics of Social Norms*. New York: Cambridge University Press.
Bicchieri, Cristina and Chavez, Alex. 2010. Behaving as Expected: Public Information and Fairness Norms. *Journal of Behavioral Decision Making* 23(2): 161–178.
Blackburn, Simon W. 1993. *Essays in Quasi-Realism*. New York: Oxford Univeristy Press.
Boyd, Robert and Peter Richerson. 1985. *Culture and the Evolutionary Process*. Chicago, IL: University of Chicago Press.
Brandom, Robert. 1994. *Making It Explicit: Reasoning, Representing, and Discursive Commitment*. Cambridge, MA: Harvard University Press.
Bratman, Michael. 1999. *Faces of Intention: Selected Essays on Intention and Agency*. Cambridge: Cambridge University Press.
Brennan, Geoffrey, Lina Eriksson, Robert Goodin and Nicholas Southwood. 2013. *Explaining Norms*. Oxford: Oxford University Press.
Browning, Christopher R. 1992. *Ordinary Men : Reserve Police Battalion 101 and the Final Solution in Poland*. New York: HarperCollins.
Cummins, Robert. 1975. Functional Analysis. *Journal of Philosophy* 72: 741–765.
———. (1983). *The Nature of Psychological Explanation*. Cambridge, MA: MIT Press.
Gibbard, Allan. 1990. *Wise Choices, Apt Feelings : A Theory of Normative Judgment*. Cambridge, MA: Harvard University Press.
———. 2003. *Thinking How to Live*. Cambridge, MA: Harvard University Press.
Gibbard, Allan and Barry Stroud. 2008. *Reconciling Our Aims: In Search of Bases for Ethics*. Oxford: Oxford University Press.
Gilbert, Margaret. 1989. *On Social Facts*. London: Routledge.
———. 2000. *Sociality and Responsibility: New Essays in Plural Subject Theory*. Lanham, MD: Rowman and Littlefield Publishers.
Haidt, Jonathan. 2012. *The Righteous Mind: Why Good People Are Divided by Politics and Religion*. New York: Pantheon Books.
Henderson, David. 1987. The Principle of Charity and the Problem of Irrationality. *Synthese: An International Journal for Epistemology, Methodology and Philosophy of Science* 73: 225–252.
———. 1991. Rationalizing Explanation, Normative Principles, and Descriptive Generalizations. *Behavior and Philosophy* 19(1): 1–20.

———. 1993. *Interpretation and Explanation in the Human Sciences.* Albany: State University of New York Press.

———. 2002. Norms, Normative Principles, and Explanation: On Not Getting Is from Ought. *Philosophy of the Social Sciences* 32(3): 329–364.

———. 2005. Norms, Invariance, and Explanatory Relevance. *Philosophy of the Social Sciences* 35(3): 324–338.

———. 2010. Explanation and Rationality Naturalized. *Philosophy of the Social Sciences* 40(1): 30–58.

Henderson, David and Terence Horgan. 2011. *The Epistemological Spectrum: At the Interface of Cognitive Science and Conceptual Analysis.* Oxford: Oxford University Press.

Henrich, Joseph. 2004. *Foundations of Human Sociality: Economic Experiments and Ethnographic Evidence from Fifteen Small-Scale Societies.* Oxford: Oxford University Press.

Henrich, Joseph and Richard Boyd. 2001. Why People Punish Defectors: Weak Conformist Transmission Can Stabilize Costly Enforcement of Norms in Cooperative Dilemmas. *Journal of Theoretical Biology* 208: 79–89.

Henrich, Joseph, Richard Boyd, S. Bowles, C. Camerer, E. Fehr and H. Gintis (eds.) 2004. *Foundations of Human Sociality: Economic Experiments and Ethographic Evidence from Fifteen Small-Scale Societies.* Oxford: Oxford University Press.

Henrich, Natalie and Joseph Henrich. 2007. *Why Humans Cooperate: A Cultural and Evolutionary Explanation.* Oxford; New York: Oxford University Press.

Horgan, Terence. 1993. From Supervenience to Superdupervenience: Meeting the Demands of a Material World. *Mind: A Quarterly Review of Philosophy* 102(408): 555–586.

Horgan, Terrence and John Tienson. 1996. *Connectionism and the Philosophy of Psychology.* Cambridge, MA: MIT Press.

Joyce, Richard. 2006. *The Evolution of Morality.* Cambridge, MA: MIT Press.

Lewis, David K. 1969. *Convention: A Philosophical Study.* Cambridge, MA: Harvard University Press.

Prinz, Jesse J. 2007. *The Emotional Construction of Morals.* Oxford: Oxford University Press.

Rouse, Joseph. 2006. Practice Theory. In *Philosophy of Anthropology and Sociology*, edited by S. Turner and M. Risjord, 499–540. Amsterdam: Elsevier.

———. 2007. Social Practices and Normativity. *Philosophy of the Social Sciences* 37(1): 46–56.

Skyrms, Brian. 2004. *The Stag Hunt and the Evolution of Social Structure.* Cambridge, UK: Cambridge University Press.

Tomasello, Michael. 2009. *Why We Cooperate.* Cambridge, MA: MIT Press.

Turner, Stephen P. 1994. *The Social Theory of Practices : Tradition, Tacit Knowledge, and Presuppositions.* Chicago: University of Chicago Press.

———. 2002. *Brains/Practices/Relativism: Social Theory after Cognitive Science.* Chicago: University of Chicago Press.

Waal, F. B. M. de, Stephen Macedo, Josiah Ober and Robert Wright. 2006. *Primates and Philosophers: How Morality Evolved.* Princeton, NJ: Princeton University Press.

Woodward, James. 2000. Explanation and Invariance in the Special Sciences. *British Journal for the Philosophy of Science* 51(2): 197–254.

11 Ecological Attunement and the Normativity of Practice

Mark Risjord

INTRODUCTION: SOCIAL SCIENCE AND DISENCHANTMENT

The social sciences have been largely responsible for shifting our view of ourselves toward a naturalistic self-understanding. Where we once imagined kingships as established by divine right, morality as flowing from human nature, or choice as arising from free will, we (or some of us, anyway) now see social processes and psychological mechanisms. This change is viewed with alarm in many quarters, and normativity has become a rallying point. As Stephen Turner argues in *Explaining the Normative* (2010), many philosophical views take normativity to be the humanistic hard core that can never be penetrated by scientific inquiry. Normativity, it is argued, always slips past scientific accounts of society, language, or intentionality. Either there is something left unaccounted for, or the social scientist illicitly sneaks normativity in by the back door. The strongest views defend a kind of value objectivism, a gap between "is" and "ought" that prevents any description from capturing the phenomenon of normativity. Turner argues effectively that these arguments fail. Humans do use the language of norms, but it is not immune to naturalistic explanation.

The social sciences are rife with talk of social norms, laws, values, contracts, and constitutions. According to Turner, these are not to be understood as genuine "oughts," commitments that somehow bind us to normative demands. As David Henderson once expressed the point, social scientific explanations do not appeal to norms "qua normative" (Henderson 2002); it is not through their correctness, or through some kind of "normative force" that norms explain. Only representations of rules, desires for a coordinated outcome, or threats of sanction are explanatory. Turner treats all talk of normativity in terms of an error theory. Appeal to norms is "good bad theory": Social norms are good for getting along, assigning responsibility, justifying actions, and so on, but norms constitute bad theory if they are treated as true of some special, normative realm.

While sympathetic to the naturalism Turner and Henderson champion, my lingering worry is that such a thoroughgoing disenchantment is bad for the social sciences. If all appeal to social norms is replaced with appeal to representations of norms, the explanatory power of the social sciences seems reduced. Does appeal to local social normativity (tacit norms, rules, laws, etc.) in the explanation of either patterns of behavior or individual action have explanatory value different from appeal to representations or regularities of behavior?

Asking about the explanatory value of norms is subject to two immediate challenges. First, normativity is typically contrasted with causality, and a standard idea in the philosophy of science is that all explanation is causal. So how could appeal to norms "*qua* normative" be explanatory? This essay will assume the adequacy of the erotetic model of explanation. I have elsewhere shown how that model can be elaborated so as to make norms and rules relevant answers to why-questions (Risjord 2000, 2005). Whether or not appeal to norms is a causal explanation is therefore not a threshold question for our inquiry. Nonetheless, the character of norms and their position within a causal picture of the world is a crucial part of the problem. Does an argument for the explanatory value of norms open the door that Turner worked so hard to nail shut? In response to this second challenge, this essay will make an assumption shared by many practice theorists in the social sciences. Social norms are not *objective* in the sense that they are not an ontologically distinct structure that stands behind practice or action. They are not a special kind of fact outside of the causal realm. Whatever the normativity of practice amounts to, it must be manifest within the scope of human ecology. At the same time, this essay will not assume that regularities of behavior alone confer normativity. Practices are regularities, but it is not in virtue of instantiating or reproducing a regularity that an action is appropriate, obligatory, permissible, etc. Some have taken this to be an anti-naturalistic point, but it will not be so taken here. Using the language of *Making it Explicit* (1994), the challenge is to split the difference between regulism and regularism. Unlike Brandom, however, I want to do so in a thoroughly naturalistic way that both assimilates and supports relevant (social) scientific knowledge.

NORMS AS THE GRAMMAR OF SOCIETY

Cristina Bicchieri's *Grammar of Society* (2006) is interesting for its attempt to provide an account of social norms that gives them explanatory power. The centerpiece of Bicchieri's account is a taxonomy of norms and a characterization of necessary and sufficient conditions for each sort of norm to exist. What she calls "social norms" get the most thorough treatment, and they are the most relevant to the questions of this essay. The conditions for a social norm to exist are formulated in this way (Bicchieri 2006, 11):

> Let *R* be a behavioral rule for situations of type *S*, where *S* can be represented as a mixed-motive game. We say that *R* is a social norm in a

population *P* if there exists a sufficiently large subset $P_{cf} \subseteq P$ such that, for each individual $i \in P_{cf}$:

Contingency: i knows that a rule *R* exists and applies to situations of type *S;*

Conditional preference: i prefers to conform to *R* in situations of type *S* on the condition that:

> (a) *Empirical expectations: i* believes that a sufficiently large sub-set of *P* conforms to *R* in situations of type *S;*
> and either
> (b) *Normative expectations: i* believes that a sufficiently large sub-set of *P* expects *i* to conform to *R* in situations of type *S;*
> or
>> (b') *Normative expectations with sanctions: i* believes that a sufficiently large subset of *P* expects *i* to conform to *R* in situations of type *S*, prefers *i* to conform, and may sanction behavior.

A behavioral rule, for Bicchieri, is a strategy. If the situation can be represented as a prisoner's dilemma, for example, one possible behavior rule would simply say "Cooperate." The agent is supposed to have a preference to conform to the rule *if* the empirical expectations and normative expectations are met. When the individual has the beliefs described as empirical and normative expectations, the social norm is said to be "activated" for that agent. When the norm is activated, the agent has a preference to conform to the rule. Bicchieri rigorously characterizes this preference by defining a utility function where the payoffs of the original game determine a new set of payoffs. This means that when the behavioral rule is activated, the agent's utility function changes. Since a game-theoretic situation is partly defined by the payoffs, changing the utility function changes the game. When activated, then, social norms turn mixed-motive games into games with dominant cooperative strategies. For example, the prisoner's dilemma is a paradigmatic mixed-motive game: The players have incentives not to cooperate, yet there are also benefits to cooperation. On a standard utility function, the rational strategy for each player in a prisoner's dilemma is to defect (not cooperate). If the behavioral rule "Cooperate" is activated for the players, their utility functions change. The game payoffs for the players change, thereby making cooperation the rational choice.

Bicchieri's taxonomy divides norms into "social norms," "descriptive norms," and "conventions." Two differentia govern the taxonomy: the type of strategic situation and the character of the preferences. As the definition above makes clear, social norms exist only in situations that "can be represented as mixed-motive games." Descriptive norms apply to coordination games, where agents are faced with multiple equilibria. The mere empirical expectation that others will conform to a rule like "drive on the right" is sufficient to conditionally motivate agents to follow the rule. For descriptive norms, then, the agents have preferences that are conditional only upon the empirical expectation, not on the additional normative expectations of a social norm. Conventions are supposed to be even weaker, applying to coordination games "without nonstrict Nash equilibria" (Bicchieri 2006, 38) and not involving conditional preferences at all. Conventions exist when there is a simple expectation that others will conform to the rule.

Social scientists and philosophers have long looked to game theory for accounts of social norms. On the classic versions of these views, for example, Lewis's account of convention, the norm is explained as an equilibrium solution to a strategic problem. In a view like Lewis's, the norm or convention does not contribute to the explanation of the individual action. The individual is merely acting rationally in the light of his/her beliefs and preferences, and the norm describes the resulting pattern of behavior. Bicchieri makes a significant departure from these views by adding a layer of cognitive psychology, and through this psychological account the social norm becomes partly explanatory of behavior. She adopts the language of "scripts" and "schemata" from cognitive psychology. When a person enters a social situation, on this view, s/he brings to it a body of anticipations about how others will behave and what others expect. The social norms Bicchieri defines are supposed to be "embedded" into these schemata. Much of the book is devoted to explaining the discrepancy between agents' actual behavior and the game-theoretic predictions of behavior by appealing to the psychological activation of behavioral rules.

Bicchieri's account of social norms seems to provide a direct answer to the main question of this essay. The existence of a social norm explains both patterns of behavior and individual actions, and it does so in a way that is distinct from straightforward appeals to the agents' beliefs, desires, or fears of sanction. Moreover, Bicchieri's explanation fits Turner's pattern for explaining normativity. Appeals to normative force (e.g., that the agents cooperate because the rule says they ought to cooperate) are replaced by something else. In this case, the existence of a behavioral rule is explicated in terms of the agents' representation of rules as part of action schemata and their beliefs and expectations about others. The rule does its work, not through the force of some kind of supernatural normativity, but through the transformation of the agents' utility functions.

REALISM AND RATIONAL CHOICE

Its novelty and power notwithstanding, three issues cast doubt on the adequacy of Bicchieri's account of social normativity. The first issue is that, in spite of the broad promise of the title, only the norms of fairness and equity get discussed in *The Grammar of Society*. Can Bicchieri's account be extended to a broader range of relevant phenomena? Second, what makes

Bicchieri's norms *normative?* This is the normativist worry about all social scientific accounts: Normativity is never explained, it is either elided or presupposed. Finally, there is a tension between realism and instrumentalism in Bicchieri's account. At some points, she explicitly says that the account is a rational reconstruction (Bicchieri 2006, 3, 48), yet at other points realistic explanatory posits appear to be playing crucial roles. As we will see, these three issues are intimately related.

Social scientific accounts appeal to a wide range of normative phenomena: rules of ritual purity and religious practice, norms of appropriate role behavior, institutional rules and regulations, and so on. It is arguable that Bicchieri's account could only apply to norms of cooperation and could not be applied more broadly. The taxonomy of social norms, descriptive norms, and conventions depends, in part, on the way in which the situation can be game-theoretically represented (as mixed motive, coordination, with or without strict Nash equilibria). The reliance on a game-theoretic representation restricts Bicchieri's norms to strategic interactions. It is not at all obvious that norms of ritual purity, for example, are relevant to strategic interactions of any sort. More tendentiously, one might treat reasons for action or norms of reasoning as social norms and it is not at all clear how the normativity of reasons could be captured as a response to a mixed-motive game. No doubt, norms of fairness are central to the problem of cooperation. The evolution of proto-humans who could be sensitive to such norms is probably a prerequisite for modern human forms of social interaction. Nonetheless, it is clear that norms of fairness do not encompass the entire domain of norms in a social order.

In response, one might point out that the question of what situations can be modeled in game-theoretic terms is an empirical issue. Game theorists have applied their tools to a surprising range of human behavior. Hence, it is an open question whether Bicchieri's account illuminates a broad class of social norms. The inadequacy of this response is manifest when we turn to the question of how we might apply Bicchieri's definitions to full-blooded social behavior. For example, suppose we observe people standing in line at a bus stop. A social scientist would want to know whether there is a local rule that requires queuing up. Is it, in Bicchieri's terms, a social norm, a descriptive norm, a convention, or mere regularity? Again, two features of the definitions are crucial: whether the individuals have beliefs about others' preferences and their willingness to sanction, and the game-theoretic representation of the situation. Identifying beliefs and preferences can be difficult, but it is not a deep philosophical issue (*pace* the problem of other minds). The question of whether a bus queue "can be represented as a mixed-motive game" is more interesting. In Bicchieri's definitions, this condition stands outside of the scope of any individual's belief or expectation. Bicchieri is clear that the strategic situation need not be part of any individual's deliberation (note that this is one of the pulls toward instrumentalism, a point to which we will return). Where, then, would the social scientist look to determine the strategic situation? Game-theoretic modeling of real-world situations is notoriously difficult and undetermined by the data. Even worse, the requirement demands only that the situation "can be" represented as a mixed-motive game. Without further specification, of course, this is so weak as to be useless. Revealed preferences in real-world situations are sufficiently incoherent that almost any situation "can be" represented by any game. Relying on the underlying strategic situation in the way that Bicchieri's definitions do arguably makes them either too limited in scope, or empirically intractable.

Let us turn to the second issue: what makes Bicchieri's "social norms" social *norms* at all? One might think that the content of the "behavioral rule *R*" involves ought-statements. When Bicchieri is discussing rules informally, they seem like maxims of an ordinary sort. In her discussion of fairness, for example, she distinguishes between fairness as sharing equally and fairness as giving to the more deserving. This is a difference in propositional content that would naturally be captured in terms of statements involving "ought" and its cognates. She also talks about rules being "embedded into scripts" (Bicchieri 2006, 57). So, one might think of the behavioral rules as either commands or ought-propositions represented by the agents, and social norms as regularities of such representation in the community. However, understanding the normativity as built into the content of the agents' representations does not square with Bicchieri's other commitments. When she turns to the technical details, it turns out that the rules are functions defined over strategy sets (Bicchieri 2006, 52). They specify the agent's strategy, given the strategies of the other players. Hence, they do not have the semantic content of ought-statements.

One might conclude that Bicchieri's account is therefore an instance of the strategy Turner endorses (in this volume and Turner 2010). Bicchieri has replaced talk of "norms" with a utility function of conditional preferences. The normativity of rules dictating cooperation has been replaced by a complex representation. This is not quite the case. A residual normativity animates Bicchieri's norms: the assumption of instrumental rationality that underlies all game theory and rational choice theory. Bicchieri is quite explicit that her account does not postulate that agents consciously deliberate about behavioral rules or the conditional preferences. Instead, she proposes a "heuristic" route from situation recognition to action. Nonetheless, she defends the rationality of the resulting behavior. There remains, then, a robust sense of normativity to Bicchieri's norms. Someone for whom a cooperative norm was activated, and yet failed to cooperate, would be irrational. The fundamental status of instrumental rationality in Bicchieri's account is a further, internal, limitation on the breadth of the theory; reasons for action cannot be among the social norms, on pain of circularity.

Let us turn to the third issue: should Bicchieri's account be taken as a realistic theory or interpreted instrumentally? Interpreted realistically, a model or theory postulates the existence of a mechanism or underlying causal law, and successful explanatory appeal to such mechanisms or laws should be taken as evidence that the mechanisms or causal relationships exist. Economists have often begged off the idea that their models capture real causal relationships. They have thereby adopted an instrumentalist reading of their theories. Instrumentalist theories may have strong predictive power, but these predictive successes are not taken to be grounds for thinking the theories literally true. The world simply behaves as if the theory or model were true. *The Grammar of Society* provides textual resources for both realistic and instrumentalist interpretations; indeed, it seems to sit uncertainly between them. Exhibit A for the instrumentalist reading is Bicchieri's claim that her theory is a "rational reconstruction":

> [It is] not a faithful descriptive account of the real beliefs and preferences people have or of the way in which they in fact deliberate. Such a reconstruction, however, will have to be reliable in that it must be possible to extract meaningful, testable predictions from it.
>
> (Bicchieri 2006: 3)

The instrumentalism is also exhibited by the utility function that substantiates the behavioral rules. It is only *phenomenological* in the physicist's sense that it is a mathematical formula which correctly describes the relationship among known (or in this case, stipulated) values. It does not purport to characterize any mechanisms.

Now, from the point of view of standard economic practice, instrumentalism is no objection to Bicchieri's view. Utility functions are supposed to be phenomenological in this sense. Something is lost, however, when we treat the entirety of *Grammar of Society* instrumentally. First, the normativity of social norms becomes attenuated once more. If the instrumental rationality of norm compliance is only an artifact of the formalism, then social norms are no more normative than any other mathematical model. This result leaves one feeling like the victim of a bait and switch. The promise was to show how "social norms are implicit in the operations of a society and make it what it is" (Bicchieri 2006, : ix). On the instrumentalist reading, the exciting prospect of a normative grammar of society becomes the rather dull result that people act as if they coordinate their behavior through their beliefs. While this is a normativist objection, notice that the discomfort is not with the disenchantment, but with the blandness of the resulting explanation. It is a problem *within* the explanatory framework of the social sciences.

A second problem with an instrumental reading arises from Bicchieri's explanations of why experimental subjects cooperate in prisoner's dilemma situations, how norms form, and so on. Her explanations rely heavily on the role of action schemata. While this could, without inconsistency, be interpreted in instrumentalist terms, a realistic construal of the causal language is not only more interesting, it accounts for the relevance of the psychological literature to which she appeals. For example, consider Bicchieri's discussion of the role of group-identity in the explanation of cooperation. Experimental evidence shows that humans have a bias to favor members of their own group, even when group divisions are arbitrary (and known by the agents to be arbitrary). In an experimental paradigm designed by Dawes and colleagues, subjects were arbitrarily divided into groups of seven. Each person was given a token worth $6. Privately and anonymously, each subject would choose to either keep the token (a defect strategy) or give it away (a cooperate strategy). If all members of the group gave away the token, each member of *some* group would receive $12. In one condition, the group believed that their group would keep the $84, in the other, they believed that the money would benefit another group (and that they might benefit from the other group's actions). Before making their individual decisions, some of the groups were permitted to discuss their choice, other groups were not. Immediately before dispersing for their private decisions, half of the groups within each condition were told that the situation had changed. If they had believed that their money would go to another group (the out-group), they discovered that it would go to their own (the in-group); if they believed it would go to the in-group, they discovered it went to the out-group. The results can be summarized as follows (Bicchieri 2006, 147):

	Initial belief that money goes to in-group		Initial belief that money goes to out-group	
	Belief at time of decision		Belief at time of decision	
	In-group	Out-group	In-group	Out-group
No discussion (% cooperating)	37.5%	30.4%	44.6%	19.66%
Discussion (% cooperating)	78.6%	58.9%	32.1%	30.4%

A standard game-theoretic analysis of this situation would predict that neither the discussion nor the recipient of the donation would make a difference. The problem is a social dilemma and the dominant choice in all conditions is for each individual to keep the $6. The experimenters made sure that there would be no mechanism by which the subjects could bind themselves to any promises made during the discussion. The discussion, therefore, was an instance of "cheap talk," and on the standard game-theoretic analysis it should be ineffective.

Dawes *et al.* argue against an explanation of this data that appeals to a norm of cooperation. Cooperation, in this instance, is cooperation with the members of one's own group (those who are donating or not donating the tokens), not cooperation with the recipients. They reason that if a norm of cooperation were invoked by discussion, then it should not matter whether the donations actually benefited the in-group or the out-group. They explain the results by appeal to group identity. Even without discussion, the discovery that the donations would go to the in-group substantially boosted cooperation.

Bicchieri argues that Dawes *et al.* conceive of norms as context-independent imperatives. On her view, activation of the norm of cooperation is conditional on the empirical and normative expectations of the subjects. Bicchieri notes that in both conditions, the discussion raised the rate of donation to the out-group. She argues that discussion "may reveal a general willingness to cooperate, and so change one's expectations about others' behavior, but it may also reveal a potential discontent with defectors, thus engendering normative expectations" (Bicchieri 2006, 148). The relatively high level of cooperation among those who discussed (58%), but who had their expectations changed from in-group benefit to out-group, is explained as a "carryover effect." Once the norm is activated, she argues, the "inertia" of the normative expectations influences the subsequent choice. Bicchieri ultimately recognizes identity as a factor, but explains its relevance as part of norm activation:

> Categorizing a situation as 'we' versus 'them' is bound to activate well-rehearsed scripts about in-group loyalty and trust. If, as I claim, norms are embedded into scripts, the categorization process will lead one to think that one 'ought to' trust in-group members and, if promises are made, trust that they will be kept.
>
> (Bicchieri 2006, 156)

Bicchieri's account of this experimental evidence is plausible. But notice that the utility function that is supposed to turn the social dilemma into a coordination problem plays no role at all. All of the explanatory work is done by the agents' expectations and related psychological phenomena. What is the status of this appeal to psychology? If it is nothing more than instrumentalist rational reconstruction, then it gains no evidential support from the experiments that establish the existence of cognitive mechanisms like scripts and schemata. Moreover, the causal connotations of words like "inertia," "activate," and "willing to cooperate" must be effaced. On the other hand, if we treat the psychology realistically, then the utility function and the game-theoretical apparatus are superfluous.

It appears, then, Bicchieri's account of social norms is hobbled by the game theory with which it begins. The utility function that transforms mixed-motive games into coordination games plays little role in the more substantive explanations that make up the bulk of *The Grammar of Society*. The game theory is the basis for the taxonomy of norms, but the representation of the underlying strategic situation as a mixed-motive or coordination game makes no difference to the account of the agents' behavior in Bicchieri's examples. One possible solution is to divide and conquer.

We might treat the game theory and the utility function as instrumentally useful representations that help relate the psychological explanations to the experimental setup. The appeal to empirical and normative expectations, the embedding of normative expectations into schemata, and so on, might be treated realistically. This bifurcated interpretation would keep the power of Bicchieri's explanations while resolving the problems identified above. The question of which game-theoretic representation is true of a particular social situation would not arise, since the game theory is instrumental anyway. And for this reason, the account would not be necessarily restricted to mixed-motive games. Any situation where the participants' cognitive schemas invoked rules, as well as empirical and normative expectations, would involve social norms.

The bifurcated interpretation of *Grammar of Society* is not without cost. Bicchieri's social norms are normative because of the role of instrumental rationality. As we noticed above, this is one of the parts of her account that sits uneasily between realistic and instrumentalist interpretations. Interpreted realistically, failure to conform to activated social norms is rationally criticizable. Interpreted instrumentally, it is not. Treating the utility function and game theory as rational reconstruction, then, strips the normativity from Bicchieri's social norms. Is there some way to reanimate Bicchieri's social norms?

BICCHIERI AS PRACTICE THEORIST?

To see another way to construe the normativity of Bicchieri's social norms, consider this prefatory remark:

> The social norms I am talking about are not the formal prescriptive or proscriptive rules designed, imposed, and enforced by an exogenous authority through the administration of selective incentives. I rather discuss informal norms that emerge through the decentralized interaction of agents within a collective. . . . Social norms can spontaneously develop from the interaction of individuals who did not plan or design them. . . .
>
> (Bicchieri 2006: x)

Bicchieri's characterization of social norms has a distinct *relational* character. Norms do not arise merely when a sufficient number of group members have some beliefs. They arise when these beliefs are the basis for their response to each other. This is surprisingly like Joseph Rouse's "normative" conception of practices (this volume, 2007a and 2007b). Rouse distinguishes between a regularist conception and a normative conception of practice. The former treats normativity as a matter of replicating a pattern. A normative conception treats a practice as a pattern of interaction among performances "that expresses their mutual accountability" (Rouse 2007a, 669). Bicchieri's conception of a social norm has some similar interactive qualities. If a social norm exists in a community, then a number of the participants have empirical and normative expectations about one another, and they are prepared to act on that basis. In so doing, their interaction constitutes the norm. If we understand her account realistically, then, she has provided an account of the underlying mechanisms of responsiveness and mutual accountability. Insofar as a norm is manifested in a behavioral regularity, the regularity supervenes on a variety of individual psychological states and responses.

Emphasizing the interactive aspects of Bicchieri's account begins to recover a sense in which her social norms could be normative without relying on instrumental rationality. However, full recovery will require the bridging of two apparent gaps between Bicchieri's project and normative practice theory. First, Rouse uses the language of "mutual accountability," and one might argue that Bicchieri's agents have attitudes that are neither mutual nor accountable. On Bicchieri's definition, the agents have no preferences about others' performance; they are only concerned with others' preferences for the agent's performance. And while others may sanction the agent's performance, the definition of a social norm provides no space to answer back. There is no critical engagement with other agents who are contributing to the practice. Second, while she emphasizes the "heuristic" route from rules to behavior, Bicchieri's formulation remains too intellectualist to be understood as practice theory. The definition relies on a complex set of beliefs. The motivational component is minimal—only the preference to conform to the rule—and there is no sense in which the agents are embodied. Indeed, while the account is cognitive, the cognitive mechanisms are entirely *cold,* relying only on beliefs and not any emotional valences. In spite of these challenges, treating Bicchieri's account as a form of practice theory provides a glimmer of hope for the explanatory value of norms. On her account, social norms explain behavior. And if we emphasize the relational character of her conception of social norms, there is a sense in which they are normative. Rouse's normative conception of practices is naturalistic (as least as I interpret it). If successful, norms would be explanatory through their specific character as norms, not as the content of beliefs nor as regularities of behavior. Hence, *pace* Turner, it would be a social scientific account of norms that did not require the social scientist to change the subject.

Bicchieri's account is intellectualist in the sense that it takes the standard conception of agency-as-rational-actor for granted. This is problematic insofar as it excludes any norms that make actions reasonable from the scope of the account. Moreover, it stands in tension with the heuristic explanations of behavior emphasized throughout the book. Taking the heuristic model seriously requires us to invert the standard order of explanation in action theory. Standard philosophical accounts of action aim to analyze intentional actions. The analyses treat intentional actions as bodily events with a causal or conceptual relationship to the right sort of psychological states: beliefs and pro-attitudes, reasons, intentions, plans, volitions, and so on. Practical (instrumental) rationality links these states to the action. Agents are then beings capable of intentional action, and *ipso facto* rational. I am not the first to suggest that this is backwards. We should begin with an account of agency, and treat intentional action as whatever it is that agents *do*.

Psychological studies of reasoning have largely converged on dual-system accounts of rationality. While the details vary, most theorists take the experimental evidence to show that our capacity to make inferences is the product of two distinct kinds of psychological systems. One is a set of "fast and frugal" algorithmic processes or heuristics. These produce quick inferences, but they are products of our evolutionary history. They can be biased and fooled by environmental conditions. The second system is more flexible, but it is slower. Deliberately invoking rules of validity to test an inference, or bringing the base rate to bear on a probability calculation engages the second system. Judgments are the product of both systems working in concert. Reasoning is thus not one, unified, thing. Since Plato's metaphor of the charioteer, philosophical conceptions of agency have postulated multi-part analyses. The particular version to be proposed here is a dual-process account of practical rationality, on analogy with the dual-processing account of inferential rationality. It conceives of the intentionality of agency as a relationship between the agent's cognitive capacities and the environment, and for that reason it may be called an "ecological" analysis of agency.

The ecological analysis of agency postulates three capacities: attunement to the environment, recognition of affordances, and a meta-cognitive capacity for linguistically mediated direction of the ongoing action processes. Each of these is intended to pick out a suite of cognitive processes that are empirically identified or identifiable. The philosophical project is to show the conceptual relationship between these facts of cognitive psychology and our understanding of agency, action, and social practice.

Agents must be attuned to specific aspects of their environment as they act. This requires perceptual capacities, but these should be thought of as capacities to recognize and track elements of the environment, not ways of representing it. Social animals must be attuned to their conspecifics as well as to the inanimate environment. For humans, this means being able to recognize and track the intentions of others, their different perspectives on the immediate environment, and their emotional responses. Bicchieri's empirical and normative expectations are better understood as attunements than as "beliefs." On her account, empirical and normative expectations are not to be understood as consciously entertained and deliberately applied to the situation. Rather, "the environment or situation we are in provides perceptual stimuli to which we respond in an 'automatic,' unreflective way" (Bicchieri 2006, 50). To say that an agent has empirical and normative expectations, then, is to say that she is attending to the regularities of behavior among her associates, and to their expectations of her.

Affordances are the possibilities for action in the environment that are recognized by the agent. Some affordances are directly provided by the environment: Turning the latch may be the only way of opening the door. When the door is the only way out, the environment constrains the agent's possibilities (with respect to an exit) to one path. Other situations are more open, such as the various ways to walk from one part of a city to another. While similar, the conceptualizing agent's active relationship to the environment in terms of affordances is superior to scripts and schemata. Again, scripts and schemata connote representations that guide the agent's action, whereas we need something more dynamic. In a social situation such as a grocery-store checkout, for example, there is a familiar routine. It is obviously not a deterministic recipe, since there are innumerable action sequences that can fit the routine. No single script will do. Rather, agents are responsive to the contingencies of the environment and to the way these change the possibilities for action. The checkout routine is better understood as a cluster of possibilities for one's own action and a coordinated set of possibilities for the other agents. That is, the checkout counter, cash register, clerk, and other aspects of the environment present a set of affordances to which the agent is responsive.

It was noted above that Bicchieri's account is cognitively cold; it does not invoke any emotional responses to norm compliance or violation. From our own experiences, however, it is clear that our responses to norm compliance and violation are always emotional, sometimes intensely so. Over the last several decades, cognitive scientists have become aware of the importance of the emotional, or *somatic,* component of thought. To say that it is somatic, rather than emotional, is to highlight the idea that what are felt phenomenologically as emotions are the conscious side of a number of processes that "range from changes in internal milieu and viscera that may not be perceptible to an external observer (e.g., endocrine release, heart rate, smooth muscle contraction) to changes in the musculoskeletal system that may be obvious to an external observer (e.g., posture, facial expression, specific behaviors such as freezing, flight and fight, and so on)" (Bechara and Damasio 2005, 339). Bechara, Damasio, and their colleagues have shown through a series of experiments that the somatic valence of both perceptions and anticipations of action are crucial to decision-making and action. These somatic valences involve the activation of the very same neural circuitry that constitutes the emotional response to a situation. Emotions that arise from experience are thus aroused when similar actions or perceptions are invoked.

Both attunements and affordances should be thought of as associated with somatic states that give the objects and possible actions a positive or negative affective character. In other words, the script associated with grocery-store checkout is not just a cluster of pure action possibilities; the action possibilities are already presented as pleasant, annoying, attractive, or fearful. One might be tempted to think that a kind of sentimentalist value theory is being proposed, but that would get ahead of the story. On a practice theoretic account, norms are social. Therefore, the somatic valences of attunements and affordances cannot be identified outright with values. They are, however, a crucial aspect of normativity, and they are what give norms their particular motivational force.

Attunements and affordances are not normally the object of attention. That is, while one is aware of the door and its handle, and one has the expectation that the handle can be turned to open the door, one may not be (and typically, is not) aware of one's awareness or expectation. That the handle is there to be turned is not something on which one would focus in the course of ordinary action. We do, of course, have the capacity to bring these things to mind, to describe them in language, to recall past experiences and knowledge, and to engage in explicit deliberation and decision-making. This third set of capacities is "meta-cognitive" in the sense that they enable agents to think about attunements and affordances, and to relate these aspects of the environment to plans, goals, rules, and general knowledge. One of the insights of practice theory, found in both Bourdieu and Brandom, is that rules do not stand behind behavior and somehow direct it. Rules are formulated by agents. Once formulated, they are new pieces in the same old game. Their power is in the way that they are used by agents in new practices of justifying or condemning courses of action. Our capacities of meta-cognition are the means through which the explicit formulation of a rule can influence behavior.

With this more robust conception of agency at hand, we can return to the two gaps between Bicchieri's account and normative practice theory: that the definition of social norms did not support mutual accountability, and that the account is too intellectualist. Thinking of agency as constituted by somatically valenced attunements, affordances, and meta-cognition permits us to bridge these gaps. Starting with the issue of intellectualism, the ecological analysis of agency follows through on Bicchieri's gesture toward a heuristic understanding of norm compliance, and permits us to embed her account in a more consistent anti-representationalist view. Insofar as social norms are followed automatically and unreflectively, the explanation will appeal to the attunements and affordances of the agents. When an agent recognizes a social norm in her community, she must be attuned to a regularity of behavior among other agents and to the expectations of the agents about the behavior of others. The action possibilities must include both the possibility of acting in the way others expect and regularly do, and acting differently. These affordances will be somatically valenced, loading the action possibilities with satisfaction, shame, pleasure, or guilt. In this way the "rule" is implicit in the agent's attunements and affordances, without having to be implicitly represented as an imperative, much less a function defined over strategies. Meta-cognition permits agents to formulate or learn explicit rules. Such rules may, in some circumstances, influence behavior by the deliberate choice to follow (or violate) the rule. Or, they may change the attunements and affordances, thereby becoming part of the agent's responsiveness to the situation.

On the ecological conception of agency, the expression of mutual accountability is not some further practice of reward or punishment (those these may exist as well). The mutual accountability is already encoded in the agents' mutual expectations about each other's behavior; in their attunements and recognition of affordances. The somatic components of these expectations provide positive and negative valences in virtue of which agents regard possibilities as right or wrong even in the absence of any threat of sanction. Such systems of mutual expectation and response can exist even if the agents do not explicitly formulate rules or norms for their behavior. Indeed, as many ethnographers have documented, the real norms of a community—those expressed by their practices—may be at odds with the official rules.

THE EXPLANATORY VALUE OF NORMATIVE PRACTICES

We may now turn to the leading question of this essay: do norms have an explanatory value over and above the representation of norms or regularities of behavior?

Let us get some purchase on this question by looking at how the foregoing section's conceptualization of practices and agents permits a distinction between social norms and non-normative regularities of behavior. Where there is a social norm, agents will be attuned to regularities of behavior, to the expectations of others, and to their emotional states, and the affordances will include both one's own possibilities for action and the possibilities for others. These recognitions of patterns and possibilities will be emotionally valenced, creating evaluative expectations for one's own and others' actions. Where there is a non-normative pattern, the affordances and attunements will not be other-regarding, at least not in the same way. The pattern arises because the agents are responding to the same dimensions of the environment, such as an easy way up the hill.

Consider an example like picking up after one's dog. In some places, this is clearly a social norm; not so in others. An agent who picks up after his dog sees doing so as a possibility of action. While the somatic valences are probably mixed (this can't be described as pleasant), he does so anyway. Perhaps he thinks the excrement will yellow the grass; perhaps he is just orderly and fastidious and does not reflect on his reasons at all. It could be that many people pick up after their dogs, and there is a pattern of such behavior. It would not be a social norm, on this account, because the agents are sensitive neither to the regularity nor to the expectations of others. A social norm arises when agents begin to form expectations for their own and others' behavior. Agents must become attuned to others' expectations, and this means that the expectations must be manifest in some way (perhaps in subtle ways like body language, or dramatic ways like verbal rebukes). When agents become attuned to others' expectations, when they come to expect such behavior of others, and when such expectations become part of the affordances of the social environment, there is the mutual responsiveness required by the normative conception of practices. A social norm to pick up after one's dog would exist[1] when the affordance of doing so is not prompted only by the excrement, but the agents' sensitivity to the expectations of others.

When the difference between normative and non-normative regularities is clear, the difference in their explanatory value becomes clear as well. When a social norm exists, we can use the norm to explain the behavioral regularity: People pick up after their dogs in my neighborhood in Atlanta because it is expected (it is regarded as good citizenship, it is obligatory). The norm also might explain why the regularity is robust, and why people are likely to react to deviations from the regularity in the way they do. If the regularity is a mere regularity of behavior, it will be explained differently: It may be due to the features of the environment, of the way agents recognize affordances, or common experiences. These regularities may be robust too, but they will be robust in different ways. Notice how this difference between explanations that appeal to a social norm and explanations that do not tracks Bicchieri's use of social norms in her explanations. The behavioral economics experiments are set up to create a conflict between cooperative behavior and self-oriented behavior that is insensitive to the expectations of others. When Bicchieri invokes a social norm, she is appealing to the responsiveness of agents, and she is explaining a pattern of behavior (e.g., unexpected levels of cooperation in a one-shot prisoners' dilemma trial).

To explain the action of an individual as following a social norm is also different from pointing out that the action conforms to a behavioral or representational commonality. For example, suppose we are in an area where pedestrians do not (in general) cross the street against the light. Let us suppose that there is no explicit or articulated social norm; it is implicit in practice in the ways described above. If an individual is sensitive to the norm, then crossing against the light will appear as a negatively valenced affordance because of the way the agent recognizes the patterns of behavior and expectations of others in the local community. The agent will act *because* of these specifically social attunements. When we ask why Jones is standing on the curb when no traffic is approaching, then, we can explain Jones's behavior by saying that it is regarded as wrong in this community to cross against the light. Notice that this explanation is different from one that looks to Jones's conscious representational states (she may have been thinking about something else), and it does not require that Jones, at that moment, is anticipating the reactions of others should she cross. Finally, it does not explain Jones's behavior by fitting it into a local regularity.

The way in which the foregoing account of the explanatory value of norms relies on an underlying psychology raises two possible objections, one related to Turner (this volume) and another related to Henderson (this volume). Reflecting on Turner's concerns, one might object that, even if we accepted such practices as constituting norms, the explanations do not rely on their normative character. The social scientist need not endorse or condemn the actions explained; no evaluation or normative judgment is involved. This is true, and it makes the account herein different from those given by Dray (1957) or Hollis (1982). These authors argued that social scientists must make normative judgments of rationality in their accounts. The distinction between a first-person and a third-person perspective on norms, discussed by Peregrin in this volume, is helpful here. When one makes a normative judgment or evaluation, one is acting as a member of a community in which norms exist. One is taking a first-person stance on those norms; one is committed to them. To say what the norms of a community are is to take a third-person stance on the norms. In the forms of explanation proposed above, a third-person stance is presupposed. Two points bear emphasizing. First, to evaluate is not to explain. So, insofar as Turner is arguing that evaluation in terms of norms is not explanatory, we can agree. Second, the burden of the foregoing argument is that there is a difference between norms existing and patterns of action or belief existing, and that this difference is relevant to social scientific explanation. So, this chapter has argued, as against Turner, that excluding norms from explanations would impoverish the social sciences.

Reflecting on Henderson, one might note that all the explanatory work of the foregoing account is being done by the lower-level attunements, affordances, and meta-cognitions, not by the social norm. In the case of Jones, above, the causal load is being carried by Jones's brain. The social norm has no additional causal force. Henderson argues that the underlying causes in the supervenience base screen off any supervening properties, and this renders them explanatorily irrelevant. However, Henderson's argument relies on an implausibly strong premise: If A screens off B from C, then B is explanatorily irrelevant to C. To screen off is to render probabilistically independent: Pr(C given A & B) = Pr(C given A). But in any chain of causes, each screens off all prior causes from its proximate effect. The same is true of any complex system where elements of the mechanism are further systems. And yet, on most accounts of causation (e.g., Woodward 2003), it is appropriate to say that "Winding the mainspring caused the clock to run," and to treat this as an explanation for why the clock is running. But of course, the turning of the final gear in the gear train screens off the mainspring. Henderson's premise would thus render most scientific explanations unexplanatory.

While the point about screening off is somewhat technical, it teaches a larger lesson. A naturalist sees the world as embedded systems, where the interaction among micro-parts brings about macro-phenomena. When science has been able to analyze the underlying mechanisms, naturalists hold that higher-"level" phenomena do not involve commitment to new kinds of stuff: There is no substance associated with social institutions, social norms, minds, or life-forces. This metaphysical commitment does not entail epistemological or explanatory reductionism. Higher-level descriptions can invoke patterns and relationships invisible from the lower perspective.

We need not treat biology as mistaken just because we can understand the workings of a cell in terms of various organic compounds. Similarly, taking normativity to be constituted by normative practices, and taking these to be analyzed in terms of relationships among agents who have specific psychological capacities, should not encourage us to treat social normativity in terms of an error theory.

If we understand both agency and the normativity of practice in the right way, social norms are explanatory. They add information and explain different phenomena than regularities of representation or behavior. It is through their specific character as norms that they explain, and in this sense, norms *"qua* normative" are explanatory. And the explanations do not remove norms from the causal realm; the account of practice and agency given here is thoroughly naturalistic. At the same time, this essay has tried to show how eliminating reference to normativity in the social sciences does leave something out or change the subject in problematic ways. Social norms (*qua* normative) have a legitimate and sometimes necessary role in social scientific explanation.

NOTE

1 The use of the word "exist" should be taken seriously here. While this account is no more than a sketch, it is intended to provide an account of what social norms *are*, and to thereby provide criteria for distinguishing situations where they do exist from situations where they do not. The position developed here is therefore an instance of the "superdupervenience" position discussed by Henderson in this volume. *Nota bene:* Since no non-naturalistic properties are deployed in either the supervenience base or the explanation of how normative practices supervene on the responsiveness and relations among agents, this position is a counter-example to Henderson's claim that there is no plausible middle position in Table 10.4 (this volume, p. 168).

REFERENCES

Bechara, Antoine and Antonio R. Damasio. 2005. The Somatic Marker Hypothesis: A Neural Theory of Economic Decision. *Game and Economic Behavior* 52: 336–372.

Bicchieri, Cristina. 2006. *The Grammar of Society: The Nature and Dynamics of Social Norms.* Cambridge: Cambridge University Press.

Brandom, Robert. 1994. *Making It Explicit.* Cambridge, MA: Harvard University Press.

Dray, William. 1957. *Laws and Explanation in History.* Oxford: Oxford University Press.

Henderson, David. 2002. Norms, Normative Principles, and Explanation: On Not Getting Is from Ought. *Philosophy of the Social Sciences* 32(3): 329–364.

Hollis, Martin. 1982. The Social Destruction of Reality. In *Rationality and Relativism,* edited by Martin Hollis and Steven Lukes, 67–86. Cambridge, MA: MIT Press.

Risjord, Mark. 2000. *Woodcutters and Witchcraft: Rationality and Interpretive Change in the Social Sciences*. Albany, NY: SUNY Press.

———. 2005. Actions, Reasons, and Causal Explanations. *Philosophy of the Social Sciences* 35(3): 294–306.

Rouse, Joseph. 2007a. Practice Theory. In *The Philosophy of Anthropology and Sociology*, edited by Stephen Turner and Mark Risjord, 639–681. Amsterdam: Elsevier.

———. 2007b. Social Practices and Normativity. *Philosophy of the Social Sciences* 37: 1–11.

Turner, Stephen. 1994. *The Social Theory of Practices*. Chicago: University of Chicago Press.

———. 2010. *Explaining the Normative*. Cambridge: Polity Press.

Woodward, James. 2003. *Making Things Happen: A Theory of Causal Explanation*. Oxford: Oxford University Press.

12 The Assassination of the Austrian Archduke, Sacred Cows, and the Conundrum of Rules

Martin Palecek

WHAT IS THE PROBLEM WITH RULES ANYWAY?

Rules apparently constitute a challenge for a naturalistic approach to the social sciences. It seems to be obvious that norms are what 'ought to be' and as such they are not easily reducible to 'what is'. Hence, social norms, rules, customs, and other forms of normativity are resistant to easy ways of explaining and reducing them. Rules are everywhere in human society. Some of them are explicit, like laws, and some of them are implicit, like the rules we apply during a visit to the neighbor's. We can use the latter as an example and we can do this with a small, strange trick—we can make some rules explicit.

Let's imagine that we are going to visit our good neighbor. When we are approaching his house we use the front path. We somehow know that jumping over the fence would be inappropriate behavior. When we stand at the front door we try to get the attention of our neighbor in some conventional way. Typically, we would use a doorbell or knock on the door. When the door opens we use some conventional sentence and shake hands or hug or kiss our neighbor. Sentences such as "Nice to see you" are almost meaningless but demonstrate our good will. The same thing happens with handshakes, etc. After greetings we wait for an invitation to come inside and our host knows that he should invite us in. As Czechs visiting the United States, we have to suppress our compulsion to take our shoes off because we know that our neighbor does not expect this kind of behavior. Our Czech habit could make our hosts feel uncomfortable. Even after we have got the invitation to come inside the house we know that this invitation does not include the whole house. We know—or possibly just feel—that there are areas of the house which are not included in the invitation. We call this 'privacy'. So we follow our hosts to the living room. If we need to use the bathroom during our conversation we ask for permission to use it, even if we already know that we are allowed to use it and to restrict the use of this place would be absurd. We could easily continue with the description, but one thing is important: During the visit our friend holds us responsible for these rules and we feel a commitment to follow these rules as well. It is similar to the behavior of our children insofar as they are responsible for their misbehavior in our eyes but we feel we are responsible for them. The friend's responsibility for our behavior ends immediately on our leaving his front yard.

We can see in the previous example what can be meant by the expression 'following rules'. It is useful to be aware that there are two kinds of such rules. Some of the rules we are expected to follow are implicit and we do not use them consciously in our behavior. During our visit we respected *privacy, private property,* and *etiquette* among other things. They were almost instinctive. These rules become visible only when we make a mistake. The awareness of having made a mistake is the realization that we are not obeying rules anymore. This might be displayed through blushing. On the other hand, some rules are explicit; we keep them in mind and try to conform our behavior to them. This happens in the case when we learn them as foreigners. We are also able to distinguish between a mere regularity or causal relationship and a genuine rule. In the case of our visit to our friend's house, spilling red wine on the white carpet *caused* the embarrassing red stain. It was *regularity* when our friend gets off the couch repeatedly to bring more refreshment. It was *rule* of correct dining to refrain from spitting pieces of chewed meat back onto our plate.

If we are able to distinguish rules from other facts so easily, why do we ask if rules are explanatory within social science? Did we not just show an example of what the explanation within social sciences can look like? Did we not just employ rules in the process of social scientific explanation? To demonstrate why we should be prudent with our conclusion, let us recall the structure of scientific explanation.

SOCIAL SCIENTIFIC EXPLANATION

What should a sufficient explanation within social sciences look like? Any explanation should go below the level of the system as a whole. We presume that a phenomenon we would like to understand is a complex system and any kind of description—simple or elaborated—of this complex system is not enough. We also presume that each part of a phenomenon is connected to the other. A good explanation exposes the mechanism, which connects parts of a larger phenomenon. These mechanisms work causally. If feature A and B does not change phenomenon F, this would not be interesting for us. In other words, the idea of causal reasoning within social science generally involves the idea of connection between causes and effects. Beside this, the idea of causality also inevitably involves the idea that one event or feature is a sufficient or necessary condition of another.

For example, suppose we wanted to explain the background to the assassination of Archduke Franz Ferdinand in Sarajevo on June 28, 1914. As a social scientist, we can start with a description of the situation. Despite this, not all of the events will be recognized as equally important for our purpose, which is to explain why the archduke was assassinated. Some events, like the illness of a common chimney sweep in Sarajevo during the visit of the archduke, did not affect anyone because the chimney sweep stayed at home with a fever. When we get rid of the events that are not linked to the assassination, we still have many connections between agents. We would mention that the archduke was planning the reform of Austria-Hungary and this reform would decrease the influence of Hungary in the Empire. We would also mention that the marriage between Franz Ferdinand and Archduchess Sofia was treated as morganatic. A morganatic marriage is a marriage between members of unequal social rank. That meant for instance that the archduchess could not accompany Franz Ferdinand in public except for the military duties of the archduke. We have Gavrilo Princip, one of the members of the group of six assassins who were also members of the Serbian nationalistic organization widely known as Mlada Bosnia (Young Bosnia). It would help to know such things as the fact that the day of the archduke's visit was also St. Vitus Day. This day was known among Serbs as the Vidovdan, commemorating the battle of Kosovo Field in 1389 between the Serbian kingdom and the Ottoman Empire. During this battle, among other events, the Ottoman sultan was assassinated by a Serb.

As mentioned above, a historian would seek the underlying causes. If she wants to explain all of the events surrounding the assassination of the archduke, she needs to employ different varieties of causal explanation: singular causal judgments ('the shockingly unprofessional behavior of the Austrian secret police, which caused the death of both the archduke and the archduchess'), generic causal relations ('nationalism causes public disorder'), causal relevance claims ('the level of education in the national language influences the rate of nationalization of the whole society'), probabilistic causal claims ('the dispute over the territory increased the likelihood of terrorist attacks'), etc. (*cf.* Little 1991, 32–34). When we look over the whole explanation of the assassination, we can see that any good historian that tries to explain why the assassination had happened, and why it was so important to the escalation of the conflict among powers, employs references to the beliefs, wants, desires, limitation, and powers that characterize the individuals whose actions influence the historical event. The historian counts these references to the beliefs, wants, desires, etc. as the parts of specific causal mechanisms that connect causes and effects. Every phenomenon that I have described above—even such a symbolic occasion like St. Vitus Day/Vidovdan—are dealt with as parts of causal mechanism.

Let us analyze the case of the archduke and Gavrilo Princip in more detail. What historians usually use for their explanation is a version of instrumental rationality. That means in fact that historians reason backwards, asking what kind of reasons, intentions, and desires someone might have had to make her action rational. Historians rarely doubt the reality of the instrumental rationality. It seems to be almost intuitive and in fact it is intuitive precisely because it is a part of folk psychology. However, even in using this reasoning, it remains a mystery why people like Gavrilo

Princip choose this kind of a suicide mission. Even the behavior of the arch-duke himself seems instrumentally irrational because the archduke had been warned about the situation in Bosnia, and he had survived the first attempt of assassination. If we employ their beliefs, wants, and desires—all parts of folk psychology—the behavior of the archduke and Princip still remains irrational. How can we solve this puzzle? Would it be better to use standard rational choice theory (RCT) instead as a way to improve our understand-ing? As Jack Goldstone (1994) who analyzes the similar puzzle about join-ing revolutions pointed out, individuals do not normally choose to join such extensive historical performances. They are more likely to be members of groups that have already formulated their own goals. And of course we have to employ norms to explain their behavior as well.

> Studies of participants in social movements confirm that individuals rely on norms of contributing one's fair share to promote collective action. . . . Participants in collective action seem quite aware that they have the option to free ride, but decline to exercise that option for fear of not obtaining the collective good they seek. . . . Group participation is critical to ordinary life. It is therefore rational for individuals to adopt and seek to instill in others norms that will lead to optimal outcomes for group action.
>
> (Goldstone 1994, 146)

This means that instead of simple RCT we should employ the more plau-sible model of structural rational choice theory (SRCT). Instead of a simple distinction between 'social level' and 'individual level', proponents of SRCT employ some 'mid-level agents' that explain the behavior of both the arch-duke and the assassin as rational. Both the archduke and Gavrilo Princip had their own goals, beliefs, and desires. They were both members of social institutions: the Austrian court and the Serbian nationalist secret organiza-tion. They both had some obligation to the Austrian state protocol or to the loyalty to Mlada Bosnia.

Nevertheless, as both Goldstone and Hechter (Hechter 1987; Goldstone 1994, 146) have argued, the existence of preferable norms within a group does not solve the problem with rational choice because both Franz Fer-dinand and Gavrilo Princip were members of more than one social group.

> What is important for solving the assurance game is the sharing of information regarding the effectiveness of contemplated actions and the views of group members. . . . That is, if the individuals in the group share the information that suggests that joint action by the group will be effective and they know that the information and the appropriate norms are shared by all (or most) members, then they know that all (or most) members will participate, leading to success. Effective group action then becomes the attractive equilibrium strategy for members.
>
> (Goldstone 1994, 147)

This means that for both actors in our Sarajevo drama what was important was their allegiance to the Austrian court or Mlada Bosnia, so-called effective groups. This also means that for a correct explanation of the assassination of the archduke, historians need to speculate about norms and rules that might be valid for all of the actors. All the actors of the Sarajevo drama made their choices and it is important not to forget such norms as *honesty* or *loyalty* for instance. Plus, for so-called 'normativists' even to employ RCT (respective SRCT) means that we must include norms. For them to be rational means to follow exact sets of rules, that imply we already need to face the problem of normativity.

If historians mention norms, does it mean that they are making a shift toward a kind of a normative explanation instead of a causal one? And if not, is this where (or why) they fail? What about a proposal that we can employ norms as the causes of someone's behavior? In fact the very message of normativism is that there is no genuine way to understand norms in the non-normative matter. We can describe this problem on the example with promising: When I promise something, I place my promise in the realm of normative. That means that expectations genuinely connected to my promise cannot be explained merely through a habit or sociological facts. "The only true 'law' that one might form about promising is a normative one that anyone who makes a promise is *bound* to fulfill it" (Turner 2002, 123). To say that promise might be a cause of someone's behavior is a categorical failure in the eyes of normativists because "Practice like promising is 'normative all the way down' in the sense that the end point for an account of promising cannot be a causal fact or process of some kind that is 'non-normative'" (Turner 2002, 123).

TURNER'S DENIAL OF NORMATIVITY

The implication of the idea that practices like promising are "normative all the way down" might be that social scientists are supposed to correct their view of norms as causes of a behavior. Would normativity make any impact on the social scientific way of explanation? Firstly, let us recapitulate what the normativists' argument usually looks like (following Turner 2010, 9–12). The ordinary way of social scientific explanation involves entities that normativists usually claim are somehow special. Those facts—such as content, rationality, and obligation—are involved in social action like behavior, learning, and talking. Normativists typically claim that these entities have some special properties. What they mean by this is that when social scientists use them for explanation, this explanation is asymmetrical. They cannot be employed in causal explanation because they are in some way substantially different. They contain something 'more' because they have consequences for behavior—what is justified, what is obligatory to do, and what is correct to say—and this 'more' is missing in such a simple causal explanation. Again, according to normativists, the existence of these (normative) entities is substantially different from usual facts.

So according to normativists, when Gavrilo Princip shot the archduke, we need to recognize two sets of ontologically different entities: (1) the physical movement of Princip's body and the trajectory of the projectile, and (2) the normative 'reason' why Princip shot at the archduke. To explain Princip's action, we need invoke the second kind of object by using concepts such as 'obligation', 'honesty', or 'virtue'. These sets of concepts, as well as reason itself, have different substantial properties to the usual facts. Normativists do not deny the existence of the sociological fact of social practices. Nevertheless, they object that such 'mere sociological facts'—that people believe a given practice to be obligatory—explain anything at all (Turner 2010, 5–6). It is the extra property of normativity that can explain one's behavior.

Stephen Turner (2010) argues that this kind of ontological difference represents something that he calls 'Good Bad Theories' (I will explain this statement later). We shall start by explaining why Turner believes that normativity does not mean any significant challenge for social science. As Turner points out, for social scientists norms are eliminable. It is possible due to the social scientific presupposition that we are always able "to read normativity back into phenomena . . . that are not unambiguously normative" (Turner 2002, 138). This is the practice of social science that goes back to Max Weber and his formulation of the process of disenchanting *(Entzauberuung)*. "We call something normative not because we think there is a normative element but because, taken together, the activity amounts to something we call normative. Calling something normative is a factual rather than a normative enterprise" (Turner 2002, 123). To explain why the archduke died or why Princip shot at him, they can employ concepts like 'obligation' or 'honesty' or 'virtue' just like other facts and count them as a combination of singular causal judgments, generic causal relations, causal relevance claims, probabilistic causal claims, as I already pointed out. This approach also brings a traditional advantage. This kind of explanation may be developed more broadly as an argument about nationalism and it may be construed as a 'conditional-probability' analysis for instance. We can collect an absolute number of violent incidences linked to the political reasons. We can see how many political decisions were connected to some of the ideas of nationalism. Finally, we can see a correlation between other public behavior based on nationalistic ideas and see if we can identify a causal relation between the absolute numbers of political decisions motivated by nationalism. We then need to identify the causal mechanism that underlies this pattern, if any.

Nevertheless, we might miss one point from the description of our problem with rules because the SRCT works to utilize the aggregate of agents. But in the case of the explanation for the assassination of the archduke we need something to explain the behavior of Princip himself. Let's evoke the whole scene of the assassination. There is a car carrying the archduke and Gavrilo Princip is on the street. Princip is disappointed that the first assassination attempt has failed. Then he sees the car with the archduke. He must decide what to do. This might be a crucial point for social scientists. What has happened and how was his decision made? In this case Princip had at least two choices—to survive or to keep his loyalty to the goal of his terrorist group—and he had to make the decision. It seems to be that rules are coming back again as the key trigger for making a decision. Hence, when Princip made his decision to shoot the archduke, he was following a set of rules constituted by social norms like as I already mentioned above—virtue, honor, love for his nation.

We know what Princip believed from what he said in court: "I am a Yugoslav Nationalist. I call for the reunification of the Southern Slavs into one state and that it be free of Austria" (Owings 1984, 56). Nationalism was the prevailing ideology for most people at that time in Europe. So we can see 'nationalism'—Yugoslavian in our case—as *R* that involves sets of behavioral practices in the way that excludes these behavioral practices that do not fall under the cluster of beliefs called (Yugoslavian) nationalism such as 'to be loyal to the Habsburgs Court' or 'to love German language'. Princip believed in nationalistic ideology and he also believed that nations are substantial entities that fight each other for supremacy. When he saw the car with His Majesty he felt himself committed to the nationalistic idea and he knew the goal of their conspiracy. He believed that his other fellows expected him to reach the goal. He also believed that the goal of their conspiracy would bring good to his other fellow citizens: "I am not a criminal, because I destroyed that which was evil. I think that I am good" (Owings 1984, 54). He probably also believed that in case they failed to assassinate the archduke, they would be punished by both remorse and exclusion from the nationalistic organization. Then Princip pulled the trigger.

And that is how we can analyze agents' behavior without presupposing any 'proper' kind of normativity distinctive from the causal world: When we spoke about nationalism, we invoked 'beliefs about nationalism'. That means that any social scientist that intends to explain Princip's behavior transforms any normative characterization of belief into a description of belief. This procedure brings the advantage of explaining any kind of phenomenon without any kind of commitment to believe in the real existence of this phenomenon. This is precisely the core of Turner's argument: When a normativist wants to speak about rules and norms as a non-reducible entity, she just disguises descriptions of common beliefs and attitudes to suggest that there is another ontological entity like the normative one. This kind of normativistic turn brings more problems than it solves (Turner 2010). In other words: To deploy rules and norms for understanding is a kind of so called 'Good Bad Theories' that I have already mentioned above. Normativists take folks explanation for granted insofar as they accept rules and norms while denying that they can be explained in causal terms.

With that qualification, we may describe these various folk conceptions as 'Good Bad Theories', meaning that they are good theories for a particular, unspecified set of purposes in a particular setting, but bad theories if we are thinking of them as adequate explanations of anything, or as proto-explanations that can be turned into genuine explanations with a little empirical vetting and some minor revision. They are, in short, kludges.

(Turner 2010: 43)

Turner therefore suggests we can analyze agents' behavior without presupposing any 'proper' kind of 'normativity' distinctive from the causal world because when we speak about nationalism, we invoke 'beliefs about nationalism'. That means that any social scientist that intends to explain Princip's behavior transforms any normative characterization of belief into a description of belief. This procedure brings the advantage of explaining any kind of phenomena without the need to commit to believe in real existence of these phenomena.

RISJORD'S CRITERIA TO BE RATIONAL

Normativists would probably be unsatisfied with Turner's account. They could object that we handled Princip as a rational agent. To recognize him as a rational agent means that we use criteria of rationality for this analysis. That also implies that we handle these criteria as normative. According to normativists, we are still missing something important: the normativity of rationality. According to normativists, the normative phenomena are not explicable in non-normative terms, and when we try to do it, we only reduce the social norm to another sort of norm, the rationality of intentional action. That means that normative phenomena are irreducible.

According to a normativist, what we need to do in the case of the interpretation of the assassination in Sarajevo is to figure out what sorts of rules of rationality Princip and the others followed. The interpreter needs to identify what "counts as a good or bad reason (for the locals) in such a context. These will be local criteria of rationality" (Risjord 2000, 154). Once we finish this job, we have two kinds of information. First, there is a cluster of beliefs that work as a model *of* reality. It is the *descriptive* model of their natural and social environment. Second, there is a cluster of rules and norms that work as a model *for* reality. That is a *normative* set of rules and norms. This is what Geertz sees as "powerful, pervasive, and long-lasting moods and motivations" that members of culture share (quoted in Risjord 2000, 156). It implies that rules and norms are explanatory in a very strong sense because norms are postulated as explanatory of group regularities. That means that an individual has reasons insofar as those individual reasons fit with the group patterns. There are at least three objections to Risjord's kind of account.

To see the first, let us recall our example of the archduke's assassination. Gavrilo Princip obviously had a very powerful and long-lasting cluster of beliefs. He articulated his model of reality directly when he said: "*I am a Yugoslav Nationalist. I call for the reunification of the Southern Slavs into one state and that it be free of Austria.*" He also expressed what counts as a good reason for him to assassinate the archduke: ". . . *I destroyed that which was evil. I think that I am good.*" It seems to be sufficient for the first condition in our analysis. Let us test the second model—the model for reality. When Gavrilo Princip decided to shoot the heir of Habsburg's empire, he followed the norms and rules he had shared with other members of Mlada Bosnia. This seems to be sufficient for the interpretation of his act. Nevertheless, when we want to understand him, we do not need to know norms and rules as such. In fact we never perceive them as norms and rules. What we have to know are his beliefs. This is exactly Henderson's (1993) objection to normativists' analysis. When norms and rules are treated as a reason for behavior, they turn into beliefs about norms and rules. They function as beliefs in the interpretation and no longer as norms and rules. Therefore, only beliefs play the explanatory role and not rules and norms.

Risjord responded to Henderson's argument by treating norms as features of a social group. According to Risjord, norms are distinct from any individual's belief (Risjord 2000, 160). He believes that this gets around Henderson's objection because it is not a *belief* about rules or norms that explains a rational action. Rather, seeing how the action fits into a social pattern of rules and norms is part of the explanation. It follows that normative explanations have a different form than causal explanations.

The second objection against Risjord is that he accepts a folk psychology of beliefs, intentions, and norms. Let me explain what I mean by the concept of folk psychology. The picture of cognition we are recently receiving from cognitive sciences is much more complicated than the philosophical view enshrined in our ordinary way of talking about the mind. The common idea is that each of us has a cluster of beliefs shared with other members of the same culture. We make our decisions in the light of rules and our behavior is thereby rule-governed. Recent findings of cognitive science have undermined this folk-psychological picture.

Most cognitive scientists argue that we have at least two varieties of cognition. The first is older, natural, fast, mostly unconscious, and automatic. The second is much younger, slower, controlled, and reflective and is a sort of *unnatural* (McCauley 2011) mode of thinking. According to McCauley, we can even recognize two types of *natural* cognition (McCauley 2011, 5). *Practiced* naturalness is a domain that becomes developed during our training within some regular activity or routine, such as any kind of job-related expertise. The second he calls *maturationally* natural cognition and that is much more interesting in our case. Maturationally natural cognition "concerns humans having (similar) immediate, intuitive views that pop into mind in domains where they may have had little or no experience and no instruction . . . ," such as "people knowing what someone is feeling or thinking on the basis of observing his or her facial expressions, and even school-age children knowing that the slightest contact with some contaminant might be enough to contaminate them fully" (McCauley 2011, 5). Maturationally natural cognition is tied up to a specific domain of our mind. As such, it is a source of making decisions and behavior that runs beyond specific rules or norms.

Several experiments run by Jonathan Haidt and his coworkers might subvert our traditional view of rule-governed behavior. Haidt shows in several cases that moral decisions are made almost instantly, but nevertheless we struggle to find a good reason for our decision (Haidt 2001; Haidt and Björklund 2008). He gives us this kind of example:

> Julie and Mark are brother and sister. They are traveling together in France on summer vacation from college. One night they are staying alone in a cabin near the beach. They decide that it would be interesting and fun if they tried making love. At the very least it would be a new experience for each of them. Julie was already taking birth control pills, but Mark uses a condom too, just to be safe. They both enjoy making love, but they decide not to do it again. They keep that night as a special secret, which makes them feel even closer to each other. What do you think about that? Was it OK for them to make love?
>
> (Haidt 2001, 814)

Haidt points out that most people who hear this story immediately say that it is wrong for siblings to make love even if there is no harm either for siblings themselves or for other people. Despite this, they have problems giving a reason why this kind of behavior is morally wrong. The implication is that our decisions might be based on moral intuition. Rational argumentation always comes later in the role of some kind of attorney.

Steven Pinker gives us another example that might be useful to demonstrate how our picture rule following or decision-making might be wrong. When surgeons cut the corpus callosum joining the cerebral hemispheres, they cut the person in two, "and each hemisphere can exercise free will without the other one's advice or consent. . . . If an experimenter flashes the command "WALK" to the right hemisphere (by keeping it in the part of the visual field that only the right hemisphere can see), the person will comply with the request and begin to walk out of the room. But when the person (specifically, the person's left hemisphere) is asked why he just got up, he will say, in all sincerity, 'To get a Coke'—rather than 'I don't really know'" (Pinker 2003, 42–43). This experiment shows us that a part of the brain (left hemisphere) can give us a coherent but false reason for behavior ordered by the other part (right hemisphere) without its knowledge.

The point is that even though our knowledge of brain activity is still rudimentary, we should doubt the folk-psychological view of rule-governed behavior (Bunge 2004; Bunge and Wallis 2008; Blais 2012). I believe that this traditional picture is an intuitive, but false view.

The third objection against Risjord's analysis is the way in which he handles the concept of 'culture'. This objection is in fact linked to the second objection. Risjord seems to believe in the deep connection between the individual and social levels. His assumption of folk psychology allows him to explain all rules and norms together. There are no mysteries and all rules and norms are conscious, at least in principle. But this is incorrect. To paraphrase Richard Rorty, we do not have 'glass substance'. And nor does culture. The view that culture consists of norms and rules when rules are behavior-governed and norms are behavior-constitutive does not help. This is the view that implicitly treats culture as kind of monolith.

NORMATIVITY NATURALIZED AND SEMANTIC

Jaroslav Peregrin (2014) also believes that normativity is necessary for the explanation of human behavior. Moreover, he believes that normativity is built into human language and human culture.

> In particular, it is already meaningful talk and our distinctively human way of thinking (which is usually called *rational* or *conceptual*) that is constituted by certain normative frameworks—just like you can score a goal only within a framework of rules, you can assert that something is thus and so, or you can have a belief to this effect, only within a certain framework of rules.
>
> (Peregrin, this volume, p. 65 italics in original)

This means that rules are essential for meaning. If you want to express something, you could see the very act of expression as reaching some kind of goal. Thus words could be seen as a set of tools, which can reach goals by following rules.

Despite Peregrin's view of language being constituted of rules, he is not following those philosophers who claim that normativity is something transcendent to our nature. In fact Peregrin as well as Risjord are some distance from this point of view. They both try to see normativity as a specific trait that evolves with the biological part of our nature. Moreover, Peregrin claims that norms and rules—the language using normativity—do not only exist as the products of our evolution, but both rules and norms are explanatory within a social scientific approach. Unlike the natural sciences, where we use causality and correlation for our explanations, within social sciences both naturalistic language and normativity are both complementary and indispensable. And this is his second step that seems to be highly problematic. Nevertheless, how does Peregrin defend his position?

Peregrin thinks that the naturalist's critique of normativism is based on a false view of the distinction between methodological individualism and holism. He correctly points out that the idea that communities have shared views or norms is plausible and noncontroversial. It is also plausible and noncontroversial to say that a newborn child has to attune her mind to something like the 'group mind' (Peregrin, this volume, p. 63). However, what is controversial according to Peregrin is the status of these shared views and 'group minds'. One extreme is known as methodological individualism or reductionism: the view that 'group mind' is just the aggregation of individual minds. The second extreme is methodological holism: the view that 'shared views' or 'group minds' are things *sui generis*. Peregrin argues that the denying of normativity is highly motivated by a critique of the second extreme (e.g., Tooby and Cosmides 1992; Turner 2010) but he disagrees that there are only these two possibilities. He argues that between them is a wide space full of opportunities to explain both society and normativity. Thus Peregrin tries to show how normativity is indispensable by the fine maneuvering between the *Scylla* of holism and *Charybdis* of reductionism (individualism).

Peregrin describes his position in this way:

> Hence the viable version of normativism we are going to defend concurs with Turner in rejecting that there would be any normative force transcendent to the social forces of human communities, and agrees that if we can talk about a normative force, normative facts, or normative explanations, then all of this must be grounded in the social facts, which are in turn grounded in the causal facts regarding the individuals forming the societies.
>
> (Peregrin, this volume, p. 64)

Peregrin calls his version of normativism *social normativism*. That means that Peregrin agrees with the fact that "the normative dimension of human affairs is all-pervasive" (Peregrin, this volume, p. 65). People behave in that way: They follow rules and they are able to explain the reasons for their behavior. Peregrin uses a soccer game as an example. What *offside* means is constituted by the rules of the game. To score is possible only if all the players correctly follow the rules of a soccer game. The correctness itself is, according to Peregrin, irreducible to non-normative language. The irreducibility of normativity is most vivid in the case of morality. The rule that people should not kill each other is not, according to Peregrin, reducible to non-normative language.

What about Henderson's argument that rules can only show correctness of some behavior but do not explain anything? Henderson argues that a norm works for the agent as a reason for his action. That means that the agent is supposed to believe that some norm and rule is a good reason for his behavior or a bad reason for his behavior. That implies that a norm and rule were replaced by a belief or disposition. Henderson says that "once we appreciate what it takes to answer a why-question, and thus to provide an explanation for an action or intentional state, we find that normative principles, qua normative principles, have nothing to contribute here" (Henderson 1993, 168).

Nevertheless, Peregrin insists that rules are explanatory. What puzzles us is the fact that we can read normativity in a purely descriptive way, and this is exactly what Henderson does. Instead of showing that rules are not explanatory, he uses a factual description of normativity. For solving this problem Peregrin uses the metaphor of two languages. If I am a player in a soccer game I can use the language of rules (the normative language of 'insiders') and I can see its normative power. On the other hand, if I try to explain the soccer game to a Martian I can describe the rules as merely the facts by the descriptive language of 'outsiders'. According to Peregrin, we have this ability to switch from one language to another—from outside to inside—without losing anything. These two languages are both complementary and explanatory. Moreover, Peregrin argues, we cannot just use the descriptive language. This is due to the fact that human acting and speaking presupposes a normative framework. So when we use the descriptive language, we can do it only partially in special cases. The 'capsule' containing the description of facts remains inevitably surrounded by a normative framework. Thus normativity prevails.

The metaphor of two languages and the fact that normative language is not reducible to a descriptive one is the key point of Peregrin's argumentation. Even if Peregrin does not want to deny a scientific approach to the study of rules (especially a psychological approach) he believes that without the 'insider view' reality remains incomplete. Of course, nobody denies that human societies consist of many norms. The dispute is whether norms are explanatory or not and I believe that Peregrin's approach still remains unpersuasive.

Notice how Peregrin uses his metaphor of two languages when he tries to define consensus: "The consensus is a matter of intersections among the members of the society holding each other responsible for what they do and answerable to the rules implicitly governing the society's functioning" (Peregrin, this volume, p. 74). This definition should be equally as valid as the cognitivist approach when, according to cognitivists, 'social consensus' is more a result of some cognitive structures than a part of individual consciousness. It seems to me that Peregrin's insider definition of consensus stresses a folk-psychological understanding of consensus only. His definition is an clear example of Turner's Good Bad Theory: Theories that are good for a specific purpose but "bad theories if we are thinking of them as adequate explanations of anything, or as a little empirical vetting and some minor revision" (Turner 2010, 43). These are folk theories that also constitute many—if not all—of our intuitions. So when Peregrin points out that cognitivists' 'social consensus' is more the result of cognitive structures rather than a part of individual consciousness, Peregrin does not use both languages. He undermines his own normativist view.

Let me recapitulate my objections to Peregrin's approach. First, when Peregrin uses his normative definition of consensus, he shows us nothing more than the fact that we can recognize who is correct or not according to his definition. This has nothing to do with the explanatory role of normativity. A normative approach just moves folk psychology around the plate. Second, when we use normativity within social sciences, we turn it into normative facts and for this purpose we use descriptive language only. Third, when we are able to stress rules and norms and test them, we have robust evidence that our intuitions about norms and explanations of our behavior are massively wrong. It seems obvious to me then that norms and rules remain explanatorily sterile.

EXAMPLE: SACRED COWS

Let us clarify the problem of why norms are not explanatory through another famous example: the existence of sacred cows. Indian society is extremely complicated. We are not able to fully describe Hinduism, as we are Christianity. It is widely accepted that Hinduism is more practiced than the religion in the Western sense of the meaning. The existence of sacred cows is peculiar to Hindu faith. The term 'sacred cows' is misleading as to far as cows are respected rather than worshiped. Consequently, cows are everywhere on the streets, blocking traffic, etc. Hindus are not allowed to slaughter them. In fact the suspicion that cows were being slaughtered has caused in the past rioting and violence.[1] The new Indian state even included a bill of rights for cows in its constitution. So there is a strong social norm not to slaughter cows in India. Can we make this norm explicit? Yes, we can. There are several hymns that celebrate cows and in a way serve as a basis for the sacred cow taboo. First of all it is *Rig Veda* and *Atharva Veda,* where the cow is usually depicted as a source of wealth and compared to a river of goddesses. In both *Brahma-samhita* and *Harivamsha* cows are connected to *Krsna*. This highly recognized avatar of *Visnu* is described as *Bala Gopala*—the child who protects the cows. Finally, there is *Puranas* and the goddess *Kamendhenu* that is 'mother of cows'(Zbavitel 1964). Indians also celebrate cows on some occasions. One of the most famous is the *Gopastami* holiday. During this holiday cows are washed and decorated and brought to the temple where they are celebrated. During the ceremony worshipers bring offerings to cows to secure that their gifts of life will continue. These depictions of the cow put cows in a very special position. The slaughter of cows is restricted and happens very rarely and only with special permission. There are several sanctions to protect cows and the cost for not obeying them is very high.

Let's test whether the social norm 'sacred cow taboo' can serve as an explanation. When we see a cow standing in the middle of an intersection in New Delhi, causing a gridlock there, or when we see a police officer trying to resuscitate a cow after it fell into a coma in the street, it seems to us that the 'sacred cow taboo' is explanatory.

It was the second wave of anthropologists that made the concept of culture explanatory. Kroeber, Malinowski, and Lowie changed the concept of culture and claimed that it was not something that could be explained in biological terms. They also claimed that culture was ontologically different from ideas or behavior of individuals, and was transmitted from one generation to the next (Risjord 2007, 406). Moreover, Malinowski thought that culture had rules, norms, and rules as backbone:

> In popular thinking, we imagine that the natives live on the bosom of Nature, more or less as they can and like, the prey of irregular, phantasmagoric beliefs and apprehensions. Modern science, on the contrary, shows that their social institutions have a very definite organization, that they are governed by authority, law and order in the public and personal relations, which the latter are, besides, under the control of extremely complex ties of kinship and clanship. Indeed, we see them entangled in a mesh of duties, functions and privileges which correspond to an elaborate tribal, communal, and kinship organization.
>
> (Malinowski [1922] 1984, 10)

This view that norms and regularities play the role of the backbone of the culture was the key for Malinowski to view anthropology and ethnography as a science. Anthropology has theory and ethnographers form a "hypothesis about cultural entities like 'rules,' 'charters,' 'functions,' 'ideals,' or 'world views.' This put ethnography on a par with other empirical disciplines in the sense that it required hypotheses that go beyond the data, and ethnographers must test or justify their claims by appeal to evidence" (Risjord 2007, 406).

Therefore, culture was perfectly explanatory at first sight according to these anthropologists (Malinowski, etc.). This was seen as perfectly reasonable. However, when we ask why people are doing this, we can only get the answer that already presupposes the existence of the 'sacred cow taboo', nothing more. The job of ethnographers is to describe norms and regularities that govern social life. But even after reconstructing rules that govern the social life of a particular group, we still have nothing that could properly explain their behavior. Even if we add more details about the diversity of social norms, the details do not increase our knowledge of this kind of social norm. With this description we have received something that is not written down in stone but is still somehow obvious, in the same way as a cartographer does not explain anything about the processes that formed mountains and valleys by describing them. Even when a cartographer adds more details to his map, he goes no further to explain how these mountains and valleys were originally formed. If we have a blurred photo of a man with a duck on his head and we are then able to sharpen the image, although the image is clearer, we are no further in our understanding of why the man has a duck on his head. This is precisely what the description of rules and norms does.

We can use rules for understanding whether someone obeys the rules or not, and that means we can use these social norms as criteria for correctness. This is important but not that important. It is due to the fact that to see people as members of culture following common rules is our instant intuition. That is so intuitive that we should be worried of this intuition and not jump to conclusions so quickly. This intuition is a part of folk psychology, and folk psychology is a powerful tool that allows us to be part of a social group. When anthropologists followed this intuition of folk psychology, they tried to develop a culture as a scientific concept and they failed. They were not able to improve this intuitive view of some unique solid group of people to scientific clarity. The most important reasons why a scientific concept of culture was not successful is that there is no single set of rules held by every member of a given group and there are no clear borders of what should be a unique culture. Recent anthropologists point out that in the closest view the connection between behavior of agent and cultural rule is always complicated (Rosaldo 1993). In fact, the rules and sources of our behavior are more complicated and based on our mental and brain activity. Rules and norms are not explicable precisely because they are a perfect example of Turner's Good Bad Theories. We want to understand the underlying mechanism. We want to know the *causes* for the installation of such social norms.

Marvin Harris offers us a very interesting causal explanation of the 'sacred cow taboo' (Harris 1974; Harris 1977). The institution of the 'sacred cow taboo' was broadly criticized back in the 1970s. Many Indians were starving at this time and there were about thirty million unproductive cows (Harris 1974, 12). The irrationality of the whole institution of the 'sacred cow taboo' seemed to be obvious. Nevertheless, Harris took this conundrum seriously and based his search for explanation on materialistic premises. He figured out that the whole Indian economy was very effective and based on what cows were able to produce without being slaughtered (i.e., milk and fuel). While the slaughtering of cows could bring a short-term supply of nutrition, it would bring famine in the long run. Vegetarianism, therefore, seems to be a very effective solution for society at this level of density of population. Harris concluded that the seemingly irrational religious sanction shrouded a causal mechanism.

Let us emphasize the whole backbone of Harris's procedure. Harris overlooks the social norm and turns it into the social *fact*. Then he builds up a basic explanatory model of the fact of the 'sacred cow taboo' and displays the causal relationships among the elements and conditions.

CONCLUSION

Norms and rules, in spite of their ubiquity, remain a kind of a conundrum for our understanding. Besides our trying to understand why norms have evolved over time, there is a more practical question as to whether norms and rules are explanatory within the social science. I claim that they are not because (a) norms and rules are a criteria for correctness, therefore they remain explanatorily sterile; (b) we want to know 'why' and therefore we have to go under the surface-level phenomena to search for causes. I am aware of the possible objection that even norms could function as causes. It seems to be less likely. A recent progress in cognitive science shows us that norms are more likely part of folk psychology than the force that drives our behavior.

What I call folk psychology is an evolved cluster of natural cognition that includes human immediate (similar), intuitive views that pop into mind even though they may have no or little training or instructions. The point of folk psychology is that this kind of cognition is tied up to a specific domain of our mind and as such is a source of decision-making and behavior that runs beyond the specific rules or norms. Hence (c) whenever cognitive science tried to go under the surface level, it discovered a causal mechanism instead. Normativism seems to be solely the final attempt to protect the obsolete idea of a body-mind dualism.

NOTE

1 For example: Binar in 1917–30 people died and 170 Moslem villages were destroyed; Delhi 1966—the 120,000 people rioted—8 people died and 48 were injured (Harris 1974, 13–14).

REFERENCES

Blais, Chris, M. B. Harris, J. V. Guerrero and S. A. Bunge. 2012. Rethinking the Role of Automaticity in Cognitive Control. *The Quarterly Journal of Experimental Psychology* 65(2): 268–276.

Bunge, Silvia A. 2004. How We Use Rules to Select Actions: A Review of Evidence from Cognitive Neuroscience. *Cognitive, Affective, and Behavioral Neuroscience* 4(4): 564–579.

Bunge, Silvia A. and Jonathan D. Wallis. 2008. *Neuroscience of Rule-Guided Behavior*. New York: Oxford University Press.

Goldstone, Jack A. 1994. Is Revolution Individually Rational? Groups and Individuals in Revolutionary Collective Action. *Rationality and Society* 6(1): 139–166.

Haidt, Jonathan. 2001. The Emotional Dog and Its Rational Tail: A Social Intuitionist Approach to Moral Judgment. *Psychological review* 108(4): 814–834.

Haidt, Jonathan, and Fredrik Björklund. 2008. Social Intuitionists Answer Six Questions about Morality. In *Moral Psychology, the Cognitive Science of Morality: Intuition and Diversity*, volume 2, edited by Walter Sinnott-armstro, 181–217. Cambridge: MIT Press.

Harris, Marvin.1974. *Cows, Pigs, Wars and Witches: The Riddles of Culture*. New York: Vintage.

———. 1977. *Cannibals and Kings: The Origins of Cultures*. New York: Random House.

Hechter, Michael. 1987. *Principles of Group Solidarity*. Berkeley: University of California Press.

Henderson, David K. 1993. *Interpretation and Explanation in the Human Sciences*. Albany: SUNY Press.

Little, Daniel. 1991. *Varieties of Social Explanation: An Introduction to the Philosophy of Social Science*. Boulder: Westview Press.

Malinowski, Bronislaw. 1984. *Argonauts of the Western Pacific*. Long Grove: Waveland Press. Original edition, 1922.

McCauley, Robert N. 2011. *Why Religion Is Natural and Science Is Not*. New York: Oxford University Press.

Owings, W. A. Dolph. 1984. *The Sarajevo Trial*. Cherry Hill, NC: Documentary Publications.

Peregrin, Jaroslav. 2014. *Inferentialism: Why Rules Matter*. London: Palgrave Macmillan.

Pinker, Steven. 2003. *The Blank Slate: The Modern Denial of Human Nature*. London: Penguin.

Risjord, Mark W. 2000. *Woodcutters and Witchcraft: Rationality and Interpretive Change in the Social Sciences*. Albany, NY: SUNY Press.

———. 2007. Ethnography and Culture. In *Philosophy of Anthropology and Sociology*, edited by S. Turner and M. Risjord, 399–428. Amsterdam: Elsevier.

Rosaldo, Renato. 1993. *Culture and Truth: The Remaking of Social Analysis*. Boston: Beacon Press.

Tooby, John and Leda Cosmides. 1992. Psychological Foundation of Culture. In *The Adapted Mind: Evolutionary Psychology and the Generation of Culture*, edited by J. Barkow, L. Cosmides and J. Tooby, 19–136. New York: Oxford University Press.

Turner, Stephen P. 2002. *Brains/Practices/Relativism: Social Theory after Cognitive Science*. Chicago and London: University of Chicago Press.

———. 2010. *Explaining the Normative*. Cambridge: Polity.

Zbavitel, Dusan. (ed.) 1964. *Bozi, Brahmani, Lide*. Praha: CSAV.

13 Self-Interest, Norms, and Explanation

Petri Ylikoski and Jaakko Kuorikoski

INTRODUCTION

A pair of loosely connected and ill-understood ideas haunt thinking concerning explanations of human behavior. According to one, behavior is inherently understandable if it can be seen as rational. Deviations from rationality may have to be causally explained in terms of cognitive limitations, momentary errors, and persistent biases, but rational behavior as such need not be further explained. Then there is the idea of self-interest as the foundational motivator of human action. The exact content of this idea ranges from a purely empirical hypothesis about what people generally care about, to a conceptual platitude that my goals and concerns are *my* goals and concerns. Often these two ideas are tightly coupled or even treated as identical: Action is rational if it competently serves the self-interest of the agent. Both notions are also heavily normatively laden. Rationality states what an agent ought to do, given her goals and beliefs, and for many self-interest defines what is good for the agent.

We will have none of this. In the first part of the chapter we argue that, first, rationality and self-interest should be decoupled. Second, in the assessment of scientific explanations of human behavior and social phenomena, neither rationality nor self-interest should be given a privileged explanatory position. Some form of principle of charity may be constitutive of our folk-psychological interpretive practices, but this alone does not justify explanatory privileges either for rationality or for self-interest. We argue that privileging rationality and/or self-interest on the basis of *intentional fundamentalism,* according to which our folk-psychological intentional attributions provide an inherently understandable fundament, is not compatible with a naturalistic approach that aims to mechanism-based understanding of natural and social phenomena. Further, we show how fundamentalist intuitions and arguments are liable to bias the investigation of human behavior. Intentional fundamentalism accords rational and self-interested behavior a status of an *ideal of natural order,* and this sets a specific heuristic for deciding what kinds of phenomena are in need of explanation to begin with. We show the dangers of such heuristics by briefly discussing behavioral economics and especially the discussion around social preferences. We further argue that the very idea of a need for an ideal of natural order rests on wrong-headed thinking about explanation and understanding.

We do not intend to do away with rationality and self-interest altogether. On the contrary, our view is that turning them into empty tautologies robs them of their explanatory power. Equating rationality with any kind of behavior describable as some form of constrained optimization and self-interest with any kind of goal-oriented action gets both concepts on the cheap. Rationality and self-interest should both be understood as empirical hypotheses and stripped from normative baggage. We argue for this on the basis of substantial psychological, social psychological, and sociological empirical research on the consequences and determinants of substantially rational and self-interested behavior.

We are not aiming to completely expunge rational choice theory from the social sciences. Sometimes rational choice theory provides a powerful modeling tool and a research heuristic, although there are also clear limitations to its use. We have discussed such limitations elsewhere (Lehtinen and Kuorikoski 2007; Ylikoski 2013; Hedström and Ylikoski 2014). Our issue here is with the foundational role accorded to assumptions of rationality and self-interest and with justifications provided for such a role. Thus, for example, economists' appeals to 'the rationality principle' when modeling markets are not a target of our discussion. In that context the rationality assumptions refer to empirical hypotheses about the efficiency of markets based on arbitrage opportunities. Such assumptions might be problematic, but the problems are straightforwardly empirical rather than being related to conceptual arguments having normative underpinnings. Only the latter are our concern in this paper.

The second part of the paper discusses an idea that could serve as an important element in a naturalistic understanding of prevalence of substantially self-interested behavior. The idea is to analyze self-interested action as a social norm (Miller 1999). According to this idea, social norms—that is, prevalent expectations about social behavior—play an important role in the generation of self-regarding actions. People's actions and opinions as well as the accounts they give for their actions and opinions are influenced by this norm. Thus, the belief in self-interested action is partly a self-fulfilling prophecy.

While this idea presented by Dale Miller and his associates still needs further elaboration and sorely requires further empirical verification, it has some appealing properties. First, rather than being based on supposedly deep psychological insight about human nature or vague conceptual argument, this idea provides a causal mechanism that can be empirically investigated. Second, it does away with the asymmetrical nature of rational choice theorizing. While appeals to social norms have become increasingly popular among rational choice theorists, they are still used only to explain divergences from rational self-interested action. This kind of ad hoc theorizing is highly suspect from the naturalistic point of view. When conceptualizing human action in terms of causal mechanisms, it is much more plausible to assume that social norms are one of the determinants of human action irrespective of its normative status (as rational). Finally, the norm of self-interest account fits nicely with a broader naturalistic picture of human agency where the ability to act consistently according to one's self-interests is an achievement rather than default state of human motivation. In this view, humans are prone to all kinds of impulses that range from selfish to altruistic. To turn these motivations into a controlled and consistent behavioral pattern requires a whole array of developmental processes that constitute an interesting object of study.

PART I: DOING AWAY WITH THE RATIONALITY PRINCIPLE

There is a long and venerable tradition of thinking about explanation of human behavior linking the explanation of action to rationality. The identity of reasons, the content of intentional states, has been taken to be conceptually constituted by some version of principle of charity: An assumption of rationality is taken to be a transcendental condition for seeing a behavior as a meaningful action by and agent with propositional attitudes (e.g., Davidson 1980).

There is also a long and (more or less) venerable tradition of social scientific and political thinking about self-interest as a central motivating factor of social action. The central idea of Mandeville and Smith, that individual virtue is neither necessary nor a sufficient condition for the promotion of the common good, has somehow morphed into a common understanding that self-interest is the best, or perhaps the only, driver of an orderly and economically prosperous society. It is not just acceptable to be self-interested; you positively *ought* to be self-interested.

It is certainly plausible that some form of 'rationality' assumption may well be built into our folk-psychological interpretive practices and that respecting basic rules of logic and being goal oriented in behavior may well be constitutive of the identity and meaning of our intentional states. To ascribe beliefs and desires to others or to ourselves seems to be (at least) intimately connected with being committed to also believing what follows from the ascribed beliefs and with expectations of pursuing reasonable means to the ascribed ends (Brandom 1994; Millar 2004). We do not want to question such a view here. We also do not want to question the common view that even though such conceptual interconnections introduce a modicum of holism, ordinary folk-psychological explanations of individual action are still causal, or at least work as if they were. We argue against two implicit explanation-related assumptions common in the social sciences. (1) Explanatory inequality: Not all things require explaining. More specifically, only 'non-rational' actions require explanation whereas rational actions are self-explanatory. (2) Explanatory fundamentalism: certain kinds of explanations are somehow privileged or final. More specifically, intentional explanations of actions are 'complete' or 'final'. These two assumptions influence the selection of the *explananda,* the search for explanatory factors and evaluation of explanations. In our view, these influences are detrimental to the goals of truly explanatory social science.

Examples of these views can be found from all social sciences, but our examples of endorsement of these assumptions come from rational choice sociology.

> Rational actions of individuals have a unique attractiveness as the basis of social theory. If an institution or a social process can be accounted for in terms of rational actions of individuals, then and only then can we say that it has been 'explained'.
>
> (Coleman 1994, p. 1)

> When a sociological phenomenon is made the outcome of individual reasons, one does not need to ask further questions.
>
> (Boudon 1998, 177)

> Not only will a rational choice explanation be parsimonious and generalizable; it will also be the end of the story.
>
> (Gambetta 1998, 104)

And, of course, there is Max Weber, who stated that the object of cognition for history and sociology was the "subjective meaning-complex of action" and that, consequently, ". . . collectivities must be treated as solely the resultants and modes of organization of the particular acts of individual persons, since these alone can be treated as agents in a course of subjectively understandable action" (Weber [1922] 1978, 13).

What these quotes suggest is that a fundamental or privileged status is to be attributed to intentional (rational) explanations. These explanations are 'rock bottom', 'especially satisfactory', or 'do not require further explanation'. In this view supra-individual explanations in terms of social structures and other macro features are either not genuinely explanatory, placeholders for individual explanations, or explanatory only when backed up by an individual-level account. There is no true social scientific explanation without descent to individual level and the explanatory regress stops there: Intentional explanations are genuinely explanatory, do not require support from sub-individual level. (Ylikoski 2012 discusses this as an argument for individualism; here we focus on special status of rational explanations.)

We do not question the place of such explanatory principles in our everyday interpretive practices. What we object to is the place of self-regarding rational action as *an ideal of natural order* for the social sciences. Stephen Toulmin (1961) argued that all sciences presuppose a conception of an ideal natural order that tells how events ought to play out if nothing impedes their natural course. The ideal of natural order determines what requires explanation and what is to be taken as inherently understandable. State of rest was the natural order for Aristotelian physics whereas Newtonian physics takes inertial motion to be the natural state not requiring further explanation. This is just the way things behave, unless otherwise perturbed. Similarly, rational and self-regarding action is presented as the way people behave, unless otherwise perturbed by errors in reasoning or special, other-regarding motives. The ideal embodies explanatory inequality (only irrational and non-selfish action requires explanation) and fundamentalism (rational explanation is self-explanatory). Rational self-regarding action would thus work as a so-called zero-law for the social sciences in providing a default baseline or contrast that guides theorizing, formulation of explanations, and empirical research.

In their introduction to a collected volume on rational choice sociology, James Coleman and Thomas Fararo explicitly make the connection to the ideal of natural order: "the idea of seeing collective life as irrationally bent . . . arises from the postulate of individual action as rational. It does not arise from the empirical generalization that all action is manifestly rational. . . . As Toulmin puts it, a theoretical discipline is often founded on a principle of natural order" (Coleman and Fararo 1992, xiv).

A similar idea can be found in John Harsanyi's work. Harsanyi (1982) claims that a normative theory of rationality is a necessary component in explanations of strategic interaction in the same way that competence in arithmetic is necessary for forming explanations of computing behavior. It does seem difficult to see how one could even formulate a mathematical *explanandum* without competence in arithmetic, and, so the idea goes, one cannot properly define the target of social explanation unless one understands what the correct strategies are. When these normative baselines are in place, behavior is always either simply (normatively) correct, and therefore self-explanatory, or a deviation to be explained.

What is wrong with such an idea of a normatively defined zero-law? There are at least three things. First, the very idea of an ideal of natural order is motivated by a mistaken idea about the nature of explanation. Second, a normatively defined baseline is not compatible with a causal-mechanical ideal of explanation in the sciences. Third, a normative baseline biases psychological and social scientific research in ways that hinder their progress.

First, the intuitive plausibility for the need for an ideal natural order in the explanation of human action rests on the following principle:

> [P] a genuine explanation requires that the *explanans* is itself explained or is self-explanatory

The underlying intuition is that understanding cannot be increased by replacing one mystery (the original *explanandum*) with a new mystery (the *explanans*). This leads to a regress of explanations, which has to stop at something that is somehow self-explanatory. Thus, in this view, nothing can be explained unless some things are inherently understandable. In the case of the individualist view of the social sciences, the regress applies to the supra-individual (macro) explanations and apparently irrational or other-regarding individual behavior, the self-explanatoriness to the intentional (rational and self-regarding) explanations (Ylikoski 2012). The self-explanatoriness of the intentional level is then given a philosophical/conceptual argument in terms of inherent intelligibility of action. Intentional action simply *is* behavior described as instrumentally rational (being goal-oriented) and trivially self-regarding (my goals being *my* goals).

The problem is that the principle [P] is false. The explanatory relation between the *explanans* and the *explanandum* is independent from the question of whether the *explanans* is itself explained. According to all causal theories of explanation, an explanation of X in terms of Y presupposes that Y is the case, but it does not presuppose that Y is itself explained. For example, according to most accounts of causal explanation, X is an explanation if and only if it is a suitable difference-maker with respect to Y. This does not require that we also have uncovered a difference-maker for X.[1]

The belief in [P] probably arises from a confusion between justification-seeking and explanation-seeking why-questions. It makes sense to ask how well justified are those reasons that one appeals to in justification of one's beliefs. It also makes sense to ask whether one is justified in believing the things that one appeals to in one's explanation. There needs to be evidence for the obtaining of X and for the causal dependency of Y on X (the mechanism between X and Y). But justifying one's belief in these claims is not the same as explaining why Y is the case. Similarly, it is clear that having an explanation for X enlarges our overall understanding, but this again is a separate issue from explaining Y itself.

It is worth noticing that while this argument for the privileged role for rationality refers to the inherent intelligibility of intentional action as the basis for the rational baseline, this is not the only way to justify the rationality assumption. For example, the standard defense of rationality in economics is based on an altogether different kind of argument. According to it, economic models are to be based on rational behavior not because it is inherently understandable, but because models of competitive markets deviating from self-interested instrumental rationality would reveal opportunities for arbitrage, which would be, or so the argument goes, exploited for profit, thus driving the modeled system eventually to the rational equilibrium. This argument is based on an assumption about the macro properties of competitive economic systems, not on the conceptual underpinnings of the interpretation of intentional states. This defense of rationality based on arbitrage can arguably serve as a basis for an appeal to disciplinary division of cognitive labor in that economics is in the business of analyzing incentive schemes, not intentional action as such. If this argument is successful, the rationality assumption in economics has very little to do with anything psychological.

The second, closely related, problem with the idea of ideal of natural order is that it is not compatible with a causal mechanistic understanding of scientific explanation. Scientific understanding of the world is increased when more is known about mind-independent causal structures. Scientists explain phenomena by uncovering their causes (or constitutive components). Most economists and rational choice social scientists are committed to providing such causal explanations. The idea that some causal explanations would be somehow inherently understandable is alien to such a view of science. While explanations at any field will bottom out somewhere, this is not a deep transcendental condition for the intelligibility of the natural world, but a pragmatic consequence of the division of cognitive labor between scientific fields.

Toulmin's prime example of a fundamental shift in the ideal order, the change from Aristotelian to Newtonian physics, is evocative, but ultimately misleading. Although especially economists are often accused of physics envy, it is highly questionable whether physics can serve as a blueprint for the structure of knowledge in the special sciences, including the social sciences. According to what is perhaps the current mainstream view, fundamental physical understanding is not causal in nature. According to at least one plausible metaphysical picture (Price and Corry 2007), (the most) fundamental physics is *not* in the business of providing explanations of why the most fundamental elements of our world behave as they do, but only aims at providing the most economical description of these regularities. Fundamental physical laws do not have (at least non-metaphysical) explanations in terms of causes and mechanisms. Therefore symmetry principles and such may well be taken as constitutive principles of understanding in foundational physics in that they are the most central axioms in the most economical way of representing fundamental regularities. Therefore changes in what are taken to be the most central organizing principles have implications for what is and what is not in need of explanation—in this sense of 'explanation'. However, it is not obvious how this has any relevance for the social sciences that arguably deal with phenomena constituted by hierarchical mechanistic complexity. Setting aside any 'physics envy', fundamental physics is not a very good model for social sciences. It is much more plausible to take social sciences as aiming to find causes and mechanisms like other special sciences. In this pursuit the idea of fundamental explanatory bedrock does not play any useful role.

Naturally it is possible to argue that the social sciences and intentional explanations are somehow special. Thus, an anti-naturalist interpretive understanding of social science could privilege folk-psychological ascription of intentional states as the relevant natural order of things. However, this strategy has two principal problems. First, in the recent debates the strong anti-naturalist position has had a hard time defending itself against causal alternatives (e.g., Henderson this volume and 2010). It might well be that the opposition of interpretive understanding and causal explanation does not really make sense. Second, it is not obvious that people advancing the rationalist position really want to associate themselves with these arguments. For example, most economists tend to portray themselves as 'hard' scientists rather than advocates of hermeneutical romanticism. Thus it would probably be philosophically easier for them to adopt a consistent naturalist position than to revert back to nineteenth-century anti-naturalist views. If the social sciences are in the business of producing causal knowledge that can be used to improve society, coherent narratives and catalogs of meanings are not enough.

The final set of problems with self-interested rational action as the idea of natural order consists of the biases it introduces into empirical research. The ideal dictates what kinds of behaviors, practices, and events require explanation and what would count as their explanation. These in turn drive the design of experiments, collection of data, and the evaluation of proposed theories. In fact, the idea of self-interested rational action provides a rather strong heuristic for doing social research, but the problem is that it is misleading. It suggests that human decision-making consists of rational core processes that are then disturbed by some additional mechanisms. If this were the case, then it would make sense to first figure out the rational baseline, then observe how the actual behavior diverges from this baseline, and then postulate theories about causal mechanisms that are responsible for this discrepancy.

However, strong heuristics are good only if their assumptions match the objects of study. In the case of self-interested rational baseline, the problem is that the match is missing. A cognitive architecture built around rational core processes would be an evolutionary miracle. It also lacks any serious neuroscientific or cognitive evidence that would support it. Its plausibility derives more from its affinity with our folk-psychological accounting practices and rationalistic philosophy, than from real empirical science. However, while its underlying assumptions do not hold, the heuristic consequences are real. Prominent examples of these biases can be found from the field of behavioral economics. This field of study has produced a variety of interesting laboratory phenomena (mostly about the ways in which human behavior diverges from the rational baseline), but it has so far been less successful in capturing the cognitive and social mechanisms behind those observations.

Behavioral economics can be defined as the pursuit of psychologically realistic economics by importing methods and results from psychological research. It is thus primarily concerned with providing a more realistic account of the individual decision-maker and consequently, but only indirectly, a better account of market-level phenomena. Nevertheless, since its conception,[2] behavioral economics has mostly consisted in providing experimental demonstrations of individual-level 'anomalies' to the standard microeconomic view of behavior. The more or less accepted body of results is made up of phenomena or 'exhibits' (Sugden 2005) such as the endowment effect, framing effects, non-linear probability weighing, and preference reversals. As an example, a prominent figure in (and a sometime critic of) behavioral economics puts the preferred division of cognitive labor between behavioral economics and economics proper in the following terms: "If principles of psychology have a role to play in explaining social choices, it must be to explain deviations from the general tendencies explained by the rational choice theories" (Plott 1996, 226). This is a clear statement of the way in which rationality as the ideal of natural order is to guide the selection of *explananda* and the organization of the division of cognitive labor. The question is whether this heuristic is the optimal one if the structure of human cognition is not in fact such that there is a central rational decision-making mechanism that usually produces rational behavior, but is now and then perturbed by other, more contingent, factors. An alternative, more naturalistic, view would start with the observation that correct and incorrect decisions are usually produced by the same psychological mechanisms. This implies that there will not be any principled asymmetry or inequality in explanations of normatively correct and incorrect decisions.[3]

Behavioral economists have also created models and theories to account for these perceived anomalies, most prominent being prospect theory. The distinguishing feature of these 'behavioral' theories of choice is that they stick to the core idea of choices being caused by maximization of expected utility and then add additional components to account for the robust experimental anomalies. In a review article, economist Matthew Rabin (1998) states that the main motivation of economists to engage with psychology is to produce a more detailed account of the utility function. Questions have been raised whether such 'fixes' to the core maximization conception add any psychological realism, since there is little empirical evidence that maximization would be a central psychological mechanism underlying choice to begin with (and a plethora of evidence falsifying related core assumptions about transforming, multiplying, and adding probabilities and values and having internal representations of all choice alternatives and outcomes, etc.). For example, Güth (2008) and Berg and Gigerenzer (2010) attack standard behavioral economics for being ill-conceived "repair programmes" trying to patch something that is fundamentally flawed as a description of the actual psychological processes driving behavior. In its place, Güth advocates an account based on satisficing and Berg and Gigerenzer a psychology based on simple heuristics. We do not need to take sides on this debate here, but only emphasize the critical point that how the psychological mechanisms of choice are structured is a purely empirical matter and that theories of these mechanisms should not be constrained by normative *a priori* conceptions of rationality.

The design of the experiments is based on assumptions about cognition: People are assumed to understand the transparently described experimental situation and then reason about it according to normative model. Only on this assumption can the experiment be said to test the highly abstract economic hypothesis. If people's cognition does not accord with these assumptions, the experiment does not test the original hypothesis. It might produce some interesting observations about influence of the various situational factors (related to framing, contexts, stakes, etc.), but generalizability of these observations is limited. When the experimental setup is designed to keep contextual influences out, the ones that manage to influence the subjects (by giving them cues about the nature of the situation) probably have much larger effect than in more natural conditions. Thus for example, cues like two dots resembling eyes on a screen have an out-of-proportion effect on the interpretation of the situation in an experimental situation. The key point here is that if we have different ideas about how human cognition works, we also design different kinds of experiments. The experiments based on the wrong model of cognition may sometimes produce interesting or surprising observations, but they are not conducive for production of data that allow progressive tracking of underlying causal mechanisms.

A range of such behavioral laboratory experiments (Ultimatum, Dictator, Public Goods . . .) have repeatedly falsified the crude picture of a purely self-regarding decision-maker. One theory proposed to explain these anomalous results is that people have social preferences, that is, their utility function incorporates arguments such as the well-being of others, fairness, or equality. Such social preferences would also be the explanation of all the apparently altruistic and pro-social behavior keeping our societies together. Although the idea of social preferences sounds plausible, even trivial, it is not the only hypothesis in the running. Other explanations offered are that people mistakenly frame one-shot anonymous interactions as repeated games in which conditional cooperation is a rational self-regarding strategy (Binmore 2006) or that it is the social norms (Bicchieri 2006) rather than the outcomes *per se* which drive behavior. What is relevant for our argument is that the social preference theory is premised on the idea that we need a separate mechanism to account for such observed choice behavior that deviates from the self-interest default. This presupposition influences the way the experiments are designed and, especially, the way in which the results are interpreted.

For example, Dana *et al.* (2007) argue that laboratory experiments do not really establish the existence of social preferences and that people act pro-socially because they care about how their actions are perceived, not about fair outcomes as such. They carried out binary dictator games with several modifications introducing moral "wiggle room" for behaving self-interestedly. The modifications included giving the dictator a (costless) option to remain ignorant about the consequences of her decision, including another dictator to share the blame (although either one could unilaterally implement the pro-social outcome), and providing the dictator with plausible deniability by introducing a randomization device that could have been, from the viewpoint of the recipient, responsible for the choice. In all cases, the fundamental incentive structure was the same, but the selfishness of the dictators' actions rose substantially.

The wiggle room experiments are in many ways ingenious and the results certainly interesting. What is even more interesting is the default interpretation of the results in the literature. The fact that providing uncertainty, ignorance, and plausible deniability as excuses for behaving more selfishly did indeed sizably increase selfish behavior is automatically interpreted as proving that apparent other-regarding behavior is only due to self-interested desire to appear altruistic, which masks the fundamental self-interested motivations. This is so even if a sizeable number of subjects, in some treatments even the majority, still managed to behave pro-socially, even though the experiment was such as to provide options (to the point of pushing) to act selfishly. An alternative interpretation of the same results free of the bias towards self-interest as the default is that the experiments show that people simply have different preferences regarding the outcomes of others and that most people also, not surprisingly, care about how their behavior is interpreted. Such experiments, along with experiments providing ambiguity (Dana *et al.* 2006; Haisley and Weber 2010) or the possibility of exiting the interaction situation (Lazear *et al.* 2012), should perhaps be seen as demonstrating the malleability of human behavior to changes in the way the subjects experience how they are expected to behave in general, rather than as uncovering the pure self-interested motivations or universal and stable social preferences.

If 'rationality' is diluted to mean the preferential use of models based on constrained optimization and 'self-interest' to simply mean goal-oriented, then one has to question the point of calling these relatively unproblematic things with such normatively loaded words. Especially since the unfortunate terminology makes important empirical questions conceptually impossible to ask. The extent, determinants, and consequences of substantial self-interest as the motivator of social action are all important empirical social scientific questions. For example, self-interest seems not to be a predictive factor for voting behavior in general, but is so in cases when the economic and social consequences of the candidate's policies have been made cognitively accessible to the voter (see Kim 2014 for references). In general, self-interest seems to be amenable to cognitive triggering by priming across a variety of contexts. In the next part we briefly lay out an alternative empirical theory of self-interest: rational self-interested action is not a foundational default mode of behavior but an achievement partly upheld by social norms.

PART II: EXPLAINING SELF-INTERESTED ACTION

When self-interested action is given up as an ideal of natural order, it emerges as a thing to be explained. It is a complex *explanandum,* not an inherently transparent *explanans*. Here we can only discuss one piece of this empirical puzzle.

Social psychologist Dale Miller (1999) has suggested that self-interested action is not a deep feature of individual psychology, but a social achievement upheld by context-dependent cultural norms. According to Miller's theory, consistent pursuit of self-interest is partly sustained by a widely accepted pseudoscientific folk theory about the 'deep' driving forces of human behavior and is as such a part of the self-fulfilling structure of the social reality. People behave selfishly because they think that others expect them to behave selfishly. Miller's theory has multiple components. The first element is a folk theory about human motivation. According to this theory, monetary incentives strongly motivate people and this is also reflected in their attitudes. This folk theory is further legitimized by scientific theories, like the economic model of *homo economicus*, that are in fact based on the same folk assumptions.

What is distinctive about this theory is that it is mostly about motivations of other people. As set of experiments by Miller and Rebecca Ratner (1998) shows, people believe that self-interest is a strong motivator for other people even in situations where their own attitudes and behavior are not influenced by it. (Similar observation is made in experiments by Justin Krueger and Thomas Gilovich 1999.) Thus people overestimate how much other people are motivated by their own material interests. They are also highly stubborn in this belief (Critcher and Dunning 2011).

The second component of Miller's theory is the idea that the folk theory of human motivation can serve as a basis for self-fulfilling prophecy in cooperative situations. If you are willing to cooperate, but believe that others will not cooperate, there is not much point in cooperation if the realization of the goal presupposes that most will contribute. This set of beliefs easily leads to behaviors that provide further support for similar beliefs in others. While public goods games do not really model collaborative situations like this, they are close. Thus in repeated games even those hopefuls who started cooperating soon learn the futility of their attempts and give up cooperation. A number of different things are going on in this situation. First, non-cooperation becomes a descriptive norm. Thus if people are sensitive to what most others do, and expect you to be as well, they will find conforming to the norm appealing. Second, being ready to benefit others (or doing chores that are pointless if others are not doing their part) when others are not reciprocating is a recipe for further exploitation. Nobody wants to be a sucker in the eyes of others. The avoidance of such situations *(sugrophobia),* with its associated self-blame (Effron and Miller 2011), is a strong determinant of behavior that is not reducible to anticipation of a pecuniary loss (see Vohs, Baumeister and Chin 2007).

The folk theory of self-interested action serves as a basis for a self-fulfilling prophecy also in institutional design (Miller 1999; Schwartz 2012). When you believe that others are strongly motivated by their self-interest, the emphasis on institutional design is to avoid situations where dishonest individuals (Hume's knaves) can exploit others or the institutional arrangement. What is not on the agenda is supporting and developing arrangements that would help people to express and cultivate their non-selfish motivations. When most situations are framed in terms of self-interested action, such behaviors are only natural, which in turn provide even more evidence for the folk theory of self-interested action.

The third major component of Miller's theory is the influence of folk theory in the accounts people give for their actions. People are constantly providing accounts of their behavior, both to others and to themselves. The format and vocabulary of these accounts is based on culturally shared views about plausible and acceptable causes of action. Now, if the vocabulary and explanatory schemes for non-selfish behavior are underdeveloped, or if they lack credibility, accounting for non-selfish behavior becomes more difficult. This is what Miller says to be the case. Usually people are ready to accept accounts that appeal to self-interested motivations as honest, but treat non-selfish accounts with suspicion. This is an interesting asymmetry that has important consequences as it supports the norm of self-interest. As people do not want to give rise to suspicion, they will attempt to normalize their non-selfish behaviors by presenting them as self-interested. We say that we want to help because it is fun (produces warm glow) or in our long-term interest (reputation gains). Miller suggests that this bias for accounts based on self-interest constrains our unselfish behavior: We tend to act on our non-selfish impulses only when we can find a self-interested frame to account for our behavior. We feel that without a relevant interest, it is not appropriate or justified to act on a purely public issue (Ratner and Miller 2001). Similarly, people tend to donate more to charitable causes if they can frame donations in terms of exchange (Holmes, Miller, and Lerner 1999). The practice of offering potential charity donors products in exchange for their donations produces more donations than appeals to charity alone. According to Miller and his associates, this is based on the opportunity the fiction of exchange provides for acting on their (non-selfish) impulse without unwanted psychological burden of providing a self-interested rationalization. Thus the candles people get in exchange for their donations are not true incentives—people do not need those candles nor they would they buy them from a store—but psychological covers for expressions of compassion. The incentives do not so much motivate charitable giving, they rather disinhibit it by providing a ready justification for it.

Disbelief and suspicion created by accounts of behavior that do not match expectations are strong negative social sanctions. Nobody wants to appear foolish, crazy, or open to exploitation. Such categorizations affect both how we think about ourselves and how others think about us as potential collaborators in various social activities. These have a strong influence on our behavior, thus providing an important path for folk theory about human motivation to mold our behavior. If we do not have a sufficient vocabulary to describe non-selfish motivations in a credible manner, or if providing such accounts takes a lot of work, we tend to avoid behaviors that lack self-oriented justification. We might tolerate, or even praise, small-scale non-selfish impulses, but in important matters such motivations appear suspicious. We might also accept that special sorts of persons—saints—might be genuinely motivated by non-selfish motivations, but these people are not ordinary people.

Now, there is a lot of work to be done with Miller's theory. For example, he is quite vague about societies that are under the spell of the norm of self-interest. Does it apply to North America, the Western world, or most known societies? There is also a lot of empirical testing to be done (Kim 2014). The most parts of the theory are still untested, and those parts that have been tested are open to alternative interpretations (for exchange fiction hypothesis see Simpson *et al.* 2006; Briers *et al.* 2007). However, there are a number of reasons why it is a very interesting theory from the naturalistic point of view.

First, in contrast to much of current theorizing about norms within rational choice theory, it does not regard norm-influenced behavior as a residual category that covers only those cases that cannot be rationalized by self-interested motivations. Rather than treating influence by social norms as an ad hoc explanatory resource, it is treated as (one) basic mechanism that influences social behavior irrespective whether it is 'rational' or not.[4] No *a priori* ideal of natural order limits its explanatory potential. It is a purely empirical matter how strong this mechanism is, and which factors modulate its influence. Naturally, it is only one mechanism that influences social behavior. Thus it is not suggested that the norm of self-interest is the full story about self-interested behavior.

Second, while the above discussion has speculated about some motivations that make people behave according to the norm of self-interest, the theory is not based on any fundamental theory of human motivation. It does not even presuppose that the talk about 'ultimate motivations' makes sense. While the rational choice theorists usually take seriously the idea that there are ultimate motives of human behavior, consistent naturalists should not take for granted that such an assumption makes sense. While it is an undeniable part of our folk-psychological accounting practices to consider hierarchies between reasons and to consider those motivations that are strong, ever-present, and general as more fundamental, there is no reason to assume that the 'ultimate motives' are psychologically real (outside of our accounting practices). If ultimate motives are real, they require a very special sort of cognitive architecture, which nobody has been able to articulate, not to mention accumulating evidence in its support. Such architectures have no justification for being treated as a default assumption. It is also very doubtful whether such ultimate springs of action could be found out by armchair speculation or by simple economic experiments. A more plausible research strategy is to follow empirical findings without prejudice and at least tentatively to assume that people are prone to act on all kinds of impulses, be they rational or irrational, selfish or non-selfish, or something that cannot be described with these terms.

Third, once the speculative psychology underlying rational choice theory is cleared away, there is room for a naturalistic account of development and sustenance of the competence for rational action. While for rational choice theorists rational (and self-interested) action is the explanatory baseline that requires no justification or explanation, for a naturalist the instances of consistent pursuit of self-interest are an empirical puzzle requiring explanation. It is not a natural state that we deviate from when we are children, when suffering from mental problems, when drunk, or when tired. Rather, it is an achievement that has many developmental precursors and is supported by significant institutional scaffolding (Hutto 2008). The emergence and development of rational and self-interested behavior can be studied in various timescales (evolutionary, historical, individual life-course), but we surmise that the norm of self-interest has a role to play in all of them. It provides a bridge that brings together psychological development of an individual (development of cognitive abilities, increasing impulse-control, development of ability to construct folk-psychological narratives of self and other) and social settings (social norms, practices of self-presentation and justification of action, institutions) in a way that allows us to consider how our ideas about human motivation could be different and how they could make a difference to the social life we live.

CONCLUSION

Our shared everyday psychological conceptualization of human behavior may well be linked to a normative ideal of rationality. To regard something as an agent is to conceive its behavior as a deliberate pursuit of ends. It is also true that much of the science of human behavior, especially of the sciences of social behavior and larger social aggregates, is conceptually based on these folk-psychological practices. We have argued that it nevertheless does not follow that scientific understanding of human behavior should be based on the normative ideal of rationality. Self-interested rationality is not an inherently understandable bedrock, an ideal of natural order, required to ground the intelligibility of social explanations. Scientific explanation does not require such bedrock to begin with: We can causally explain phenomena without yet having an explanation for the cause. We have further argued that the normative conception of rationality should not even be considered as a baseline defining the deviations in need of explanation. Using such a baseline biases the scientific study of human behavior if it does not correspond to the way in which our psychological mechanisms are in fact structured. We should not systematically offer different kinds of explanations to correct and incorrect decisions, if they are causal products of the same psychological processes.

When self-interested rationality is stripped of its special explanatory status, it itself becomes an interesting object of explanation. We have given an example of one particularly interesting theory of self-interested behavior, which regards such behavior as being caused by self-fulfilling beliefs in self-interest as a fundamental motivational factor. As an object of scientific inquiry, self-interested action is not a normative baseline for explanation, or precondition of, agenthood, but a behavioral pattern requiring explanation in terms of social and cognitive causal mechanisms.

NOTES

1 Notice that this explanatory dependence is based on local facts about causal dependence. Thus whether or not an explanation of a particular phenomenon captures the right causal factors is a local matter having little to do with subsuming the phenomenon under a broader unifying framework. The regress intuition drove Michael Friedman (1974) and Philip Kitcher (1989) to explicitly advocate a view according to which understanding was a global feature of belief systems. Such a global conception of understanding has been the subject of devastating criticism.

2 An important ancestor of behavioral economics is a branch of early cognitive psychology in the 1970s called 'behavioral decision research' (BDR), which applied the newly emerged ideas about computational manipulation of internal representations to explain deviations from rationality (Angner and Loewenstein 2012).

3 This is essentially the same symmetry principle as proposed by the proponents of the strong programme of sociology of scientific knowledge (Barnes, Bloor and Henry 1996). If the goal is the production of scientific causal explanations, then normative attitudes towards the *explananda,* whether it be correct and incorrect decisions or correct and incorrect scientific theories, should not influence the selection of causal *explanantia.*

4 It is important to notice that this account of social norms is not based on the Parsonsian story about psychological internalization of norms. In our view, social norms are based on agents' beliefs about other agents' behaviors, expectations, and tendencies to sanction one's behavior. Thus it is important to distinguish social norms and motivations for following them. The existence of a social norm is a social fact, but the motivations to follow it might vary. People might follow a social norm because they attempt to avoid negative sanctions or aim to be rewarded by positive sanctions, they attempt to please others by fulfilling their expectations, they might find the norm legitimate or morally justified, they might have internalized it as a personal moral principle, or they might just follow their habit (Bicchieri 2006).

REFERENCES

Angner, Erik and George F. Loewenstein. 2012. Behavioral Economics. In *Philosophy of Economics,* edited by Uskali Mäki, 641–689. Amsterdam: Elsevier.
Barnes, Barry, David Bloor and John Henry. 1996. *Scientific Knowledge. A Sociological Analysis*. London : Athlone Press.

Berg, Nathan and Gerd Gigerenzer. 2010. As-If Behavioral Economics: Neoclassical Economics in Disguise? *History of Economic Ideas* 18: 133–165.

Bicchieri, Christina 2006. *The Grammar of Society: The Nature and Dynamics of Social Norms.* Cambridge: Cambridge University Press.

Binmore, Ken. 2006. Why Do People Cooperate? *Politics, Philosophy and Economics* 5: 81–96.

Boudon, Raymond. 1998. Social Mechanisms without Black Boxes. In *Social Mechanisms: An Analytical Approach to Social Theory,* edited by Peter Hedström and Richard Swedberg, 172–203. Cambridge: Cambridge University Press.

Brandom, Robert. 1994. *Making It Explicit.* Cambridge, MA: Harvard University Press.

Briers, Barbara, Mario Pandelaere and Luk Warlop. 2007. Adding Exchange to Charity: A Reference Price Explanation. *Journal of Economic Psychology* 28(1): 15–30.

Coleman, James. 1994. *Foundations of Social Theory.* Cambridge, MA: Harvard University Press.

Coleman, James and Thomas Fararo. 1992. Introduction. In *Rational Choice Theory: Advocacy and Critique,* edited by J. Coleman and T. Fararo, ix–xxii. Thousand Oaks: Sage.

Critcher, Clayton and David Dunning. 2011. No Good Deed Goes Unquestioned: Cynical Reconstruals Maintain Belief in the Power of Self-Interest. *Journal of Experimental Social Psychology* 47(6): 1207–1213.

Dana, Jason D., Daylian M. Cain and Robyn M. Dawes. 2006. What You Don't Know Won't Hurt Me: Costly (But Quiet) Exit in Dictator Games. *Organizational Behavior and Human Decision Processes* 100: 193–201.

Dana, Jason, Roberto Weber and Jason Xi Kuang. 2007. Exploiting Moral Wiggle Room: Experiments Demonstrating an Illusory Preference for Fairness. *Economic Theory* 33: 67–80.

Davidson, Donald. 1980. *Essays on Actions and Events.* Oxford: Clarendon Press.

Effron, Daniel and Dale Miller. 2011. Reducing Exposure to Trust-Related Risks to Avoid Self-Blame. *Personality and Social Psychology Bulletin* 37(2): 181–192.

Friedman, Michael. 1974. Explanation and Scientific Understanding. *Journal of Philosophy* 71: 5–19.

Gambetta, Diego. 1998. Concatenations of Mechanisms. In *Social Mechanisms: An Analytical Approach to Social Theory,* edited by Peter Hedström and Richard Swedberg, 102–124. Cambridge: Cambridge University Press.

Güth, Werner. 2008. (Non-) Behavioral Economics—A Programmatic Assessment. *Journal of Psychology* 216: 244–253.

Haisley, Emily and Roberto A. Weber. 2010. Self-Serving Interpretations of Ambiguity in Other-Regarding Behavior. *Games and Economic Behavior* 68: 634–645.

Harsanyi, John. 1982. Subjective Probability and the Theory of Games: Comments on Kadane and Larkey's Paper. *Management Science* 28(2): 120–124.

Hedström, Peter and Petri Ylikoski. 2014. Analytical Sociology and Rational Choice Theory. In *Analytical Sociology: Norms, Actions and Networks,* edited by Gianluca Manzo, 57–70. New York: Wiley.

Henderson, David. 2010. Rationality Naturalized and Rationalizing Explanation. *Philosophy of Social Science* 40: 30–58.

Holmes, John, Dale Miller and Melvin Lerner. 2002. Committing Altruism under the Cloak of Self-Interest: The Exchange Fiction. *Journal of Experimental Social Psychology* 38(2): 144–151.

Hutto, Daniel. 2008. *Folk Psychological Narratives: The Sociocultural Basis of Understanding Reasons.* Cambridge, MA: MIT Press.

Kim, Anita. 2014. The Curious Case of Self-Interest: Inconsistent Effects and Ambivalence toward a Widely Accepted Construct. *Journal for the Theory of Social Behaviour* 44(1): 99–122.

Kitcher, Philip. 1989. Explanatory Unification and the Causal Structure of the World. In *Scientific Explanation,* edited by P. Kitcher and W. Salmon, 410–505. Minneapolis: University of Minnesota Press.

Kruger, Justin and Thomas Gilovich. 1999. 'Naive Cynicism' in Everyday Theories of Responsibility Assessment: On Biased Assumptions of Bias. *Journal of Personality and Social Psychology* 76(5): 743–753.

Lazear, Edward, Ulrike Malmendier and Roberto Weber. 2012. Sorting in Experiments with Application to Social Preferences. *American Economic Journal: Applied Economics* 4: 136–163.

Lehtinen, Aki and Jaakko Kuorikoski. 2007. Unrealistic Assumptions in Rational Choice Theory. *Philosophy of the Social Sciences* 37: 115–138.

Millar, Alan. 2004. *Understanding People: Normativity and Rationalizing Explanation.* Oxford: Oxford University Press.

Miller, Dale. 1999. The Norm of Self-Interest. *American Psychologist* 54: 1053–1060.

Miller, Dale and Rebecca Ratner. 1998. The Disparity between the Actual and Assumed Power of Self-Interest. *Journal of Personality and Social Psychology* 74: 53–62.

Plott, Charles. 1996. Rational Individual Behavior in Markets and Social Choice Processes: The Discovered Preference Hypothesis. In *The Rational Foundations of Economic Behaviour,* edited by K. E. Arrow, M. Colombatto, M. Perlman and C. Schmidt, 225–250. New York: Macmillan.

Price, Huw and Richard Corry. (eds.) 2007. *Causation, Physics, and the Constitution of Reality.* Oxford: Oxford University Press.

Rabin, Matthew. 1998. Psychology and Economics. *Journal of Economic Literature* 36: 11–46.

Ratner, Rebecca and Dale Miller. 2001. The Norm of Self-Interest and Its Effects on Social Action. *Journal of Personality and Social Psychology* 81: 5–16.

Schwartz, Barry. 2012. Crowding Out Morality: How the Ideology of Self-Interest Can Be Self-Fulfilling. In *Ideology, Psychology, and Law,* edited by J. Hanson, 160–184. Oxford: Oxford University Press.

Simpson, Brent, Kyle Irwin and Peter Lawrence. 2006. Does a 'Norm of Self-Interest' Discourage Prosocial Behavior? Rationality and Quid Pro Quo in Charitable Giving. *Social Psychology Quarterly* 69(3): 296–306.

Sugden, Robert. 2005. Experiments as Exhibits and Experiments as Tests. *Journal of Economic Methodology* 12(2): 291–302.

Toulmin, Stephen. 1961. *Foresight and Understanding.* London: Hutchinson.

Vohs, Kathleen, Roy Baumeister and Jason Chin. 2007. Feeling Duped: Emotional, Motivational, and Cognitive Aspects of Being Exploited by Others. *Review of General Psychology* 11(2): 127–141.

Weber, Max. 1978. *Economy and Society.* Edited by Roth, Günther and Claus Wittich. Berkeley: University of California Press. Original edition, 1922.

Ylikoski, Petri. 2012. Micro, Macro, and Mechanisms. In *The Oxford Handbook of Philosophy of the Social Sciences,* edited by Harold Kincaid, 21–45. Oxford: Oxford University Press.

———. 2013. The (Hopefully) Last Stand of the Covering Law Theory—A Reply to Opp. *Social Science Information* 52: 383–393.

14 Can Expected Utility Theory's Notion of Rationality Be Explanatory?

Lina Eriksson

THE NORMATIVE NOTION OF RATIONALITY

The notion of rationality is normative—there is something *wrong* with a person who is not rational. This is so even though we disagree somewhat about what exactly rationality requires. Our folk-psychological notion of rationality involves many different aspects of the concept, but most importantly, it includes some reasonable level of instrumental rationality and consistency. Within Expected Utility Theory (EUT), this folk-psychological notion of rationality has been sharpened; rational behavior is seen as expected utility-maximizing behavior, which involves, among other things, quite stringent requirements of consistency and appropriate responses to changes in probabilities of various outcomes. I will refer to this notion of rationality as *strong rationality*. EUT can be, and sometimes is, understood as just a normative theory. But it has also played a very important role as an explanatory and predictive theory in social science. When we discuss whether—and if so, how—social science should be naturalized, we therefore need to address whether—and if so, how—social science can be naturalized with respect to the normative notion of rationality.

Paraphrasing Kornblith on naturalizing epistemology (Kornblith 1994), we can ask:

1. How ought we to reason?
2. How do we reason?
3. Are the processes by which we reason also the ones by which we ought to reason?

Advocates of the view that we should naturalize rationality usually claim that scientific explanation of human behavior only requires an answer to question (2). Question (1) is irrelevant for the explanation of human behavior. Let us therefore call the view that social science can and should be naturalized with respect to the normative notion of rationality *Irrelevance*.

Opponents of the view that we should naturalize rationality of course hold somewhat different views about what role rationality plays in explanations.

But I take the main such view to be what I will refer to as *The normative is explanatory*. According to this view, when we explain somebody's behavior, it is not enough—or at least not always enough—to provide an answer to question (2), namely, an account of how that person actually made their decision to behave in that way. Some reference to an answer to question (1) about how we *should* make decisions plays a part, even if only a minor one, in the explanation of behavior too. The conflict between advocates of *Irrelevance* and advocates of *The normative is explanatory* thus concerns how we should answer the question: what, if anything, is gained by using the notion of rationality to describe people's decision-making rather than just describing what it is that they do in non-normative terms?

I will argue that a standard principle of charity argument cannot establish an explanatory role for strong rationality, even if it might do so for a weaker notion of rationality. But there are other reasons to think that strong rationality has a legitimate explanatory role to play. I discuss three. I then turn to objections against the view that strong rationality can be explanatory, including the standard one that people often and systematically violate strong rationality. My conclusion is nevertheless a qualified yes in favor of an explanatory role for strong rationality.

RATIONALITY AND THE PRINCIPLE OF CHARITY

A common argument in favor of using an assumption of rationality to explain people's behavior is that such an assumption is necessary if people are to be understood as *intentional* agents. We understand behavior as action because the behavior followed in particular ways from the desires and beliefs we ascribe to the person in question. If it does not follow from these desires and beliefs, we either revise the desires and/or beliefs we ascribed to the agent so as to achieve the fit between desires and beliefs on the one hand and the behavior on the other, or, when this is not possible, we fail to understand the behavior as expressing an intention at all. Daniel Dennett has argued that in order to at all ascribe such things as beliefs and desires to others, we need to first determine that it is appropriate to take what he refers to as an 'intentional stance' towards them. That is, we must presume that they are rational: that they will not accept contradictory beliefs, etc. Because if they happily "believe" both that it rains and that it does not rain, for example, then we cannot make sense of what they are doing as *believing* something about the weather (Dennett 1978).

The argument that a notion of rationality is necessary in order to understand people as intentional agents is usually not made to defend strong rationality *per se*. But can an explanatory role for strong rationality be defended in the same way? The problem would be, of course, that if people are not fully rational, in the sense outlined by strong rationality, then perhaps we cannot see them as agents acting with intentions. And people are seldom fully rational . . .

Stephen Stich is among those that point out that our decision-making often is far from perfect. But he claims that this does not mean that we cannot understand people as intentional agents. What is required for such understanding is not that people conform to an objectively correct notion of rationality, but that they are people *like us*. What matters is that the mistakes they make are the kind of mistakes that we ourselves could easily make. And some violations of rationality are mistakes we could easily make, others are not (Stich 1994). If Stich is right, then perhaps what is needed for a good explanation is not that behavior is understood as rational, but that it is understood as behavior that we ourselves could perform.

I think Stich is correct in that people do not need to be perfectly rational in, say, the sense of strong rationality, in order to be interpreted as intentional agents. However, the choice is not between *that* very strong notion of rationality, and no notion of rationality. If we did not think of our own behavior as somewhat directed to goals, where means were chosen because they had some reasonable chance of making us achieve those goals, and where beliefs were updated in a way that tracked truth in at least an approximate fashion, then I don't think we would be able to think of ourselves and others as intentional agents either. What is required is however not that we comply with a very strong notion of rationality, such that we perform probability calculations with ease and update our beliefs as perfect Bayesians. A much weaker notion of rationality is sufficient. Notice that Stich's claim is a problem only for a rather demanding notion of rationality, one that we systematically violate, but is perfectly compatible with the claim that a weaker notion of rationality is required in order for us to understand ourselves and others as intentional agents.

It is thus important to recognize that we operate with more than one notion of rationality at the same time. The kind of rationality that is necessary if we are to understand each other as agents who act on intentions is a rather basic one: a sufficient instrumentally rational connection between actions and the desires and beliefs that motivated those actions, plus possibly some broad notion of what counts as intelligible goals and some reasonable constraints on belief formation. The kind of rationality that researchers find that we regularly deviate from, on the other hand, is not like this. *That* kind of rationality is usually strong rationality, and presupposes a significant ability to deal with probabilities, perfect information, or familiarity with Bayesian epistemology, and finally, it tends to concern cases presented to people in abstract terms, rather than in realistic, concrete terms that are more similar to what people encounter in real life. This is, so to speak, a sharpened notion of the kind of rationality required to make sense of ourselves and others as agents.

When we discuss whether the normative notion of rationality can be 'done away with' in social science, I therefore think it is important to keep in mind which notion of rationality we are talking about. There is a multitude of such notions, some sharper, others more basic. The proponents of the view that the normative notion of rationality for explaining human behavior tend to rely on a more basic notion, the critics tend to draw attention to the common violations of the requirements of much sharper notions of rationality, like strong rationality.

If I want to defend an explanatory role for *strong* rationality, I can thus not rely on the argument that a notion of rationality is necessary for us to understand people as intentional agents. However, I will argue that even this notion of rationality can have a role (or rather, several different roles) to play in explanations of human behavior.

REASONS TO THINK EUT CAN PLAY AN EXPLANATORY ROLE, AFTER ALL

One such role is as a standard of comparison and evaluation. It is illustrative to consider the way the strong notion of rationality is active 'in the background', so to speak, in the literature on bounded rationality.

Beginning with Herbert Simon's work in the 1950s (for example, Simon 1957), it has grown to become an important and major part of the literature on decision-making. It is based on the recognition that real people don't have perfect calculation abilities, unlimited time to devote to decision-making, perfect information, etc. What is needed is therefore a theory of 'rationality for real people'. Real people do not have the time, energy, money, and/ or ability to ensure that each decision they make is the best possible one. Instead they make decisions under a whole lot of constraints that means they aim for decisions that are good enough, rather than best. To spend the time, energy, and money necessary to really make the best possible decision of what toothpaste to buy, you would lose time, energy, and money needed for more important decisions (Byron 1998). And in many cases, we simply do not have the capacity for reasoning that would be required for optimal decisions; we thus have no choice but to get by as best as we can with the limited cognitive abilities that we have. In Simon's later work, he offered yet another interpretation, namely, that bounded rationality was not so much about the product of thought, but the procedure of thought. People do not aim directly to maximize—or even to satisfice—utility, but rather, they make decisions according to reasonable decision-making procedures, and go with whatever decision those procedures result in (Simon 1978, 1995).

The theory of bounded rationality has given rise to a lot of research on how people actually make decisions. One prominent example is the research by Gerd Gigerenzer and his colleagues on the decision heuristics people use (Gigerenzer and Sturm 2012). Instead of trying to go through conscious calculations of what the best option is, we use heuristics—rules of thumb—to make decisions quickly and without a lot of cognitive effort. We could of course talk about any kind of fast decision-influencing strategy we have (for example, when buying a house, you could rely on astrology rather than do your financial research) as a 'fast and frugal heuristic'. But (apart from the fact that 'frugal' means 'achieving the good results with less resources', which implicitly already relies on a normative standard for results) this would not be helpful for researchers in this field. They are interested in heuristics that give the same, or similar enough, results as conscious, deliberate, clear thinking, not in just any kind of quick, random hunches. It is thus not the case that strong rationality becomes irrelevant: Rather, it is underlying the development of the concept of bounded rationality, determining the interpretation of what counts as a reasonable decision under limitations, rather than as stupidity.

Further, presumably we have these decision heuristics and not others *because* they tend to give these results. With '*because* they tend to do so', I mean the following: because an evolutionary process has equipped us with the tools for making decisions that are not completely detrimental to us getting what we want (compare with Rouse's discussion in this volume) and because of learning. This is thus the second reason that rationality can have a role to play in social science: not only as a standard of comparison, but also as part of an explanation for why we have the psychology we do, indeed, as a reason to expect us to *be* approximately rational. Instrumentally rational and consistent behavior is important because it is such behavior that is likely to make agents successful. Similar arguments have been made in regards to other areas of human cognitive abilities. For example, Quine argued that because the kind of people who regularly made incorrect inductive inferences would not survive for long, a result of evolution was that we are the kind of people who tend to make correct inductive inferences (Quine 1969). Evolution has equipped us with tools that make us approximately rational in indirect ways.

The third reason why rationality can have a role to play is that not only do we happen to have rules of thumb that allow us to make approximately rational decisions, we often also deliberately, consciously *try* to be rational. We think about appropriate means to ends, consider chances, worry about risks, compare the magnitudes of what we might gain or lose, and so on—in short, we try to be rational. If it is pointed out to us that our choices are inconsistent, or that there are much better means to our goals than the ones we've chosen, we often (although not always) try to modify our behavior. And this, too, provides a reason to expect us to *be* approximately rational, at least sometimes, and therefore, to give rationality an explanatory role.

Recent literature on decision-making has focused to such a great extent on how our decisions fail to be rational, that it might seem as if rationality has no role to play. But it's important to keep in mind, just as Quine noted with respect to induction, that even though we certainly make mistakes, not all decisions (or inductive inferences) are mistaken. Evolution has made us the kind of creatures who are reasonably good at instrumentally rational thinking, and who are reasonably consistent, and who are at least somewhat responsive to probabilities. Not perfect. But not completely irrational either. The mere fact that we make a lot of systematic reasoning mistakes should thus not be allowed to hide from view another fact, which is just as indisputable, namely, that we also often manage to reason relatively rationally. We could see the glass as half empty and focus on all the mistakes we make; but we could also see it as half full and focus on the fact that we routinely make reasonably rational decisions. The here outlined reasons for why rationality can have a role to play are certainly not the result of deep, original thinking on my part. But that shouldn't make us ignore them.

POSSIBLE OBJECTIONS

However, that said, there is also reason to be skeptical about how much these reasons can in fact justify. It certainly seems like forming reasonably accurate beliefs about things such as the danger of car crashes would be conducive to our health, at least if we are also rational enough to act on those beliefs in a reasonable manner. But it nevertheless remains true that a lot of people do underestimate the danger, and/or overestimate their driving abilities, and as a result drive too fast, sometimes with horrific consequences. Similarly, although a proper understanding of probabilities and good causal reasoning would doubtless be of value to us in many situations, it nevertheless remains true that the evolutionary pressure on us to develop such an understanding has not been strong enough to result in behavior that always conforms to the rationality dictates of EUT. Take for example the representativeness heuristic, discussed by Stich in the article mentioned above (Stich 1994). The tendency to match 'like with like'; to think that a major event must have a major cause, or, to use Stich's own example, to think that the burnt skull from a red bush-monkey is an effective treatment of epilepsy because the monkey's movement pattern reminds us of the jerky movements of a person who is having an epileptic seizure (Stich 1994, 348, original example from Nisbett and Wilson 1977), is not even indirectly rational. And there is now plenty of research from behavioral economics and psychology that shows that the representativeness heuristic is not a rare case. For example, according to Kahneman and Tversky's prospect theory (1979), people systematically violate the dictates of EUT by being more averse to losses than they are motivated by opportunities to gain. And there is substantial data that supports this (for a discussion, see Qattrone and Tversky 1988).

Despite the reasons I outlined above for thinking that we can expect people to be at least approximately rational, it is thus also obvious that sometimes, we are not. We must therefore ask what value strong rationality has, if many of our decision-making tendencies are not, in fact, rational, even in this indirect evolutionary sense.

Some answer this question with a resounding "Not much!" People violate the dictates of rationality to such an extent, they argue, that we would do better to explain decisions without categorizing those decisions as rational or irrational. And there are also other possible worries about using the categories of rational and irrational behavior: Such categorizations might lead us to mis-identify what it is that we observe or miss relevant facts because our attention is directed elsewhere. Further, some people argue that explanations ought to be symmetrical: We should not use one type of explanations for rational decisions and another type for irrational ones, but rather explain all decisions in similar ways (see for example Ylikoski and Kuorikoski, this volume).

Perhaps we should therefore drop any reference to rationality whatsoever, and instead develop a description of the psychological tendencies, biases, etc. that we systematically exhibit without comparing our decision-making with a normative ideal. Taken to its extreme, this view would suggest that we compile a list of decision-making tendencies, like that of loss aversion, and use this list as a mere description of how people tend to make decisions, rather than as a list of ways in which people do, and do not, act rationally. We do thus not need to use the notion of rationality, strong or otherwise, to explain human behavior.

Responses to Observations That Violations of Rationality Are Systematic and Common

People seem to treat a change in probabilities from 0.9 to 1 or from 0.1 to 0 differently than a change in probabilities from, say, 0.6 to 0.7. Without invoking a normative notion of rationality to evaluate this tendency, we can simply refer to it as a 'certainty effect'. Someone attempting to avoid the use of normative notions in explanations of people's behavior would thus explain that patients tend to react differently to information that a particular medicine changed their risk of dying from their disease from 0.1 to 0, than to information that the medicine changed the risk from 0.7 to 0.6, by saying that the patients' behavior reflected this certainty effect. A person who did not share this ambition, however, would probably try to make sense of the reactions by giving an explanation that made them rational: For example, knowing for certain that you're not going to die from the disease gives you a peace of mind that a risk decrease from 0.7 to 0.6 does not. If we include peace of mind in what counts as utility, then it might be rational to give priority to being certain, rather than to treat all equally large changes in probability as equally important.

Reinterpreting what utility consists of is a very common response when confronted with violations of EUT. And there are good reasons for at least some of these reinterpretations, I believe. Providing an account of what the agent considered to be valuable and worth trying to achieve (that is, an account of what the agent saw as utility) is often part of a satisfying explanation of the agent's behavior. When we reinterpret utility to include more than just money, lives saved, or some other objectively identifiable benefit, in particular, to include psychological factors such as peace of mind, regret avoidance, self-respect, and pride, then many of the apparent violations of EUT disappear (see for example Loomes and Sugden 1982 on Regret Theory).

However, this strategy also risks making EUT tautological (Levin *et al.* 2013). A tautological theory is obviously of little use, and if there are no restrictions on what can count as a goal or concern that people might try to maximize, then for any behavior no matter how crazy, we can always come up with some goal that the agent might have been pursuing, at least if we are a little creative. But insisting that only, say, money counts as utility, and that all other things that people care about (and that we have no problem understanding people as caring about and striving towards) should be delegated to the realm of irrationality, is not very helpful either. Expected utility maximization then only becomes expected monetary gain maximization. Unfortunately, I do not think there is a natural and strict border between what goals we count as belonging among those that a person can be rational in pursuing, and what goals do not. And it is worth noticing that the question of the rationality of goals, which is what underlies the debate about how utility might be reinterpreted, is something that is explicitly not answered by EUT.

This reinterpretation of utility is often in line with plausible speculations about what might have been advantageous behavior from an evolutionary point of view. Consider again prospect theory and the results that indicate that people are averse to losses. It seems plausible that it often makes sense to be more concerned with avoiding losses than to achieve risky gains, and to try to protect what you have: If you can get by with what you have, but risk losing it if you stretch for more, then being cautious if you can, and taking risks to avoid losing your livelihood if you must, can be perfectly sensible. If, say, $10 that you have is worth more to you than another $10 would be because the $10 you have is necessary for survival, whereas an extra $10 would just make living a little easier, then it makes sense to be prepared to fight harder to keep the $10 you already have, than to gain an extra $10. As economists would say, money has a decreasing marginal utility. And since most things have a decreasing marginal utility, loss-averse behavior might be sensible (or might no longer be defined as loss averse).

Experiments to demonstrate the irrationality of the behavior described by prospect theory normally get around this by structuring the situation in such a way that this interpretation of loss aversion is not plausible—for example, showing that people ask a higher selling price for a mug than they are prepared to pay to acquire it (as in the experiments on the Endowment effect, see Kahneman *et al.* 1990). Obviously, one can live perfectly well without any of the mugs, and it therefore makes no sense to interpret the behavior as a sensible reaction of the difference one versus two such mugs make to people's lives.

But evolution does not always generate very fine-tuned psychological mechanisms, so it is to be expected that sometimes the same mechanisms that make us cautious of losing what we have can lead us to very odd behavior indeed (as in some of the experiments that have been used to demonstrate the descriptive accuracy of prospect theory). If this interpretation of what is going on in these experiments—that they are the results of the lack of fine-tuning of overall beneficial psychological tendencies—is correct then prospect theory is not proof that we are irrational *per se,* instead the theory is result of an evolutionary past that has endowed us with cognitively cheap but reasonably efficient psychological tendencies (various suggestions along similar lines are nowadays quite common in the literature, for example see Aumann 2008). It is of course always a bit dodgy to claim that since we have trait *x,* therefore trait *x* must be advantageous, at least overall, from an evolutionary point of view. Evolutionary drift, changes of function, and a developmentally plastic mind are just a few of the factors that should make us cautious of jumping to conclusions. But nevertheless, the tentative suggestion about the lack of evolutionary fine-tuning of our psychology is at this stage still a possible interpretation of what is going on in some of the experiments on which prospect theory is based. Doubtless others will—and do—think it is the wrong interpretation. And perhaps further work will show that it does not, in fact, normally help people to be cautious of losses. But it has not been demonstrated yet, I believe.

RESPONSES TO THE CLAIM THAT THE LABELS 'RATIONAL' AND 'IRRATIONAL' CAN BIAS EXPLANATIONS

A focus on whether behavior is rational or irrational might lead us to mis-identify the mechanism that led to the behavior. The certainty effect sometimes results in rational behavior, sometimes in irrational. If we assume that rational behavior is the result of a deliberate attempt to be rational, and reinterpret utility accordingly, we risk missing that the real cause was the certainty effect. The problem is thus similar to that pointed out by Ylikoski and Kuorikoski (this volume) about how the assumption that people are self-interested has led researchers to mis-interpret data that, without the assumption of self-interest, would quite sensibly have been taken to indicate that agents were motivated by altruism or a sense of fairness. Elsewhere, I have discussed the self-interest assumption at length (Eriksson 2011), and I am generally sympathetic to many of Ylikoski's and Kuorikoski's claims. But although I agree that the self-interest assumption has led researchers to sometimes mis-interpret their data, I believe the case is more complicated in the case of rationality. Behavior that is in line with the dictates of rationality, or at least approximately so, does not have to be the result of a deliberate attempt to be rational, so we do not have to ascribe a particular, conscious mechanism as the explanation of the behavior. Indeed, we have already discussed that evolution can have equipped us with decision heuristics that result in approximately rational behavior even though the decision-making process looks nothing like careful calculations of complicated equations about probability and utility. Saying that behavior is rational does thus not commit one to a particular view about the mechanism that led to it, whereas the assumption of self-interest usually leads researchers to claim that people are consciously and deliberately trying to further their self-interest.

But of course, the fact that evolution is not perfectly fine-tuned does not solve the problem that characterizing behavior as 'rational' or 'irrational' can make us more likely to miss when rational and irrational behavior alike are driven by the same mechanism. One has to recognize that it is indeed the same mechanism before one can investigate whether this might be due to evolution's lack of fine-tuning. And even if, say, the certainty effect is indeed the result of evolution's lack of fine-tuning, it is still the case that some of the results of the certainty effect are irrational. But this does not mean that rationality has no explanatory role to play for those results. It is not that we should explain those particular results as being rational. That would obviously be absurd. Rather, rationality plays a role in explaining why it is that we have the psychology we do. So yes, there is a risk that we miss that rational and irrational behavior alike are driven by the same mechanisms in many cases. But some legitimate kind of explanation still involves a role for rationality.

Similarly, one could criticize bounded rationality's focus on heuristics that make us behave approximately rationally, because that focus directs attention away from all the other heuristics that do not make us even approximately rational. And they are part of our decision-making psychology too. But whether this really is a problem depends on how one formulates the research question. The research on fast and frugal heuristics, for example, investigates heuristics with an eye on whether they enable us to make rational decisions. Associating an heuristic with rationality is thus normally the end result, not a criterion for choosing which heuristics to study, even though the heuristics that people tend to write about are the ones that turn out to enable us to act rationally.

Responses to the Claim That Explanations Should Be Symmetrical

However, one could still argue that explanations ought to be symmetrical. Our focus on rationality tends to make us give one type of explanations for some behavior (rational behavior) and another for other behavior (irrational behavior): Rational behavior (with a possible reinterpretation of what utility is) is seen as the end of the matter (people behaved rationally because they had evolved in that way and/or deliberately tried to), whereas irrational behavior is seen as in need of some further explanation about why the agent deviated from the standard of rational behavior. And that asymmetry, some argue, biases our explanations (Ylikoski and Kuorikoski in this volume seem to hold that view). A worry about asymmetrical explanations in this context might have its basis in a more general sympathy with the concerns about asymmetry raised by for example Bloor (1991/1976) and Barnes, Bloor and Henry (1996) in the debate about the "strong programme," but it could also be based on the more specific worry that by focusing on whether behavior is rational or irrational, we become blind to the fact that sometimes the same factor that can generate rational behavior can at other times generate irrational behavior (as discussed above). I will put the general debate about the strong programme aside, and focus here on what we can say in response to the second worry, apart from what we already said above.

The two reasons I've outlined above for why people can often be expected to be approximately rational are also reasons to think that there are different mechanisms that explain rational and irrational behavior. People are not machines, they take themselves to be normatively bound by rationality ideals, and they are often guided by those ideals in their decision-making, even if they sometimes make mistakes (Jones 1999). A person acts rationally partly because they think they ought to behave rationally, and if you point out to them that they have acted irrationally, they usually modify their behavior. Of course it is possible that people are delusional about their own ability to align their behavior with a rationality ideal, and that in fact their behavior is determined by the same mechanisms regardless of whether it turns out to be rational or irrational. But I see no (strong) reason to expect this, and in particular, no (strong) reason to ignore the reason for asymmetrical explanations that people's own endorsement of the rationality ideal constitutes. Similarly, evolution sometimes gives us reason to provide asymmetrical explanations, even when people are not deliberately trying to be rational.

Finally, I don't think there is an answer to whether explanations ought to always be symmetrical or not, based only on some facts about the world and the psychology of those whose behavior we are trying to understand. Explanations are obviously about such facts. But there are different ways of describing the same thing, and what counts as a good explanation depends only partly on features of the phenomenon we are explaining, because the needs, interests, and cognitive abilities of the person doing the explaining matters too. And part of what makes us feel that an explanation of human behavior was good is that the explanation makes sense of the behavior. However, that said, I argued earlier that although some notion of rationality might be necessary for behavior to 'make sense', strong rationality is not. This is thus not a defense of an explanatory role for strong rationality, just an objection to the claim that we ought always to prefer symmetrical explanations.

I also do not intend my argument to amount to an unqualified endorsement of a claim that a reason explanation (a rationality explanation) is always the end of the matter; that nothing else needs to be explained. Yes, rendering a behavior understandable as based on reasons is often the basis of a satisfactory explanation, but sometimes we do ask further questions. When it requires a great familiarity with probability calculations and other technical aspects to arrive at the rational course of action, we will be surprised when someone who, as far as we know, lacks the required knowledge and ability behaves rationally. An explanation is obviously not satisfactory just because someone acted rationally, if there is a puzzle about why or how they managed to act rationally. Being motivated to act rationally does not guarantee the ability to do so. The alleged explanation thus generates more questions than it answered. Something similar might be said about common reasoning mistakes; if almost everyone is susceptible to give a disproportionate emphasis to certainty, in comparison with what EUT would dictate, then it might very well be that what needs explaining, when someone treats probabilities *in accordance* with EUT, is how it is that they were not influenced by the certainty effect. Perhaps they had been trained in probability theory. Perhaps they had come across discussions of the framing effects that the certainty effect can give rise to, and were determined to not display such behavior themselves. But some sort of explanation of why they did not give such disproportionate emphasis to certainty, even when most others did, would be called for. Further, if we have good reason to believe that the person whose behavior we are trying to explain does not, in fact, endorse the same notion of rationality as we do, we are—or should be—perplexed if that person nevertheless behaved in a way we considered rational (although evolution might of course have made it the case that whatever this person consciously *endorses*, s/he will still exhibit some rationality in their actual behavior, just as most people who claim to believe in fate still look for cars before they cross a road).

SOME THOUGHTS ON NORMATIVITY AND EXPLANATION

Normative principles do not work in mysterious ways. The causes of human behavior are obviously natural (a point stressed by, for example, Henderson 2002). So if normative principles are going to be explanatory, it is not by having some supernatural causal force, which replaces normal psychological processes. Rather, normative principles explain by how those psychological processes are shaped.

Rationality is explanatory because we are the kind of creature that is responsive to facts about means to ends and to the result of our actions. I don't mean to claim that the normativity of rationality reduces to facts about means-ends efficiency, etc., and our responses to such facts. I want to leave deeper questions about the ontological status of normativity aside. But when we discuss whether rationality can be *explanatory,* it is the connection between rationality and such facts and our responsiveness to them that is crucial. It is the case that some behavior will lead to us getting what we want, and other behaviors won't, and whether a behavior is likely to be conducive to us getting what we want is going to figure in at least some explanations of that behavior.

You might argue that since there is nothing normatively required about our achieving our goals, there is no normativity here, just facts and our responsiveness to such facts. It obviously does not give us an independent normative principle of the kind that trouble people who worry about the existence of normative 'facts' like 'It is wrong to commit murder" or "Correct behavior is behavior that conforms to causal, not evidential, decision theory." But then, when we are concerned with how to explain behavior, I don't think we need to settle such ontological issues.

Still, why not just explain by citing the psychological processes that people go through when making their decisions? Because when those processes lead to rational results, the rationality of those results is not a coincidence. It is part of the explanation of why we went through those processes rather than others. And this is not merely a justification of the behavior, it is about more complete and satisfying explanations. When the result is not the rational outcome, we are instead left with the nagging further question in need of an explanation: but why behave like *that*? Or perhaps rather, why go through *those* psychological processes?

CONCLUSION

I have made the claim that a notion of rationality like that found within EUT—what I refer to as *strong rationality*—can play an important role in a good explanation of human behavior, despite the fact that human beings often are not rational in that sense.

However, my claim cannot be defended by a standard principle of charity argument, because even if this argument is correct, the kind of rationality required in order to be intelligible to others as an agent would be a weaker kind of rationality than strong rationality.

Instead, I looked at three other reasons to think that strong rationality can have an explanatory role to play: that strong rationality can play a background role as a standard of comparison and evaluation, as it does within bounded rationality, because evolution is likely to have equipped us with a psychology that will make us at least approximately rational a lot of the time, and because people try to be rational (at least sometimes).

Despite these reasons to expect rational behavior, several objections can be made, objections that, if successful, mean that strong rationality should not be used to explain people's behavior. I've looked at three: Data shows that people often and systematically violate the dictates of strong rationality (and if they are not rational, how can we use a notion of rationality to explain their behavior?), when we categorize behavior as 'rational' or 'irrational' we risk mis-identifying what it is that we observe and to be blind to important phenomena, and finally, explanations should be symmetrical in the sense that rational and irrational behavior should be explained in the same way, not in dramatically different ways. I discussed each of these objections, finding that they can be met to some extent (although not all the time).

In the last section, finally, I claimed that we can refer to rationality in explanations of human behavior without necessarily committing ourselves to any particular view about the ontological status of normative principles.

On the basis of the claims made in this chapter, I think that strong rationality has a legitimate explanatory role to play, and I thus side with those who endorse the view *The normative is explanatory,* rather than with those who endorse the view *Irrelevance.* But I do so a bit hesitantly, because although I think most of the objections can be met quite successfully, some nagging worries remain. I think the main problem is that the labels 'rational' and 'irrational' can lead us to give asymmetrical explanations where symmetrical would be more appropriate, namely, when it really is the case that both rational and irrational behavior was caused by the same psychological mechanism. I see no reason to expect that this is always the case, because quite often, rational behavior is likely to be driven by other mechanisms than irrational behavior. But when it *is* the case, we risk missing important and interesting aspects of our psychology, because we look for different mechanisms when there really is just one, one that sometimes leads to rational, sometimes to irrational behavior.

REFERENCES

Aumann, R. J. 2008. *Rule-Rationality versus Act-Rationality.* HUJ Center for the Study of Rationality, Discussion Paper #497.
Barnes, B., D. Bloor, and J. Henry. 1996. *Scientific Knowledge: A Sociological Analysis.* Chicago: University of Chicago Press.
Bloor, D. 1991. *Knowledge and Social Imagery,* 2nd edition. Chicago: University of Chicago Press.
Byron, M. 1998. Satisficing and Optimality. *Ethics* 109(1): 67–93.
Dennet, D. 1978. *Brainstorms.* Cambridge, MA: MIT Press.
Eriksson, L. 2011. *Rational Choice Theory—Potential and Limits.* Houndmills: Palgrave McMillan.
Gigerenzer, G. and T. Sturm. 2012. How (Far) Can Rationality Be Naturalized? *Synthese* 187: 243–268.
Henderson, D. 2002. Norms, Normative Principles and Explanation: On Not Getting is from Ought. *Philosophy of Social Sciences* 32(3): 329–364.
Jones, B. D. 1999. Bounded Rationality. *Annual Review of Political Science* 2: 297–321.
Kahneman, D., Knetsch, J. L. and Thaler, R. H. 1990. Experimental Tests of the Endowment Effect and the Coase Theorem. *Journal of Political Economy* 98(6): 1325–1348.
Kahneman, D. and Tversky, A. 1979. Prospect Theory: An Analysis of Decision under Risk. *Econometrica* 47(2): 263.
Kornblith, Hilary.1994. "Introduction". *In Naturalizing Epistemology,* 2nd edition, edited by Hilary Kornblith, 1-14. Cambridge, Mass.: MIT Press
Levin, Y., A. Cahen and I. Aharon. 2013. Naturalized Rationality, Evolutionary Psychology and Economic Theory. *Journal of Cognition and Neuroethics* 1(1): 39–72.

Loomes, G. and R. Sugden. 1982. Regret Theory: An Alternative Theory of Rational Choice under Uncertainty. *Economic Journal* 92(4): 805–824.

Nisbett, R. E. and T. D. Wilson. 1977. Telling More Than We Can Know: Verbal Reports on Mental Processes. *Psychological Review* 84: 231–259.

Qattrone, G. A. and Tversky, A. 1988. Contrasting Rational and Psychological Analyses of Political Choice. *The American Political Science Review* 82(3): 719–736.

Quine, W. V. 1969. Natural Kinds. In *Ontological Relativity and Other Essays*, 114–138. New York: Columbia University Press.

Simon, H. 1957. A Behavioral Model of Rational Choice. In *Models of Man, Social and Rational: Mathematical Essays on Rational Human Behavior in a Social Setting*, 241–260. New York: Wiley.

———. 1978. Rationality as Process and as Product of Thought. *American Economic Review* 68(2): 1–16.

———. 1995. The Information-Processing Theory of Mind. *The American Psychologist* 50(7): 507–508.

Stich, S. P. 1994. Could Man Be an Irrational Animal? Some Notes on the Epistemology of Rationality. In *Naturalizing Epistemology*, edited by H. Kornblith, 337–357. Cambridge, MA: MIT Press.

15 Trust, Norms, and Reason

Ladislav Koreň

THE PUZZLE OF COOPERATION AND TRUST

Humans are ultrasocial beings whose unique mode of coexistence hinges to an unprecedented extent on cooperation. Cooperation often creates positive externalities that could hardly be realized via solo efforts. However, it is well known that there are often incentives for shirking or free-riding on the positive externalities so created, promising even higher net payoffs for opportunists who want to avoid costs. So, for efficient cooperation to materialize in such social dilemmas, a modicum of trust would seem to be needed on the part of interdependent agents acting under conditions of social uncertainty, disposing them toward putting their stake in cooperation under the control of others and relying on their trustworthiness. The fact is that cooperation is far from uncommon in real-life social dilemmas. Though people are sensitive to material incentives, this indicates that they act on other motives as well, trusting others to be disposed to act on like motives.

According to a widespread view in the social and behavioral disciplines, if we want to explain robust patterns of intentional behavior, we need a model of the decision-maker that equips human agents with empirically plausible motivational and cognitive capacities responsible for that pattern of behavior. It is often assumed that explanation at this level should be a rationalization of intentional behavior in terms of interlocking tastes (desires, preferences) and beliefs (expectations). Hence the hot question discussed in contemporary social and behavioral research: what kind of empirically plausible tastes and beliefs can account for people's disposition to cooperate, trust, and reciprocate (paradigmatically, in social dilemmas or similar mixed-motive interactive situations)?

A great deal of attention has centered on the ambitious model of economic rationality depicting people as instrumental decision-makers maximizing their expected material payoff (typically money or something convertible into money). For both sympathizers and critics, the main issue has been: how far can we get with this parsimonious model of *homo economicus* when it comes to explaining robust patterns of cooperation, trust, and reciprocation across various social domains? Though proponents of the model have been ingenious in devising self-interested models of social behavior, it has long been suspected that it runs out of steam when it comes to explaining robust rates of cooperative behavior in social dilemmas (without imputing to agents empirically implausible cognitive deficiencies). Indeed, its claim to methodological hegemony in social and behavioral sciences has been challenged by the 'behavioral-experimental revolution' in economics, game theory, and neighboring disciplines. Its practitioners have urged systematic use of controlled lab-experiments to identify motives that might bring about observable social behavior, and which would otherwise be difficult to sort out in real-life situations. Specifically, they have focused on one-shot experimental games (under various protocols) designed to control for various selfish incentives to cooperate, arguing that behavioral evidence elicited from them indicates that people often care about other things than their own material payoff—for example, the well-being of others, relative differences in material payoffs, fairness, equity, etc.—even when this induces them to sacrifice their material payoff.

This marriage of theory with experiment has been timely and fruitful, but it is a matter of ongoing controversy what inferences about proximate motives driving real-life social behavior we are warranted to draw from people's behavior under laboratory conditions. That said, one powerful empirical hypothesis that has found considerable support in experimental and field research is that populations of human agents are motivationally heterogeneous, containing, in particular, a sizeable proportion of agents who behave as *conditional cooperators*. Conditional cooperators are types disposed to cooperate with others on the condition that others are willing to cooperate, being sensitive not just to likely outcomes of interaction, but also to past actions, opportunities, beliefs and intentions of interaction partners—and, importantly, to social norms framing the context of social exchange. With such types being sufficiently represented in a pool of agents interacting in social dilemmas, it is arguably easier to account for robust rates of cooperation.

This chapter aims to further explore the potential of this approach in application to trust-based social interactions. I first review pertinent experimental evidence to the effect that cooperation in dilemmas of trust is due (in part) to conditional cooperators willing to establish and maintain mutually beneficial trust-reciprocity relations. Then I discuss the influence of social norms on trust-reciprocity relations, in particular, their vital role in coordinating intentions and beliefs of conditional cooperators under the conditions of social uncertainty. With this in place, I finally explain how this approach allows us to explicate many trust-reciprocity–based social exchanges as reasonable, which are prima facie problematic from the parsimonious perspective of the *homo economicus* model.

TRUST AND RECIPROCITY IN THE LAB

Many theorists have suggested that social dilemmas highlighting the problem of trust can be modeled by mixed-motive games with a payoff structure of *prisoner's dilemma* (PD).

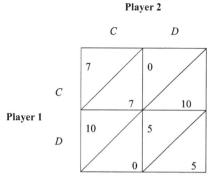

Figure 15.1   PD in material payoffs—normal form[1]

Assuming that players 1 and 2 are narrowly self-interested players maximizing their expected material payoff, being mutually aware of this fact, the traditional game theoretical analysis (henceforth TGA) utilized in the *homo economicus* model predicts mutual defection in PD-type interactions. Since the strictly dominant strategy for 1 (symmetrically for 2) is defection, the standard solution of TGA assumes that rational players 1 and 2 should reason themselves into the unique Nash-equilibrium in pure strategies (defect; defect) via elimination of strictly dominated cooperative strategies. But, then, they end up with the outcome (5; 5) that is payoff-dominated by the Pareto-efficient outcome (7; 7). However, looking at the strategic situation from the collective perspective, it seems that if only players 1 and 2 could *trust* one another not to defect, they could hope to reach the efficient outcome. But the fact of their being made from the same strategic stuff, along with the fact that they are mutually aware of that,[2] precludes emergence or persistence of mutually beneficial trust and hence cooperative ventures between them.

It is a great merit of TGA that it allows us to model in precise and illuminating ways when trusting or cooperative transactions might materialize between narrowly self-interested agents. On the one hand, TGA predicts that in PD-type interactions with common knowledge of rationality on the part of players it is never prudent to cooperate, not even when 1 and 2 play them with one another repeatedly over a finite horizon.[3] On the other hand, it is consistent with TGA that conditions favorable for trust or cooperation might materialize (1) when the PD-type game is played repeatedly over an indefinite time horizon, or (2) when it is played repeatedly over a finite horizon while involving incomplete (asymmetric) information on the part of players about their rationality,[4] or (3) when the PD-type interaction is being watched by onlookers who might eventually turn out to be the players' partners in similar interactions, or could share valuable information about one's performance (reputation) with other prospective interaction partners. In all three cases, it may in the long run pay off to play trust (cooperate) and gain the reputation of being a conditional reciprocator of trust (cooperation) rather than that of being a myopic opportunist.

Though the *homo economicus* model armed with TGA has proved quite successful in competitive market-type interactions, behavioral economists and game theorists have subjected it to a systematic experimental testing of how well it fares as a positive theory that allows us to predict and explain real-life interactions. Human behavior in strategic situations with a PD-type structure of material payoffs (as well as its *n*-person variants such as the *public goods* game) has been studied and compared under various experimental conditions: both in one-shot and repeated versions, involving anonymous or non-anonymous players, with or without observers recording players' performance, with or without a threat of second- or third-party punishment, allowing players to communicate or not, etc. While observed data have more or less significantly varied with respect to various controlled variables (and across cultures[5]), one thing has not been confirmed: namely, the pessimistic prediction of TGA that people, *qua* maximizers of their expected private payoffs, should mutually defect in one-shot PDs (or, for that matter, in finitely repeated PDs of complete information). In fact, it has been observed that 40–60% of subjects tend to cooperate in one-shot PD-type games (or in the first round of repeated PD games). To the extent that we can interpret players' willingness to cooperate in such interactions as revealing a degree of trust on the part of interaction partners, experimental data of this sort may tell us something revealing about the problem at hand.

Important as PD-models are, many paradigmatic trust-based social transactions—such as sequential exchanges of goods or services between players 1 and 2 that are not (completely or efficiently) regulated by enforceable contracts and usually involve a time-lag between 1 doing her part first and 2 doing her part later—are better modeled by *sequential games* in extensive form, in which player 1 can initiate the transaction by trustingly cooperating, and then 2, usually knowing beforehand about 1's decision, decides whether to reciprocate (honor) trust or abuse. What, in the literature, is often called *the basic trust problem* concerns precisely dilemmatic situations in which player 1 chooses whether to initiate a potentially efficient cooperative interaction with 2 and faces a behavioral risk in choosing the cooperative option, since she thereby transfers to 2 control over her cooperative stakes, who then decides whether to reciprocate while having a salient material incentive for opportunistic exploitation. Because player 1's choice of a cooperative option puts interaction and its outcome (partially) under 2's control, the basic problem of trust involves risk and vulnerability on the part of 1, which, indeed, are commonly considered to be its essential ingredients.

Figure 2 represents a dynamic model of such an interaction, in which player 2 chooses her move based on her information about the previous move of player 1, provided that 1 decided to initiate the transaction.[6] In a

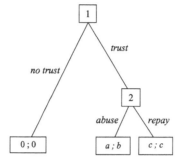

Figure 15.2 Trust game in extensive form

situation having this incentive structure, 1 and 2 are both aware that they can reap mutual benefits from the transaction (*viz.* (c; c)), compared to the status quo outcome (0; 0) when the transaction is not even initiated. However, 1 faces the risk that 2 may choose to inflict on her a harm/loss (*viz.* $a < 0$) by opportunistically exploiting her trust, since this maximizes 2's payoff (*viz.* $c < b$) at that decision point.

Assuming $a < 0 < c < b$ is a structure of material (monetary) payoffs over which Players 1 and 2 maximize—both knowing this in common ground—TGA predicts their play at the subgame perfect equilibrium *(no trust, abuse)*, which leads to the Pareto-inferior outcome (0, 0).[7] Again, however, relatively high rates of cooperation and reciprocation have been observed in laboratory implementations of one-shot trust games of this type. This casts a *prima facie* doubt on the accuracy of TGA utilized in the *homo economicus* model.

The binary trust game models trust in an *all-or-nothing* manner. Presumably, though, people are disposed to trust and reciprocate in various degrees. To measure degrees of trust and trustworthiness respectively, there has been an intense experimental industry focusing on so-called *investment games*. In the baseline setting first described by Berg *et al.* (1995),[8] the game involves two anonymous players. Player 1 is assigned the role of the sender (or trustor) and player 2 the role of the responder (or trustee). The experimenter then endows 1 with x (e.g., 10) tokens and the responder with n tokens.[9] Player 1 starts the game by deciding whether to send to player 2 some positive sum $y \leq x$ or to keep all the tokens in her private account. In case 1 opts to send nothing, the game is over, each player keeping his/her initial endowment (converted into money at a specified exchange rate known beforehand). If player 1 sends something, the experimenter multiplies y by a positive factor k (usually y is doubled or tripled) so that 2 gets ky. At this point, 2 may either transfer back to 1 some positive amount z ($\leq n + ky$) or keep all the tokens in her private account.

Under this protocol, 1's investment y (relative to x) is taken as a measure of 1's degree of trust, while 2's return of z (relative to the surplus ky)

measures 2's degree of trustworthiness (willingness to reciprocate). Significantly, a number of experimental studies replicating this protocol have shown that a sizeable portion of first movers are disposed to send positive amounts to second movers. Indeed, on average, first movers invest between $0.4x$ and $0.5x$. However, returns from respondents have turned out to be more problematic. Although z has been positive more often than not, on average it has approximated $0.95y$, which indicates that trust (as measured by y) has not quite been repaid. Still, the fact remains that a considerable number of respondents transferred back $z > y$.[10]

These findings fly in the face of the standard prediction of TGA about one-shot dilemmatic games, assuming that the maximandum of players is their material payoff. Player 2 should abuse trust in case player 1 "naïvely" places it, this being 2's maximizing choice at the relevant decision point. But, as a self-interested maximizer who knows (or believes) that 2 is made of the same stern stuff, player 1 is in a position to predict 2's defection. Accordingly, reasoning herself back to the initial decision point via a backward induction, player 1 should realize that she will be better off by not sending anything. Hence, the prediction of TGA is that there should be no transaction under these conditions. In which case, however, 1 and 2 would forego the opportunity of reaping higher benefits.

It is important to note at this juncture that the difficulty for the economic model does not hinge solely on behavior observed in one-off interactions between strangers. It remains even if we introduce social elements such as face-to-face contact or pre-play communication. Unlike one-shot interactions under the veil of anonymity (single- or double-blind designs), social interactions of this sort—in which social distance is lower—are frequent in real life and they often lead to beneficial outcomes. This has been amply confirmed in the controlled experiments, where introduction of such factors has been found to correlate with increased rates of cooperation (*cf.* Ostrom 2003). However, according to TGA, such "cheap" verbal signals should not really change the underlying incentive structure of the interaction.

CONDITIONAL COOPERATION AND TRUST-RECIPROCITY RELATIONS

If the *homo economicus* model runs out of steam when it comes to explaining observed cooperative behavior in trust dilemmas in the laboratory as well as in real life, what plausible explanation can social and behavioral theorists offer? To answer this question, a considerable number of alternative proposals (not necessarily exclusive)—based on various modifications on the basic trust and investment games—have been made. Discussing and comparing their merits and demerits is beyond the scope of this paper. In what follows, I shall discuss two recent studies, both of which gesture toward one pertinent hypothesis: a sizeable portion of people behave as conditional reciprocators using social-normative reasoning of a sort to induce and interlock their respective intentions, beliefs and actions so as to reach efficient cooperative outcomes.

The first study of McCabe *et al.* (2003) focuses on the potential impact of a trust-reciprocity mechanism in generating and sustaining cooperation in social dilemmas of trust. The authors conducted and compared what they call the *voluntary trust game* and *involuntary trust game* (both under the single-blind design), whose structure is represented by Figures 3 and 4 respectively.

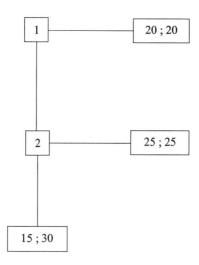

Figure 3   Voluntary trust game

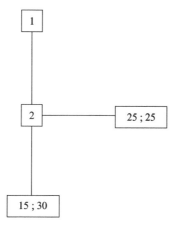

Figure 4   Involuntary trust game

In the voluntary trust game, player 1 can choose between two options. *Move right* is the exit option that leaves both players with 20 tokens. *Move down* is a potentially costly option for 1, since 1 risks losing 5 tokens (compared with the sure thing guaranteed in the exit option) in case 2 chooses to defect (by *moving down*), which earns 2 thirty tokens. But it is also an action that, if reciprocated by 2, leads to the Pareto-efficient outcome (both earning 25 tokens). In the involuntary trust game, by contrast, player 1 does not have the exit option of moving right, not facing any positive opportunity cost (1 can only gain, the only issue — to be settled by 2 — is how much).

As for the predictions of TGA, the strategy-profile (*move right, move down*) is the unique subgame perfect equilibrium of the voluntary trust games (in pure strategies), should players care only about maximizing their expected material payoffs (under the standard assumption of common knowledge). This prediction, however, was not confirmed. What is more, the authors report a significant decrease of mutually beneficial transactions in the involuntary game compared to the voluntary game: in the voluntary game 17 of the 27 first movers moved down and 11 of the 17 second movers reciprocated, but in the involuntary game only 9 of the 27 second movers choose to move right. Importantly, this difference cannot be explained solely in terms of players' other-regarding preferences over material payoffs, in accordance with outcome-oriented social preference models such as Fehr and Schmidt (1999) and Bolton and Ockenfels (2000) inequality aversion models.[11] The trouble is that player 2 has available exactly the same options with exactly the same payoffs in both games. Hence, the probability that 2 will reciprocate should be the same in both games.

As a viable middle way between the *homo economicus* model and purely outcome-oriented models of social preferences, the authors put forward their own *trust-reciprocity hypothesis* (*TR hypothesis*). Assume a proportion of people behave as cooperators (reciprocators) disposed to cooperate with partners—being kind and reciprocal—on the condition that others are willing to cooperate too. Suppose these people face a sequential cooperative dilemma modeled by the voluntary trust game. Realizing that cooperation can produce a mutual benefit, player 1, who is a conditional cooperator, might want to realize the beneficial exchange by cooperating, provided she believes that player 2 is prepared to sacrifice something in order to repay kindness with kindness, being able to "read" cooperation as a signal of 1's kind intention to realize a beneficial transaction relying on 2's positive reciprocity. These, then, are the conditions for trust to materialize, leading 1 to signal her willingness to enter the trust-reciprocity relation with 2, thereby intending to induce positive reciprocity on the part of 2 due to her recognizing this very intention of 1.

Given this recursive structure of intentions, and drawing on Baron-Cohen's (1995) work on *mind-reading* (as a version of *theory of mind*), the authors suggest that the pertinent mechanism of signaling and decoding intentions might be a matter of the players' mutual beliefs about one another's potential gains from the social exchange as well as about their opportunity costs:

> Under the TR hypothesis, it follows that the formation of the second mover's beliefs about the intentions of the first mover must be understood to include the opportunity cost of the first mover's action.
>
> (McCabe *et al.* 2003, 269)

Importantly, should player 1 not have a choice-option with a positive opportunity cost to her—or should 2 not know about 1 having one—2 could be at a loss to interpret 1's action as one that is intended to establish the trust-reciprocity relationship. According to the *TR hypothesis*, we would expect that in such situations there should be less cooperation and reciprocity between players than in situations in which such 'signaling' opportunities are available to first movers. As it happens, the aforementioned difference between cooperation rates in the two treatments is consistent with, indeed predicted by, the *TR hypothesis*.

What the numbers from one-shot voluntary trust games (compared with involuntary trust games) can be interpreted as revealing is that a sizeable proportion of human agents (as represented in experiments) behave as conditional cooperators ready to cooperate and reciprocate given their assessment of opportunities, intentions and beliefs of their social partners, in addition to their assessment of respective material payoffs. Admittedly, a significant proportion of subjects behave consistently with TGA model—choosing non-cooperative strategies recommended by the subgame perfect equilibrium (in pure strategies). Still, the pool does not seem to consist only—or even predominantly—of myopic opportunists.

First, reciprocal actions of second movers are not payoff maximizing strategies. Second, though calculative opportunists in the role of first movers can try their luck by moving down, they can rationally choose to do so only if they believe that not everybody in the pool is a rational opportunist—indeed, that the probability of meeting a cooperator (reciprocator) in the given pool is sufficiently high for them to take the risky cooperative option. Third, although other-regarding preferences (such as pure altruism, inequality aversion, etc.) might play a role in motivating first movers to give away something to second movers, experimental evidence indicates that the willingness of first movers to place their trust in second movers positively correlates with the first movers' expectations of reciprocity on the part of second movers (indeed, investments tend to increase with the strength of their expectations of reciprocity). Fourth, it has been found that subjects who tend to reciprocate in the role of second movers also tend to invest in the role of first movers, but not vice versa.[12] This asymmetry is explicable on the assumption of heterogeneity of types. While a portion of conditional reciprocators who behave as trustworthy types are also ready to trust in the role of first movers (giving cooperation a chance), rational opportunists who are not trustworthy and have no reason to form a reputation for trustworthiness in one-off games can also give away something if they expect their partners to repay their investment but defect in the role of second movers.

TRUST MODULATED BY SOCIAL NORMS

There is further evidence gathered from closely related experiments with social dilemmas in the lab, as well as from field studies, to the effect that a sizeable proportion of people are conditional cooperators (reciprocators), who (a) expect more people to reciprocate once having entered social dilemmas and (b) are themselves more willing to enter social dilemmas with cooperative intentions when having a choice to enter them. Thus Elinor Ostrom sums up:

> Given both propensities, the feedback from such voluntary activities will generate confirmatory evidence that they have adopted a *norm* that served them well along the long run... a substantial proportion of population drawn on by social sciences experiments... do have sufficient trust that others are reciprocators to cooperate with them even in one-shot, non-communication experiments.
>
> (Ostrom 2003b, 49. Italics mine)

What Ostrom has in mind here is that the norm adopted of conditional cooperators—one that served them well along the long run—is the norm of *reciprocity*. As she also points out, since norms are primed via socialization-enculturation processes, their effect on behavior is likely to be sensitive to various contextual variables. For instance, it has been amply documented in experimental studies that the levels of trust and reciprocity among conditional cooperators are sensitive to factors such as face-to-face contact and pre-play communication about the nature of the game allowing formation of promises and commitments, presumably because conditional cooperators are sensitive to signals indicating that their prospective partners in cooperative ventures are conditional cooperators with requisite beliefs and intentions (emotional signals are likely to play a significant role here[13]).

McCabe *et al.* do not make any connection between their mechanism of trust-reciprocity for conditional cooperators and social norms, but in a study closely related to their research program Hoffman *et al.* (1996) highlight the connection with reciprocity norms defined as implying:

> ...that if one individual offers a share to another individual, the second individual is expected to reciprocate within a reasonable time.
>
> (Hoffman *et al.* 1996, 341)

The idea that a norm of reciprocity might exert a pull on conditional cooperators facing dilemmas of trust is quite appealing, but it needs much more elaboration if it is not to be a mere truism to the effect that reciprocators prefer to reciprocate. For a specific positive proposal we now turn to the research of Bicchieri *et al.* (2011) focusing on the role of *social* norms in dilemmas of trust.

Based on Bicchieri's own (2006) influential account of social norms, Bicchieri *et al.* assumed that, to the extent *social* norms (as opposed to *personal* norms) are operative in trust dilemmas—inducing players to cooperate and/ or reciprocate—players should have (a) *empirical* expectations that sufficiently many others conform to the norms, as well as (b) *normative* expectations that sufficiently many others expect them to conform to the norms, eventually being ready to sanction transgressions. If, then, players come to interpret the interactive situation as cuing a salient social norm (categorizing it as relevantly similar to certain prototypical situations they are familiar with), they might want to exhibit behavior sanctioned by the norm, *conditionally* on having interlocking empirical and normative expectations.[14] Based on this view of social norms, the approach of Bicchieri *et al.* was to elicit normative expectations of subjects upon being told that trustors (or trustees) in a previously conducted investment game sent (or sent back) either nothing or some (increasingly) positive sums to their interaction partners. For each scenario described to them[15], subjects were asked, (1) with what payoff fine (if any) they would punish this or that type of zero or positive investment (return) by a sender (responder), (2) how many participants in their session they expect not to punish such behavior and (3) what punishment, on average, they expect from other participants in their session.[16] In addition, to test the hypothesis that *thick* relationships of trust might have specific norms of their own (*e.g.*, a norm of trusting between friends) that need not be operative in situations of 'generalized trust' (between non-related parties, absent formal or informal contracts, enforcing institutions, etc.), the authors also conducted and compared *the friend treatment* and *the stranger treatment*. The only difference between the two treatments was that participants in a given session were told either that the interaction to be evaluated occurred between friends, or that it occurred between strangers.

Having subjected to analysis responses from 62 subjects (30 in the *stranger* treatment and 32 in the *friend* treatment), the authors report that the data do not statistically support the hypothesis that a social norm of *trust* is being operative in such trust dilemmas (not even in the *friend* treatment!). Their analysis reveals that, on average, subjects expected that most people in their session won't punish zero transfers by trusters. At the same time, their data do seem to lend some support to the hypothesis that a norm of *reciprocity* applying to second movers might be operative, as, on average, subjects expected that most people in their session would punish zero returns with a payoff cut. By contrast, subjects did not expect returns of

$z > y$ to be punished. At the same time, they found no evidence for normative expectations supporting a social norm *prescribing* beneficial (or fair) returns, as sending back $z = y$ was not expected to be sanctioned either. Here, once again, the differences between the stranger and friend treatments were statistically insignificant.

Based on their findings, Bicchieri *et al.* conclude that there is some evidence to the effect that a social norm of reciprocity is operative in mixed-motive games of trust:

> If, indeed, a reciprocity norm exists and is commonly shared, then it makes sense for the truster to try to focus the trustee on it, in the expectation that he will reciprocate and thus benefit the truster.
>
> (Bicchieri *et. al.* 2011, 173)

At this juncture, the studies of Bicchieri *et al.* and McCabe *et al.* can be interpreted as complementing one another. Putting these two lines of research together, I submit that something like the trust-reciprocity mechanism described by McCabe *et al.* might be of help to first movers to focus second movers on a norm of reciprocity in one-shot trust games—in particular when first movers and second movers are strangers—helping them to 'read' (fallibly, of course) one another's cooperative intentions, given a set of available opportunities (including opportunities that were not actually taken but could have been taken) (McCabe *et al.* 2003). McCabe *et al.* describe one plausible mechanism of *social* reasoning focusing players on a salient social norm of reciprocity that might be operative even in one-shot anonymous interactions, in which participants cannot draw on visual or verbal clues.

CONCLUDING DISCUSSION

Several alternative explanations of trust-based cooperation have been proposed in the received literature, many of them appealing to *social preferences* of one sort or another (*e.g.*, the inequality aversion model of social preferences) or to proximate mechanisms such as risk-orientation, guilt-aversion or betrayal aversion.[17] Let me now highlight the comparative merits of the hypothesis of conditional cooperation sensitive to social norms. For a lack of space, the intended comparison will be confined to outcome-oriented models of social preferences.

Models of social preferences typically assume that social preferences such as altruism or inequality aversion are relatively robust traits of people, distinguishing them from selfish types. Being such, they should translate to relatively robust pro-social behavior in the common games of life as well as in related experimental games played in the lab. We have already seen one problem pertaining to purely outcome-oriented models of social preferences noted by McCabe *et al.* (2003): cooperation rates in the voluntary trust game are significantly higher than in the involuntary trust game. In general, several authors have argued that there is so far little evidence that social preferences extrapolated from a particular one-shot experimental game or a set of games (*e.g.*, from the ultimatum game) are robust enough in that they continue to be reliably expressed in related one-shot games or repeated games, being relatively stable with respect to manipulation of framing, information, social distance, or grouping effects (*cf.* Bicchieri 2006; Binmore 2007; Woodward 2008, 2009a, 2009b; Binmore and Shaked 2010).

Observed variability of people's behavior across different (but related) games, on the other hand, is consistent with, indeed predicted by, the hypothesis that a sizeable portion of human agents behave as conditional cooperators sensitive to social norms coordinating their intentions, beliefs and actions in interdependent situations of social exchange. It has been amply documented in social psychology that normative framing of social situations is a ubiquitous phenomenon highly sensitive to contextual clues that may activate in participants different social norms in mixed-motive situations that might have the same structure in material payoffs but their contextual background varies. Also, social norms vary significantly across cultural groups. If so, one should not be surprised at observing variable behavior across different games in the lab and real life, depending on the social nature of the social exchange, which itself depends on information to be gathered from cues present the context. This meshes well with reviewed experimental evidence to the effect that players are often concerned about (signals of) intentions, beliefs and opportunities of co-players, trying to figure them out in situations of social exchange in which social norms of reciprocity—general or specific—might be expected to induce and/or reinforce the trust-reciprocity relationship.

Furthermore, if the trust-reciprocity mechanism indeed works, we could expect, first, that levels of cooperation between players might decrease when second movers have less than complete information about strategy-sets of first movers and/or their associated opportunity cost. As it happens, there is some evidence for this effect (see McCabe *et al.* 2003, 274). Moreover, as perfect anonymity allows for the impact of the "Gyges-effect" of making players "invisible" (in the lab simulated via double-blind protocols), the pull of shared norms on subjects interacting under such conditions might be less strong than in conditions of imperfect anonymity (single-blind protocols), except for individuals with sufficiently internalized norms of conduct. In fact, the impact of the "nobody is watching me" factor on decreasing reciprocity levels has been reported in a couple of studies recording a statistically significant decrease in cooperation in double-blind treatments compared to single-blind treatments.[18] The upshot of this is that social context and, in particular, social distance matters: the higher the social distance between players and between players and onlookers (e.g., experimenters), the weaker might be the pull of social norms.

The foregoing account, however, raises for us three issues that need to be addressed. First, one may wonder how behavioral variability across different social games, which is predicted by Bicchieri-style account of social

norms, can be reconciled with the disposition for conditional cooperation that, we assume, is a relatively stable trait of its possessors (perhaps
an evolved trait developed by ancestral humans). Second, what accounts
for cooperative behavior of people who might not condition their preferences on empirical and normative expectations supporting genuinely social
norms? Third, in what sense can we say that trust and reciprocity in social
dilemmas is rational?

As regards the first issue, Woodward's (2009b) intriguing analysis of conditional cooperation shows that there need be no real conflict, since conditional cooperators are bound to face social uncertainty (or indeterminacy)
regarding the goals, intentions and beliefs of social partners. As he explains,
conditional cooperators may need certain focal points around which they
could coordinate their beliefs. Now one salient rationale of social norms is
to provide such reference points: shared expectations as to what, in a given
social exchange, counts as a trustful and reciprocal behavior, or when a positive or negative sanction is in order. Otherwise mutually beneficial cooperation in social dilemmas might have a hard time getting off the ground
or might unravel even among appropriately motivated conditional cooperators due to their failures to coordinate. Since social norms, in this role,
coordinate specific types of social exchange—often, culturally variable—we
should expect (1) significant differences in the behavior of conditional cooperators across different types of social games or across similar social games
played in different cultures and (2) sensitivity to various framing effects.
Both predictions have found empirical support: framing effects as well as
contextual and cultural variability of behavior have been reported in several
studies based on laboratory experiments as well as on field research.

Woodward's analysis, though, suggests one *prima facie* difficulty for the
research of Bicchieri *et al.* reviewed above. As he argues, the hypothesis
that social norms perform a vital coordinating function for conditional
cooperators—as reference points—would seem to imply that considerable variation in contributions of subjects in social exchanges of a certain
type indicate that no *specific* social norm efficiently coordinates such social
exchanges. Though Woodward does not make this point with reference to
the study of Bicchieri *et al.*, he mentions evidence from experiments with
one-shot investment games to this effect: there is, in fact, a significant
variation in contribution levels by both first movers and second movers.
This would seem to indicate absence of *specific* social norms of trust and
reciprocity—specifying how much it is appropriate to give away and to
send back.

As we have seen, Bicchieri *et al.* concur with the conclusion that no specific social norm of trust is being operative in investment games. But they
may resist the conclusion about the absence of a specific social norm of
reciprocity coordinating subjects' play in investment games, since normative
expectations elicited by them can be taken to indicate a specific reciprocity reference point of $z = y$ (quite consistently with replicated data from

investment games that show that, on average, first movers' investments tend to be at least repaid).

The second issue is more pressing, particularly for the approach of Bicchieri *et al.* that implicitly hinges on the idea (explicit in Bicchieri 2006) that preferences shaped by *personal* norms—in marked contrast with those shaped by *social* norms—fail to reliably translate in actual behavior, precisely because they are not conditioned on empirical and/or normative beliefs. That said, the experimental design of Bicchieri *et al.* does little to disqualify the hypothesis that a proportion of trusters and reciprocators can be motivated by a personal norm of trust or reciprocity with a moralistic spin.[19] Shaun Nichols (2010) urges a related point when reviewing Bicchieri and Xiao's (2009) research on dictator games studied under two treatments: dictators in the first group were told that 60 % subjects participating in the session of the same experiment previous year gave away 20% or less of the windfall to receivers, while dictators in the second group were told that 60 % subjects participating in the session of the same experiment previous year shared the windfall with receivers approximately equally. Consistently with Bicchieri's account of social norms, Bicchieri and Xiao can explain higher rates of equal division of the windfall in those subjects whose empirical expectations were manipulated in favor of the likelihood that enough others in their session would divide the windfall equally. Still, what accounts for the fact that one third of subjects divided the windfall equally even if they did not expect enough others in their session to divide the windfall equally? Nichols speculates that the norm of equal division of a windfall might be a personal norm for a sizeable proportion of humans, which tends to be moralized and resonates with a natural tendency to feel negative emotions (outrage) when one's social status is harmed (as with unequal division of a windfall). This is not the place to examine this intriguing proposal or Nichols' specific arguments. Aforementioned considerations suffice to make it clear that personal values or internalized norms cannot easily be dismissed as determinants or co-determinants of cooperative behavior in social dilemmas. Methodologically, then, to sort out the relative impact of personal and social norms on cooperation in dilemmas of trust, a more complex experimental design is needed, comparing correlations between (a) personal values and actual behavior and (b) empirical and/or normative expectations and actual behavior.

Finally, what is the lesson of our argument so far for the issue of rationality of trust and reciprocity in dilemmas of trust? Bicchieri *et al.* suggest the following:

> Trust is grounded upon reciprocity norms. Their very existence provides grounds for the expectation of being reciprocated. We expect people to help those who have helped them, and therefore we expect those whom we trust to have an obligation to honor our trust. This is the reason why we have argued that trusting can be rational, insofar as the truster

expects, by her action, to focus the trustee on a reciprocity norm and thus trigger an adequate response.

(Bicchieri *et al.* 2011, 181)

Information about the past behavior and reputation of interaction partners often provides conditional cooperators with a sufficient reason to enter a risky social exchange that is potentially beneficial. However, we need to explain also moderate levels of cooperation in dilemmas of trust in which people lack this personal information about partners. Since social norms explained *à la* Bicchieri hinge on empirical and normative expectations that are general in nature, they are suited to influence people's choices in extended social networks.

Thus, conditional cooperators are disposed to trust/reciprocate in social dilemmas given their beliefs about particular others as well as their generalized expectations about the *types* of agents they are likely to interact with in a given environment, both of which are subject to continuous updating in the light of day-to-day experience. If they have experienced a great deal of trust and reciprocity in certain social environments, they may, as it were, attach a high enough probability p of interacting with cooperators (sensitive to a social norm), it then being worthwhile to them to induce their social partners, including strangers, to enter mutually beneficial trust-reciprocity relations. In addition, partner choice (clustering effects) can further enhance their chances of reaping mutual benefits from social exchanges, allowing cooperators to interact with similar types (avoid or shun opportunist types), based on reputations and signals of various kinds (communicative and emotional).

So, in the longer run, conditional cooperators are not naïve fools to be easily taken advantage of. Admittedly, in populations comprising a mixture of selfish and cooperative types, extending one's experience-based expectations of reciprocity to interactions with strangers is, objectively, a *risky* extrapolation (though, subjectively, it need not be perceived as such). Yet, there is hardly any other way to reap gains from interdependent cooperative ventures other than being at least moderately 'optimistic'— that is, trusting. What evidence we have indicates that a sizeable proportion of real decision-makers act as if they are hardwired for conditional cooperation—indeed, that these dispositions pay, on average, even though they are vulnerable to opportunistic exploitation in hostile environments.[20]

To this extent, I conclude, trust-based cooperative interactions beyond the narrow scope of the *homo economicus* model are within the reach of a more *social* model of decision-maker that takes into account dispositions for conditional cooperation and cognitively bounded mechanisms of decision-making, in particular, explaining some social behavior in dilemmas of trust as modulated by normative heuristics of social reasoning (*cf.* Messick and Kramer 2001; Ostrom 2003b; Bichierri 2006). It turns out that conditional cooperators whose preferences and expectations interlock in social norms fare, on average, fairly well, in spite of the fact—or, perhaps, due to the fact—that they do not consciously calculate, on a case-by-case basis, "what's in it for them."[21]

NOTES

1   C and D label respectively the strategies "cooperate" and "defect." Numbers in the payoff-cells specify the prisoners' respective material (monetary) payoffs for given strategy-profiles (intersections of two action-options C and D available to 1 and 2). Number in the left-hand part of a cell specifies payoff to Player 1, number in the right-hand part specifies payoff to Player 2. Ordinal ranking is assumed here, not measuring how much a particular outcome is preferred by a player compared to other outcomes.

2   According to the standard rationality and common knowledge assumptions embodied in TGA.

3   As the players are modeled as knowing at which—*n*th—round the game ends, they can look forward to the end of the game and then use backward-looking induction to successively eliminate dominated options much like in the one-shot version. It turns out that the Nash equilibrium in pure strategies is, again, the strategy-profile *(defect, defect)*.

4   PD is indefinitely repeated if there is a positive probability *p* of playing the same game after each round and the probability *p*—1 that the game will end after each round. It can be proved that if *the shadow of future* represented by the probability *p* is not too small (equivalently, if players are patient enough and do not discount the future too heavily) cooperation is sustainable in a stable Nash-type equilibrium. Indeed, the so-called *folk theorem* states that such an indefinitely repeated PD has a vast number of stable (Nash-type) equilibria. Some of them instruct players to reciprocate cooperation (or trusting move) at every turn until the interaction partner defects. In fact, every intermediate possibility between full cooperation and full defection—one of them being to play the famous *tit-for-tat* strategy—can occur in the equilibrium strategy profile, so that there is a delicate issue of equilibrium selection (*cf.* Fudenberg and Maskin 1986). For the second lesson see Kreps *et al.* (1982), who show that cooperation (or trust) may materialize even between prudential players when there is a tiny chance that the partner might be "irrational" (e.g., a consistent follower of the *tit-for-tat* rule), so that players could both induce their partners to play tit-for-tat for quite a few rounds and adjust their strategies in light of updating their subjective priors as the game iterates. Under such conditions, cooperation (or trust) may emerge and be sustained for quite a few rounds—as part of a sequential equilibrium—in the finitely repeated PD with incomplete (asymmetric) information, because even prudential players have incentives to build reputation as if they were committed players (followers of *tit-for-tat*). However, toward the end of the supergame, when the threat of inflicting future losses on defecting players by denying them opportunities to benefit from future transactions is removed, conditional cooperation (trust) unravels and players return to playing the strategy-profile *(defect, defect)*.

5   *Cf.* Camerer (2003) and the cross-cultural study of Henrich *et al.* (2004). Ostrom (2003b, 2014) provides a superb survey of research in this area.

6   Unlike in PD, in the normal (strategic) form the moves of the players are not modeled as made independently. The game is based on Kreps (1990). See also Güth and Kliemt (1998) and Messick and Kramer (2001).

7   *Subgame perfect equilibrium* is a refinement of a Nash-type equilibrium for sequential games containing well-defined subgames. A strategy-profile is said to

be a subgame perfect equilibrium of a given game if it is a Nash equilibrium in each of its subgames. The idea behind it is that in sequential games containing subgames some Nash equilibria are based on incredible hypothetical threats, which, however, the player has no payoff-based incentive to realize at relevant decision points of the game. Subgame perfect equilibria are refinements of Nash equilibria in that they are not based on such incredible threats. A typical method of finding a subgame perfect equilibrium for a given game is to use backward-looking induction, assuming common knowledge of players' rationality.

8 Camerer (2003) and Chaudhuri (2009) provide reliable overviews on the later research under various replications and modifications of the original investment game.

9 We let n be equal to x, as in Berg *et al.* (1995) original design.

10 Though even those responders only rarely sent back z equalizing the profits of both players, for example, 15 tokens, if $x = 10$, $n = 10$, $y = 10$, $k = 2$. For a discussion of this issue see Woodward (2009a, 2009b).

11 In the Fehr-Schmidt model, for instance, it is assumed that the two basic measures of inequality aversion—*viz.* how much a player dislikes inequitable outcomes (a) favoring her partner and (b) favoring herself—are uniformly distributed in the heterogeneous population. So if x_i denotes the material payoff of player i and x_j the material payoff of player j, and α_i measures how much i dislikes disadvantageous inequality while β_i measures how much i dislikes advantageous inequality, then the utility of player i in a two player game is given by $U_i(x) = x_i - \alpha_i(x_j - x_i)$ if player i is worse off than player j $(x_j - x_i \geq 0)$, and $U_i(x) = x_i - \beta_i(x_i - x_j)$ if player i is better off than player j $(x_i - x_j \geq 0)$. Fehr and Schmidt assume that, in general, players dislike advantageous inequality less than disadvantageous inequality. In his important study stressing the role of players' beliefs and intentions, Rabin (1993) also shows that 2 can form a judgment about whether 1 has sacrificed something to benefit (eventually harm) her (*viz.* positive opportunity cost). If, then, 2 is the type that likes to repay kindness with kindness—and meanness with vengeance—2 can benefit from reciprocating that kind act.

12 For more on this issue see Chaudhuri and Gangadharan (2007) and Chaudhuri (2009).

13 Frank (1988) is a classic study on the strategic role of emotions.

14 According to Bicchieri (2006, 11), a behavioral rule R for mixed-motive interactions of the type S is said to be a *social norm* in a population P, if a sufficiently large subpopulation P_{cf} exists such that each member i of P_{cf} (1) believes that R exists and applies to S-situations, and (2) i prefers to conform to R on the condition that (a) i believes that a sufficiently large subset of P conforms to R in S-situations and either (b) i believes that a sufficiently large subset of P expects i to conform to R in S-situations or (c) i believes that a sufficiently large subset of P expects i to conform to R in S-situations and may sanction behavior. The norm R is then said to be *followed* in P if the conditions (2a) and either (2b) or (2c) are satisfied for enough people in P_{cf}, which leads them to prefer conformity to R.

15 As in the original investment game of Berg *et al.* (1995), both players were supposed to start with 10 tokens. However, the strategy set of the sender (values of y) was restricted to $\{0, 1/2, 1\}$ in terms of fractions of her initial endowment (x), while the responder repayments (z) could be in the range $\{0, 1/3, 2/3, 1\}$ in terms of fractions of her earnings $(3.y)$.

16 Possible fines correspond to increasing percentages of players' respective earnings in the range $\{0\%, 10\%, 30\%, 50\%, 70\%, 90\%, 100\%\}$ of a player's earnings.

17 An up-to-date review of the relevant literature is provided by Chaudhuri (2009).

18 For this effect, see Hoffman *et al.* (1996) for dictator games and Cox and Deck (2005) for trust games. Note that McCabe *et al.* (2003), who report a significant

proportion of conditional positive reciprocity on the part of second movers, used a single-blind protocol. However, based on extensive data from their experimental treatments, Barmettler *et al.* (2012) argue that differences in reciprocity levels in investment games are statistically insignificant between single-blind and double-blind protocols. As far as I can see, the debate continues to be indecisive.

19 In a related spirit, the studies of Cox (2004), and Ortmann *et al.* (2000) confirm the hypothesis that a trust-reciprocity mechanism is operative in trust and investment games, but they also identify a number of other factors—e.g., unconditional altruistic preferences or inequality aversion—influencing cooperative choices in dilemmas of trust.

20 Decay of cooperation in environments in which a mixture of conditional cooperators interacts with selfish types is also explicable: If their cooperative actions are repeatedly exploited in specific domains of social interaction, conditional cooperators become vigilant, adjusting their repertoire of behavioral strategies accordingly. On the other hand, both real-life experience and 'restart' effect observed in the laboratory experiments indicate that they are often willing to give cooperation another chance, preferentially with like types, monitoring reputations, opportunities, and emotional and behavioral signals helping them to estimate cooperative intentions of their prospective interaction partners. The 'decay' effect has been repeatedly confirmed for repeated PD-type games (including public goods variants) played for a finite number of rounds, typically under random rematching of interaction partners after each round. While the level of cooperation in the first round is between 40–60%, over next rounds it declines, in the last round being quite low. The standard explanations consistent with the *homo economicus* model explain the decay either in terms of initial confusion and subsequent learning on the part of self-interested agents, or in terms of a lack of common knowledge of self-interested rationality among players that may induce rational opportunists to form a temporary reputation of "nice guys" (*cf.* Binmore 2007; Kreps *et al.* 1982). The story sketched above provides an alternative account of the decay effect, which is favored, among other considerations, by the restart effects. Restart effects (*cf.* Issac and Walker 1988, Andreoni 1988) document that when subjects are given a chance to play a new repeated PD game after they have experienced a decline of cooperation in a previous repeated PD game the initial level of cooperation tends to be as before (between 40–60%). For a good discussion of this issue see Woodward (2009a, 2009b).

21 My work on this study was supported by the grant GA13–20785S, *The nature of the normative—ontology, semantics, logic.* I would like to thank Jaroslav Peregrin for helpful comments.

REFERENCES

Andreoni, James. 1988. Why Free Ride? Strategies and Learning in Public Goods Experiments. *Journal of Public Economics* 37(3): 291–304.

Ashraf, Nava, Iris Bohnet and Nikita Piankov. 1988. Decomposing Trust and Trustworthiness. *Experimental Economics* 9(3): 193–208.

Barmettler, Franziska, Ernst Fehr and Christian Zehnder. 2012. Big Experimenter Is Watching You! Anonymity and Prosocial Behavior in the Laboratory. *Games and Economic Behavior* 75(1): 17–34.

Baron-Cohen, Simon. 1995. *Mindblindness.* Cambridge, MA: MIT Press.

Berg, Joyce, John Dickhaut and Kevin A. McCabe. 1995. Trust, reciprocity, and Social History. *Games and Economic Behavior* 10(1): 122–142.

Bicchieri, Cristina. 2006. *The Grammar of Society.* Cambridge: Cambridge University Press.

Bicchieri, Cristina and Erte Xiao. 2009. Do the Right Thing: But Only If Others Do So. *Journal of Behavioral Decision Making* 22(2): 191–208.

Bicchieri, Cristina, Erte Xiao and Ryan Muldoon. 2011. Trustworthiness Is a Social Norm, but Trusting Is Not. *Politics, Philosophy & Economics* 10(2): 170–187.

Binmore, Kenneth G. 2007. Does Game Theory Work? The Bargaining Challenge. Cambridge, MA: MIT Press.

Binmore, Kenneth G., and Avner Shaked. 2010. Experimental Economics: Where Next? *Journal of Economic Behavior & Organization* 73(1): 87–100.

Bolton, Gary E. and Axel Ockenfels. 2000. ERC: A Theory of Equity, Reciprocity, and Competition. *American Economic Review* 90(1): 166–193.

Camerer, Colin F. 2003. *Behavioral Game Theory: Experiments in Strategic Interaction*. New York: Russel Sage Foundation.

Chaudhuri, Ananish. 2008. *Experiments in Economics*. New York: Routledge.

Chaudhuri, Ananish and Lata Gangadharan. 2007. An Experimental Analysis of Trust and Trustworthiness. *Southern Economic Journal* 73: 959–985.

Cook, Karen. (ed.) 2001. *Trust in Society*. New York: Russell Sage Foundation.

Cox, James C. 2004. How to Identify Trust and Reciprocity. *Games and Economic Behavior* 46(2): 260–281.

Cox. James C. and Cary A. Deck. 2005. On the Nature of Reciprocal Motives. *Economic Inquiry* 43(3): 623–635.

Fehr, Ernst and Klaus Schmidt. 1999. A Theory of Fairness, Competition, and Cooperation. *Quarterly Journal of Economics* (114): 817–868.

Frank, Robert. 1988. *Passions within Reason*. New York: Norton.

Fudenberg, Drew and Eric Maskin. 1986. The Folk Theorem in Repeated Games with Discounting or with Incomplete Information. *Econometrica* 54: 533–554.

Güth, Werner and Hartmut Kliemt. 1998. The Indirect Evolutionary Approach: Bridging the Gap Between Rationality and Adaptation. *Rationality and Society* 10(3): 377–399.

Henrich, Joseph, Robert Boyd, Samuel Bowles, Colin F. Camerer, Ernst Fehr and Herbert Gintis. 2004. *Foundations of Human Sociality: Economic Experiments and Ethnographic Evidence from Fifteen Small-scale Societies*. Oxford: Oxford University Press.

Hoffman, Elizabeth, Kevin A. McCabe and Vernon L. Smith. 1996. Social Distance and Other-regarding Behavior in Dictator Games. *American Economic Review* 86: 653–660.

Isaac, Mark and James M. Walker. 1988. Group Size Effects in Public Goods Provision: The Voluntary Contributions Mechanism. *Quarterly Journal of Economics* 103: 179–200.

Kreps, David M. 1990. Corporate Culture and Economic Theory. In *Perspectives on Positive Economic Theory*, edited by James E. Alt and Kenneth A. Shepsle, 90–143. Cambridge: Cambridge University Press.

Kreps, David M., Paul Milgrom, John Roberts and Robert Wilson. 1982. Rational Cooperation in the Finitely Repeated Prisoners' Dilemma. *Journal of Economic Theory* 27(2): 245–252.

McCabe, Kevin A., Mary L. Rigdon and Vernon L. Smith. 2003. Positive Reciprocity and Intentions in Trust Games. *Journal of Economic Behavior & Organization* 52(2): 267–275.

Messick, David M. and Roderick M. Kramer. 2001. Trust as a Form of Shallow Morality. In *Trust in Society*, edited by Karen Cook, 89–118. New York: Russell Sage Foundation.

Nichols, Shaun. 2010. Emotions, Norms, and the Genealogy of Fairness. *Politics, Philosophy & Economics* 9(3): 275–296.

Ortmann, Andreas, John Fitzgerald and Carl Boeing. 2000. Trust, Reciprocity, and Social History: A Re-examination. *Experimental Economics* 3(1): 81–100.

Ostrom, Elinor. 2003. Toward a Behavioral Theory Linking Trust, Reciprocity, and Reputation. In *Trust and Reciprocity: Interdisciplinary Lessons from Experimental Research,* edited by Elinor Ostrom, 19–79. New York: Russell Sage Foundation.

———. 2014. Collective Action and the Evolution of Social Norms. *Journal of Natural Resources Policy Research* 6(4): 235–252.

Rabin, Matthew. 1993. Incorporating Fairness into Game Theory and Economics. *The American Economic Review* 83(5): 1281–1302.

Woodward, James. 2008. Social Preferences in Experimental Economics. *Philosophy of Science* 75(5): 646–657.

———. 2009a. Why Do People Cooperate as Much as They Do? In *Philosophy of the Social Sciences: Philosophical Theory and Scientific Practice,* edited by Chrysostomos Mantzavinos, 219–265. Cambridge: Cambridge University Press.

———. 2009b. Experimental Investigations of Social Preferences. In *The Oxford Handbook of Philosophy of Economics,* edited by Harold Kincaid and Don Ross, 189–202. Oxford: Oxford University Press.

About the Authors

Janette Dinishak is an assistant professor of philosophy at the University of California, Santa Cruz. She works primarily in the philosophy of psychiatry, the philosophy of psychology, Wittgenstein, and the epistemology of other minds. She has published papers on Wittgenstein, philosophical questions concerning autism and perception, and deficit views of human differences.

Lina Eriksson is a senior lecturer in philosophy at Flinders University. She has a background in political science, and has published books and journal articles on explanations in social science, including *Rational Choice Theory—potential and limits* (2011) and the co-authored *Explaining Norms* (2013). She has also published work on decision theory and political philosophy.

David Henderson is the Robert R. Chambers Distinguished Professor of Philosophy at the University of Nebraska, Lincoln. He works in the philosophy of science and the social sciences and in epistemology. He is the author of *Interpretation and Explanation in the Human Science* (SUNY 2013) and, with Terrence Horgan, *The Epistemological Spectrum: At the Interface of Cognitive Science and Conceptual Analysis* (Oxford University Press 2011). In recent work he has been interested in the social scientific and psychological work on social norms and cooperation. Also, relatedly, he is working on understanding epistemic norms as social norms, and on the character of epistemic evaluation and self-regulation. Some of this work is reflected in "What's the Point?" (with Terry Horgan) in David Henderson and John Greco (eds.) *Epistemic Evaluation: Purposeful Epistemology* (Oxford University Press, 2015). He has long had an interest in how normative matters feature (and do not feature) in social scientific explanation and understanding.

Ladislav Koreň has been the chair of the Department of Philosophy and Social Sciences of the University of Hradec Králové. He was also a holder of the Alexander-von-Humboldt research fellowship at the Munich

Center for Mathematical Philosophy. He is the author of several papers in the areas of epistemology, philosophy of language, philosophy of logic, and philosophy of social sciences.

Jaakko Kuorikoski is currently a professor in social and moral philosophy at the University of Helsinki and a research fellow at TINT Academy of Finland Centre of Excellence in philosophy of social science. He has published on explanation, models and simulations, mechanisms, and causality in, for example, *BJPS*, *Erkenntnis*, *PhilSci*, *PPR*, and *Synthese*.

Mark Okrent is professor of philosophy at Bates College in Maine. He is the author of *Heidegger's Pragmatism* (1988) and *Rational Animals: The Teleological Roots of Intentionality* (2007), as well as of numerous articles. Although he has published on a broad range of topics in the history of philosophy and the metaphysics of mind, his work tends to more particularly focus on issues concerning the nature of intentionality and the place of intentionality in nature.

Martin Palecek is an assistant professor of philosophy and social sciences and director of the Language, Mind, and Society Center at the University of Hradec Kralove. He held the Fulbright-Masaryk Fellowship at Emory University. His research examines issues of philosophy of social sciences, theory of cultural anthropology, and cognitive sciences.

Jaroslav Peregrin's research is located at the intersection of logic, analytic philosophy, and semantics; he has authored papers in these areas for *Australasian Journal of Philosophy*, *Erkenntnis*, *Journal of Philosophical Logic*, *Pragmatic and Cognition*, *Philosophia*, *Philosophical Topics*, and *Studia Logica*. Aside from a couple of books in Czech, he is the author of *Doing Worlds with Words* (Kluwer 1995), *Meaning and Structure* (Ashgate 2001), and *Inferentialism* (Palgrave 2014). His current research focuses on both logical and philosophical aspects of *inferentialism*, *viz.* the view that meaning is essentially a matter of inference. He is also working on more general questions related to normativity, especially in the context of evolution theory. He is the head of the Department of Logic of the Institute of Philosophy of the Academy of Sciences of the Czech Republic and a professor at the Faculty of Arts and Philosophy of the University of Hradec Králové.

Mark Risjord is a professor in the Department of Philosophy at Emory University and the University of Hradec Kralove, Czech Republic. His research in the philosophy of social science has concerned the role of rationality and normativity in explanation, the explanation of intentional action, and the role of values in the sciences. His books include *Woodcutters and Witchcraft: Rationality and Interpretive Change in the*

Social Sciences (SUNY 2000), *Nursing Knowledge: Science, Practice, and Philosophy* (Wiley Blackwell 2010), and *Philosophy of Social Science: A Contemporary Introduction* (Routledge 2014).

Paul A. Roth is a professor in the Department of Philosophy at the University of California, Santa Cruz. His research focuses primarily on philosophy of history, philosophy of social science, philosophical naturalism, and Quine. He has published over 70 articles and reviews. Representative works include "The Silence of the Norms: The Missing Historiography of *The Structure of Scientific Revolutions*" (*Studies in History and Philosophy of Science* 2013), "The Pasts" (*History and Theory* 2012), "Hearts of Darkness: 'Perpetrator History' and why there is no why" (*History of the Human Sciences* 2004), "Mistakes" (*Synthese* 2003), and *Meaning and Method in the Social Sciences* (Cornell U.P. 1987). He co-founded the Philosophy of Social Science Roundtable and continues to serve as a member of its executive committee. With Stephen Turner, he co-edited the *Blackwell Guide to the Philosophy of Social Science*. Roth is currently completing a book on the philosophy of history—*The Pasts*, under contract with Northwestern University Press.

Joseph Rouse is the Hedding Professor of Moral Science in the Philosophy Department and the Science in Society Program at Wesleyan University. A specialist in the philosophy of science, the history of twentieth-century philosophy, and interdisciplinary science studies, he is the author of *Articulating the World: Conceptual Understanding and the Scientific Image* (Chicago 2015), *How Scientific Practices Matter: Reclaiming Philosophical Naturalism* (Chicago 2002), *Engaging Science: How to Understand Its Practices Philosophically* (Cornell 1996), and *Knowledge and Power: Toward a Political Philosophy of Science* (Cornell 1987). He also edited John Haugeland's posthumously published *Dasein Disclosed: John Haugeland's Heidegger* (Harvard 2013).

Karsten Stueber is professor of philosophy at the College of the Holy Cross. He publishes in the areas of philosophy of language, philosophy of mind, and philosophy of the social sciences. He is the author of *Rediscovering Empathy: Agency, Folk Psychology, and the Human Sciences* (MIT Press 2006, 2nd edition 2010) and *Donald Davidsons Theorie Sprachlichen Verstehens* (Anton Hain 1993). In addition he has co-edited three anthologies: *Philosophie der Skepsis* (1996), *Empathy and Agency: The Problem of Understanding in the Human Sciences* (Westview 2000), and *Debating Dispositions* (DeGruyter 2009). A fourth anthology, *Moral Sentimentalism*, is forthcoming with Cambridge University Press.

Stephen Turner is Distinguished University Professor in Philosophy at the University of South Florida. He has written extensively on the history and philosophy of the social sciences, including such books as *The Search for a Methodology of Social Science: Durkheim, Weber, and the Nineteenth-Century Problem of Cause, Probability, and Action* and *Max Weber and the Dispute Over Reason and Value: A Study in Philosophy, Ethics, and Politics*, with Regis Factor. His books relating to normativity include *The Social Theory of Practices: Tradition, Tacit Knowledge, and Presuppositions; Brains/Practices/Relativism: Social Theory after Cognitive Science;* and *Explaining the Normative.* A collection of his writings on tacitness has recently appeared with the title *Understanding the Tacit.* Currently he is publishing on Wilfrid Sellars. His paper "Durkheim, Sellars, and the Origins of Collective Intentionality," with Peter Olen, will appear in the *British Journal for the History of Philosophy.*

Petri Ylikoski is professor of science and technology studies in the Department of Social Research at the University of Helsinki and Professor of Analytical Sociology at the Institute for Analytical Sociology at Linköping University. His research interests range from sociological theory to foundational issues in philosophy of science. His papers have been published in journals such as *Annual Review of Sociology, Philosophical Studies, Erkenntnis,* and *Synthese.*

Julie Zahle is associate professor in the Section of Philosophy at the Department of Media, Cognition, and Communication, University of Copenhagen, and Research Fellow at the Academy of Finland Centre of Excellence in the Philosophy of the Social Sciences (TINT), University of Helsinki. Her research focuses on various topics within the philosophy of the social sciences, including the individualism-holism debate, theories of practice, the method of participant observation, and values in social science.

Index

272   *Index*

McCabe, Kevin, 251–3
McCauley, Robert, 202–3
meaning: of action, 46–7, 87–8, 124; of words, 35, 54, 66
methodological individualism, 204–5. *See also* norms, reality of; reductionism
methodological naturalism. *See* naturalism, epistemological
mistakes, 3, 50, 137, 140, 142, 216, 235, 241. *See also* error theory
moral norms. *See* norms, moral
motivation, 43, 69, 138, 188; reasons as 20, 106. *See also* reasons

naturalism: philosophical, 2, 28, 29, 39–40, 98; epistemological, 2, 68, 78–80, 97; metaphysical, 3, 44, 54, 66, 100–2, 156–9, 165
normative practice. *See* practice
normativity: criteria for, 3, 10–11; of inference, 10–11, 14, 23, 99, 102; perspectival character of, 47, 71, 90, 191, 206. *See also* error; norms; rule-following
norms: explanatory role of, 97, 147, 155–6, 190 (*see also* normative explanations); moral, 5, 9, 11, 13–16, 72–3, 96–7, 99, 105, 109, 156, 161, 166, 203; reality of, 14–15, 100–2, 156–9, 205, 241–2; responsiveness to, 37, 55, 100, 138, 153, 254, 258; social, 145–6, 153, 255; as standards, 137; Turnerized, 44–5, 180. *See also* rule-following

obligation. *See* norms, moral

participant observation, 80–6
Peregrin, Jaroslav, 204–7
practice, 22, 35–9, 147; linguistic, 35; normativity of, 35, 47, 190; as regularities, 36, 184; scientific, 29, 43
pro-social attitudes, 221–2, 256. *See also* emotions

rational choice theory, 197, 215, 225, 235–7. *See also* game theory

rationality: bounded, 233–4; in explanation, 197, 216–17, 231–2, 234, 241–2; instrumental, 106, 142–3, 166, 180, 186, 196, 214–15; theoretical, 150, 166–71, 179
Raz, Joseph, 16–20
reasoning, 10–11, 21–4, 32, 73, 186, 234–5. *See also* rationality, theoretical; rules, of inference
reasons, 4, 9, 16–19, 68–9, 86–9, 98–9, 101, 106, 121, 126, 142, 168, 179–80, 189, 199, 201, 205, 215, 225. *See also* rationality
reductionism, 14, 44–5, 60, 64, 67–70, 156–7, 191, 205. *See also* norms, reality of
Risjord, Mark, 201–4
Rouse, Joseph, 185
rule-following, 68–9, 188, 195. *See also* norms
rules, 178–9; of etiquette, 99, 194–5; of games, 64–9, 97, 101; of inference, 21–2, 32, 100, 186, 179, 214. *See also* norms

Sellars, Wilfred, 28–9, 54–5
simulation, 103–4, 107, 115–16. *See also* empathy; *verstehen*
Smith, Adam, 105
social norms. *See* norms, social
Spohn, Wolfgang, 90–2
Steuber, Karsten, 86–7, 115–16, 120–2
supervenience, 157–9

teleology, 3, 36, 46–7, 49–51, 54–7, 145
Turner, Stephen, 103, 180, 190, 199–201, 205

verstehen, 4, 86–9. *See also* empathy; simulation

we-intentions. *See* joint action
Woodward, James, 258

Ylikoski, Petri, 238, 239

For Product Safety Concerns and Information please contact our EU
representative GPSR@taylorandfrancis.com
Taylor & Francis Verlag GmbH, Kaufingerstraße 24, 80331 München, Germany